CHRISTIANITY IN ROMAN BRITAIN
TO AD 500

For
C.A.R.R.
in gratitude for so many years of
help, advice, and encouragement

CHRISTIANITY
IN
ROMAN BRITAIN
TO AD 500

CHARLES THOMAS

University of California Press
Berkeley and Los Angeles

University of California Press
Berkeley and Los Angeles

© Charles Thomas 1981

Printed in Great Britain

Library of Congress Cataloging in Publication Data

Thomas, Charles, 1928–
    Christianity in Roman Britain to AD 500.

    1. Great Britain—Church history—To 449—
Addresses, essays, lectures.   2. Great Britain—
Church history—Anglo Saxon period, 449–1066—
Addresses, essays, lectures.   3. Ireland—Church
history—To 1172—Addresses, essays, lectures.
I. Title.
BR748.T43   274.1'02   80–26003
ISBN 0–520–04392–8

Contents

The illustrations

Author's foreword

The origins of this book lie in a lecture-series that I was invited to give in Truro Cathedral, during the Lent season of 1977, by the Dean (the Very Reverend Henry Lloyd) and Chapter. In my native Cornwall, it is more or less inescapable that any such lectures have to be titled 'The Age of the Saints'. The first two covered the period and topics discussed here; and the whole series, obliging me as it did to clarify my thoughts, revealed to me (though I hope not to my audience) how many questions I had evaded and how little I really knew. During an attempt over the last three years to rectify some of that ignorance, I committed myself to a longer and publishable account. In thanking Dean Lloyd, and Dr Graham Webster (as general editor of the series), I must also thank my publishers for their patience, helpfulness and confidence.

It will become apparent to the reader that my experiences in both archaeology and history have lain in those bands of time that enclose, and too often can exclude, the Roman occupation of Britain – prehistory and protohistory. I can only hope that extensive reading and site visits will together have compensated a little for my lack of direct involvement in Roman studies. Where the study of Christianity is concerned, this shortcoming may be less marked than in passages dealing with the secular aspects of the Roman empire, since I can claim some familiarity with Christian archaeology, history and writings in the post-Roman period. The task of catching up with the literature of Romano–British researches – one for which a conventional classical upbringing does little to fit one – was immensely eased by the spread of so many excellent modern publications. Since, however, hardly any of them mention our early Christianity, I could quote a much earlier historian, and say *forsan placide libellus adiungeretur* 'perchance another little book may quietly take its place'.

In giving, as I have done, so much weight to the evidence derived from the study of language, particularly in the form of place-names, I have tried to avoid what seems to be a common failing in Romano–British studies – a tendency to rely over-much on the sketchy witness of archaeology when conventional historical sources run dry, to ignore linguistic evidence because it is unfamiliar, and therefore to close the accounts somewhere between 383 and 410, tailing off very much not with a bang, but a whimper. To me, as I think to many others, the true division in the story of Insular Christianity ('Insular' means 'British and Irish', together) comes not around AD 410, but with the opening of a new phase of full monasticism centred about a hundred years later. This statement may seem to beg the question of continuity. I have no doubts myself, and have not had for years, that continuity from Roman Britain into the sub-Roman fifth century demonstrably took place in many ways and was not confined to Christianity. The last six chapters therefore discuss fifth-century Christianity, and a certain amount of secular history, in southern Scotland and in Ireland as well as much of England and Wales. This strikes me as needing no particular justification; if we have to label people, Patrick was a Roman Briton, and presumably Ninian or Nynia was one as well.

The revision and re-typing of the book and the preparation of all the illustrations was facilitated by a short period of study leave (for which I am glad to thank the University of Exeter and its Board of Cornish Studies). The work has been planned and composed for a specific readership, and it will save both critics and reviewers a little time if I explain this. I had in mind, naturally, students in British (and, I hope, Irish) universities, since the last textbook of this kind appeared in 1912; but with them, that vast studentship in the world of adult education and extra-mural studies – one for which I am bound to feel a special affection, after so many years of involvement with it, and for which I have frequently written. There are also many people, perhaps more today than at any other time in the past, who are clearly interested in Roman history, and Britain's Roman past. They will find very little space devoted to Roman Christianity in the existing literature, and they may like to have this account, placed in its Romano–British setting. Others, by no means necessarily in Holy Orders nor at theological colleges, have already shown great interest in works on post-Roman Insular Christianity, and I hope that here I have supplied the previously lacking initial chapters.

Lastly, I have borne in mind friends, colleagues, and fellow-students abroad – in the United States and in Europe. For the latter's benefit, dimensions have been given in metric as well as Imperial, and some aspects of the subject have been related to European contexts. I hope that, accepting at least the new material evidence, it will no longer be supposed that Christianity in Britain effectively opens with St Augustine in AD 597. If (apart from the odd reference to St Alban) this has too often been the case, it is largely because no-one has bothered to contradict it in detail.

It is useless to pretend that parts of the subject-matter are not complicated. They are, and I have therefore included explanatory matter which will be known already to archaeologists, early historians and linguists, but not necessarily to informed and interested persons who happen to work outside those disciplines. Where, by way of illustration, I have cited passages in Latin, I have almost always provided literal translations; and where possible I have tried to cite sources and references which the ordinary reader, certainly in Britain and the United States, might hope to find through the system of public libraries.

Very many friends have helped me in numerous ways. I begin by thanking those who in asking me to produce papers, chapters for books, extra-mural and symposium lectures, and broadcast talks, forced me into a beneficial process of re-writing – Professors Barrie Dobson and Philip Rahtz, Drs David Dumville, Peter Fowler and Warwick Rodwell, and Messrs Geoffrey Bryant, John Casey, Roy Hayward and Trevor Rowley. I am particularly grateful to those who have allowed me to see unpublished material – Professor John Mann, my Exeter colleague Professor Malcolm Todd, Dr John Chandler, Miss Catherine Johns, and Messrs Jim Gould and John Hedges; and, in the cases of John Mann and John Chandler, further thanks for allowing me to cite them. Plates 1, 7 and 8 were most generously provided, with other photographs and advice, by my old friend Professor Barri Jones, whose aerial reconnaissances in the North are adding new chapters to Roman Britain; and Mr Stanley West, with great kindness, has allowed me to use the original Icklingham drawing (fig. 40).

The list of those who provided me, often unasked, with relevant information or clarification is quite possibly defective and in expressing my warm gratitude to them all I offer my apologies for any inadvertent gaps. They have been: Lord Fletcher of Islington (Eric Fletcher); Professors Peter Brown, Rosemary Cramp, M.J. O'Kelly, Stuart Piggott and Etienne Rynne; Drs Tania Dickinson, Margaret Faull, Isabel Henderson and Harold Taylor; Misses Dorothy Charlesworth, Jennifer Price and Ann Wells; and Messrs Brian Gilmour, Christopher Green, Mark Hassall, Jock Macdonald, Donald Mackreth, Donnchadh Ó Corráin, Oliver Padel, Kenneth Painter, and another old friend and former colleague John Wacher. None of these persons must necessarily be thought to be committed to any interpretation made in respect of their own views, finds, or corrections, but I trust that none of them has been misrepresented. I am, as always, grateful to Mr John Hopkins and the staff of the Library of the Society of Antiquaries of London, and (in Cornwall) for the resources of the Courtney Library of the Royal Institution of Cornwall, and the Bishop Phillpotts library – it gives me pleasure to remember that my own college at Oxford was also the college of Henry Phillpotts, Charles Plummer, Ian Richmond, E.A. Lowe and Daniel Binchy.

Where all and any aspects of the Christian archaeology of Britain and

Ireland, not to say most of western Europe, throughout the first millenium AD are concerned, I can only acknowledge my profound debt to the published work, and the generous advice, help and encouragement of Dr C.A. Ralegh Radford. In pointing out – though only in terms of the most affectionate reproof – that this is really a book he should have written, it hardly needs to be added that his would have been a very much better and more authoritative one. Finally, without the protection and forbearance of my wife, herself a busy author, and all my children, it would have been almost impossible to compose or to write this book; and I leave it to them to decide if the end has justified the means.

CHARLES THOMAS
Cornwall, May 1980

Abbreviations
in the text and references

ASC *The Anglo-Saxon Chronicle – a revised translation*, ed. Dorothy Whitelock, with D.C. Douglas & S.I. Tucker (London 1961)

CIIC R.A.S. Macalister, *Corpus Inscriptionum Insularum Celticarum*, 2 vols, consecutive numbering: *i* (1945), *ii* (1949), Dublin

Conf. St Patrick's *Confessio*

DEB Gildas, *De Excidio Britanniae*: see Williams 1912, Winterbottom 1978

ECMW V.E. Nash-Williams, *The Early Christian Monuments of Wales* (Cardiff, 1950)

Ep. St Patrick's *Epistola*

HE Bede, *Historia Ecclesiastica*. see Plummer 1896

HF Gregory of Tours, *Historia Francorum*: see Dalton 1927, and Chap. 7, note 2

LHEB K.H. Jackson, *Language and History in Early Britain* (Edinburgh, 1953)

RCHM Royal Commission on Historical Monuments, England – as prefix to dated and named *Inventory* volumes

RIB R.G. Collingwood and R.P. Wright, *The Roman Inscriptions of Britain, I. Inscriptions on Stone* (Oxford, 1965)

The symbol * prefixed to a name, or word (thus: *bern-*), implies that it is a name or linguistic form not actually attested in surviving writings or inscriptions, but can be legitimately inferred from the known operations of linguistic principles. These are often known as 'starred forms'.

Where dates are cited in the form (e.g.) '425 × 435', or a person's age as '50 × 55', it is implied that the true date, or true age at a given event, has an approximately equal chance of falling in any one year in the bracket of time so indicated. The form '425–435', on the other hand, means 'the whole period of time between 425 and 435'.

The names of English, Scottish and Welsh counties given in the text are those in force before the 1974 local government boundary reorganisations.

CHAPTER ONE

The Approach and
The Religious Background

As works of imagination, the historian's work and the
novelist's do not differ. Where they do differ is that the
historian's is meant to be true.
R.G. Collingwood *The Idea of History*

When the author used to teach the principles of archaeology to first-year undergraduates, helping them to master such distinctions as that between relative and absolute dates, one favourite essay question went something like this: You are an intelligent and mobile inhabitant of the planet Sirius, familiar already through pictures and video-tapes with Earth's physical content. You cannot however read or understand any Earth language. You are now to be teleported to a British city, intact, but temporarily denuded of all its usual inhabitants – somewhere like Birmingham, or York. All the principal places of worship will be indicated. Ascertain, from the visual and architectural clues alone, the nature of the dominant religion followed by the momentarily absent citizens.

This question invariably produced some most ingenious essays, but the correct answer is: Sun-worship. It could hardly be anything else. Virtually all the clues point that way, and that way alone. Consider the obvious facts. The major temples are rectilinear, with their longer axis east-west, on the Sun's daily path. Inside, the higher and more important end is related to the position of Sun-rise. The emphasis upon the vertical – towers, spires, and long upright elements – marks an obeisance to the mid-day position of the great Orb. Some of the spires are even topped by gold (Sun-coloured) pieces of metal.

Within these temples, a common fitting is a kind of desk, in the form of a large Sun-coloured bird upon a pedestal. This devotion to the idea of the sky, its fiery Ruler, and all its lesser inhabitants, is carried a stage further. There are pictures of doves; of happy-looking humans, with bird-like wings; and of important people with Sun-like circles in gold or yellow or white behind their heads. The cruciform dazzle of the Sun's rays seen through the glass windows – with glass whose very colours echo the Sun's spectrum – is imitated by another widely-employed symbol, simplified to the shape of a cross. And as well as these brilliant windows, which need the Sun to bring them to life, various lamps or little model Suns abound. If one looks around just outside, one sees that when humans die, they appear to be buried in pits which are also aligned east-west. What seem to be descriptive stone tablets (often enriched with doves, or crosses) are placed, either pointing Suñ-wards, or laid flat where the Sun can easily inspect them. (Continue the exercise for yourself.)

Ridiculous as this recital may seem, it is a readily supportable interpretation of visible and tangible data, and it is one that lies within those limits of archaeological 'inference' that most students would be told were legitimate ones. It warns us that the explanation of observed phenomena solely through such attributes as their shape, colour, disposition and ornament can constitute an exercise fraught with intellectual peril. In the absence of other specific indications, things can too easily seem to be what they are not and never were. Where we deal with artefacts whose functions are not at once apparent, and whose purpose may have been 'ritual' – beyond the obvious functions of a life-support system – we can very readily compound errors from the first guess. If there can be an archaeology of the results of past *actions*, there is no archaeology of past *thought*.

Nowhere is the lesson of the extra-terrestrial enquirer and his or her pardonable Sun-worship blunder more applicable than in our own human approach to the archaeology of religious activity here on Earth. We should remember all those speculations – so often unfettered, and so often dribbling away into the sheerest lunacy – that have been linked to Stonehenge, to Silbury Hill, and to the Pyramids. We have to accept that without some guidance from classical literature, from inscriptions, and from external analogy, our inferential picture of any cult or religion practised in Roman Britain could be so lop-sided as to be almost worthless.

Though this book is meant to be read as a straightforward narrative, and one in which the complexities arise from the very nature of the subject-matter rather than its treatment, we are from the outset faced with certain choices. There are at least three distinct ways of approaching the question, 'What form did Christianity take in Roman Britain?'. One could, like Hugh Williams in 1912, try to give a plain historical answer. Now, minor inscriptions on stone, metal or wood apart, it seems most unlikely that any new written sources of any length or substance will ever come to light; and therefore further work in this direction can only consist of re-interpreting the historical material that we possess, or of trying to establish likelihoods through recourse to analogy – by studying records of Christianity as it was in other and more fully documented parts of the Roman empire.

The position is very different when we turn to archaeology. In the last few decades the volume of both discovery and excavation in Britain has increased enormously (though for reasons which have no particular connection with either Christianity, or Roman Britain). It is now a quarter-century since the archaeological material bearing upon our subject was assessed,[1] and those assessments can stand revision. It is a different matter again when we look at a third possible approach – one that lies through what we can call 'linguistics'.

The language of early Christianity in the western part of the Roman empire was Latin, the formal Latin of the Scriptures. The everyday speech of most Romano–British Christians was on the other hand British. British was not a written language. Latin was however both written and spoken (though the two forms were not always the same). Any discussion of how Christianity in Britain *worked* obliges us to explore the extent to which Latin was spoken in Britain, and for how long, and whether for instance all Roman Britons were bilingual. The fact that we ourselves can read Latin without obstacle is not in itself enough to ensure that we always know precisely what certain words meant in the fourth century AD, or precisely which Latin words were most commonly used in fourth-century Britain to express certain common Christian ideas. Again, a most important branch of language study is that of place-names – onomastics. The degree to which this can shed fresh light on early British history, Christian history included, is by no means universally appreciated. All in all, the linguistic approach to the question posed above must go alongside, and no longer be seen as ancillary to, the historical and archaeological enquiries.

The first chapter of a general study is probably no place for too extended an essay upon archaeological method; but the reader is entitled to know what the author thinks is the distinction between *evidence* and *inference* – words that will recur. The topic of early Christianity (or any other religion), and never more so than when related to Britain, is one where this distinction is of great importance. It may seem a little like that old puzzle – What is the difference between history and archaeology?

The term 'history' can mean several things, though currently it has two principal meanings. It could be all that happened in the past, theoretically represented by the full, highly-detailed record of past events – something that by its very nature, of the Past as it really was, we can never expect to recover. Or it can mean selection and interpretation, the outcome of historical research and assessment; an investigation into all source-material and previous comment about some particular aspect of the past, and then the creation of new history by casting one's results in yet more writing. Both definitions are very imperfect. Collingwood, who described the second definition as the scissors-and-paste method, argued himself (and much of British historical effort) into an impasse from which later historians have, though with difficulty, rescued us[2]. When Carr defines history,[3] for himself, as 'a continuous process of interaction between the historian and his facts', he does not absolve the modern student from an obligation to read what Carr regards a historical 'fact' as being; nor Collingwood's own and more pessimistic definition.

When we juxtapose history and archaeology as concepts, and deliberately leave unexplored the deeper philosophical worries about history as such, we can extract one particular characteristic. The historian, to whatever extent he sees himself as selector and interpreter, relies in the main upon statements made in the past by fellow-humans – statements which have survived, in any form, and which he can comprehend. These may be as close as we can expect to find them to factual objectivity, like a 1602 rent-roll or an 1851 railway timetable, in neither of which is there very much room for the compilers' personal views or prejudices. They may however be overwhelmingly subjective, like the memoirs of a former Cabinet minister or a dismissed general, and will required from any interpreter as much selectivity as was exercised by the compilers.

But there is a common factor, if we are prepared to agree that what history gives us can be described as 'evidence'. Not all would agree, even to this; Collingwood, one of whose typical pensées stands at the head of this chapter, held extreme views about the inferential nature of evidence[4] which, if wholly followed, would render the next few pages meaningless. On the other hand, what history (as here opposed to archaeology) must provide – and we shall call it 'evidence' – is information processed by some mind in the past; what we receive is what someone, standing in for our much later selves, believed to have taken place, even *ought* to have taken place. Historical philosophy continues to explore this idea, and all its implications. It must suffice to say that we now select, as a particular criterion of what will be distinguished as 'historical evidence', the independent fact that its mere existence implies human, mental agency. This has no relevance to questions of truth, or reality in times past, or (historical) 'fact'. If the 1851 timetable belonged to a railway that had no trains, or was not even built, and had been issued to deceive shareholders, it is still evidence – of an 1851 fraud, not an 1851 railway operation.

The term 'archaeology' also has several meanings. One expresses no more than the apparent existence of past structures and artefacts, perhaps a quarry for scholars, perhaps just a visual amenity ('Greece is full of archaeology'). Another sums up the concept of a large, ever-growing set of techniques, excavation being merely one of them, used to discover things about the otherwise unrecorded past. The third meaning can describe the creation of informative narratives that present the information gathered when archaeological techniques have been applied to archaeological material. Such narratives can take the shape of notes, articles and books, but they can also be museum displays, films, or radio and television programmes. The commoner presentations, like this book, are closely akin to historical writing.

Archaeology and history are not divided in any way by our perception of time. We are now being regaled with histories of the 1950s, 1960s, even the 1970s. If archaeology is popularly associated with the 'otherwise unrecorded past', because in that context the results are spectacular or exciting, it is clear that archaeological techniques and any rapportage based on them can just as well be applied to the partly-recorded and recent past, or anywhere that history stammers or is perforce silent. Even if we had a string of supposedly reliable eye-witness accounts of the battle of Hastings in 1066, there would be ample reason for a medieval archaeologist to acquire knowledge in a dozen different directions, through controlled excavation of the battlefield. In such ways, archaeological and historical techniques may support each other, and even offer independent confirmation of the 'reality' of specific points.[5]

But where we will now separate history and archaeology is in that what was earlier called 'evidence' in the case of history proves to be of a very different nature where archaeology is involved. The radical distinction is that archaeological discoveries have not been previously processed by any human mind. The processing will involve, not the assessment of what someone else in the past raised (by any means) to the status of potential historical evidence (however close to, or far from, reality); but another activity, necessary to raise a discovery to a higher level where it can be fully employed. This act is the *inferring* of all possible circumstances that could have brought about whatever new fact or past state of affairs is now being observed, and usually justifying the selection or preference of one or more such circumstances. If history, putting it very broadly indeed, deals with *evidence*, then archaeology has to deal with *inference*.

Our opening example, of the extra-terrestrial who constructed a full hypothesis of sun-worship entirely from observations, is a fair pastiche of an archaeologist in unfamiliar territory, proceeding to a narrative statement by the inferential method. To be valid, such a process must begin with certain premises – that humans do habitually combine for the activity called worship, that they tend to construct buildings for this purpose, that religion is the mental or spiritual counterpart of these physical acts, and that religion can regulate the ways in which humans dispose of their dead. Since we agree that these are valid (true) premises, we can agree that they were valid for the inferential process fictionally described.

Philosophically-minded readers who, at this point, may speculate as to whether inferential processes in archaeology are mainly deductive, or inductive, will have to go back to Collingwood.[6] In the main, archaeologists do not concern themselves with the distinction, but neither do they often distinguish between philosophical categories of evidence – any methodological work will show pages devoted to 'evidence' in archaeology, discussed in pragmatic, even social, terms. The answer is that the initial inferential process usually is (or should be) deductive; the subsequent narrative often is (and should not always be) increasingly inductive; and that there is a great need for a full-scale enquiry on these lines into the last fifty years of archaeological writing.

Let us look at a second example – the excavation of a Romano–British villa-house, in a part of which is found a human skeleton irregularly disposed and with a jagged hole in the back of the skull. No direct historical evidence of any kind bears upon this discovery, and the villa was previously unknown. A villa-house (to avoid further debate) is the Roman equivalent of a country-house of decent standing, and one does not expect to find a skeleton on the floor of a country-house kitchen. There must be an explanation.

The chief guides are those so fruitfully exploited by Sherlock Holmes: commonsense, deductive logic, and analogy. If we so wish, we can give them a portmanteau label: inference. Commonsense instantly narrows the range of explanations for the hole in the skull; one rejects assault by pterodactyls, suicide, or the impact of a meteorite. Examination of the setting will determine, and it must do so to the satisfaction of any other competent observer, whether or not the body was laid to rest clothed or unclothed, and in any kind of grave; whether this took place before, or after, the villa-house was deserted or its roof had collapsed for any reason (preferably, for what reason); and also whether the skeleton is that of a man or a woman, and approximately what age.

Things which fall to the ground and remain further undisturbed will lie above things which had so fallen previously; this, the long-agreed principle of stratigraphy, is the mainstay of geology and to a large extent of archaeology too. It is probable that we can demonstrate a sequence involving the building of the house; its use or occupation; collapse of the roof through decay or fire; and lastly the placing of the body in collapsed material. It is possible that absolute dates will be procured for stages in this sequence. These will be won from analogy; from discovery (in profusion or scarcity) and in precise positions of objects such as coins and distinctive pottery – objects whose counterparts have elsewhere been consistently and repeatedly found to be reliable indicators of measured time past.

All this is commonplace in archaeology, if descriptively rather than analytically made public. In such an instance, one can go a long way towards establishing the outline of an historically-unevidenced happening, without committing the (archaeological) fault known as 'exceeding the limits of inference'.

The unaided human senses are not the only tools. Laboratory work can now produce the most arcane and surprising conclusions, and without leaving room for much argument. The skeleton could be assigned age, sex, state of health and a great deal else by way of firm statement or with very high probability.

But what of the actual death? Experts examining the hole in the skull can (as in forensic medicine, a most useful analogy) suggest whether a blunt or pointed instrument was used. They may point to clear signs as to the shape of that part of the object which penetrated the skull; hence to the general character of the weapon. Inferences combine, like rabbits, to breed other inferences. Was the implement a tomahawk-like object notably favoured by Anglo-Saxons, and was the dead person a Saxon slain by fellow-Saxons? Was the corpse stuffed into the débris of a ruined villa-house to conceal the slaying? Why should any Saxons, at a period estimated to lie between AD 400 and 450, have been in this place at that time?

The whole story, insofar as any story can be constructed (and there have never been lacking those who could write pages of the most persuasive prose about similar discoveries), rests on *inference*, most of it of the deductive kind. This may have sprung from logical and rational thought, and be defended by reasonable argument, but it still remains stubbornly archaeological inference and not historical evidence – or (note the quotation marks) it is inference from archaeological 'evidence', and not 'inference' from historical evidence. It has been pointed out, and it will once more be pointed out now, that the ultimate skill of the archaeologist (if this label possesses a precise meaning) lies not only in the construction and handling of inferences, but in knowing at what point he or she must cease to infer anything at all.

There is a small and rather difficult area where evidence and inference, in the senses previously described, seem to overlap, or are presented to us willy-nilly in overlapping guises. It is one which especially affects the Roman period, and the subsequent few centuries. It contains all those things which offer us both some form of historical evidence (as written statements, however curt), and grounds for the exercise of archaeological inference. We may expect that these will mainly be found in connection with a period at which a given society becomes literate, an extended horizon which in some though not all modern countries is used to mark a divide between 'prehistory' and 'history'. Coins are the best examples. Inscriptions upon metalwork and stone form others, as do (this is often overlooked) writings upon prepared materials like animal-skins.

The complication, for us, is that a coin, say a Roman imperial coin, exhibits in abbreviated written form what we have to regard as being unquestionably historical evidence: title and honorifics of some emperor, place of minting, and what amounts to a direct statement of some bracket of absolutely-dated time. But from the size and metal and physical state of wear of such a coin, and this is in addition to any context in which it was found, non-historical inferences can be made, using special archaeological techniques included in the discipline of *numismatics*. An inscription upon a stone will in itself be historical evidence (and very possibly linguistic evidence as well). There is however what could be called 'an archaeology of inscriptions', *epigraphy*, which can study an inscription in a classificatory sense not wholly dependent upon the individual meaning; and there can even be, say, 'an archaeology of milestones'[7] involving *petrology* (where did the actual stone, geologically speaking, come from? what can be inferred from its shaping, and its location at a supposed date?). Even a piece of what might seem to be pure historical evidence, like a ninth-century cartulary written on parchment, has its own inherent and far from negligible archaeology. There is the archaeology of all forms of early writing, and of the techniques and materials used, or *palaeography*. And it so happens that the close study of historically dated sheepskin parchments has had profound inferential value for animal geneticists, reconstructing the Old World history of breeds of sheep.[8]

All this is entirely, sometimes a little uncomfortably, relevant to the study of Christianity in Roman Britain. In trying to make plain his own distinction between evidence and inference, the writer can but express his hope that in the chapters that follow it will be made sufficiently clear which technique of enquiry is, at any point, being pursued. Most of this study will have to depend upon inference, and analogy. The facts, some of which a historical philosopher like R.G. Collingwood would deny as factual, derived from what is conventionally regarded as the historical evidence could be summed up in a couple of pages. They could be re-arranged, and discussed interminably, but no such exercise would expand the core. If we are to pursue the subject, and set out a framework of possibilities in the hope and the expectation that further research will assist others to get closer to historical realities, we have to walk along what amounts to a tightrope. That rope is anchored, at both ends, in time; the origins of the Christian religion in the first century AD, and predominantly Christian Britain and Ireland about six centuries later. We try very hard to remain upon this rope along its whole and narrow length. Otherwise, of course, we shall fall off; on one side, into an excessive timidity that restrains any enquiry or exploration at all, and on the other into formless quaking wastes that lie beyond the bounds of inference.

A third and final cautionary tale, a forerunner of Chapters 4 and 5, can round off this section. In Eastern lands where Islam is the ruling Faith, one sees displayed in various fashions texts from the *Qur'an*, set out in the graceful and beautiful calligraphy of the classical Arabic scripts. They have instant significance within their parent culture, one whose history is fully recorded. If I chance to visit in Cheltenham a retired colonel, in the hall of whose home I observe a brass dish or a majolica bowl adorned with such a text, what can I infer? That its owner, whose appearance certainly suggests membership of the Anglican Church, has embraced Islam? Or that he obtained the object during his residence in a land where objects so inscribed are widely available? Which inference is the least improbable? And what if all this happens, not in Cheltenham, but in Woking, Surrey, where there happens to be an Islamic mosque or temple? Does this proximity lend weight to the first inference?

Precisely analogous problems arise, again and again, in the study of Christian archaeology in the Roman empire, and in a most acute form when that study takes place about Roman Britain. Early Christianity had its texts and symbols, analogous in their use to the texts of Islam (the *Qur'an* forbids the making of images, as strictly did both Jewish and early Christian teachings). We can at least tactfully question the retired colonel, in English (or Hindi or Arabic). We cannot question our Roman forebears in any tongue. Do similar Romano–British objects, and discoveries are very often of this sort, permit the inference that the owners of objects with Christian ornament were necessarily Christian? Can we even infer that such were originally made or decorated exclusively by Christians, within or without Britain? Could a pagan have made one such, for sale to a Christian, from whom it was stolen by another pagan (as the infidel Colonel got his trophy), who then lost it a hundred miles away?

Unless we accept the clear challenge to clarify and refine our thinking about this, and other equally fundamental, problems (and they are archaeological problems), even so basic a tool of fresh research as the distribution-map will be just another useless construct, teetering on the border of inferential propriety. This particular challenge is faced below, not wholly with resolution, in Chapters 4 and 5. But facing it does not absolve one from the need to answer many other and awkward questions, such as, What was a Romano–British church like, and how can we now recognise one? One could end simply by laying out, within compartmented subject-headings presented as separate chapters, a list of probabilities; and by way of concluding, only what scientists tell us to call 'a model', which has to be clearly labelled as that, and nothing more. This is perhaps inevitable, just as it has long been inevitable in a great deal of archaeological writing, and noticeably so in those dealing with regional aspects of the rise and fall of the Roman empire (too often misleadingly represented as 'histories'). But the realisation of all these hurdles strewn along the road must not always daunt the new enquirer. If a credible narrative of any kind needs some further justification, perhaps one could cite the wise and pertinent comment of Sir John Summerson, that 'readability goes along with the spirit of enquiry, rather than the sense of repletion'.

Our account of Romano–British Christianity must be prefaced with a summary of the wider religious picture. It has become a convention to depict Christianity, when viewed dispassionately as only one of many religious manifestations in Roman Britain, as lying within a third division of all such manifestations, that comprising all the introduced Oriental mystery cults. Any summary must explain why.

At the time of the Claudian conquest, Britain and Ireland were mainly inhabited by peoples who spoke and thought in Celtic languages – British, and the ancestor of Irish – and who can be properly called Celtic. All these Insular Celts included groupings, or tribes, who were relatively recent immigrants, and were related to others in Gaul. They shared, as far as we can ascertain, in the language-family, many personal names and customs, and religious beliefs, of the Celts of western Europe. The ethnography of the latter had long been a matter of interest to the Graeco–Roman world. In the setting of more general comment about their picturesque barbarian neighbours, into whose lands Rome had intruded, the cults and beliefs of the Celts find particular mention in works of classical writers. Nor does it much matter whether this appears in ethnography (a tradition which was begun by the Greeks), general or natural histories, military memoirs, or formulaic productions like rhetoric and panegyrics. If we now possessed no other sources of information (beyond such references) about native life and manners in Britain between Augustus and Theodosius, we should still have some idea of the religious beliefs and practices of the British, and that idea would be on the right lines.

But we do, as it happens, possess a great deal of information from other sources. We have numerous inscriptions (listed in RIB), a very enlightening range of small finds and statuary,[9] excavated pagan temples and shrines,[10] and studies of native cults which can proceed, not so much directly from Romano–British research, but backwards from post-Roman native studies – in particular, of Old Irish, whose literature contains some of the oldest and most important specialised evidence, in this light, about any European people.[11] All this has helped us in making a useful tripartite classification of 'Romano–British religion'. We distinguish the native cults; the Roman religion introduced from the first century AD (itself, really no more than highly evolved native cults of Greek civilisation and the Italian peninsula); and later within this period the various Oriental mysteries. Since the philosophies and practices of the last-named were not much less complex than those of (say) the Church of England, we can designate them as religions.

The native cults of the Celts make up a subject far too elaborate to be examined fully here. The most convenient short introduction is probably still that by Marie-Louise Sjoestedt.[12] At their peak, these cults produced a corpus of some religious thought, externally influenced by higher civilisations, and maintained by that exclusive priesthood which we know as Druids.[13] But in general we can claim that there may have been as many 'gods' as there were notionally separate tribes. This contention would exclude the possibility of amorphous, but national, deities; and also the certainty of hundreds of lesser beings, Shakespeare's 'Elves of hills, brooks, standing lakes and groves', perhaps (rather like the Roman *lares familiares*) also domestic hobgoblins. Nor was such a catalogue ever static. Gods, like the fame of human heroes, waxed and waned, those of defeated or expunged tribes being forgotten or humiliated. Further, the Roman practice of recruiting non-Roman military forces, from native peoples whose males were prised from non-British settings and drafted as units to Britannia, meant that new (often Germanic) native gods arrived with their worshippers, and had then to be accommodated.

The impact of Rome, with her much more organised religion, had a profound effect; one quite apart from the introduction of such purely Roman concepts as devotion to the *numen*, the named and divine aspect, of a recently-deceased and deified emperor. John Mann has defined this impact. 'The role of Rome was probably, in fact, to assist in the *creation* of Celtic deities as individual personalities . . . . The Romans had an extensive collection of deities, covering every aspect of nature and of human life. The Celtic peoples on the other hand had not yet travelled so far along this road. What seem to be the names of different Celtic gods may, at least to begin with, have not really been names of individuals at all. They were rather merely descriptions of a local manifestation of a wider and as yet undifferentiated divine power.'[14]

Outwardly, the most persuasive piece of evidence for this view is the process called *interpretatio* (*Romana*), in which native deities were equated and jointly titled with Roman, or Graeco-Roman, ones. The process was deliberate, and the Latin phrase is the one employed. Tacitus[15] describes a German grove belonging to the Naharvali, staffed by a transvestite native priest, and says that *deos interpretatione romana Castorem Pollucemque memorant* 'what they call these gods would be, by *interpretatio*, Castor and Pollux'. But, he goes on to point out, this just identifies the type (for his readers), the native Naharvali name being *Alci*. When Rome had absorbed a country into her empire, this process moved onward from mere literary comment to outward public advertisement on altars and dedicatory slabs. Roman Britain could show many a shotgun marriage, with such dualities as *Mars Belatucadros*, *Sulis Minerva*, and

Apollo Maponus. These, and others like them, overshadow but do not entirely conceal traces of Celtic deities whose cults were sufficiently deep-rooted or widely based (like *Brigantia* in the north of England, or perhaps the Severn estuary healing god *Nodens*) to allow ideas of rather more independent identities.

Roman religion operated on many levels, both social and spiritual. Though the charge so often brought against it, that '. . . by the time of the Empire it had lost most of its spiritual force – it had become an agent for political and social unity, based on loyalty to the family, the Emperor, and to Rome'[16] is partly true, its complexities had not noticeably lessened because of any loss of driving force, or growth of sophisticated private unbelief. The hard core was still the old Roman pantheon – Jupiter or Jove, sky-father, greatest and best, with all his outsize male and female companions – now joined by the deified Roman emperors, so well placed to intercede on Rome's behalf directly with their divine drinking-partners. On the doorstep (or under it, or behind the house) were all the spiritual household pets, the *lares et penates*, nymphs of the villa springs, godlings of the private shrines.[17]

Where Rome may also have brought about a fundamental change, and British Christianity was not unaffected here, was in the national *attitude* to the divine world. Belief, if often vague and all-pervasive, in some form of cosmic balance has found many expressions in history. The ancient Chinese, whose deceptively primitive and colourful pantheon affords here and there the odd instructive parallel, held a conception (philosophical rather than religious or superstitious) to which one might apply such words as balance, harmony, cosmic rhythm and equipoise. This in (say) Han times way by no means incompatible with a massive display of rural shrines, facilities for sacrificing, a state priesthood, ancestor-worship, or the age-old quest for personal immortality.

It must be doubted whether the Iron Age British, who in terms of material culture alone were a good many stages behind their contemporaries in early Imperial Han China, would unaided by Rome have gone past a spiritual stage that was, at best, propitiatory, and viewed man as wholly in subjection. 'In Celtic religion, the aim seems to have been to propitiate the immense powers of nature *in advance* – that is, by performing elaborate rituals, to persuade the divine powers to bring about that which was desired, or to ward off that which was not desired' (John Mann).[18]

Rome's contribution was to jolt this supine view of the other world, one pervasive of everyday living, into its own next phase; for it can be argued that Roman religious practice, starting from remote origins very similar to those of the Celts, had merely reached a more advanced stage of development than that of the Britons. In this stage – one where of course we cannot ignore the climate of thought that produced the Roman legal system, 'surely the most impressive intellectual achievement of Roman civilisation'[19] – the Gods, who had drawn a little nearer to Man when they permittcd the Augusti, warts and all, to join their ranks, were humanised still further. They now connived at, or did not overtly punish the idea of, fictions of a contractual state. Unlike the cringing Celts, imprisoned in their apotropaic fears and fantasies, the Romans by announcing vows made bargains with individual deities, shopping around for appropriate and supposedly the most efficacious figures. These vows or promises were to perform some action, make some gift, or undertake some event, in return for favours granted by the deities involved. Such vows were manifested on a simple *ex voto* plaque or through an inscribed stone altar (within the means of an average substantial citizen), and at the top end of the scale entire temples could be promised, built and dedicated. The common formula VSLM, *votum solvit libens merito* '(so-and-so) has (hereby) willingly and deservedly fulfilled his promise', made it known to all who read that a piece of business, a cure, or a restitution, had now been brought to a mutually satisfying end. It is the social (Romano–British) equivalent of the handshake and the glass of sherry in the lawyer's office, or the registration of a land-title after some conveyance finally reaches completion.

For any such system to be credible, it had to operate and bc seen to operate in a state of equilibrium, one that minimised any chance of unilateral caprice. This, too, the Romans appreciated. Their own version of the Oriental equipoise, the balanced forces of *Yin* and *Yang*, was their *pax Deorum*; the slightly vulnerable relationship attained with the gods, not so much by men as by the Roman empire, with Roma Aeterna at its centre. This stands a little nearer to ideas of national fortune and stability, and thus to any other desirable *pax* concluded with non-Roman entities, than to abstruse ideas worked out in cosmic terms. 'The Romans had no need to apologise for the growth of Roman power, or try to excuse Roman rule over other Peoples. Expansion could not have taken place if the gods disapproved. Therefore, the gods *did* approve, and no one could challenge their will. Rome had prospered precisely because the Romans had paid the correct cult to the gods, and so long as the *pax deorum* was maintained, Rome would prosper – and expand. Hence, of course, the vital importance of ensuring that the cult of the gods was always maintained.'[20] As we shall find in Chapter 2, not least of the crimes laid at the door of the over-enthusiastic early Roman Christianity was that, by endangering the *pax deorum*, the Church directly threatened the State.

Since so much of our evidence for British Christianity comes to us through archaeology, it is proper to ask – though here without wanting too much detail about matters considered further below – what were the physical reflections of the native cults, the Roman religions, and the extensive rustic conflations of both, in Romano–British towns and countryside. A Christian church is, when all has been said, only a specialised building that uses everyday materials and crafts; a chalice is a cup to hold liquid; and all mosaic pavements were made in the same way, whatever pictures, Christian or pagan, they displayed.

The superiority in outward form, over their pre-Roman equivalents, of monuments proper to Romano–British religions is very much the same as for domestic architecture or roads and bridges. There were many pre-Roman temples and shrines, expressed in their own technology of timber posts and planks, ditches and holes in the ground, cobbles and flags, thatched roofs and baked-clay hearths. The temples and shrines which accompanied the Roman occupation ranged from bucolic little constructions scarcely better than those of the pre-Claudian days, up to classical, virtually Mediterranean buildings in major towns and cities. This range took in all the Romano–British instances of a much wider regional type, the square-plan 'Romano–Celtic temple'.[21] The Roman stone altar, sacrificial in origin, was one innovation; Roman sculptured statuary ran alongside a great catalogue of wholly local depictions-in-the-round, most of the pieces assignable to one deity or another through particular character or accessories.[22]

Where we might see special relevance to Christianity is in the matter of siting, especially urban siting. Temples in towns occupied lots, bounded spaces, within the *insulae* or blocks produced by any town-plan that involved a grid of streets within a boundary earthwork or wall. Insulae, or parts of them, were at bottom parcels of urban property. In varying degrees of what we would now call 'freehold', a citizen could own such a parcel, for his house, even a house and Roman-inspired garden. He might well wish to add a shrine.[23] He and his friends might also come to own a walled plot in the town cemetry, as the property of their little burial-club. While some of the interesting walled cemeteries of Roman Britain[24] may have been the private plots of wealthy families, a phenomenon well-known elsewhere in the empire,[25] it is possible that others were indeed the property of local *collegia*, clubs or guilds. It is in this framework, and especially in the third and fourth centuries of urban Britain, that one bears in mind the likelihood of ownership by Christians of parcels of land, upon which stood buildings used as (or, after AD 313, actually constructed for) churches.[26]

A pagan temple of any standing, within the official forms of Roman religion, would have been publicly or municipally owned. A *Mithraeum* seems more likely to have been the property of its adherents, in this particular cult usually persons of wealth and position. That Christian groups, *ecclesiae*, had attained a rather similar socio-legal standing already by the third century is implicit through surviving documents. Imperial rescripts in the fourth century confirm this. As Ste. Croix points out,[27] whatever the legal basis for this may have been, there is no real evidence that a Christian group as such ever constituted a *collegium illicitum*, an association illegal in itself; and in plot-ownership terms it was in the same position as a mercantile guild or a pagan fraternity.

In the very much more extensive countryside, it is the rise during Roman centuries of the private, organised estate – farms, and villas small and large – and even the appearance (though still inside the Roman religion) of what we have to call 'private temples', that offers some pointers. Much play has been made in recent decades, within oecumenical Christian thought, of something called 'the house-church', applauded as a true return to the Apostolic period. As we shall see (Chap. 7), the Romano–British Christian version arose from motives of privacy, and earlier perhaps of secrecy and poverty, rather than from any urge to simplify matters. The privately-founded episcopal churches, *tituli*, with names that could perpetuate their donors and proprietors, form in spiritual terms quite another matter, and though these played a great part in the development of Christianity in cities like Rome, they are probably irrelevant to Britain. Rather should we think of (in pagan times) a villa-house with its own well-shrine or *nymphaeum*, and an earlier shrine in the grounds, as at Chedworth (p. 219); or, still higher in the scale of gracious living, the second-century circular shrine replaced by the grander fourth-century temple-cum-mausoleum, both hard by the Lullingstone villa in Kent.[28]

Many functions have been attributed to Romano–British temples and shrines – for instance, those of major centres of pilgrimage, notably in connection with healing or medicinal cults (Lydney, and Bath), and as localities for what later would be called fairs, festivals and markets. The aspects which do bear some relevance to Christianity are those just described, however; the idea of the cult building as an integral, owned, plot, part of a properly-managed town, and the idea of the private (family or estate) cult-building, as an adjunct to a rural holding.

We have very little information as to how, if at all, pagan detail may have been mirrored in actual Romano–Christian practice. The pagan altar, *ara*, was rigidly avoided, even the very word being excluded from Christian terminology. It is possible (Chap. 7) that, in so far as we can determine them, ground-plans of Romano–British churches are related to those of certain late pagan temples, apart from the more general debt owed by churches, as architectural forms, to secular models. Specifically, the extraordinary feather- or leaf-shaped votive plaques in the Water Newton hoard, indubitably Christian in nature, but pagan in form, call for deeper examination (p. 118). But, in this topic of overlap, we are drawn, before a final short look at the Oriental mystery religions, to *syncretism*.

This useful seventeenth-century word, with its adjective 'syncretistic', describes the personal mental process of reconciling different if not directly opposing spiritual tenets within one philosophy. For Roman Britain it arises, not so much in the meeting of native and Roman cults, but in that more subtle zone where religion becomes involved with ethics, with abstract belief and arguments, and true philosophy.[29] It is well exemplified by problems arising from the study of late Roman villa mosaics, only a very few of which can be claimed to show direct allusions to Christianity, but rather more of which contain scenes or figures, where an indirect allusion has been suspected.[30] Now one might point out that the Gospel story involves a young adult male, born of woman but claimed as an avatar of the True God, who through redemptive self-sacrifice overcame the dark powers of death and evil, and offers places to his devout believers in a spiritual otherworld. This presentation does no great injury to the message of the New Testament. It does however align that message with those of other religions which involve all or most of such features, particularly those of the Young God, the conquest of co-extant evil, and the eternal reward of the believers.

It is therefore possible to wonder whether sophisticated Roman Britons, familiar with secular classics, and enjoying a cultured existence in town and country after AD 313, might not have included what John Chandler[31] describes as 'nominal Christians'; adherents, in principle and where necessary in public, to the most fashionable and swiftly growing *religio licita*, the Church, but unable to perceive any real inconsistency in the displaying of Orpheus taming the wild beasts, as Christ tamed the beasts in men, on the pavements of their main rooms.[32] Just such a man might have been privately reluctant to destroy, for sheer destruction's sake, a nearby shrine piously erected by his grandfather; particularly if it could be shrugged off as something maintained for the sake of the servants.

A further stage of multiplicity, one in which such casual syncretism would have been less probable, occurs with the arrival of fully-developed cults originating in North Africa or the eastern provinces. These are frequently discussed[33] and can be quickly mentioned.

Mithraism, in the late Roman period, hardly less complicated to the newly converted than Christianity would have seemed; the cult of the Anatolian mother-goddess Cybele and her divine son Atys; of Egyptian deities, Isis in particular; and from Syria, a group of intermingled cults springing from a local *interpretatio* of powerful figures in Jupiter guise – these represent the rather more flamboyant forms. On the intellectual side, a corpus of beliefs known as 'Gnosticism'[34], rich ground for future heresies, had elsewhere interpenetrated Christianity and may have reached Roman Britain. And it is also possible that, given the presence of enough settled Jews to form communities, Jewish temples or synagogues could have been found in certain towns (*cf.* p. 174). What most of the Oriental mystery cults and religions had in common with the Christian church, certainly during the third century and to a much lesser extent in the fourth, was an appearance – to the total outsider – of exclusivity. This had little to do with the jollities at the local temple. It all hinted at dark ceremonies conducted in private, things accessible only to initiates; it might well be inimical to the *pax Deorum*, despite the official toleration of such cults; and in bureaucratic eyes, as so often now, all that is not patent is presumably being deliberately hidden.

The historical process whereby Christianity rose to become the principal religion of the Later Roman Empire, and thus the main highway (together with a remnant administration) along which Roman civilisation could propel some of its accomplishments towards early medieval Europe, is outlined in the next two chapters. No such chapters can be substitutes for, in his own day, the writings of Edward Gibbon, nor in our own those of A.H.M. Jones.[35] And we are left with one question that every writer upon this subject must answer for himself. What precisely was the appeal of Christianity?

It may seem trite to point to the wretched conditions under which the vast majority of late Roman citizens, of all nationalities and creeds and through all the provinces, passed their often very short lives. We think of the burden of increasing taxation laid on all those still in any position to be taxed; that constant fear – no stranger to Roman Britain – in so many areas, of barbarian incursions, unchecked or checked too late; and the progressive inadequacy of the entire body of Roman paganism, the *prisca religio* of nostalgic apostates, to provide any solace consonant either with the dignity of the human individual, or his pathetic hopes of an ameliorated afterlife. Trite all this may be; but we can see how, in this very area of little reward and less hope, the news of a religion with a difference struck a spark. The difference was multiple. *This* religion now offered to all, without exception and without payment or levy, a promise of personal salvation. One was asked to believe in a single God: was that really so difficult? This God had, moreover, become manifest as Man, not all that long ago, and within the Roman empire; he had lived, he had died, and *mirabile dictu* he had overcome Death itself. His followers now spoke of a Second Coming, redemption of a Divine vow, after a period of notable turmoil which (as everyday life and politics strongly suggested) might even now be in progress. The very dead would be resurrected. If therefore burials instead of cremations, burials in the style of Christians, burials *with* Christians, could assist that particular process, why not go along with the custom? All religions possessed holy places, temples; why should not the Christians have them? Those who could not read, or were confused by details, could avail themselves of instruction in the new creed. It cost nothing except time. One was initiated after baptism in water; there was nothing all that new in the idea of water, especially running water, having sacred qualities. What Christianity was offering, and what almost no other religion had ever offered *in toto*, was unrestricted membership and salvation to men and women, rich and poor. The poor would not be excluded, as in other temple-owning cults, because they were unable to make frequent financial contributions. All would be saved; there was a real, personal involvement, spelled out in a simple form that any ordinary downtrodden Roman could easily understand. In John Mann's words, 'the difficulties of his oppressed condition in a vast impersonal society were simply washed away'.

If this spiritually ideal picture of the Faith in its first centuries refers to Roman Britain at all, it refers to the earlier third century, between the most likely date of a Christian foothold in Britain (give or take a generation, AD 200), and the trauma of the first full persecution in the middle of that century. One might even propose that the later story of British Christianity is one of a decline, a steady fall from grace in the face of worldliness, down to that disgraceful position described – without specific detail, but in adequate degree – by Gildas, writing of the later fifth century. Any such comments ought to form a postscript, rather than a preface, to our account; the more so when the declared aim is to chart the progress of Romano–British Christianity, not to draw moral precepts from each descriptive stage. The chapters that follow will try to put together such an account. Only the final one need return to the theme of where Romano–British Christianity succeeded, and where it failed.

CHAPTER TWO

The Historical Evidence

A candid but rational inquiry into the progress and
establishment of Christianity may be considered as a very
essential part of the history of the Roman empire . . . . But
this inquiry, however useful or entertaining, is attended with
two peculiar difficulties. The scanty and suspicious materials
of ecclesiastical history seldom enable us to dispel the dark
cloud that hangs over the first age of the church.
Edward Gibbon (1776)

The historiography, the analytical study of the published histories, of
Christianity in Britain before AD 600, is in its own way instructive. If we
confine it further, to what are now England and Wales (for both Scotland
and Ireland possess their own distinct historiographic traditions), it is at
once remarkable how slender the list seems to be. This observation itself
suggests a reason; and we further realise how very little material for any
such history exists. Virtually all the historical evidence has been known
to specialists for centuries, and apart from rare and usually marginal
enlightenment afforded by recognition of some fresh manuscript variant,
there is nothing else to look for. Progress has to rely, not on the despatch
of scouting-parties of palaeographers to comb the scriptoria of obscure
religious foundations, but on rigorous dissection of what we already
possess.

Any form of Christian historiography in the past has been an easy
target for later historians; Collingwood[1] considered all such histories as
'of necessity universal, providential, apocalypitc, and periodized', and in
relation to most of them he went on to justify this criticism. Only with
Edward Gibbon, whose famous 'Fifteenth and Sixteenth Chapters' (on
Roman Christianity) of Vol. I of his *Decline and Fall of the Roman
Empire* (published 1776) marked a watershed, did the course of the whole
tradition change. Gibbon, quite apart from casting the early stages of
Christian history in the Roman empire within the same causative mould
as secular history, and thus denying any special 'providential or
apocalyptic' guidance, also depicted the Church as (in J.M. Robertson's
words) '. . . not a preservative but a dissolvent of all ancient civilisation
as such' and one whose eventual domination of the Later Roman Empire
'could not possibly preserve it' (the empire) 'as against races unweakened
by its sacerdotal spell'.

We need not follow the long debate, involving Gibbon's critics and his pulverising treatment of those critics, or all the subsequent attempts to assess this particular aspect of Gibbon's rôle within European history.[2] But, after Gibbon, no historical account of early Christianity could safely discuss the Church save as one of numerous, though in this case vital, facets of the classical past. Gibbon of course hardly adverted to Christianity in Britain, of which he could know nothing save the existence of scattered mentions from Tertullian onward. In the last century, perhaps in part inspired by easier access to Bede's historical writings and by the appearance of appropriate Irish and Scottish sources, Christianity started to be of rather more concern to native historians. Its early British phases were, however, so frequently seen as a means of justifying contemporary ecclesiastical politics, and doctrinal wranglings, that we can today largely disregard the output. There are occasional points of interest. The self-educated Cornishman, George Smith (1800–68), in his *The Religion of Ancient Britain*,[3] struck a balance between the Roman, (Celtic-speaking) British, and converted English aspects of his Gibbon-directed study that would not again be found for a good half-century or more. It has to be added that Smith, who also wrote the first standard three-decker history of Wesleyan Methodism, saw fit to sub-title his *Ancient Britain* with such revealing sentiments as '. . . including an investigation into the early progress of error in the Christian church, the introduction of the Gospel into Great Britain, and the state of religion in England *till Popery had gained the ascendancy*'.

As Gibbon's discourse on the Church was set in the much larger backdrop of Rome's secular imperial decline, so fresh treatments of the early British church waited upon the rise of a separate *genre* – that of the 'national history'. This is exemplified by such works as John Richard Green's *A Short History of the English People*.[4] The tale of the Church begins, not in Roman days, but in 597 with the landing of Augustine: 'The march of the monks as they chanted their solemn litany was, in one sense, the return of the Roman legions who had retired at the trumpet-call of Alaric.' Now enriched by the arrival of the Apostle of the English, 'the new England was admitted into the older commonwealth of nations'. Green, as E.H. Carr points out,[5] may fairly be assessed as pedestrian, but he was among the first to advance towards a view of history as the history of the whole national community. In this respect, Green may have trodden unwittingly in the footsteps of a very much earlier British pioneer – not in this case the eighth-century Bede, but the sixth-century Gildas, whom Edward Thompson now describes[6] as 'an innovator . . . in the history of British historiography he was the greatest innovator of all . . . He was the first man in the entire West to write a provincial history.'

Virtually all the known sources for our oldest Christian history had been collected, edited and classified by 1869, by A.W. Haddan and William Stubbs.[7] Newer historians were given the materials, and progressively the comparanda as well. Gradually, tome by tome, the corpora of all the relevant European sources became available; the *Monumenta Germanica Historiae* (monumental, indeed), the *Corpus Inscriptionum Latinarum* (with the seventh, Roman Britain, volume in 1873); and one must not pass over our own *Rolls Series*. But the first attempt at a full history of Insular Christianity, Hugh Williams' *Christianity in Early Britain*, did not appear until 1912, sadly just after the author's death.

Dr Williams has not always received his rightful due; those more recent writers who have too readily dismissed his work as being obsolete have, in some cases very patently, not necessarily been equipped either to judge it or to profit by it. Williams wrote, it is true, from a Welsh viewpoint. He was Welsh, his career (as a professor at Bala) lay in Wales, his book itself sprang from a very Welsh event, the 1905 Davies Lecture, and the author was most at home in the central stream of Welsh scholarship. If one would today counsel caution to the beginner or lay student, it would be because it needs maturer scholarship to redress subtle balances of various interpretations; and because, inevitably in the long period since 1912, most of the linguistic, and some of the hagiographical, conclusions demand adjustment in the light of subsequent research. This said, *Christianity in Early Britain* remains a magnificent study replete with strong and original thought. In its moderate and sensible style it closely recalls the work of another great scholar, Charles Plummer, editor and translator of Bede's historical works.[8] And Williams was displayed, unconsciously, at his very best in a now forgotten (but still important, and extraordinarily prescient) review article[9] – his handling of that most controversial of essays upon the Celtic Church, the 1901 views of Heinrich Zimmer, a man whom Kenney could call 'the Ishmael of Celtic studies, whose hand was against every man's'.[10]

Hugh Williams took the word 'Britain' to signify the homeland of the post-400 British, outside the gradually-increasing regions of the former Roman Britannia which were being settled by the English. His History ended, effectively, in AD 603, the occasion of Augustine's meeting with the British bishops at 'Augustine's Oak'. After that event, he wrote,[11] 'there were two Churches in Britain, the old British, the new Roman'. In his final double-chapter ('Two Churches'), he summarised the state of Christianity in the early seventh century. Having reached his intended limit, Williams left by implication the unitary tale of the later Church, within the whole British mainland, from then up to Norman times, to another hand. It cannot be said that this challenge has ever been taken up, in the form that Williams probably had in mind. But if, in the interval since 1912, scholarship has been enriched through such aids as LHEB, RIB, the creation of further national and international series (like *Scriptores Latini Hiberniae*, and *Codices Latini Antiquiores*), and by the productive careers of so many whose works are cited below and in the Bibliography, then justice demands that we realise Hugh Williams, if alive today, would have produced a better synthesis than this present volume. Critical assessment of his *Early Britain* which fails to see Hugh Williams' intellectual power and receptivity is as inequitable as the much commoner criticism levelled at the late Karl Marx in his rôle as an economic historian.

'British' (that is Celtic and English) early religious history was from the early 1930s to the late 1940s marked by the attention paid, in many university circles, to the Church in Anglo-Saxon England; and perhaps already overshadowed by realisation of the increasing complexities of protohistoric studies. These now necessarily involved linguistic enquiry and critical review, rather beyond conventional training and resources. The late H.M. Chadwick, exceptionally, straddled the traditional boundaries. There were, none the less, at all times a few persons able to proclaim that British Christian history did actually begin rather earlier than AD 597. In singling out names, one incurs of course some risk of slighting others. It would never be right to overlook a few notable minds whose owners, their contributions still relevant, continued to proclaim that much of fifth-century Britain was the product of preceding ages, and that there was even potentially a British history in the sixth century. One recalls, naturally, C.E. Stevens, whose championship[12] of an older fellow-historian precedes the present powerful revival of attention paid to Gildas.[13] Mortimer Wheeler, whose largeness of interests always matched his own personality, explored and published several major sites, Lydney[14] and Verulamium[15] in particular, with Tessa Verney Wheeler; and these if nominally Roman in emphasis were invariably interpreted within much wider temporal contexts. Wheeler's grasp of the post-400 side of those contexts, and his politico-military conception of sub-Roman British history that could at its least lift the whole topic clear of befogging localised details, led to such formative essays as his rightly-famed *London and the Saxons*; facing squarely the enigma of the British in fifth-century south-east Britain.[16]

For far too long, the standard curricular emphases of many British schools and universities meant that works entitled *The Pre-Conquest Church in England*, *Roman Britain and the English Settlements*, or *Roman Britain and the Early English*, were economically feasible ventures. Such comment, far from intentionally slighting any of these, points out by contrast that a reprint of Hugh Williams's 1912 *History* would not have been such. But one must also record that the Chadwicks (Hector Munro, and Nora Kershaw) were up to the times of their deaths in 1947 and 1972 respectively, and particularly from the mid-1940s onward, responsible for the initiation and the presentation of combined studies – severally and jointly, and with their colleagues and pupils – which most firmly united the related protohistories of Scotland, Wales, post-Roman Britain and Anglo-Saxon England. It is not easy, at so short a remove, to give full and objective assessment of their achievements,[17] particularly from anyone who was close to either of them. It is however compellingly necessary to point out that there is no longer any hope of real progress through old-style 'separatist' studies, as opposed to the Chadwickian model of unified topics, regions, and disciplines. As for the preciser qualification of periods of absolute time, the Chadwicks, and their school, were mainly concerned with events after AD 400. Sadly, a detectable gully still yawns between this, very much the Chadwick period, and the continuous study of Roman Britain. The difficulty is to discern sufficient contemporary scholars (who, if still few numerically, are mainly very high in quality) prepared to look – like Hugh Williams in 1912, and in broader vein Kenneth Jackson and the late John Morris – specifically at the centuries between AD 300 and 600.

Since the 1950s, and this must be linked to post-War development throughout Britain's towns and countryside, publication of both factual records and synthetic accounts of discoveries illustrative of the British past has striven – but with only partial success – to keep pace with chance finds and the results of all forms of excavation. This is especially the case with Roman (and to some extent, also post-Roman) studies, simply because the enormous quantity of material can so rapidly surmount our national capacity to process it. In the restricted compass of this present book alone, it will be seen (Chaps. 4 – 7) how much of the evidence for the presence of Christians in Roman Britain has only come to light in the last quarter-century.

What has so emerged has also stimulated, since about 1950, sufficient papers and essays to warrant (if no more) a complete factual revision of Williams's 1912 volume. Again one risks injustice to the meritorious by selective reference; but the impact of particular papers, such as Toynbee (1953) and Frend (1955) set this particular ball rolling. One could go on, legitimately, to particularise such events as the 1961 *Art in Roman Britain* exhibition (which led to Jocelyn Toynbee's two major works here);[18] the 1967 Nottingham symposium, ostensibly to examine 'Christianity in Britain, 300 to 700', with its collected papers;[19] slightly on the sidelines, the Patrician Year (1961) with its alarming rash of publication;[20] and a steady range of fresh comment on Roman Christianity generally.[21] Individual discoveries of outstanding merit – the Lullingstone wall-plaster, the Hinton St Mary pavement, and the Water Newton hoard – not only prompted speedy, and generally very thorough, publication; they performed, even if this was not at once apparent, the much more valuable function of bringing the whole notion of 'Romano–British Christianity' into (one can hardly write *'back* into') the sphere of European scholarly interest. The British Museum's 1977 *Wealth of the Roman World* exhibition[22] could by that time, and with total justification, place the Water Newton objects, as the earliest hoard of Christian silver in the empire and by no means the least significant, right alongside the Casket of Projecta and the Kaiseraugst Treasure.

There is no particular call to list all the closely parallel output of papers, on related themes, from neighbouring European countries over the same period. Some, notably from centres and museums in the Netherlands and the Rhineland, have had the same beneficial effect upon British scholarship, as (one likes to suppose) the British traditions of systematic fieldwork and rescue and salvage archaeology are by way of return exerting within the Continent. What *does* bear comment is that this same period has seen the appearance of many syntheses of early Christian history and archaeology; as works which, rather like Gildas' in Edward Thompson's view, are preferred by learned native scholars, concerned with national identity and native endeavour, in native languages. This is an observation, and not any form of lofty supra-national criticism; the majority of histories appears in precisely such a guise. Those one has in mind would range from the almost entirely historical, like Émile Mâle's *La Fin du Paganisme en Gaule* (1951), to others couched in a mixture of classical-style archaeology and art history (for instance, de Palol's 1967 *Arqueología Cristiana de la España Romana*). As a backdrop, this same period has seen – remaining with archaeology, in the broadest idiom – works writ on larger canvas, and powerfully influential ones. A list would have to begin with such names as André Grabar[23] and persons in his own circle, for example Khatchat-rian;[24] Krautheimer,[25] and, since the present work is to some extent couched in the Gildasian national idiom, one includes J.G. Davies[26] and John Ward Perkins.[27] All these now readily permit, and indeed require, however, that new provincial studies of early Christianity be placed in a much broader Late Roman imperial format.

What has been said so far in this chapter must not be construed either as some personal justification for this book, shortcomings and all, or still less as an oblique harangue aimed at the writer's various colleagues for not having produced, among them, a better book at an earlier date. It is simply an individual historiographic view of the present state of studies in early British Christian history, and it may well afford (if it has to) an explanation of why and how yet one more summary, however imperfect and however personal in tone, should be attempted. In making that attempt, and in rounding off the historiography at 1980, the author's main reflection is one of gratitude; that the present existence of so much published information – in *Britannia, Medieval Archaeology*, the BAR and CBA reports, in corpora like RIB, in national and local journals – facilitates the task of search and collation which, in Hugh Williams' day, would have been hardly and dearly accomplished.

As we move on to examine the first records of Christianity in Britain we must isolate at once, and very sharply, a body of legends concerning British Christian origins.[28] These myths, not all of them interconnected, do include some of great antiquity. A common factor, that many of them were given written form by such medieval authors as Geoffrey of Monmouth – something that accorded them a currency, and a longevity, that they might not otherwise have attained – does not preclude completely the chance that certain of these stories have an older genesis.

A few of these legends can be relatively easily disentangled. The belief that (Flavia) Helena, mother of Constantine the Great, was a British princess and the daughter of Coel Hen, 'Old King Cole,' and eponymous king of Colchester, may partly have sprung from confusion with another and later Helena – very probably well-born and British – who was the wife of Magnus Maximus (ruling 383–8) and who also had a son by the name of Constantine. Again, the possibility that Constantine the Great, the precise date of whose birth, and age at death in 337, were facts not agreed by early biographers, was actually born in Britain is aired occasionally. It is remote in the extreme. His father Flavius Valerius Constantius Chlorus, governor of Dalmatia in 282–4, became Caesar or junior emperor in the West in 293, moved to Gaul in 297 from Britain, and returned to Britain as Augustus in 306. Constantine I as a child was sent to Diocletian's court (in 292). The powerful York bust (Pl. 2), if really of Constantine, and dateable to 306, is enigmatic; is it a youth of nineteen? a man in his mid-twenties? The commonly accepted idea is that he was born in 288, in Moesia (now Yugoslavia). Did he visit Britain as a child? His attachment to Britannia, the chance that he was ever personally influenced by (British) Christians, and even the depth of his own religious commitment, are matters of uncertainty; all we know is that it was at York, on his father's death in July of 306, that Constantine I allegedly first disclaimed the title of Augustus thrust upon him by the army, and then assumed that of Caesar with Galerius' agreement and recognition.

The Helena stories at least treat of historical persons, Old King Cole excepted. Though in a rather different sense, Our Lord, St Paul, and Joseph of Arimathea were also historical, the supposition that they personally visited Britain – during the first century AD – underlies a corpus of picturesque myths of uncertain age; possibly medieval as we have them, conceivably the reflection of something much older. More easily explained is the tale of Lucius, a British king, whose second-century appeal for the grace of conversion, addressed to Eleutherius,

Pope *c*.174–89, was incorporated in Bede's *Historia*;[29] Plummer thought
it likely Bede obtained this, ultimately, from informants who had picked
it up in Rome. It has been shown to be a muddled version of a Papal
contact with another Lucius, prince of Edessa, older *Birtha* or *Britio
Edessenorum* – hence the ascription to Britannia.[30]

Lurking a very long way within another body of beliefs, one whose
tap-roots must go far behind the Anglo-Norman poets and chroniclers, is
that mysterious, shadowy, autochthonous mythos which never really
dies; has a constant appeal to the romantically-minded; and, for want of
any better name, is best labelled 'the Matter of Britain'. Where Christian
origins are concerned, part of all this is specifically linked to Glastonbury, in Somerset – the spot where Joseph of Arimathea's staff took root
as the Glastonbury Thorn. It has been slightly surprising, during the
whole long period of excavation to which Glastonbury Abbey, the Tor,
and other sites (Chalice Well, Beckery, etc.) in the immediate area have
been subjected, that so far one cannot bring any of this into Roman
Christianity at all; the first Christian phase appears to be an (?) early
sixth-century monastic foundation.

Possibly another common factor in many of these origin-legends is
that they attempt to fill a vacuum, to explain the unascertainable by the
incredible. In the sixth and seventh centuries and one need look no
further than Gildas and Bede for confirmation – no-one had any real
notion of how Christianity in Britain began. If such oral traditions had
ever existed, the thread of their transmission across the Late Roman
period was so slender, and so often stretched to breaking-point, that no
details survived. This was not universally the case in what had been the
Roman empire. There were churches claiming descent from individual
Apostles. In Gaul, most people knew about the martyrs of Lyon in 177,
and the seven episcopal founders – Trophimus, Saturninus and the rest –
sent by Pope Fabian in the middle of the third century to the major cities
(St Dionysius or 'St-Denis' of Paris among them). Is it too far-fetched to
suspect that the Church in post-Roman, non-English Britain, aware that
it lacked the named founding-fathers of more fortunate provinces, began
at a popular level to form its own retrospective apostles? And – we shall
consider this below – is the prestige accorded to Albanus, already surely
to be discerned in the fifth century as the equivalent of a national martyr-
hero, partly a corollary of Britannia's lack of any other, or earlier, named
Christian pioneer?

More acceptable history begins with very general allusions to the Church
in Britain. These are conveniently listed, though without translations
from the Greek or Latin, in Haddan & Stubbs[31] – some, with more up-to-
date textural references, are repeated now by Rivet and Smith[32] – and
they were discussed by Hugh Williams.[33] The allusions to the presence of

Christianity in Britain are, alas, neither isolated nor particularly specific. When the North African convert Tertullian, a man whose literary output and stylistic influence upon Christian Latin terminology have often earned him the sobriquet 'Father of Latin Theology', wrote his Tract against the Jews (*Adversus Judaeos*), he chose to make the point that Christianity was, by about AD 200, already established in the remoter fringes of the empire – seen from Carthage, that is – as in provinces whose intellectual centres could embrace and extol the Faith. Tertullian's rhetorically-phased string of such marginal lands runs, partly clockwise, from the Persians, through the Gaetuli (representing the North African hinterland), Mauretania, north to Spain (*Hispaniarum omnes termini*), then to the diverse peoples of the Gauls. Here, before he moves around to the northern barbarians (Sarmatians, Dacians, Germans and Scyths), we find *Britannorum inaccessa Romanis loca* ('places of the British not approached by the Romans') which, like all the other regions, are said to be now *Christo vero subdita* 'made subject to the true Christ'.

This cannot possibly be taken at face-value. Nor is there reason to suppose that a Church Father in sunny, urbane Carthage – who went on to add a clause sweeping up into a heap '. . . all the peoples I have not bothered to mention and all the many provinces and islands of which we are ignorant' – was in the least concerned to ascertain, either the state of the Roman frontiers in Britain in AD 200, or the exact locations of the few Christians Britain may have by then possessed. Tertullian's contemporary Origen, an ascetic and productive Alexandrian writer and philosopher, also chose (in various Homilies) to bring in *Britannia*, or *terra Britanniae*, in very much the same light – a region at the end of the civilised world. It was one of several such place-names, used to hammer home the joyous fact of the triumph of the Church; a Church, indeed, *quae mundi limites tenent* 'which is now established at the very ends of the (Roman) world'.

If one is prepared, with Frend and others,[34] to look upon individuals travelling mainly for commercial purposes, to Gaul and Britain from Mediterranean lands, as at least one very likely channel for the diffusion of Christian ideas, then given the importance of both Carthage and Alexandria in spiritual and intellectual (as well as commercial) ways, we could agree that people like Tertullian and Origen were in a position to be told – and would have been told – of even minor Christian triumphs and footholds in westermost lands. The opening years of the third century offer us a date not inconsistent with reasonable guesses on other grounds; for example, the presence of Christianity in Gaulish cities in the preceding quarter-century.

The Christian writers of the fourth century, like Eusebius ('Father of Church History') writing sporadically up to about 323 and mentioning the British connections of Constantine, and his father Constantius, and

Lactantius, who died about 320, and whose work forms a major source for the Diocletianic persecutions, allude to Christianity in Britain. So, too, do a number of Greek patristic writers rather later in the century. Their remarks are however less relevant to the Church in Britain, as such, than to the praiseworthy orthodoxy of Britain's stance during the mid-fourth century Arian controversies (these had to do with the exact nature of Christ's divinity);[35] but these, and other documents, include reference, and this is important and valuable, to British bishops and to British participation in fourth-century ecclesiastical councils outside Britain. Together they confirm, though without offering very much enlightenment about matters where all other forms of revelation are lacking, the existence of an established but unquantified British Roman church.

Nor, when we turn to another giant of Latin letters, St Jerome, are we much wiser through seeing that, like Tertullian before him, Jerome also like to employ rhetorical and geographical tropes to depict the idea of the Church Universal (sample: *et Galliae et Britanniae et Africa et Persis et Oriens et India . . . unum Christum adorant*). This may be thundering prose, but it is derivative; it is not necessarily what we seek.

What is so very pointedly missing, and in the lack there may be a lesson, is any particular recourse to British Christianity by way of illustration in works of third-century Christian writers; or those which, after Constantine's conversion, belonged to a more developed historiographic tradition. One thinks of specific points, illustrative of Christ's triumphs, after long struggle, *inter barbaros* or *inter provincias longinquissimas*, Rome's notoriously remote satrapies; Britannia high on anyone's list here. This is bound to reinforce a long-standing suspicion: that until post-Constantinian times, British Christianity was numerically very insignificant, had no particular geographical focus, and had up to then produced no one Christian thinker, martyr, or expatriate champion whose name could be snatched up in polished circles as that of a distant soul prominently gained for Christ. It is one more reason for declining to believe (as against John Morris) that public martyrdom of the citizen Albanus, at the hands of a Caesar and within a day's posting from the capital, could ever have occurred – as a notable and isolated happening – as early as AD 209. If it had, it seems scarcely conceivable that news of it would not have reached Christian circles in Rome and Alexandria within a year, and that someone would not have seized upon it. We shall return to the martyrdoms again; but that Albanus's more probably formed part of, and was historically thus concealed within, a widespread persecution of later date, may be suggested by this negative evidence alone.

Questions of the British bishops, the first direct mention of whom is to be found in the textually variable recensions of the *Acta Concilii Arelatensis*, the AD 314 ecclesiastical council of Arles,[36] ought not to be taken apart from considerations of episcopates and dioceses in Roman Britain. Discussion of them is deferred to the relevant place (Chap. 7).

The Greek word *martyros*, later *martyr*, meant 'one who bears testimony; a witness'. In a Christian sense, borrowed into Latin because this has been the term used for the disciples who were directly witnesses of Our Lord, it developed special meanings: Christians who, because they bore witness to the Faith, underwent persecution, and (as more generally in later centuries), persecution ending in their deaths.

The persecution of Christians – that is, the hostile actions of non-Christians that gave rise to martyrdoms and thus to the whole cult of martyrs in the early Church – was rather more than just a matter of brave but tear-stained faces in some Roman arena, and of voices raised in hymns as the hungry lions rushed forward. As William Frend has fairly convincingly demonstrated,[37] on any proper and full historical assessment the persecutions were actually a failure. Ste. Croix's useful analysis[38] may profitably guide us. From the non-Christian angle, there were as a start two, quite distinct, forms of persecution: the popular, and the official. We should not so much ask why Christians were persecuted at all, as 'Why did the Roman government – emperors, Senate, civil and military administrative machineries – persecute Christians?', and, separately, 'For what reasons did ordinary pagans demand persecution?'

For Britain, as for Gaul, where the history of Christianity possesses little substance before the early third century, the initial phase of persecutions (involving Nero's choice of Christians as a mass or collective scapegoat for the great fire of AD 64 at Rome) does not concern us. Until the middle of the third century, the low-key latent popular anti-Christian sentiment that could and did surface, from time to time and from place to place, though not after any pattern, had as its kernel what might be described as the stubborn *exclusivity* of the Christians. The common answer to the two questions set out above is this;[39] it was not so much the positive beliefs and practices of the church that aroused pagan resentment, as the negative element in that religion – the Christians' total refusal to worship any God save their own. Such an attitude, in non-Christian eyes, could only endanger the *pax Deorum*, the essential equipoise between gods and men. If the lofty but generally beneficent indifference of the gods was to be disquieted in this fashion by the Christians' private, inexplicable monotheism, then it might well follow that natural disasters (flood, fire and pestilence) would be so brought about.

Official, or State-directed antagonism is harder to pin down.[40] But here again, in the framework of the Romans' legal system, the offence was not the positive practice of Christianity. It was more a matter involving any one of a great many detailed charges that could stem from the application of Christian exclusivity, monotheism, or plain unacceptable behaviour in everyday life and affairs. These could, at the gravest, involve *maiestas* (treason). As Ste. Croix puts it,[41] if the Roman state – for any cause at all, pressures of popular hostility at a period of pronounced anti-Christian feeling included – wished to drag some Christian before the law, no legal foundation was needed, 'other than a prosecutor, a charge of Christianity, and a governor willing to punish on that charge'. Nor, as was mentioned earlier, is there persuasive reason to think that Christians were ever seen as belonging to groups outlawed *per se*, irremediably illegal associations. What *was* in conflict was the external, pantheon-insulting, socially disruptive or even insurrectional behaviour of citizens, whose private spiritual get-togethers might otherwise be readily tole-rated in the same way as those of half-a-dozen other major pagan cults. The most offensive form of this behaviour could be manifested by near-hysterical crowds offering, or even demanding, to be martyred for Christ; a spectacle then, as now, perhaps more easily imagined in the Near East and Hither Asia than in Gaul, or Britain.

We must go back to Britain in the context of those particular episodes of state-inspired anti-Christian hostility commonly recalled by the labels of relevant emperors, or else as 'general persecutions' and (for that under Diocletian) the 'Great Persecution'. Here, we must ask: did these extend to Britain? and during which such events were British Christians martyred?

The persecution under Decius, from about January 250 to his death in June 251, was in part characterised by doubts as to whether Christians, as loyal Romans, could afford sufficient proof that they sacrificed loyally to the emperor's *numen*. As in the later (257–9) persecution under Valerian, the irreconcilable conflict sprang out of the, by now wholly evolved and rigid, Christian monotheism. This in official eyes was unreasonable. Christians were not being required to surrender any part of their faith, or (initially) of their ecclesiastical property, still less their physical selves; merely, at a period of some disquiet in the larger tide of the empire, to pay due respect to the gods on whom the welfare of their empire rested.[42]

Frend has underlined the extent of the apostasies, or backslidings, that occurred as a result of such persecutions,[43] even in those provinces where the Church had become widespread, well-organised, and with follow-ings already large enough to give rise to sectarianism. At this juncture, the continuity of the Faith depended (as it has done in more recent centuries) on the steadfastness of a few, mainly the clergy, rather than on the massive resistance of a public following.

After 260, under the Rescript of Gallienus,[44] Christianity enjoyed a new status as a *religio licita*, an officially approved cult. The course of the next half-century – during which churches, some as we know of considerable size, were built, cemeteries openly resorted to, and the whole impedimenta of Christian life and worship now publicly and legally deployed – goes some way to explain the ultimate failure of the Great Persecution. This began in 303 when, as Eusebius tells us, the main issue was once again 'that all the people should without exception sacrifice in the several cities and offer libations to the idols'.[45] The emphasis on the positive restoration of the *prisca religio* 'Our Faith from Ages Past', that is the various forms of official State-favoured religion, reminds us (as aspects of fourth-century Britain will do) that paganism was far from extinct. Revival in this light culminated, during the next eight years, in the reported policies of Maximinus II, emperor in the East, who ordered the full-scale re-erection of temples and the appointment of a formal pagan hierarchy to serve them.

The end of the Great Persecution was marked, less by any single event, than by the eventual implicit admission that Christianity was now beyond the stage where it could be expunged, or all its adherents effectively subdued. The very administration was riddled with Christian sympathisers. Upward social mobility in the later empire,[46] bringing to positions of influence Christians from the lower and middle classes, may have been an important factor. In the further dioceses and provinces, orders to destroy, confiscate, fine and imprison might, as they passed through Christian hands, be locally modified, deferred and even lost. Since 260, the expansion of the Church in terms of population – Frend has particularly quantified this for North Africa[47] – meant that Rome was half-way to a dilemma, comparable to that facing any modern industrial nation which toys with the idea of outlawing General Strikes; you cannot arrest an entire population.

The landmarks that close the Diocletianic episode began with Galerian's grudging edict of 311 (the Galerian Edict, or the Edict of Toleration)[48] where once more the heart of the matter becomes apparent. The Christians are recognised, but this is providing they do nothing to offend against public order; and accept that it is their duty as Roman citizens to pray (to their own Deity) for the continued well-being of the State. The much more positively worded edict issued in March 313 from Milan by Constantine the Great and his fellow-Augustus, Licinius (the Edict of Milan)[49], raised Christianity to 'our first and principal concern'. It announced a general religious tolerance. It ordered the restitution of all church property, and, where this had been destroyed, compensation. Surviving letters of Constantine[50] to the African churches, letters which must exemplify a wider issuing of such directives, specify the return of buildings, land, and all other property. We know, too, that actual funds, for the maintenance of orthodoxy in areas now further disturbed by the rise of the Donatist heresy,[51] were sent to Caecilianus, since 311 bishop of Carthage.

That somewhere, at some date, Christians who were Roman citizens were martyred in Roman Britain is not in doubt. The most probable opinion in fifth-century Britain was that this occurred under Diocletian. Gildas, in a rare burst of detail,[52] says as much, alluding to 'the nine-year persecution by the tyrant Diocletian'. This took place in a civil diocese where God was able to save his nascent Church solely through *clarissimos lampades sanctorum martyrum* 'the most brilliant lamps of the holy Martyrs'. Gildas then names *sanctum Albanum Verolamiensem . . . Aaron et Iulium legionis urbis*, and, almost certainly because he knew no more names, other citizens of either sex *diversis in locis* 'in various other places'.

Since, by the time he wrote, or by that of the previous generation in the late fifth century, it is safe to suppose that the graves of at least some such British martyrs would have become the nuclei of *martyria*, martyrial shrines in the shape of churches, we are not surprised that Constantius' Life of Germanus written about 480 mentions, referring to AD 429, the shrine of the blessed martyr Alban; nor that Gildas, referring to the period after 313, pictures the British Christians reconstructing their damaged churches and also building *basilicas sanctorum martyrum* 'churches of the holy martyrs'.[53] The martyrdoms were then early enough to give rise to fourth-century martyria.

Bede's own account of the British martyrs, which is necessarily taken from Constantius, Gildas, and also one version of the *Passio Albani* (below), adds nothing. Bede repeats that Aaron – whose name suggests a Jewish Christian – and Julius were from *legionum urbis cives*.[54] As Colin Smith now shows,[55] it is very likely that Bede did not know where this place was, and had no means of finding out or adding further comment. The idea that Caerleon, in south-east Wales, is far and away the most probable location has been adequately explored, and agreed, since Hugh Williams.[56]

But what *is* far from certain is that the persecution which led to the martyrdoms of Albanus, Aaron, Julius, and others un-named was that of AD 303–11. Hugh Williams, who had already edited and annotated Gildas' text,[57] reminded his readers – as others since have done – that, in linking mention of the named martyrs to Diocletian's persecution, Gildas qualifies the ascription with the words *ut conicimus* 'as we conjecture: so we suppose'. He did not therefore know for certain. And historical opinion has hardened against this acceptance, because such other comment that survives strongly indicates that Britain, under Constantius and (from 306) Constantine, was virtually spared the persecution that marked other Christian regions.[58] If we were to assume that persecutions at the times of Decius (250–1) or Valerian (257–9) really formed the setting, then this would go some way to explain, as was hinted earlier, the near-total loss by the late fifth century of actual names; the gap is two centuries, rather than a century and a half.

The cult of St Alban is of very great interest; not only because of the present concern, with the potential, archaeological and historical, of the cult centre (St Albans Cathedral), but because it is so widely evidenced at such an early period. Apart from the mention by Gildas (and through him Bede), Alban's fame survived the collapse of Roman Britain and certainly reached the Continent. Constantius' 480 text assumed that his readers, imagined mainly as Gaulish, will know who the blessed martyr Albanus is; the name is not further glossed or explained. The numerous church dedications (*Albanskirche*) in the post-Roman cities of Germany may, in the hagiographical mazes, have swept up the odd, purely local, figure bearing the same name; but it is quite probable, from such evidence as the coincidence of patronal feast-dates, that some of the older and more important Rhineland foundations (like that at Albansberg, Mainz) represent the Verulamium hero. The poet Fortunatus – Venantius Honorius Clementianus Fortunatus, the Italian aristocrat who towered over the world of polite letters in Gaul, dying about 600 after a period as bishop of Poitiers – versified Alban, in the line[59] *egregium Albanum fecunda Britannia profert* ('And fertile Britain, famous *Alban* yields'). Britannia's protomartyr was in distinguished company.

The most intriguing aspect of the legend is the inferred reality of a lost, but very early, original account or *Passio* (a description of saintly death, rather than a *Vita* or quasi-biographical Life), perhaps composed a little before AD 500. It can be no more than a guess, but an intelligent one, that it might have been composed in northern Gaul, by a British immigrant.[60] Wilhelm Levison's paper[61] has said virtually all that one imagined could be said on the subject, starting with the reminder that it was Gildas, and not the slightly earlier Constantius, who was the first specifically to link the martyr to Verulamium (*A. Verolamiensis*, DEB 10); and that Gildas may have been remembering, perhaps from his youth, part of some text in which he had seen this detail. Hence one line of reasoning could point to such a pre-Gildas source, an exemplar lying well behind the surviving *Passio Albani* recensions (Turin, late 8th century; Paris, early 10th). Levison himself thought it most improbable that the British martyrdoms were Diocletianic, and therefore they must have been earlier; but he regarded this problem as insoluble.

John Morris, in demonstrating[62] that the reconstructable, factual portion of the surviving texts actually describes the setting of Veru-lamium, the little river Ver, the hill outside the city where the Abbey or Cathedral stands, and even the myriad wild flowers consistent with 22 June (Alban's feast-day), took an entirely new line of reasoning. From the Turin text, which starts with a visit to Britain by Septimus Severus (193–211), Morris leant heavily upon the use of the name *Caesar*, as that of the figure who accused Alban, vainly commanded him to sacrifice, condemned him, and after the miracle-attended martyrdom on the hill, ordered the persecution to be stopped. All this, Morris argued, if indeed it fell within the known dates of Severus' British visit (summer 208, to early 211), pointed more specifically to the year 209. Severus and his son Antoninus were then campaigning in Scotland, leaving the other son Geta, who had been accorded the formal title *Caesar* by his father (an Augustus), as governor of the civil diocese. Therefore it was Geta Caesar in 209 who was involved; and Morris found other turns of phrase in the reconstructable text to support this. The later expansion of Alban's grave into a church, or martyrical basilica, was connected by Morris to a date 'about 396' and a visit to Britain by Victricius of Rouen, of whom more below. This is not really relevant, and is linked to Morris' particular views about Victricius, and about the history of Whithorn – ideas which the present writer finds, respectively, dubious and untenable. All that we really know is that, by 429, some aggrandisement of the site had taken place.

If Morris' hypothesis about a martyrdom in 209 has been gratefully taken on board at present-day St Albans, it has failed to overcome scholastic doubts. Arguments which place Aaron, Julius and Alban to the period 251–9, the next persecutions earlier than 303, do explain our lack of general detailed traditions. They hardly lead us to suppose that an earlier, and localised, episode in 209 – a phase when Verulamium still had a fair spread of non-Christian temples – could have given rise to quite so detailed an account 300 years later; an account which surely coalesced, albeit on the spot, in the latter part of the fourth century, and was fully recoverable through continuous oral tradition over two or three generations only. In short, while accepting with Levison that we cannot expect to be enlightened further – at least, not until St Albans is excavated – the middle of the third century is still the least improbable period.

In the latter part of the fourth century, and again during the fifth, we encounter other Christians by name. The few whose claims to attention are in connection with the Pelagian heresy will be mentioned in the last section of this chapter. One or two others, more properly part of any prefix to a history of British and Irish Christianity from AD 500 onward, will appear in the second part of this work.

Victricius of Rouen, bishop of that city (*Rotumagus, Rotumagensium*), an ardent champion of Martin of Tours and the author of a tract on early saints, was not a Briton. (The suggestion that he was 'perhaps of British birth',[63] is seen, on closer inspection, to have no more foundation than the identification of his particular name with that scratched on a piece of pewter-ware in the Appleshaw hoard, p. 110). His relevance here is that he is known to have visited Britain, and as a metropolitan Gaulish bishop coming to see (?) other bishops, in the mid-390s. Whether or not Victricius was then able to introduce 'elementary concepts . . . of radical egalitarianism' arising either from his own writings or his personal enthusiasm for Martin's brand of self-isolative monasticism forms a point about which we do not have much by way of hard fact.[64] Any answer will depend as to whether one believes – in the author's view, wholly against the trend of present evidence – that full Insular monasticism began, at some such place as Whithorn, around 398. If that were so, the elevation of Victricius to the stance of an innovating founder 'seems a likely conjecture'.[65] It cannot however be any more than a conjecture. Since poor Victricius is to be continually, if marginally, found, interred in speculative footnotes, it should be added that there is no cogent reason to see him yet again, perhaps a half-century after his death, in the guise of 'a man coming as it were from Ireland, by name *Victoricus*', in the dream related by Patrick (*Conf.* 23) (see Chap. 13). Late Roman personal names in the stem *Victr-* are not too rare; and as Ludwig Bieler can be allowed to conclude,[66] 'The Victoricus here mentioned is not known from any source independent of the *Confessio*'.

Swept by a reverse current, centripetal rather than centrifugal, we find a scatter of Britons (or British and Irish persons) in Gaulish ecclesiastic affairs during the fifth century. Cumulatively, they have a certain importance. If there was any desire to maintain contact with, to seek news about, or to reinforce, the British church from its stronger and far less severely disrupted counterpart in Gaul, then Christian activists of British birth or attachment are most likely to have had some hand in this.

Mansuetus, who was a signatory to a church council held at Tours in 461, styled himself *episcopus Britannorum*;[67] he is identified as a Mansuetus who was also bishop of Toul, in eastern France. Since Hugh Williams' day, it has been recognised that the *Britanni* in question are very much more likely to represent fifth-century immigrants, from southern Britain to northern France, than any section of the British populace at home. The setting has been discussed by Jackson,[68] as well as later by John Morris (*cf.* p. 247).

Other persons, like Faustus, who became bishop of Riez in 462; Riocatus or Riochatus, who visited Faustus in Gaul, and whom Sidionius Apollinaris called[69] *antistes et monachus* 'priest and monk', and *hic ipse venerabilis* 'this truly venerable man', further implying that he was returning to *Britannis*, 'the British', whence presumably he had come; and the earlier Fastidius, who was involved with the Pelagians, all possess some interest, but do not particularly advance our study. One minor point is the slight uncertainty as to whether between about 420 and 470, words like *Brit(t)o* and *Britanni* always have to mean 'a Briton, the British' in the absolute sense of belonging to Britannia, the old Roman civil diocese. This arises mainly in the slightly rarified world of late Gallo-Roman letters, verses and tracts that conjointly form the source for our knowledge of these, and even more shadowy, people.[70]

Large numbers of British Romans, later augmented by children of such parents born abroad, were by the second half of the century in scattered settlements over much of northern France. Thousands settled, over a couple of hundred years, in the Armorican peninsula, implanting their own late British language (now Breton), as the very names Bretagne and Brittany remind us. Some even seem to have wandered as far as north-west Spain, a region still then more 'Celtic' than truly Roman.[71] If the late fifth century writer, Gennadius of Marseilles (*Massilia*), chose to add the epithet *Britto* to Fastidius' name, then the *Britto presbyter*, whose tombstone at Mertola, in the south of Portugal, records his death in AD 546,[72] is an even later, nostalgic, Christian expatriate. The trouble is that we are removed, in time and space, from late Roman Britain. Some of these fifth century 'British' may never have set foot in Britain. They never lose a certain fascination for students of the period. The curious may like to know that Mrs Chadwick explored the possibility that Faustus was the son of the fifth-century British *tyrannus*, Vortigern.[73]

In this realm of doubt, it is (if one can be permitted a moment of chauvinism) a pity that Britain cannot claim parentage for the lady once known as 'Aetheria' and even 'Silvia', though now more correctly *Egeria*, whose incomplete account of her long pilgrimage to the Holy Places in the early 380s is among the brighter gems of early Western literature.[74] Her work, a veritable quarry of both liturgical and architectural information about the Levant, was not again matched in the West until Adamnan's late seventh-century version of Arculf's *De Locis Sanctis*. Because Egeria's particular vocabulary is of great interest in rather a specialised direction, we shall come back to it in Chapter 6. Though there is no doubt that she came from the West, and belonged to some form of late fourth century Christian sisterhood, the slender clues point to Spain, or less supportably Aquitaine.

What her journal illustrates is that, by her day, it was perfectly feasible for distant, if hardy, provincials to undertake this kind of pilgrimage; and a generation later British Christians *were* doing so.[75] Egeria's narrative includes remarks which are directly addressed to those she left at home. 'Now I do want you to realise, my revered lady sisters', she writes,[76] 'that from this *very* spot where we were standing, that's from all round the walls of the church, or should I say perhaps from the very top of the central mountain, all these other mountains could be seen all around us . . . ' This is after her party, a 'guided tour', had slogged and puffed their way up Mount Sinai (8664 ft) '. . . and you don't go up them slowly, round and round like a snail, you go straight up them as if you're climbing a wall!'

One is reminded of that eighteenth-century *genre*, Memoirs of My Travels, in the form of Letters to a Friend. As this brave, eager little soul, so full of unquenchable enthusiasm and unalloyed delight at being allowed to *see* the very places mentioned in her Bible, scribbles away in her journal, in her vivid and deplorable Latin, we hear an authentic voice across the centuries – as possibly we only do again in Patrick's *Confessio*. John Wilkinson, her sympathetic translator, assumes (surely with every justification) that 'Egeria wrote much as she spoke'. This is important, and bears on matters discussed in Chapter 3; if we had a contemporary British *peregrinatio*, it would resolve problems, not only of church life and affairs in the Holy Land, but of Christian terminology in Roman Britain. Much may be learnt from this unique document.

If one had to construct a précis of the matter of Pelagius, and the problems of Pelagianism, in the equivalent of a single page, it would be as follows. Pelagius, a late fourth-century Briton, preacher and philosopher, propounded views which elevated the rôle of Man as possessor of free will and considerable responsibility for his own destiny, against stronger views held by people like St Augustine that stressed God's eternal, overwhelming, predeterminism. Rapidly, Pelagianism became a heresy. It attracted converts and publicists, among them apparently Britons, though its main intellectual spread was Mediterranean. Some have seen in it a spiritually-couched protest against social oppression, and corruption; and (after Alaric's sack of Rome in 410) special relevance in an age of tumult and uncertainty. Since Britain at this period exhibited civil unrest and ecclesiastical divisions, it can be argued that until at least 429 (Germanus' British visit to combat this heresy) Pelagianism came to dominate British Christian thought. Others however prefer to see Pelagianism as a matter of conflict mainly confined to theological or intellectual circles, with little relevance beyond Pelagius' personal origins to Britain at all, and even less to British social and political history, AD 400 to 430. It would be incorrect to suppose this debate is conclusive one way or another, or has been concluded. The whole subject has attracted an extensive literature of its own.[77]

Over-long expositions, either of the complex natures of the views attributed to Pelagius, or the various surviving writings said to be his, or his circle, or an aftermath movement known as 'semi-Pelagianism', would all be out of place. None would directly advance the study of Christianity in Britain. We can take particular points, beginning with the heresiarch himself.

Pelagius must have been born in the second half of the fourth century. Contemporaries, as opponents, all had no doubts that he was British. Myres[78] believed the implied background of advanced formal education points to 'the civilized lowland zone' (as opposed to north or west Britain). He studied law in Rome probably in the 380s, but around 386, according to Jerome, *forum negligens se ad ecclesiam transtulit* 'abandoning the Courts, he betook himself to the Church'. It is clear that he was individualistic to a degree, very much a free theologian.

An interesting sidelight is that Pelagius does seem to have been in every way, to use Myres' felicitous wording, 'an outsize personality, whose extravagant opinions were felt in some way to match an extravagant physical appearance'. We hear much of this. The Spaniard Paulus Orosius, Augustine's supporter, called Pelagius 'a most monstrous great Goliath of a man', and claimed that 'he confronts one, head-on, with his great solid neck and his fatness' (*robustamque cervicem praeferens etiam in fronte pinguedinem*). An unnamed opponent of Jerome – argued by de Plinval to be Pelagius – was, in Jerome's words, 'a most obtuse fellow, weighed down with Irish oatmeal', 'an Alpine dog, vast and fat', and a person having 'the general build and strength of athletes, though also pretty stout'. Both physically and mentally, Pelagius impressed himself upon those who chanced to befriend or to oppose him.

Pelagius expounded his ideas, mainly in Rome, from 394 to 410. After the Sack of Rome, he fled to North Africa, and thence to the Holy Land. He spread his views through sermons and lectures, and a series of tracts and pamphlets; though the extent, and even the real authorship, of so much of Pelagian literature remains problematical.[79] Myres clarified the general perception of these ideas, in the context of their time, by emphasising that 'to his lawyer's mind it was inconceivable that God could have placed men in the world without giving them both the capacity to understand his purpose and power to carry it out'.

This was a time, however, when another very powerful thinker, Pelagius' close contemporary St Augustine of Hippo, was clarifying man's relationship to God, and to God's purpose, in a very different light; and was in a position to enforce theological views which were intrinsically opposed to those of the British humanist. Augustine, the development of whose theology must be seen against the course of his life and career,[80] taught that man was entirely subject to, dependent upon, and personally helpless within, the Divine Will and Plan. Divine Grace (*gratia*) could alone provide means of salvation, if and when salvation was individually appropriate. To suppose, with Pelagius and his followers, that any man could take initial and fundamental steps towards his personal salvation, had to this end been provided with 'free will', and might through his own conduct pre-empt the degree, nature, even the actuality of his reward or punishment after death, was an idea peculiarly monstrous and impudent to Augustine. Such a view eroded the very concept of Divine Will, and God's timeless omniscience.

Had this controversy, which at its height affected a period no longer than a couple of decades, been confined to an intellectual battle between côteries centred on the two giants of ecclesiastic thinking, one could stop here; with only the reiteration that a late Roman British society able to produce a Pelagius must, after all, have had its more interesting side. But debate has accumulated around the application of Pelagian doctrines to political, as well as to Christian dogmatic, movements; around the chance that such application affected historically-detectable events; and around the possibility that such effects were felt in fifth-century Britain, where they played a part in political as well as ecclesiastical history.

If we can now look back again at Victricius of Rouen, his visit to Britain has been presumed (though this is nowhere so explained) to have been made necessary by local theological quarrels. There is a strange little entry, found in the Laud MS, 'B', or Peterborough text of the *Anglo-Saxon Chronicle*, a Latin interpolation under the year 403, which notes that Pope Innocent sent a decretal letter to *Uictricio Rotomagensi archiepiscopo* – who is our man. But, at the most, we can only see this as a fortuitously-preserved witness that the controversy, whatever it was about, was an important one, perhaps a complex one, and that it took several years to resolve. That it had anything to do with Pelagianism in Britain is nowhere implied. It is just as, and perhaps more, likely to have concerned metropolitanships in the Church in Britain (p. 198); and within the old Gaulish prefecture, the way in which any such were to be related to the older metropolitanships in Gaul.

The next such visit to Britain is a much clearer one: it was the visit by Germanus, then bishop of *Autessiodurum* (Auxerre), supported by bishop Lupus of *Trecassina* (Troyes), in 429. Constantius, who was a monk at Lyon, in writing Germanus' Life about 480, was in a position to get the salient facts correctly. He tells us[81] that a British deputation had visited bishops in Gaul and had reported that, over a large part of the province, the heresy of Pelagius had taken hold; and the visitors asked, as matters of urgency, that powerful external support be now given to the ranks of orthodoxy within their own Church. Later chapters in the same Life describe Germanus' visit. He, with Lupus, undertook a preaching tour, a public debate, the working of a miracle, and the expurgation of this 'damnable heresy'. Crude and simplistic as the narrative is, and it reports these events in lurid terms with a wealth of pejorative and superlative adjectives, it is directly concerned with Pelagianism in Britain. The heresy's hold, and its extirpation, is pictured as a politico-religious struggle.

Orthodoxy is represented by Constantius' hero, Lupus, and a large popular following. Heresy is seen in the form of 'teachers of perverse doctrines' (*sinistrae persuasionis auctores*) who 'flaunted their wealth. . . in dazzling robes' (*veste flugentes*). They had attracted crowds of flatterers and hangers-on – including at least one man of high military rank (*quidam tribuniciae potestatis*) – and at a lower level, ordinary (and speedily reconverted) persons who had lapsed, had been deceived, and were now redeemed by Divine conscience. The debate comes to its inevitable end. The tribune's blind ten-year-old daughter, for whom the Pelagians are by now too scared to do anything at all, is restored to sightedness by Germanus's personal reliquary. The heresy is expelled, uprooted, wholly destroyed (*deleta est*).

In terms of the British Church alone, and putting considerations of British political life aside, it is difficult to suppose that if Pelagianism was already deeply enough rooted in 395 or so, to warrant (as has sometimes been suggested) Victricius' visit, the older, mainstream, orthodox side of British Christianity then waited another thirty-four years before again asking help from the Gaulish episcopate. This would be a long run for any heresy, in a diocese which, for the first decade of it, was still very much part of the empire; and if this were the case, it is also remarkable that, in the interval, no Christian chronicler mentions the presence of so powerful a deviation from the true Light in relation to Britannia. One explanation could, of course, be that Pelagianism, by 429, had not long been current at all, and that the orthodox reaction arose, understandably, immediately there seemed to be any chance of heretical ideas getting out of hand. There are circumstances, to be mentioned below, which suggest that this *is* the explanation.

In the meantime, we go back from 429 to the earlier period of much of the actual Pelagian writings. Myres began his own exegesis[82] by examining their use of the word *gratia*, 'Grace'; a term to which, ostensibly, and with its strict theological meaning of 'the supernatural assistance of God bestowed upon a rational being with a view to his sanctification',[83] the Pelagians attached only Augustine's concept of the Divine Will. Augustine's school, in their turn, held *gratia* to be a matter of such supreme, central importance that *inimici gratiae*, 'Enemies of Grace', became their main anti-Pelagian slogan.

But, rather in the fashion that the English word *perquisite*, one that formerly to Pepys (an administrator) and Blackstone (a lawyer) was precise and unobjectionable, has now come to take on – mostly in the colloquial abbreviation 'perk' – a very different, equally precise, and pejorative meaning, so Myres showed with dated contexts that *gratia* at this time had as its most obvious popular value 'judicial corruption in the courts; official hanky-panky of all kinds in public life'. In short, it meant corruptibility with a price-tag. Myres then asked, 'Is it possible that Pelagius and his friends may have been attempting, however confusedly, an attack on the social corruption inherent in a totalitarian regime, rather than initiating, as Augustine suggested, a barefaced assault on the fundamentals of the Christian faith?'[84]

The application of this idea to Britain requires, once again, the assumption that at some date after 394 or so the teachings of Pelagius took hold in his native land. Is there any support for this, in the belief[85] that Britannia produced not only the author of the heresy but also 'the *majority* of the Pelagian authors that we can identify'? (These include, in Morris' terms, 'perhaps Coelestius, the Sicilian Briton, the author of the *de Virginitate* unless he be the same individual, Bishop 'Fastidius', and Faustus of Riez, the architect of semi-Pelagianism'.) Those who are prepared to credit the assumption can, if they wish, see Pelagianism as having had a run of at least thirty years, in 'the very home and nursery of Pelagianism', where 'it never became heretical; it was absorbed into orthodox thought' (John Morris). In Britain, then, 'it had the profoundest effect', and it had this 'in the one part of the Roman world in which for a brief and not wholly inglorious moment an attempt had been made to put its founder's reforming notions into practice' (Myres).

To make these assertions, either (with Myres) as illustrating a responsible and rational early fifth-century revolt against a distant and irremediably diseased régime; or (with Morris) as an early and extraordinary case of British radicalism and egalitarianism, is one thing. To find at the same time, among the bare bones of the British historical record, specific events whose courses might convince a dispassionate observer that Pelagian ideals, rather than self-interest or sheer opportunism, formed the commoner motives, is quite another. In so matching history with Pelagius, the outcome will rest entirely on anyone's personal reconstruction of what happened in Britain after AD 400.

John Morris, whose fascinating study of Pelagian literature has to be read in its original form,[86] rather than in the greatly-curtailed digests later set out,[87] managed to breathe life and reality into his 'Sicilian Briton', in a way slightly reminiscent of Rome giving shape through its heightened concepts of god-head to some dimly-perceived but hitherto amorphous native Being. The person in question, a young, lettered aristocrat, residing in Sicily but unwilling to return to his native Britain, writes, in his tract *De Divitiis*, on the precept 'If though wouldst be made whole, Go, sell all that thou hast' (Matth., XIX.21). He takes this quite literally, and he preaches a direct Christian egalitarianism. Now his style of writing, the advanced nature of the sentiments, even certain citations, all link this tract and its author to a cluster of Pelagian broadsides, dated at around 410. They are powerfully worded statements, from 'a senatorial milieu', composed by persons who knew exactly what they were writing about, and what lessons they wished to draw. One longer piece, *De Vita Christiana*, given by Morris an 'approximate date . . . of 410–11', might, it is claimed, actually have been written in Britain; and perhaps by 'Fastidius', who stands either for the Fastidius mentioned earlier, or a comparable figure.[88]

Morris saw *De Vita Christiana*, not so much as a religious Tract for the Times, as a 'political pamphlet'; issued shortly after, and describing, an actual historical rebellion. In it, a government had been violently overthrown. It had been replaced not by a popular party, but by a new government, headed by *iudices* (magistrates). In its turn, this, an arguably short-lived power, had also been replaced, by a fresh régime also involving men of property and further *iudices*. There had been, of course, a repetition of violence, and of confiscation of property and estates. On this latest government, the pamphlet now urges its (Pelagian) ideals of the Christian Life, the *Vita Christiania*, as the basis for all forms of political and public conduct from now on.

Morris believed that these circumstances, inferentially reconstructed from the text itself, could only refer to the circumstances of Britain in AD 410. The British, after some three years of allegiance to the usurper Constantine III, renounced their contumacy, and appealed to the rightful Honorius for protection. When Honorius refused to help, the discredited, remnant-Roman governing class was violently overthrown. Now (in 410–11? in 415?) a generally similar government, of leading citizens, having just replaced the previous dissidents, seems to offer (because it is Pelagian in outlook?) rather more prospect of putting Pelagianism to the test, and this the author urges on them.

It may simplify this digest if we observe that John Morris is arguing for three successive British 'governments', which can be labelled *A*, *B*, and *C*: *A* being the conventional ruling machinery, if technically in a state of rebellion, that backed Constantine III from 407 to 410, *B* a movement of upper-class dissidents that replaced *A* in (?) 410–11, and *C*, perhaps more susceptible to Pelagian ideas, another such, replacing *B* in the period (?) 411 to 412/15. The many assumptions – that *De Vita Christiana* was composed in Britain, that its date was as stated, that it really allows this reconstruction, etc. – were challenged by Hanson[89] who thought the evidence 'very frail indeed'.

Myres' slightly earlier application of Pelagianism to British history will be seen to differ from Morris', not in principle but in detail, and in the other sources used – that section of Zosimus' (post–425) history of the Roman empire touching Britain,[90] and the very much later compilation ascribed to Nennius, particularly the legendary British life of Germanus.[91] Myres thought it probable that 'the classes mainly affected by Pelagianism at this time in Britain were precisely those best placed to take the initiative in ousting the officials charged by Constantine (III) with the maintenance of the old regime';[92] and that the, typically, well-to-do landowners of Pelagian outlook remained as the chief supporters of the movement for at least another twenty years, historically surfacing again in 429 to confront Germanus and Lupus as *conspicui divitiis*.

This telescopes, into a single post–410 party, Morris's *B* and *C* as just defined. Myres then saw his *B/C* Pelagian movement, the native government of Britain, as behind an even later cause of dissension, one where 'the Pelagian issue can still be seen' – we are perhaps around AD 440 – 'bedevilling politics and paralysing the efforts of the civitates to maintain a united front in the barbarian invasion'. And this leads, as it must, to a further view of 'Pelagians' as a British grouping of the mid-fifth century, its leadership personified by Gildas' *superbus tyrannus* and the 'Vortigern' of Nennius; the survival of the heresy is then seen as the reason for a *second* visit by Germanus – probably in 448. In this model, where stood the ranks of Orthodoxy, the anti-Pelagian British? They are not Morris' short-lived national government (*B*). They are not really political at all, because their base is the 'Catholic', orthodox church of fourth century Britain, maintained in the face of later political and heretical turmoil. This Catholic opposition brought over Germanus and Lupus in 429, and Germanus in 448, the second time to weaken Vortigern's authority. Internal Catholic resistance, combined with a revolt of his own barbarian *foederati* – the earliest, licensed Germanic soldier-settlers – overthrew Vortigern. So Roman Britannia fell, and so (with the *adventus Saxonum*, the arrival of many more English), red tides of heathendom began to flow westward over a Britain that had, more than once, boasted the Imperial purple.

The puzzled reader who has followed all this digest – and it has been most carefully simplified – and who perhaps goes on to read Morris' and Myres' own words, may well ask plaintively. But what on earth did the proud tyrant Vortigern in his bone-strewn North Welsh redoubts have in common, theologically, with Pelagius and such men as the firebrand Christian socialist author of *De Divitiis*? The weakness of all such reconstructions lies precisely here. It begins, moreover, with real doubt – already mentioned – that such heresies, Pelagius' in particular, *were* ever applied socially to the extent where they governed or modified history. These 'nationalist and socialist theories', A.H.M. Jones wrote,[93] looking at the Donatists in north Africa, and Arianism among the converted Germans, 'seem to me to be based on a radical misapprehension of the mentality of the later Roman Empire. . . . Modern historians are, I think, retrojecting into the past the sentiments of the present age when they argue that . . . the real moving force behind these movements must have been national or class feeling.'

What exactly occurred in Britain between 406 and 450 is a matter that never fails to attract fresh enthusiasts, but the solutions – and Morris' later interpretations lie among them[94] – can be and usually are couched in the guise of historical models mainly using Gildas and the few European chroniclers. They do not depend upon Pelagianism as a major factor, nor often as any factor at all. Without Prosper's entry for the year 429 (below) or Constantius' direct explanation for Germanus' visit, then in all likelihood Pelagianism would hardly ever be mentioned. For the history of the British church, our deduction must be that a formal, organised Church continued to exist. It is indeed in this light that we interpret the record of 429, which portrays not only a British church in contact with Gaul but an orthodox one triumphing over heresy.

For Pelagianism itself, the tendency of scholars has been not to decry the importance of the movement, as purely an ecclesiastical one; but to confine it to theological circles in the Mediterranean and Levant, and to remove it from early fifth century British politics altogether. Partly this arises from a careful questioning of whether the movement really did possess any socially-translatable aims;[95] and of what evidence there is to support its presence in early fifth-century Britain.[96] Who, for that matter, *were* 'the Pelagians', if we seek influential exponents of its aims, outside theological circles?

The most marked objections to what can be called (their common thematic factors being greater than the specific variations) the 'Myres and Morris' hypotheses of British history, 406 to 450, have come in two contributions[97] by Edward Thompson. Their content and significance will be appraised later (Chap. 10); but they offer, on a basis of strictly-selected early sources, an interpretation of the fifth century turmoils that may be social, but has nothing to do with the social application of heretical doctrines. Thompson dismisses Pelagianism as an effective force. Those who have had recourse to it to explain otherwise seemingly-motiveless events are, one by one, winkled out of their *spelunculae* and stripped bare.

To explain the record of AD 429, we must allow the presence of some wealthy heretical element in (at least) south-east British Christian circles. But it need not have been long inspired. Prosper[98] tells us that *Agricola Pelagianus Severiani Pelagiani episcopi filius ecclesias Britanniae dogmatis sui insinuatione corrupit* 'Agricola, a Pelagian, son of a Pelagian Bishop Severianus, by his underhand ways, corrupts British Christianity'. We know nothing of either man except from this one entry; neither is described as British; and the appeal from British orthodoxy for help in 429 can be construed, as was implied above, that the corruption was probably reaching only its first flush of localised success. Prosper also knew that 'at the instance of Palladius the deacon, Pope Celestine sent Germanus, bishop of Auxerre, to act on his behalf; and having put the heretics to rout he guided the British back to the Catholic faith.' The episode is to be seen in correct perspective – a confined one, confined in both time and space. Thompson[99] points to the failure of Pelagianism to impress itself upon British memory – 'we may take it as an ascertained fact that when Gildas was writing . . . Pelagianism was dead, buried and forgotten'. We need not ourselves forget Pelagius; but the British Church, and Britain, in the fifth century (Chap. 10), are matters where his heresy and its social applications cannot at the moment be portrayed as central factors.

CHAPTER THREE

Languages, Literature and Art

The etiolated voice of the B.B.C. announcer has become a
regular joke. It is probable that we have too much of one
thing – the Oxford accent. I am sorry to have to think this
. . . But I find by experience that it is apt to annoy those who
do not possess it, and it might quite well be wise to adulterate
the pure Oxford liquor with some provincial accents.
Raymond Postgate *The Listener*, Feb. 1930

'Aquae Sulis', he repeated. 'The best baths in Britain. Just as
good, I'm told, as Rome . . . You meet fortune-tellers, and
goldsmiths, and merchants, and philosophers, and feather-
sellers, and ultra-Roman Britons, and ultra-British Romans,
and tame tribesmen pretending to be civilised.'
Rudyard Kipling *Puck of Pook's Hill* (1908)

The vernacular speech of Britain when the Romans came was the Celtic
tongue called today 'British'. In Kenneth Jackson's telling phrase, this
was spoken all the way from Penzance to Edinburgh. Though most
imperfectly evidenced in written form, enough is known about its
immediate post-Roman descendants, and about the working of linguistic
rules applicable to the Indo-European languages, to give an adequate
idea of what British, during the Roman period, was like. Over five or six
centuries, this language was no more static, of course, than contemporary Latin, or than English from Chaucer to Winston Churchill;
Jackson has shown[1] that there are indications of regional dialects even
within the 'British' period (up to the early sixth century). This, we can
see, would have been expected, if we envisage a large and unevenly
dispersed population, throughout the present England and Wales, recent
and heightened estimates of whose total favour a figure somewhere
between three and four millions.[2]

The prehistoric and early protohistoric linguistic content of Britain
and Ireland may have been rather more complex than these remarks
suggest.[3] We need not be concerned with this here, nor with the limited
evidence that from time to time Roman Britain contained speakers of
Greek,[4] Hebrew, Aramaic, and even the odd case of Phoenician and
Coptic. These, known from inscriptions, mainly reflect commercial

mobility within the empire. But the principal tongues of the Roman empire were Latin, in the west, and Greek, in the east, the boundary between these cultural halves being sharply defined,[5] even if (in Europe) it did not entirely coincide with political and, later, ecclesiastical frontiers.

The link between Latin, and Christianity, is fundamental; and two-fold. Latin was *the* language of the Church in the western empire. Since, as we shall see, Latin was virtually the only language used for writing, the entire body of Christian evidence – from the Bible down to the simplest Christian peasant graffiti – comes to us in the form of the Latin language. In a study of early Christianity, this justifies our spending a little time in exploring this principal medium of Christian transmission.

The linguistic history of protohistoric Britain, a subject fascinating enough in itself, therefore holds a very special relevance to the story of British Christianity. Well into our Middle Ages, Latin was the primary, frequently the only, language of Christian worship, liturgy and litera-ture. But there is another, special reason why we need to give so much attention to this fact; though to some extent Roman Britain was (to use the term without further qualification) a bilingual region – in Latin and British – and though literacy was both widespread and variegated, *only* Latin was both spoken and written. British remained no more than a spoken tongue. Any British Christian writing is therefore Latin Christian writing.

We shall be looking again at this bilingualism, but the comment that British was confined to speech alone needs expanding. No-one doubts that this is true. The question has been fully, almost axiomatically, delineated by Jackson.[6] His comment, that 'British was not a written language, and that the *only* language of writing was Latin; it would not occur to anyone to write in British, nor would they know how to do so', nevertheless remains a comment, not an explanation. Rivet and Smith point out[7] that an early effort *was*, regularly, made to write British sounds in Latin characters – they have in mind coins, and personal names on inscriptions – and that the Celtic languages did, eventually, become fully written languages, using for the purpose forms of the Latin alphabet; Irish, after about AD 600,[8] and Welsh about a century later.

It hardly helps to explain one puzzle by adducing another; but the solution would today be seen by many students in social, or perhaps in sociolinguistic, terms rather than as purely a matter of historical linguistics. It is as much a factor of the relevant prestige of languages, as one of the actual feasibility of whether an arbitrary set of symbols (letters) can convey all or part of specific meanings. There are familiar and illuminating cases of much more recent tongues, spoken by several millions, which could perfectly well be reduced to writing in a 26-letter alphabet, but which remain, essentially and socially, only *spoken*. A good instance is 'Alemannic' or Schweizerdeutsch (Schwyzertüütsch), in which most German-Swiss converse, think, and even broadcast; but which is hardly written at all, save for the odd village shop-sign or (recently) for very self-conscious 'folksy' dialect purposes.⁹ The official written language is the standard German, or Hochdeutsch. The Swiss, even if they so jealously guard all their classic rural values, are by no means unsophisticated. Schweizerdeutsch and Hochdeutsch are of course closer to each other – but in degree, rather than fundamentals – than spoken British and Latin ever were. They do however form, within one language-area, an example of a 'higher/lower language' pair, the complications of modern Swiss multilingualism apart. In a different, but comparable way, British and Latin did the same. It could in fact, *pace* all those who have quoted from LHEB without sufficiently careful reading of all Jackson has written on this point, never have been technically impossible to write the bare bones of an official letter, or a memorial, or a love-poem of sorts, in British, using the Latin alphabet. It does seem to have been socially and in some mysterious way psychologically something that, as far as we can see, just was not done; and it follows that such a block could eventually be better explored and described in this light.

The status of Latin in Roman Britain has been fully described.¹⁰ It is not necessary to do more than summarise Jackson's findings. Latin was the language of government and the law, and the first (generally, the only) language of actual Romans in Britain. Where the native British, who in the later empire were Roman citizens as much as any Italian, participated in national and local sides of government in the civil diocese, or were involved in law, the official religions, and education, they were within contextually Latin-only situations; and there was an overwhelming incentive to master correct Latin, written and spoken.

There were various other circumstances in Latin's favour. Even if the Roman army had not been, as it was, an integral part of the Roman *imperium* and thus bound to the Roman language as much as the whole civil administration, its composition became, ethnically, more and more heterogeneous. Latin was as essential to its functioning, as a military lingua franca, as Hindustani (Urdu) became alongside and slightly below English in the sole comparable phenomenon of later times, the old Indian army within the British *imperium*. There must have been a very large linguistic spin-off from standing garrisons with long-term soldiery, and civilian settlements of time-expired warriors and their families, the *coloniae* (Colchester, Gloucester, Lincoln and York). There was also a Latin currency emphatically concerned with trade and commerce; where visiting traders came, as many did, from eastern provinces, Latin would be the language of the dock-office, warehouse and market-place. All this would have extended the use of Latin well beyond the mainly upper middle-class British Romans likely to be involved in the civil administrative machine. Education was a minor factor, perhaps; formal schooling of a kind in Britain went back to Agricola's day[11], and was coloured by the Romans' long-standing dissective interest in their own language, as well as of their literary culture and its place in the known world; as means of social progress, and less overtly as a vehicle for *romanitas*, limited and fee-paying urban schools would have affected only the native governing circles. (Though Britain, as a country, would have to go on waiting for Joseph Lancaster and 1798 for anything that approached the genesis of mass national education, some form of schooling may have continued into the fifth century.)

The only proviso one would now dare to add to Jackson's view is that any such assessment has to be made within a large number of (non-liguistic) factors; factors which have always been variable and are now debatable, and which since 1953 have been subject to increasing disagreements.[12] One such concerns the degree of Latinisation of the British population, and the evidence for it. When Jackson wrote[13] '. . . whether the industrial and other lower-class British population in the towns was really Latin-speaking is problematical'; or 'it would be a more probable view' (that is, than Haverfield's, and R.G. Collingwood's) 'that in most cases the peasants of the Lowland Zone hardly knew Latin at all', these do appear to be only partly assessments cautiously reached by arguing backwards from linguistic inferences and observations relating to post-Roman times. They must also in part depend – as did earlier assessments, by Romanists who would have disclaimed any pretensions to Kenneth Jackson's *auctoritas* here – upon the evidence of archaeology and social conditions; the shades of Romanisation apparent as between town and countryside, between 'Highland' and 'Lowland' Roman Britain, and upon all the instances of written Latin made plain by non-official scribbles. These can take the form of graffiti, informative or rude; short notes of names, measurements, and even sentiments; and Latin, in any guise, on pots and pans and sherds thereof, on tiles and bricks, building-stones and quarry-faces, and up to the Romano–British equivalent of the schoolchild's slate and the letter-card. Now here the surprising volume of all this material, recovered in post-1950 excavation of all sorts, together with the frankly demotic character of much of it, might alone predispose anyone (as it did Richard Hanson in 1968) to propose some modification to older views of Latin penetration.

If we take 'the Highland Zone' to mean, without further elaboration, parts of northern and western England, Wales, and southern Scotland, Jackson's view was that in the Roman period 'it is fairly certain that the [Highland Zone] inhabitants knew and used practically no Latin, except what little was necessary for relations with the occupying army'. But, in the fifth and sixth centuries AD, it is not disputed that in this great zone, Latin continued alongside British (by then 'Late British', moving from dialects to separate regional languages) as both a written and spoken language. There will be endless debate, and it is right and necessary that there should be, on the precise situational forms this not wholly clarified aspect of bilingualism took – in a few areas it was further complicated by the introduction of the speech of Irish colonists[14] – and also how far down the social scale any use of Latin extended; also why, and where, and for how long, Latin was needed.

But, in order to provide a basic explanation, to account for the presence of Latin at all in regions where, given the conventional view of Britannia before about 400, 'the language of the Highland Zone (apart from the army and its native camp-followers) was to all intents and purposes exclusively British',[15] obviously one is forced to postulate a substantial movement of motivated Latin-users into the relevant zone. If this could have taken place after the period of, say, the *barbarica conspiratio* and Theodosian restoration of 367–8,[16] it has to be earlier than *c*.500, the childhood of men like Gildas and a date within the established era of the Highland Zone inscribed memorial Christian Latin tombstones.

The long preferred explanation has been that upper-class and upper middle-class Roman British (for, in modern terminology, this is usually implicit) did migrate, in considerable numbers, from regions agreed to have been Latin-using in the fourth and early fifth centuries, to regions where the presence of Latinity in the fifth and early sixth centuries requires some such premiss. As for the Church, a movement where Latin quite apart from its universal practical application had taken on added spiritual significance (all Christian literature; all formal worship), then if the circumstances that inspired the mass movements just postulated put paid at the same time to Christianity in the Lowland Zone, its subsequent and clearly Latin-using religious predominance in the Highland zone might be explained by a post-400 reintroduction of the Faith.

All this, to be summed up briefly, rather than disparagingly, as the 'refugees and Gaulish missionaries' hypothesis, not only begs a whole roomful of purely historical questions and answers; it has now become embarrassingly difficult to reconcile it with re-interpreted evidence, and attractive inferences, that might look to very different models. Such models would tend to discount the 'refugee movement' as a major factor. The model of the present book would of course deny the very constricted view of Christianity formerly held. Was the Church so wholly expunged in Lowland Roman Britain? Was it so wholly absent from the Highland Zone in the late fourth century? All these models would offer transformed views, not just of those regions that became Lowland Scotland, Cumbria and Northumbria, Wales and the south-west; but also, and much more radically, of what became Anglo-Saxon England.

Parts of these ideas, which concern more especially the fifth and early sixth centuries and are not fully rooted within the earlier period, will be taken up in a later chapter (Chap. 10). But here, in making what appears as criticism of an established view, one consistently and uncritically repeated in popular works about Roman Britain – and not noticeably modified in academic ones – it is legitimate to ask precisely how else the evidence, even the increased modern evidence, could otherwise be deployed.

The short answer is that we might very well concern ourselves, not with the *quantitative* examination of Latin in Roman Britain (i.e., how many citizens among 3.5 millions knew any Latin in AD 350, or what are the distributions of the contents of RIB, and all Latin graffiti known up to 1980), but with the *qualitative*.

The currency, and life, of any spoken language, things affected by but not wholly dependent upon concomitant written form, are human and societary phenomena. When we want to discuss them, we cannot ignore such factors as prestige, secular and religious values, the machineries of acquisition and transmission, and – where, as in Roman Britain, we also have bilingualism, a term that covers many and diverse language-relationships – the situational and behavioural use of one or other speech when a choice is available. It may at once be objected that high-flying statements of this nature are all very well, if we are talking about contemporary bilingualism – for example, in Wales, where thousands are not only bilingual (in Welsh and English) but can also be *diglossic*, able to choose between appropriate and different forms, in the former tongue, which now has two distinct linguistic diatypes, Literary and Colloquial; a state of affairs sometimes claimed as exceptional.[17] Here, of course, techniques of investigation are applied at a most advanced level to living speakers, and enquiries of this kind can also be diachronic, that is extended backwards through time by careful use of documentary evidence. The languages of Roman Britain not only lie wholly in the remote past; one was not written at all, and the other we know from an inherently defective record. Insofar as any diachronic aspect can be pursued, it is through retrospective and inferential studies based on later records (of the post-Roman Insular languages) which are themselves also partial.

Rather similar objections, if one wanted to find them, could be levelled *mutatis mutandis* at the whole of Romano–British archaeology as opposed to Victorian architectural studies, or to early British social history as opposed to mass-observation techniques. If we heeded them completely, we would presumably abandon all interest in our past. The point is, perhaps, that by an analysis or assessment of existing evidence in new ways, we may be guided toward the creation of fresh hypotheses, and new interpretations of that past.

It should be unnecessary to defend the proposition that Romano–British society was stratified, in any terms one chooses. In AD 325, one could have come across a rich, cultivated man, supping with his guests, swapping Virgilian tags and taking good care to employ the pluperfect tense, in a villa mansion redolent of taste and discernment – Rudyard Kipling's 'ultra-Roman Briton'. Two hundred *milia* away, a none-too-clean though substantial sheep-farmer, absent-mindedly scratching himself, might be rather noisily enjoying mutton broth and pressing a further portion upon a visitor, in the smoky, flame-flickering interior of a stone-walled heather-thatched *casa*. Both hosts could be Roman citizens, *cives Romani*; both ethnically British by birth and immemorial ancestry; and both speaking Latin, one because the social setting exclusively called for Latin speech, the other because he was trying to sell some beasts to any army purveyor. The physical components and the accessories of these contrasted scenes are like those very fully revealed by archaeology. Expanded nationally, the entire matériel would reveal also, through being translated into terms of value, capital outlay, maintenance and replacement costs, etc., a corresponding range of purchasers and users. It would do so even in the absence of any historical guidance.

If we leap ahead sixteen centuries, we could now picture a tea taken in a Bloomsbury *salon*, where the tinkle of bone china and the tinkle of Lytton Strachey's discourse to a circle of right-thinking friends might be overheard against a background even more overtly literary than that of a Romano–British villa-house with an Aeneid scene on its pavement. Contrast this with a coarser and certainly less neatly consumed meal, involving persons whose unenviable lives left little room for attention to anything save personal survival, in a Glasgow tenement kitchen. In both London, W.C.I, and Glasgow, W., the vehicle of communication is English. This is so in written form, whether it be as a mint copy of *To The Lighthouse*, or a jam-smeared football page from the *Daily Record*. And both these groups of British citizens speak English. In Lytton Strachey's case, it is a high mandarin literary English; in Glasgow, something which is English mainly in the sense that it is not French or Lithuanian.

We have looked at extremes, and if the point they make·is now an obvious one, it is a necessary preliminary. (Readers who may be familiar with the principles illustrated in the next few pages will perhaps excuse their inclusion on the grounds that most people – and this appears to cover at least some historians and archaeologists interested in early Britain – will not be.) The English of the British Isles in 1980 is a good place to explore next, because 'English' is not any single unitary phenomenon. There is still an official, literary, correct English, and its existence still worries many kind-hearted commentators just as it did Raymond Postgate fifty years ago. It undergoes some continuous but relatively slight changes, and in the main it is a written language found in literary magazines, legal judgements, heavy novels, and the best kind of official report. Limited numbers of citizens can and do speak this. We might also call it a continually-updated form of the English of the King James Bible and it constitutes a standard, so it can be labelled *Standard English* (= SE). Insofar as SE can be said to have a homeland within Britain, this might be depicted as a sort of oval, the longer axis joining London to Oxford. Here, and of course widely elsewhere, the acoustic character of the spoken form of SE is labelled *Received Pronunciation* (= RP). Its transmission through time is selective and the agencies involved are social, educational, and 'work-situational'.

But some distinguished High Court judge, when at home during weekends, will not hesitate to call out to his nearest and dearest, 'Come on, you lot, don't hang around and keep me waiting; don't you realise I'm dying for my tea and I'm jolly well frozen?' This may be delivered in RP; but it is not strictly SE at all, since it involves colloquialisms (lot, hang, jolly) and contractions (don't, I'm). (The judge would not use this phraseology in the House of Lords, urging a part of visiting Commonwealth jurists to leave the terrace and to follow him as swiftly as possible to the imminently-closing tea room.) A judge whose origins lay in Yorkshire might, both in speaking SE in RP, and colloquially, as above, in RP, use in the word *hang* a vowl which is detectably not the same as *hang* in London-originating RP; or if using the word 'eighteen', might pronounce it as if it had an Italian *-tt-* in the middle of it, 'eight-teen'. Or, if the judge were Scottish, he might have stressed the word 'realise' as rea*li*se, stress-pattern 2–1–3, instead of the normal, SE in RP *ré*alise (stressed 3–1–2).

The intensive dissection of language, particularly spoken, in this direction – all the rich and fascinating variations within a single speech, the circumstances giving rise to those variations, or more simply the interaction of *language* and *society* – has long since reached the stage where it can constitute a distinct academic pursuit, sociolinguistics.[18] Those who feel like joining Joseph Crabtree in opining that '. . . the appearance of the prefixes *socio-* or *social* is a warning that whatever comes next has lost any real meaning' will, in this case, be in error. At its broadest, sociolinguistics now embraces, to begin with, dialect study; better defined as the study of the varieties of a given language differentiated mainly on a geographical basis. In Britain, dialect studies have attained a level where both historians and protohistoric archaeologists would do well to acquaint themselves with recent findings. But if 'dialect study' tends to suggest the analysis of regional speech-patterns at peasant levels, for lexical ends, given an aura of respectability because all this is mixed up with the academic exploration of Middle English and its developments, it must be made clear that this is by no means all that goes on. There are other kinds of dialects, or diatypes, that have very little to do with such sentences as *He scalled on the caunce and scat hes chacks* or *If thi iver does owt for nowt do it for thisen.* Any large city, British cities included, today contains within the total speech of its inhabitants 'dialects' which are to be distinguished in terms of social class, occupations, confrontations and special situations, and even down to gender and family groupings. When to this one adds the dimension, as in Wales, or Switzerland, of people speaking two or more languages as well as internal dialects, and when one points to very precise studies of how and why people change or 'switch', often very suddenly, from one form to another, it can be appreciated that what (for want of any better name) is known as sociolinguistics covers an enormous field relating to a major human activity. This field is relevant to every human society of any appreciable size, past as well as present. The comment covers, and it is meant to cover, speech in Roman Britain.

That the Latin language ranged extensively from its own mandarin literary form to extremes of popular colloquialism has long been appreciated. The variety of spoken Latin at the colloquial level is labelled 'Vulgar Latin' (= VL) and can be studied as a speech-aspect in itself. It is not, to use French terminology, a *patois*, a 'social dialect' that serves a population in its least prestigous functions. It corresponds to grades of spoken English that we shall indicate in a moment; though over an area as large as the western part of the Roman empire VL must have been manifest in a good many regional forms, even if it is now difficult to detect them all as filtered through writing. The important thing is that by no means all those who spoke or wrote Latin in the empire necessarily and consistently chose, or were uniformly well equipped, to speak and write the literary, classical, or what might be called 'Standard' Latin.

Though statements somewhat to this effect are implicit in LHEB, new light dawned in 1971 when John Mann collected and published,[19] out of what he called the sub-literary tradition of Roman inscriptions, a series of written forms which arguably illustrate *spoken* usage, of VL in Roman Britain, covering some four centuries (up to AD *c.*500). His paper encouraged others,[20] though the raw material is by its nature limited. It also attracted the notice of a major linguist whose writings, even when they sheer off into dazzling and scarcely-comprehensible complexity, are very firmly anchored in his own appreciation of all speech, at all times, as a reflex of real human actions and settings. Eric Hamp offers[21] a fresh view of the phenomena of Latin as spoken or used in Britain. No apology need be offered for dwelling on these two, quite exceptionally important, papers, the significance of which has yet to be properly appreciated.

Hamp, using Mann's 'rich listing . . . very complete . . . a very valuable collection', kicked the whole subject of spoken language in Roman

Britain into the sociolinguistic field. What he sees is, in his own words, 'evidence, in short, for a gradient of speech varieties which probably matched a spectrum of social groups and situations'. Students of language as such, rather than those of Roman Britain, will have recognised at once in Hamp's paper a reflection of a well-known passage from a standard textbook.[22] Let us agree that it *is* highly probably that Roman Britain exhibited, in respect of Latin alone, what Bloomfield called 'a complex speech community', and recall his (English) likely types.

These are in roughly what amounts to descending order of social prestige, and will be referred to as *grades*. They are:

1 *Literary standard*. Written SE; SE spoken in RP; Lytton Strachey, or the judge in his robes.
  'I have none.'
2 *Colloquial standard*. Speech, in RP, of the 'privileged class'.
  'I haven't any' or 'I haven't got any'.
3 *Provincial standard*. As 2, but differing slightly from province to province.
  'I haven't any' (where the vowel-sounds possess a (regional dialect origin) difference from RP vowel-sounds).
4 *Sub-standard*. In England today, *not* in RP, mainly in social classes D–E, subject to limited regional variations.
  'I ain't got none.'
5 *Local dialect*. Spoken by the least privileged class in society – this takes us to the Glasgow tenement again.
  'A hae nane.'

Hamp, in what he modestly called 'notes containing materials towards the substantiation of such a grading', works under a great relative disadvantage. Contemporary sociolinguistic work is largely based upon fieldwork, with repetitious interviews of selected informants, careful situational observations, and deployment of the entire battery of sound-recording and phonetic notational aids. From Roman Britain, all that anyone has is an imperfect and devious written miscellany, surviving in part through unequal chance, and originating with now socially-unclassifiable citizens. None the less there is just enough to drag something from the shades. Hamp, whose presentation generally follows the Bloomfield list, has set up his own, as follows:

1 *Literary standard*. 'An official or careful kind of Latin which we may call public or literary or schooled.'
  Example: *Genio sancto centurie Aelius Claudianus opti votum solvit* RIB 448.
2 *Colloquial standard*. 'Characteristic of folk spoken Latin throughout

most of the Empire . . . Britain clearly shared such features' (= Vulgar Latin).

Examples: *soldus* for *solidus* (gold coin); *coniux* for *coniunx* (spouse); *Banniesses* for *bannienses* RIB 1905.

3 *Provincial standard*. 'Truly regional British . . . regardless of whether . . . speakers were bilingual or not' (this is what was cited as geographical dialects of VL or, as Hamp says—'regional [within the 'empire] in the sense that not all spoken Latin shared [these forms]').

Examples: *defuntus, santus,* for literary *defunctus, sanctus; posivit, posiviit, for* posuit; and other words whose spoken British Latin existence has to be postulated by the shapes they assumed after being taken as loanwords into British (later Welsh).

4 *Sub-standard*. 'Probably branded as sub-standard rustically provincial or 'ghetto urban', only occurring in the speech of bilinguals or in the borrowings of (British) monolinguals.'

Examples: *solidus* as *solt-* (postulated from Welsh *swllt* 'wealth, treasure'); *sacto* for *sancto*, if this represents spoken *saXto*, the [X] being approximately as in Scots English *loch*.

5 *Local dialect*, where 'bilingual speakers in relaxed moments sprinkled their Latin so liberally such with bastard formations that only the core syntax and abstract structure could indicate which language a given sentence was spoken in'. The ironic and quite unintentional resemblance in Hamp's words to what a monotype SE speaker of RP might think about extremes of urban dialects (Glasgow, Liverpool, older Dublin) apart, this grade is by its nature the least likely to be detectable in *written* form anywhere. Hamp points to evidence from later Welsh of widespread 'theft' of, e.g., the Latin termination *-at(us)*, tacked indiscriminately on to Latin (and British) nouns to make collectives, or give indications of measure/duration.

Examples: Welsh *pyscawd* (now *pysgod*) 'fish', coll. plur., from *piscātus* rather than *pisces*; Welsh *diod* 'drink', from British **digā*, extended to **digātā*,[23] as French *bouchée* 'mouthful' is explained from VL **bucātā*. (At this free-for-all level, one could adduce as *formational* analogies only – not truly social ones – current colloquial American–English spoken bastard forms as *dullsville*, etc. (place, person, event) analogously created from 'Hicksville', or the termination *-wise* = 'in respect of, with reference to', which is an old but not very common one in 'correct' SE (contrariwise, likewise, otherwise).)

Hamp makes it very clear that, in cautiously setting up these grades on the convenient Bloomfield model, he merely wished to put forward 'a different, and I hope more adequately realistic, picture of the use of Latin in Roman Britain than has heretofore received emphasis'. Bloomfield chose his examples from Modern English, in monolingual England.

Hamp's come from a place and time where we know that two spoken languages of much the same degree of complexity were used. But it should be evident that Hamp's grades *1–5* do not all imply the same *kind* of bilingualism. Grade *5*, in particular, raises the possibility of direct comparison with certain 'pidgin' or 'Creole' sociolinguistic patterns, where two languages (one at least in a very sub-standard format) are indiscriminately mixed in speech, the spoken units being phrases or sentences, rather than single words. Those instances of Grade 1, and possibly grade 2, need not have and to a significant degree may not have included bilingualism with British at all; or to no more extent than a senior Colonial official who bawls for a drink from or urges haste upon a native servant. That spoken Latin of 2 and marginally of *1* could outlast AD 400 or AD 410 or AD 425 – and that they did so is an argument at the heart of Jackson's view here – is something that calls for a socio-historical explanation, quite apart from linguistic inferences.

Hamp emphasises, as at the same time he points to the recent growth of interest and effectiveness in studies of bilingualism, language contact, and what is called 'areal diffusion', that even a provisional acceptance of his postulated social gradience reflected by such forms implies, over four centuries or so, a speech history within Roman Britain no less complex than those of more recent, roughly comparable and much more closely explored societies. The complexity has always been there. It is for instance possible to identify[24] a large number of Latin loanwords into British. Aspects of this process show very well a 'higher/lower language situation',[25] with Latin as the higher (H) tongue of technologically and socially superior conquerors. Given this, there is nothing very surprising in finding that H *maceria* 'masonry walling' was taken on board by people to whom this was a Roman novelty, or that H *pont-* 'constructed bridge' should replace L **briva* 'plank over a stream (or similar)'. The entire Christian terminology, as we shall see, was expectably borrowed from the Christian Latin vocabulary. But this hardly clears up the mystery as to why it was felt necessary to borrow Latin *bracchium* 'arm' or *bucca* 'cheek; mouth', now seen as Welsh *braich, boch*, in the same way that these gave rise in Latin-descent Romance speech to, e.g. French *bras, bouche*, Ital. *braccio, bocca*, etc.

We begin to glimpse a very complicated picture indeed, almost all aspects of which are the familiar currency of sociolinguistics. In the degree of bilingualism implicit in Hamp's grades *3* and *4*, there is just sufficient (for example), taking into account the virtual certainty that Late Roman Britain had a population large enough, and socially complex enough, to provide the appropriate background, to suspect we can glimpse 'styles' or niceties of social-dialect choices, exemplified by such forms as (1) *sanctus* and the (3) *santus* presupposed by, e.g. Welsh *sant* – if still Latin, a specifically British reflex. If a villa proprietor could write Latin 1, and among his other ultra-Roman British cronies at the baths talked in Latin 2, even 3, his options in addressing his farm staff might be: to talk to them in British (like certain Anglo-Welsh counterparts), or Latin 3, or in jocular moments Latin 4. Decent, established field-hands, whose home speech was British, might manage Latin 4 when bringing produce to the house, or going with the *dominus* to market-days. But, if Hamp is right, the *dominus* has access to a linguistic range permitting speech 'coding', in which his choice of spoken form could carry implicit messages (reproof, approval, friendliness, shared concern), as in monolingual settings a Scots or regional English gentleman-farmer can if he wishes deploy coded speech today.

This is not wild speculation at all. It may sound like, and it is, a far cry from the simple Latin/British dichotomies which figure in earlier accounts of Roman Britain. That it probably stands, as Hamp suggests, very much closer to the observed realities of other and later language provinces (simple and bilingual) as these are being clarified by sociolinguistic work is both important and encouraging. The picture, whichever way it is eventually drawn, of language in fifth-century Britain can no longer be supposed to centre around a 'Lowland Zone' in which the incoming English met only those rustic British monolinguals who had failed to escape in time to the hills, or to arrange a passage to France. At the very least, Latin was around wherever and whenever any Christians were around. We turn back, however, to Jackson's conclusions about the survival of British Latin, and the nature of (and evidence for) that survival.

The evidence, fully and clearly given in LHEB, comes to us in two ways. There is the observation of surviving writings of all kinds; and the inferences made from borrowed Latin elements in post-Roman aspects of the British language and its descendants.

The writings bear witness to a sporadic but continued tradition of literacy. Physically, this was expressed in a legacy from Roman Britain – rustic, even formal, capitals used for inscrptions, the informal (cursive) hands, such as *New Common Writing* and its many later varieties, and a range of book-hands or formal lower-case writing styles, the earlier with such names as *Uncial* and *Half-uncial*, the later regional developments with others like *Insular Majuscule*. Memorial stones and a very few late sixth-century Irish instances apart, little has survived, though the reasons are archaeological ones; the point is that writing, as such, did survive somewhere. The continued composition of literary Latin is implied by a long-drawn-out (though probably unrepresentative) catalogue; correspondence with Honorius in 410, with Gaulish bishops in 429, with Aëtius in 446 × 454; some British correspondence with Patrick in Ireland (Chap. 14); Patrick's *Epistola* and *Confessio*; any material known to

Gildas; Gildas' writings (e.g., DEB); and so on, to a late sixth-century horizon of ecclesiastical canons, and annals and chronicles which, outside Ireland, may begin in mainland Britain with the postulated works at Iona, perhaps Bangor (?), and certain South Welsh foundations. (We can omit the mythical British 'Easter Annals' from AD 455 onwards!)[26] Most of this material is ecclesiastical in content or context.

The second type of evidence, beginning with the vocabularies taken into British from Latin, concerns the *nature* of the Latin – one might now re-word this as 'the grade' of Latin – so borrowed, as revealed by the precise Latin forms, necessary to explain the precise forms seen or legitimately inferred in the earliest Welsh.[27] Much of this is clear and is shown by straightforward examples. The Latin *oleum*, 'olive-oil, cooking oil' – a Roman innovation – appears as Welsh *olew*, which has to be explained as if one British Latin manner of saying this word was a very careful and pedantic trisyllable, *ol-e-um*, with a -w- sound inserted between the last two syllables (*ol-e-wum*), and treatment as a British loan with the customary British stress on the second syllable, *oléwum*. Elsewhere in the empire words of this shape became in spoken VL *olium* (*ol-yum*) and produced, e.g. Italian *olio*, Spanish *óleo*. Britain was different. Again, to take up a point which has bedevilled generations of schoolboys, the classical Latin V, v (as in *Victor*, *via*) was originally produced like English -w-, but by late Roman times was pronounced like English -v- (as was, almost, Latin -b- between vowels; hence Latin *laborare*, Italian *lavorare* 'to work'). But in Britain, these sounds were kept apart and distinguished; because Latin *plebem* was taken into British with a -b-, not a -v-, sound, and a word like Latin *civitas* must still have been spoken in its older, Augustan, classical fashion as 'ci-wit-as', not 'civitas' as elsewhere, because it gave rise to Welsh *ciwed*.

From these and many other examples, Jackson concluded that the Latin from which British drew 'would have come from the speech of an educated or conservative reservoir of society'.[28] He went on, 'To the ordinary speaker of VL from the Continent, the language from which the loanwords in Brittonic were derived must have seemed stilted or pedantic, or perhaps upper-class and 'haw-haw'. It is remarkable time and again that they [the British Latin peculiarities] tend to agree with the pronunciations recommended by the grammarians as distinct from those of ordinary colloquial Vulgar Latin.' They are, in other words, spoken, and rather archaic, Grade I Latin, a sort of island in a sea that one would suppose to be composed of Grades 2 and 3.

We have to be clear that there are two faces to this matter – the linguistic *demonstration*, which is not open to question and which since LHEB appeared in 1953 has been appreciated as a set of observations of the greatest importance; and the social or historical or even sociolinguistic *explanation* of why this should have been the case. Jackson put the rhetorical question, 'What class of people would speak or be anxious to learn the semi-artificial Latin of the learned or upper classes, and at the same time be in a position to transmit the words in their pronunciation to the British language'? His answer has remained:[29] the native British squirearchy, whose Latin was acquired artificially in schools from pedantic grammarians, or by contact with 'genuine high-ranking Romans'; the native upper classes of town and country, villa-proprietors, *magistratūs*, *curiales*, 'ultra-Roman British'. The interlingual transmission, from Latin to British, arose because they were specialised bilinguals to whom British was their native tongue. Speaking to their house serfs and villa labourers, the Latin nouns they used – and Jackson has stressed that the borrowing is lexical (names of things or concepts) not affecting the syntax or morphology (the actual structure) of British – would be in their correct, classically-pronounced forms. In taking on board the Latin loans, the British-speaking, largely monolingual peasantry would have done so with a pronunciation 'on the whole the educated semi-classical one of their masters'. Kenneth Jackson then adduces the case of Czarist Russia, where the aristocrats affected French and where 'if Russian house serfs acquired any French words from their masters, it would inevitably be the French of Paris, not that of Provence or Gascony'.

Since, given this social setting, it is historically likely that the initial absorption of these Latin words (and the early stage of their phonetic and structural development in spoken British) took place mainly east and south of a line drawn from Hull to Gloucester, any view which locates the subsequent intensity of this development, and the principal homeland of the language that betrayed it, west of the same line, must also explain the shift. Jackson considered that one result of the Anglo-Saxon onslaught in the Lowland Zone was that the Highland Zone 'underwent a temporary access of Latin influence' (we are now in the fifth century, of course). 'Refugees must have flooded into the safer hill country, bringing with them a more Roman civilisation and a greater knowledge of Latin; Latin loanwords into British that had not yet found their way into the dialects of the Highland Zone may have come there now.'[30]

Something of this explanation must still stand; but it has to be said that three decades of research have signally failed to clarify the details, let alone the general shape, of this refugee movement. Indeed the tendency, fed by archaeology and place-name studies, if less plausibly by history, is now to place considerably more emphasis on another social phenomenon, the outlines of which are, increasingly and annually, rather more perceptible. This is one of continuity (in the sense in which German scholars of the same period use their word *Kontinuität*): of the way of life of those formerly–Roman British, in England, in the Lowland Zone, who did not apparently fly to the hills but continued to inhabit their pre-English territories and even towns. Since we do not yet perceive very much beyond their mere existence – and in terms of their social condition, little save that the further to the east or south-west they were the more likely their condition was to have become servile[31] – we cannot fully match this against the LHEB model. What we can perhaps now suspect is that relatively few Grade I Latin speakers fled west to the hills – some at least may have crossed to Gaul (or, if Edward Thompson is right, to Ireland); and that not everyone proper to Hamp's spoken Grade 3 (or even Grade 4) was necessarily expunged from the regions settled by AD 500 by the English; that a dwindling element of spoken Latin was retained and that Anglo-Saxons may even have acquired place-name elements from such people, not necessarily always in assimilated British forms but in spoken VL of some kind.[32]

The original discussions gave very little prominence to the rôle of the Church. This is comprehensible when one remembers that up to 1953, when LHEB appeared, Christianity in Roman Britain had hardly been explored, and was itself the subject of models in which, barely extant anyhow by *c.*AD 400, it was rapidly exterminated by the advancing pagan English; formed the most insignificant component of any fifth century westward Flight to the Hills; and when the Faith was subsequently encountered over most of northern and western Britain, the Highland Zone, it had to be explained as stemming mainly from a reintroduction of Christianity from Gaul. Since one purpose of this book is to correct this now untenable idea, we reach the point where we can wonder if the Church, bastion of Latinity, is a relevant factor in the debate.

Jackson more recently pointed out[33] that, following the later fifth- and earlier sixth-century advance of the England across the Lowland Zone 'there is indeed little evidence that Latin survived at all as a living speech in these parts of Britain *after the elimination of the upper classes, except among the clergy*' (the present author's italics). This last proviso raises various questions. Did any such clergy, whose presence, numbers, and distribution at this period would presumably be connected with the state of British Christianity before *c.*450, deliver their sermons and homilies, or give baptismal instruction, or hold meetings among themselves, in *Latin* (recalling that – if we can believe any details given by Constantius – St Germanus preached to crowds of immense size, in or around Verulamium in AD 429, in this language)? If their psalters and Holy Writ were in Latin, and liturgical worship took place in Latin, did this preclude an increasing element of homilies given in Vernácular British (like the cases in Wales and Cornwall in much later periods)? The contemporary Church in Egypt rapidly went over to Coptic, the vernacular, and it did this before the split between the (Coptic-speaking) Monophysites and the (Greek-speaking) Orthodoxy.[34] In other regions, where the rural population were just not exposed (as the British were) to Latin, or in the east, Greek, native languages – as A.H.M. Jones has shown – were perforce employed for Christian worship independently of, and before, any such regional Churches became embroiled in schisms or heresies that might have induced the adoption of deliberate non-Latin or non-Greek language. For British, we do not know. One has in mind, of course, districts neither markedly 'Lowland' nor initially within the areas of early English settlement; and yet quite outside Atlantic Britain with its admitted, though marginal, later fifth century external Christian links. Such include Cotswold and the Severn basin, 'the Chester region' if that was Gildas's later base,[35] and the kingdom or state of *Elmet* in north-central England.[36] What went on here, in Christian terms? Were spoken Latin and spoken British ever *not* used together at a rural service in the fifth century?

The ecclesiastical Latin loanwords in British are of much interest in themselves because they embrace just about the whole range of Christianity.[37] There are the major festivals like Easter and Christmas (*Pascha, Natalicia*); the offices (*episcopus, diaconus, presbyter*, and the curious British Latin by-form *premiter*);[38] aspects of the liturgy (*baptizo, benedictio, offerenda, psalterium*); some tangible elements (*altare, clocca*); simple theology (*diabolus, paradisus, trinitas*); and reflections of Christianity in society (*caritas, eleemosyna*). The period of these loans must have begun in the fourth century, if not the later third; and it would now be argued by some (p. 303) that elements of this British Latin vocabulary of the Church were strong enough and widespread enough to have reached Ireland rather before AD 400. Independently, the fourth century Christian archaeology of Britain (Chaps. 4 and 5) supplies us with what seem to be instances of *altare, cl(erus), epi(scopus), Xt(us)= Christus*; and with *Dominus, sanctus, orare* and *vivere* used in Christian senses. These can only be the tip of the iceberg.

David Greene, discussing some of the evidence relating to the early British church from a linguistic standpoint,[39] felt able to complement Jackson's (LHEB) views with some of his own; these stressed his observations that there had been a period when the dominance of Latin in Britain was 'overwhelming', and though it was earlier stated (from Jackson) that the loans into British were in the main confined to vocabulary, Greene saw even the possibility of morphological ones – for example, evolution of a British pluperfect modelled on Latin, and what are called 'compound prepositions' in Welsh, copying the spoken VL usage that produced French *devant* from VL *de ab ante* – as we might say 'out front of' instead of 'before'. The 'distinctive British variety of (spoken) Latin', Hamp's Grade 3, led to Latin *planta* (whose meanings include 'offshoot, slip (of)') being borrowed into Welsh and Irish, in colloquial form, to mean 'children' – still with us in the noun 'clan', through Scots English from Gaelic. This with similar examples points to 'a vigorous Latin speech, both classical and vulgar', at one stage (the fourth century?) – genuinely parallel to what was happening elsewhere; for example in Gaul, where (to take a very familiar case) it was the regional VL *testa* 'hard shell, 'nut' ' and *manducare* 'to gobble', not the Classical Latin *caput*, *edere*, that emerged in French as the words for 'human head' and 'to eat' (*tête*, *manger*).

There are elements within the specifically Christian terminology that raise the idea that the Church, as a repository of colloquial spoken Latin in addition to the Classical format of its literature, may have played a larger part than has been envisaged; and perhaps that the diffusion of Christianity from its (under-estimated) late fourth-century Lowland Zone base might have been not that much less important a factor than the refugee squirearchy. It provides a plausible milieu for the transmission of a quite large vocabulary at a near-colloquial level. The matter of the actual literature, and its physical forms, will be dealt with in the next section; but here one could hazard the guess that any Gospels, for example, were commonly known by the Classical word *scriptura*. This however passed into (eventually) Welsh *ysgrythur*, showing[40] that Grade 2 or VL *scrittura* was the source. We could similarly guess that formal addresses or sermons, perhaps baptismal instruction as well, Latin *praecepta* 'moral instructions, precepts', were commonly so called in Late Roman Britain. But – unlike French *précepte*, Spanish *precepto* – it was a Grade 3, regionally British VL *precetta* that led to Welsh *pregeth*; the bilingual British had no -pt- cluster in their own tongue.[41]

The phenomena which properly belong to the later fifth century will be more fully examined in a later chapter; in this section, however, we can just take this argument a stage further with a preliminary glance at some of the inscribed memorial tombstones which, in the latter part of that century, began to appear within 'Atlantic Britain' rather than the Highland zone; that is, west Devon and Cornwall, south Wales, north-west Wales, and south-west Scotland. Obviously these regions lie open to Atlantic seafarers and, as it will be explained, the re-appearance of inscribed tombstones (which become rare in late Roman Britain) may in all probability be due to transmarine influence, derived from other lands where the custom had not lapsed. That apart, it will be argued that these inscribed stones allude to British Christian dead, were erected by British, were an aspect of continuous British Christianity, and insofar as Latin (in rustic rather than formal monumental capital letters) was used, the Latin was the Latin current in that form of British Christianity.

We could select a limited group, having in common (*a*) an early – between AD 450 and 550 – date, estimated on grounds of epigraphy, actual linguistic forms (LHEB), and rather rarely context; (*b*) the inscription still displayed in Roman style, that is in *horizontal* lines. (The corpus numbers refer to CIIC, not to RIB.) John Mann included Latin forms taken from this group in his collection,[42] some of which Hamp particularly discussed.[43] They provide further evidence that the Latin so employed, which must have been current in the specifically Christian background involved – the clergy who oversaw the Christian burials, the Christians so buried, the provision of models or chalked lines for the stone-cutters – was a living, spoken, developing colloquial Latin. Some of the unfamiliar forms are probably only graphs, errors in writing – *ani* 421, *ic* 520, *pientisimus* 360, *fidaei* 360. Others show the normal development of spoken Latin that one would expect in Britain, elsewhere – *iacit* 479, 500, 514, *nipus* 520, *patrieque* 360, *coniux* 320, *sinum* 520, *emereto* 445, *Rostece* (=Rusticae) 421, and *ficerut* 520; very much a written expression of Grade 2. There may be, even in this limited sample, traces of regional British treatment of VL: as *protictoris* 358,[44] *Caelexti* 413,[45] and *Ingenavi* 455 – the last an indicator that, even in remote east Cornwall in a generation around AD 500, 'Latin was known by these people as a living tongue'.[46] 'These people' can only have been the local Christian hierarchy, in this particular time and place.

There seems to be, all in all, reason to reconsider the part played by the Church in maintaining foci of spoken Latin during the fifth and early sixth centuries; if not so much in bilingual contexts, then in numerous settings where British speakers were exposed to Latin, and where constant opportunities for the process behind loanwords occurred. The rôle of the Church, rather than that of refugee aristocrats and their retainers, may have been under-estimated. The transmission of spoken Latin (and Latin writing), westward and northward in space, and from Late Roman to sub-Roman Britain in time, may not have been so simple as a 'from Lowland to Highland Zone' progression; nor, in social terms, need it necessarily have centred on the sub-Roman *tyranni* and their courts. Classical (Grade 1) Latin, buttressed by the possession and use of mainly ecclesiastical literature, doubtless was transmitted and maintained, the kind of context one has in mind being the major later fifth century monastic schools (as that of Illtud in South Wales).[47] But very many more Britons, if they carried over their spoken VL, with its regional (Grade 3) character, would surely have done so – particularly when true urban life generally collapsed after the mid-fifth century – around their churches. And all the evidence for the continued use of spoken Latin, in itself, and as a source of loans, may again suggest a much more widespread, more firmly-established, late Roman British church than has hitherto been supposed to be the case.

The author recently had occasion to attend a morning service in a Church of England building of medieval origin, conducted by its Rectorial incumbent for a large congregation. Not a line of the normal prayer-book service was followed. Hymns were sung from a demotic paperback work, lessons read from a totally unfamiliar (and equally demotic) 'translation' of the Bible, impromptu and colloquial addresses punctuated the proceedings, and the Rector twice played his guitar. Only the Lord's Prayer seemed homely. The service was not irreverent, and the faces of all present showed pleasure and enthusiasm, if hardly deep spiritual uplift.

The experience was a timely reminder, when one considers (from what amounts to virtually no evidence) the *literature* of the Romano–British church, that it is possible to conduct Christian worship without overmuch recourse to written form. The parallel cannot be taken too far. There is a tendency today, at its most marked in the rising fundamentalist sects, to level down the English so used, from a literary standard whose archaic lexis and morphology may well confuse many of the devout, to a colloquial language also represented by tabloid newspapers and weekly magazines. At a rather higher level, the 1961–1970 *New English Bible* is merely the latest in a series of responses to this tendency.[48]

In Roman Britain, granted that a late fourth-century service would ideally have been conducted in Latin, it is possible, as we saw, that more than one grade of spoken Latin may have been employed. The scriptural and liturgical elements, however colloquially phrased their exegeses to a popular congregation may have been, were fixed by their written form to a classical literary standard. They were central and essential; the whole matter of Christianity was contained in the Gospels, and the forms of the Mass, and the combined sacrament of baptism and confirmation (Chap. 8) with other necessary liturgies, demanded (with the Gospels) that the written exemplars were there, were available, and were used. To this extent we see that there must have been a literature of Roman British Christianity. None of it survives, but it is not credible that there was none. All we can do today is to discuss its more likely shape.

Hugh Williams[49] approached this problem both by the use of analogy – evidence of what had been used elsewhere in the empire at this time – and retrospective inference (loanwords in Welsh). In admitting what was tantamount to defeat in the search for details, so he like both previous and subsequent writers was obliged to argue from what we know of this topic in Britain and Ireland in post-Roman times. The linguistic arguments are not, in this particular case, informative. Obviously there was a service for the Mass. From later Welsh *offeren* it can be inferred with near-certainty that late Roman Christians in Britain spoke of the eucharistic service as *offerenda*;[50] and that this was the commonest, perhaps universal term could be guessed because Middle Cornish *oferen* and Breton *oferenn* ought to go back to a phase before the political and geographical separation of South-West Britain from Wales, and the early phase of the migrations to Armorica. We can also guess that *offerenda* 'those-things-which-must-be-offered' was, in spoken British Latin, as sharply differentiated from the pagan *sacrificium* as Christian *altare* was from pagan *ara*. But this tells us nothing about the Mass itself.

The slightly later Irish evidence might seem a particular attractive quarry, since by the seventh century we begin to see evidence for the circulation, consumption and scholarly regurgitation of a very large body of Christian literature – patristic commentaries as well as Biblical studies. There is an objection, and it is sufficient to remove further discussion of the point from this book. Virtually all the indications point to post-Roman introductions, wholly independent of contemporary Britain; the sources may have included the Church in contemporary Gaul, but also involved Spain, and through Spain the Mediterranean lands.[51] There are persuasive historical and archaeological contexts for such an introduction.[52] If we are then forced back to the early fifth century, before the appropriate period of such introductions, we arrive at Patrick and Palladius. All that we know about the latter (Chap. 12) is that he did not come to Ireland from Christianity in Britain. On the other hand, Patrick did; since the supportable chronologies for his time in Ireland do lie within the gap between fourth century Roman Britain, and the Continental re-introduction of letters to Ireland, study of Patrick's writings and their textual allusions could be important to a study of Late Roman British Christian letters.

Examination of Patrick's familiarity with the Bible[53] clarifies this a little. The question of what else he knew of Christian Latin writing[54] takes us into realms of greater uncertainty. But where Patrick and his Bible are concerned, analysis would support the conclusion that the Old and New Testaments were known in late Roman Britain; and that quotations, either from memory or a written text, in the work of both Patrick and the later Gildas show that it was in the form called the *Vetus Latina* or 'Old Latin' Bible. Roman Britain shared the particular textual versions which, from the third century, had been used in Gaul (as opposed, say, to the 'African Old Latin' version used in the north African provinces).

It is pure chance that the next stage, the deliberate supersession of what had by then become a very heterogeneous collection of Biblical texts, coincided roughly with the last years of Roman Britain. St Jerome, the principal translator-author (and what would today be called general editor) of the replacement, the *editio Vulgata* or Vulgate, had revised the Gospels on the basis of older Greek texts by 384. The Psalms, as necessary to Christian worship as the Gospels, were reconstituted several times, the 'Gallican' psalter of *c*.392 certainly being Jerome's work, as were fresh versions from the Hebrew of the remaining canonical Old Testament books. The Apocryphal books were also revised, their later journeying as far as Ireland forming a most interesting study in its own right.[55]

In practical terms, the whole Biblical text, the equivalent in scope of a present-day machine-printed Revised Version in English, would have been both vast and costly. A fourth-century British church cannot necessarily be supposed to have had much more than the Gospels, the Psalter, and perhaps certain of the Prophets; the actual instances, constantly used, would be as constantly part-copied and replaced. The first unambiguous reference to a collection of Biblical books within one cover[56] occurs in the sixth-century *Institutiones* of the Roman patristic writer Cassiodorus. Extraordinarily, the oldest extant MS of the complete Vulgate is British, the early eighth century Codex Amiatinus written around 700 at Jarrow-Monkwearmouth, sent as a gift by Abbot Ceolfrith to the pope. Its textual standing is such that it has formed the basis of post-medieval recensions of the Vulgate.

The form of any such text in a Romano–British church would have been what is known as a *codex*. Originally this meant one of a series of wooden tablets – the older *caudex* meant 'piece of wood' – perforated on the margins, and strung together concertina-fashion, like those recently found at first-century *Vindolanda* (Chesterholm) on Hadrian's Wall.[57] By late Roman times something very close to the medieval and modern book had evolved, with ink-on-parchment folios or pages cased in some sort of cover; and we can guess that Biblical and liturgical codices in Roman Britain were of this kind. The Vulgar Latin nomenclature varied regionally. In the Romansch of the Swiss Grisons 'a book' is still *il cudesch* (VL *ille codex*); French *livre* on the other hand is VL *liber*, the -b- becoming almost a -v- sound. *Liber*, retaining the Classical Latin value of the -b-, underlies, for example, Old Cornish *liver*, Modern Welsh *llyfr*. *Psalterium*, the book containing the psalms, gave rise to Irish *saltair*, Welsh *sallwyr*. Earlier, it was suggested that VL *scrittura* could have been the common term in late Roman Britain for the Bible.

There is a chronology inherent in the replacement of the Vetus Latina by the Vulgate. Most recently, this was called into play by Hanson;[58] collation of the evidence for Patrick's Biblical sources, against the established dates of the Vulgate, could perhaps offer if not fixed points then at least valuable pointers to Patrick's own relative dates. Hanson's conclusions support his own view of the latter. But the burning question remains: when did Jerome's New Testament in the Vulgate form reach Britain? Was this before, within, or after the period when Patrick is likely to have been instructed in this, rather than in the Vetus Latina, text? Hanson thinks it reasonable to suppose that the Vulgate New Testament would not have been widely current in Britain until 'at least thirty years' after its translation in the mid-390s, and that '. . . it would not be surprising if it was 40 years before the British Church assimilated this new translation'. The word 'assimilation' does not imply total replacement; and it cannot, since it is also known that Gildas, educated presumably around AD 500, may have been familiar with parts of the Vulgate Old Testament, but leant rather upon the Vetus Latina for the New. Both were still in use; this, notably with evidence for the use of a very early Vetus Latina literal rendering of Job, 'presupposes in itself a continuous history of Christianity reaching well back into Roman Britain'.[59]

But, once again, there are too many variables at work. Bieler's conclusions were[60] that, if we take Patrick's education between roughly ten and sixteen as representative of the Christian curial classes in very late Roman Britain, he knew a psalter text which was 'Gallic', the version used in Gaul; the Old Testament in the Vetus Latina and pre-Jerome form (pre-404, plus any time-lag involved in this reaching Britain); a Vulgate text of the Acts, something which might possibly have reached Britain around 400; and, for the remaining New Testament allusions, Patrick's text was essentially pre-Jerome, corrected here and there by the Vulgate.

In the first place, we do not know what period precisely we are discussing (though, for this phase of Patrick's life, a date in the 420s will be suggested later); secondly, there is uncertainty as to whether Patrick is quoting from memory, and if so from which stage in his memory, or from whatever texts he happened to have by him in a rather isolated setting. None of this possesses real cogency for the chronology of British Christian literature, since its sole outcome is to confirm the idea that Patrick's writings are later – a half-century later – than the decade or more in which Jerome supervised the preparation of the Vulgate Bible. What it does underline is the strong possibility that the basic textual equipage of the Romano–British Church was derived, through Gaul, from late Roman western Christendom; that, eventually, most of the Vulgate text reached Britain, probably rather before c.450; and that ecclesiastical circumstances in the fifth century were not such as to encourage speedy and universal substitution of Vulgate versions for the surviving Vetus Latina ones.

When we look at liturgy – set forms of wording for the Mass, for baptism and confirmation,[61] marriage and burial, ordination, etc. – we have almost no information. That any British liturgical forms are likely to have remained in standard use after the fourth century, their users increasingly deprived through isolation from access to later forms, is perhaps the best inference to draw from the slight evidence that in later centuries British practices could be stigmatised as irregular; irregular, because archaic and out-of-date.

Both Hugh Williams and David McRoberts[62] made brave attempts to reconstruct the likely form of certain sacraments. This is within the province of the ecclesiastical and liturgical specialist, but the exercise contributes sadly little to history and the present writer is certainly not qualified to pursue it. We are confined, through circumstances, to a discussion of the physical reflections of burial (Chap. 9); and the only sacrament which can be examined at all widely is that of baptism and confirmation (Chap. 8), because its outward reflection is direct, interesting, and isolative.

Can we hope, even against expectation, for fresh light? We do know that one priceless legacy from Roman Britain – writing – was never lost; and though, having passed through the removes of being marked out larger-than-life (by a literate hand) and then being cut or chiselled (possibly by an illiterate one), they are not the same as anyone's *ipsissima scripta*, it is interesting to remind ourselves of this by looking at the earliest post-Roman evidence, the rustic capitals and lower-case letters used on the first group of inscribed memorial tombstones from the late fifth century (fig. 1). Others, of course, wrote directly on other material. It is just conceivable that, under favourable environmental conditions, as archaeological work extends still further into urban Roman Britain, the odd scrap of textual evidence could be found. Several possibly relevant Romano–British towns are still notoriously under-explored.

A likely model is provided by the so-called Springmount Tablets. These were discovered some time ago in that classic Irish mode, a man cutting turf in a bog (near Ballymena, Co. Antrim). They are a set of latter-day *caudices* – wooden tablets some 3 by $8\frac{1}{2}$ in (7.5 by 21 cm), the edges pierced for binding, each tablet with one face recessed and filled with wax. They are thus erasable, and re-usable; and like the pupil's slate, were designed for practice and instruction. It may be imagined that Illtud's pupils in late fifth century Llanilltud Fawr (Llantwit, Glamorgan) were familiar with such; and that they were also used in Roman Britain.

The Springmount tablets[63] contains Psalms 30 to 32 in the Vulgate enumeration. The text is the Gallican one – Jerome's – but with a few readings from Vetus Latina, and others arising, it would appear, from

1 Examples of 'rustic capitals' and evolved half-uncial lettering, used in inscribed memorial stones, west and north Britain, from the mid-5th to 7th cent. (after ECMW)

carelessness in transcription or from the fact that the writer depended upon his memory; leading to one recent commentator's suggestion that this may be the work of the instructor (!) rather than of his pupils. The hand used – the wax surface is incised with a point or stylus – is a composite one, a mixture of New Common Writing and Half-Uncial. The date, which has long been regarded as seventh century, may perhaps be earlier; around AD 600,[64] or possibly 'rather earlier . . . it is not unreasonable to place them in the 6th century, and indeed, they may well represent a type of hand common in Ireland as early as St Patrick's day' (so Bella Schauman).[65] On this last reckoning, it is permissible to demonstrate, using the same Springmount hand, what such a tablet containing the first dictated text of Patrick's *Confessio*, sect. 1, might have looked like in the latter half of the fifth century (fig. 2). One day, sub-Roman, or fourth-century, Britain may disgorge something similar.

We could preface any mention of Christian art in Roman Britain with the paradoxical remark that, on a strict interpretation of the rulings of the early Church, there should be none. Jewish teaching observed the Mosaic prohibition of graven images, whether as 'the likeness of any form that is in heaven above, or that is in the earth beneath, or that is in the water under the earth'; even though later Jewish practice felt able to reconcile this with the ornamentation of its temples. Orthodox Christian views, certainly from Tertullian to Augustine (and later), saw no reason to abrogate such rulings.[66] That they were continually and popularly transgressed is probably implied by specific condemnations. The Canons of the pre-Constantinian Council of Elvira in southern Spain (*c*.305) contains the ruling that 'there shall be no pictures in church, lest what is reverenced and adored be depicted on the walls'.[67] Among the signatories to this was Hosius (Hossius, Ossius), bishop of Cordoba, a man who was later to be close to Constantine himself.

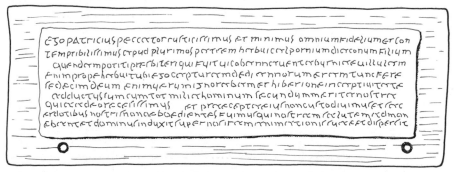

2 Reconstruction: wooden tablet with inset waxed face, of Springmount type, with initial section of Patrick's *Confessio* ('Ego Patricius peccator rusticissimus', etc.) in the Springmount hand (after Schaumann)

Jocelyn Toynbee points out that the Church's prime concern, quite understandable in an age where pagan worship was generally centred on visible hierophanies – depictions of pagan Beings, directly or through obvious attributes – was the danger that images themselves might be publicly worshipped. (What would St Augustine have made of any Spanish cathedral; or a modern Irish one containing simulacra of such men as Padraig Pearse and John F. Kennedy?) It was apparently not possible, and perhaps would never have been possible, to remove from Christian contexts all traces of the purely decorative side of Late Roman art. In Britain, even the floor of the Silchester church, though free from *imagerie*, bore three-colour geometric design. But there is another dimension altogether, in that the slender repertoire of truly Christian art (and this is so in Roman Britain) was always symbolic, rather than specific. At least some of these symbols, hardly grand enough to fall within the category of graven images, and also not the kind of object any rational person would be likely to worship as such, were older commonplace components of ornamental art.

The British examples will be found in Chapters 4–9. Here, we might classify and examine them in a more general way, having in mind the early, archaeologically-weighted comment that it is frequently only the presence of such ornament that permits us to see Christian meaning.

Far and away the most important of the *symbols* is that known variously as the Constantinian symbol, the monogrammed or monogrammatic Cross, Christogram, *chrismon*, *labarum*, and *Chi-Rho/chi-*

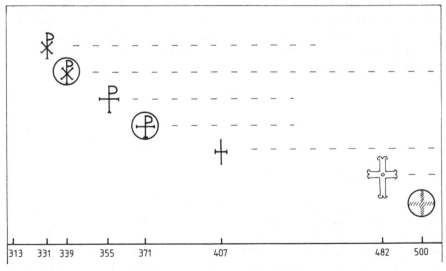

3 Relative introductions of chi-rho forms, and initial crosses, based on Rome catacomb inscriptions (from De Rossi 1861); dates AD are shown on the bottom axis

rho. The earlier version is the Greek capital *Chi*, like our 'X', with the Greek capital *Rho*, like our 'P', superimposed with its stem through the X-intersection. These two letters, ch-, r-, are those that begin the word *Christos*, Latin *Christus* 'the Anointed One'. It is not always sufficiently emphasised that to the vast majority of western Christians, who neither spoke nor read Greek, this was essentially no more than a symbol; it would not have been perceived as containing actual and separable letters.

The chi-rho (from here onward, this will be treated as a normal technical word not requiring to be italicised) originated in contexts where written Greek *Christos* was current. We need not explore the slightly difficult question of its origin; *chi* and *rho*, like other Greek letters, could stand for numbers (600 and 1000; 100), and when ligatured could also imply *chronos* 'time'. This particular Christian conflation probably took place before 312, however. The event that raised it to particular prominence occurred in that year; when Constantine the Great (Pl. 3), before his defeat of Maxentius outside Rome at Ponte Milvio ('the Battle of the Milvian Bridge'), underwent an experience, described for us by Eusebius and Lactantius in slightly different ways. The emperor may of course have undergone that particular inner conversion so fully explored by William James, though nothing else in Eusebius' remarks leads one to suppose this, and there is the possibility that in his own way Constantine was already a Christian. He had, before this battle, a dream (Lactantius), or else a noonday vision experienced during prayer and then repeated in a dream (Eusebius). In it, Constantine saw a celestial cross, and the words *In hoc signo vince* 'In this Sign, conquer'; and understood a Divine command to ensure that the symbol be placed forthwith on the shields of his troops. (The old term *labarum* – a word meaning the chi-rho symbol, not used here – probably refers to the (*vexillum*) *laureum*, the Roman military standard wreathed to indicate victory, assuming that the chi-rho was painted on the vexilla of his army.) Eusebius mentions only 'a cross of light' seen in the noonday sky. Lactantius has this as a cross-shaped X (perhaps rather + ?) with its top bent over. Both accounts are slightly later than the battle; if one wished to pursue the details of what was obviously a real happening, the range of symbols used (painted, daubed, or scratched) probably included half-a-dozen chi-rho approximations. What matters is that, from 312/3, the Roman world overwhelmingly believed that Constantine's victory was partly or wholly the result of Divine intervention; that the symbol had been ☧; and that the *religio licita Christianorum* might be so symbolised.

There are various ways – apart from the precise delineation (simple lines, double lines, splayed terminals, and open or closed rho-loop) – of portraying the chi-rho monogram. It could appear by itself, or encircled, the surrounding ring even taking the form of the *corona*, the civilian and military festive and triumphal wreath. As a very general guide, fig. 3

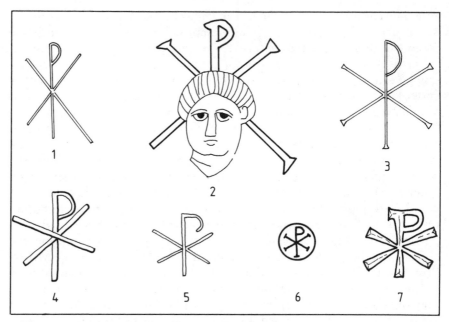

4 The Constantinian chi-rho in Romano–British art
  1 Maryport stone   2 Hinton St Mary mosaic   3 Lullingstone wall-plaster (without
  wreath)   4 Walesby lead tank   5 Ashton lead tank   6 Frampton mosaic   7
  Chedworth stone slab

shows from one specialised source-area, the Christian catacombs of
Rome, the relative order (and some idea of currency through time) in
which particular versions appeared. This is only a guide (it is based on a
nineteenth-century corpus)[68] but it serves as an indication, and also
demonstrates the later and secondary use of the Cross. In Roman Britain,
the earlier, or as it is usually called, *Constantinian* type, ☧, is what one
would expect to find during the fourth century and what one does find
(fig. 4). It is instructive to look at the much more widespread and more
casual use of the symbol in the form of graffiti, where perhaps we see the
equivalent to Grade 4 'sub-standard' Latin currency in these portrayals,
some of which may be by virtual illiterates. There is a tendency to graphic
simplification; something which eventually produced the later fourth-
century simplified, or *later*, chi-rho, ☧ . Not too much chronological
value should be attached to the replacement of one form by the other.
Fig. 5 shows a range of such graffiti, and also some more careful
representations, cut by masons on stone, from fourth century Britain.
   Accompanying the chi-rho from an early stage are two further
alphabetical symbols, which to a limited extent may be found on their
own (as fig. 5.8) – though they can be interpreted as Christian only when
together. These are the Greek letters whose names are *alpha* (vowel -a-)

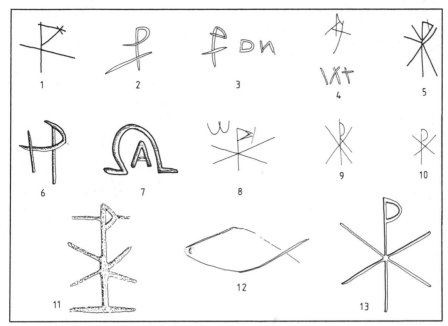

5 Graffiti in Roman Britain (from rubbings or photographs, unless otherwise indicated) 1 Richborough sherd (after Greene K.) 2 Exeter sherd 3 Canterbury sherd 4 Gatcombe sherds (after Branigan) 5 Copthall Court, London, bowl 6 York tile 7 Wickford tile (after Wright) 8 Welney bowl 9 Caerwent bowl (after Boon) 10 Appleshaw dish 11 Catterick stone 12 Rockbourne stone 13 Chedworth stone slab

and *omega* ('Great O' – the long -ō-), which begin and end the Greek alphabet. Their significance, which began as a Jewish revelation of Divinity, is to be seen in *Revelations*, and may have been orally popular in Jewish-Christian circles from the first century; 'I am Alpha and Omega, saith the Lord God, which is and which was and which is to come' (*Rev.* 1.8); 'I am the Alpha and the Omega, the beginning and the end' (*Rev.* 21.6). The Greek letters α, ω (lower case), and A, Ω (capitals) were not all familiar objects in the western Empire; they were easily assimilated to Latin formal or rustic capitals, A, Λ or a cursive form α, and to a double or ligatured Latin V, as W, w. There is a rare instance of the correct Greek capital on the Wickford tile (fig. 5.7).

Roman Britain provides cases of the chi-rho accompanied by these symbols (fig. 6), one obvious model being imported silverwork from eastern provinces, examples of which are discussed in the next two chapters. To underline the point that these must have been regarded as accessory *symbols*, and only to a minor degree in the light of their Greek nature and the *Revelation* passages, we can notice a few other instances (fig. 7) where alpha and omega are inverted, or reversed, or both. In

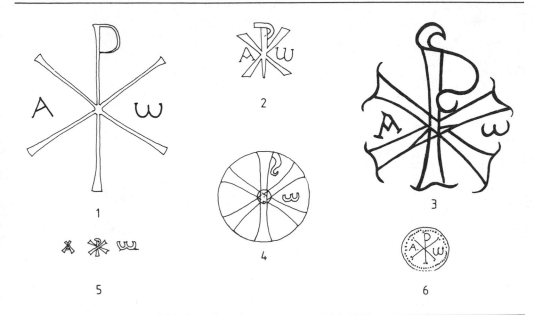

6 The chi-rho with flanking Alpha and Omega in Romano–British art
  1 Lullingstone wall-plaster 2 Isle of Ely bowl 3 Water Newton silver bowl (no.
  8) 4 Water Newton silver dish (no. 3) 5 Biddulph silver spoon 6 Water Newton
  strainer handle (no. 7)

casting a lead tank from reverse, this is explicable; but the Richborough
ring (no. 3) suggests a pretty fundamental muddle.

In addition to A and W (as these will be textually indicated), there may
be traces of other 'alphabetical' symbols. Marks on the base of a bowl
from Lankhills, grave no. 250 (Chap. 9), make up a motif possibly to be
seen elsewhere disguised as linear ornament (fig. 13.3), a conflation of I
and X, the Greek capitals of *Iesous Christos*, Jesus Christ. Graffiti on a
jar from Gatcombe,[69] from the same building that produced the beaker-
rim with a chi-rho graffito (fig. 5.4), which read I X +, might possibly be
seen in this light, rather than as numerals. Another remote possibility is
the contraction DN (*dominus noster*), known as a secular phrase but
used to imply 'Our Lord' in a Christian sense. (In the geminated plural,
DDNN = *dominorum nostrorum*, this was seen as an Imperial stamp on
a late Roman tin-ingot from Cornwall, where tin-extraction was
probably a State monopoly.)[70] What appears to be DN, the N reversed,
occurs as a Canterbury graffito (fig. 5.3) and DN may be involved with
other letters on a Poundbury lead coffin (Chap. 9). This could have
escaped briefly from the world of the *nomina sacra*, the orthographic
conventions for writing and contracting the Divine Names. But

Romano–British 'DN' forms must be distinguished from post-Roman occurrences (DNI, DNO, DNS – *dominus*, inflected) on Insular memorial stones, which derive from later literary sources.[71]

The absence of the Christian cross – either the equal-armed 'Greek' cross, like our plus-sign, or the 'Latin' cross with lengthened vertical stem – reflects the strong probability that this had not yet come into wide or general use as a Christian symbol in Late Roman times. Its earlier history, as a symbol, is complex. By about AD 400, it was beginning to appear in Italy, Mediterranean North Africa and the Levant as a small initial symbol, a subsidiary motif, and a structural element in decoration, but (lengthy inscriptions apart) mainly on metalwork and ceramics. The eventual spread of the Cross to post-Roman Britain and Ireland is imperfectly documented,[72] and further confused because the encircled later chi-rho could on occasions give rise to an encircled cross (this happened on inscribed memorial stones in the Rhineland).[73] The straightforward cross is unlikely to have been significant in post-Roman Insular art before the sixth century. Simple linear crosses of any kind on Romano-British objects cannot be regarded as Christian; if not just crossed lines at right-angles, they could occasionally be seen as numerical (X=*decem*, ten).

The representational and pictorial designs which occur in Britain, sometimes very much in a Romano-British idiom, belong to a complex range of Christian symbols, the roots of which lie in the Mediterranean and Near East, and even beyond in earlier centuries. Some of them have been explored, massively, by Erwin Goodenough[74], an excellent bib-

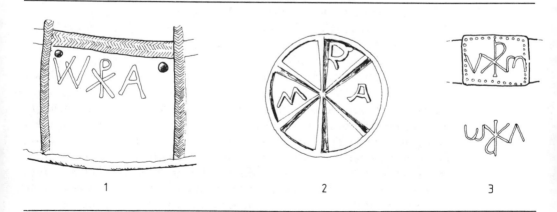

1   2   3

7 Reversed and inverted Alpha/Omega forms
  1 Icklingham lead tank   2 Water Newton *Iamcilla* plaque (no. 12)   3 Richborough finger-ring

liography being provided by André Grabar.[75] Late Christian and
Byzantine aspects were well covered by O.M. Dalton.[76] For Roman
Britain, they fall within the general conspexus authoritatively laid out for
us by Professor Jocelyn Toynbee.[77] Some of these symbols are pictorially
derived from the New Testament – like the *vine*, or parts thereof, after
John 15.1 ('I am the true Vine . . .'), 15.5 ('I am the Vine, ye are the
branches'). Others express similes or interpretations, broadcast through
patristic teachings from Tertullian onward. The *Fish*, born in water, is
related to the idea of Christian spiritual birth in baptismal waters; and
though this may have been over-subtle for the average British convert,
the Greek word for 'a fish' (*ichthūs*) was linked to an acrostic
(romanised, *I*esous *Ch*ristos *Th*eou *U*ios *S*oter) reading 'Jesus Christ, son
of God, Saviour'.[78] It is just worth mentioning that one, known, very
quick and simple way of drawing this symbol – two shallow curves,
meeting at the head end, and crossing at the other to form the tail – was
found incised on a block of stone at the Rockbourne (Hampshire)
Roman villa.[79] About 6 in (15 cm) long, this is shown – but with reserve,
as there is no other evidence that the context need be Christian – in fig.
5.12.

The *dolphin*, a beast whose taxonomic status was not clear in the
Classical world and which had gathered its own mythology around itself,
represented in its animal-fish duality the temporal and eternal, physical
and spiritual dualities of Man. Other objects had qualities, real or
supposed, to which Christian meaning or illustration might be
attracted. The myriad seeds contained within a *pomegranate*, and the
belief, used in his teachings by Augustine, that the flesh of the *peacock*
was undecaying, both indicated in their several ways the idea of
immortality. Fronds or branches of the *palm* take us back to Psalm 92
('The righteous shall flourish like the palm tree') and, in the New
Testament story, Christ's entry into Jerusalem. This (*John* 12.13)
appears in the Vulgate as . . *acceperunt ramos palmarum et pro-
cesserunt obviam ei*. *Doves*, quite apart from the numerous New
Testament allusions to the Holy Spirit in this shape (*columba*), shown
pecking at grain, or berries as in the Lullingstone wall-paintings, stand
for men gratefully consuming the broadcast supply of God's teachings.
The archaic symbol called the *Tree of Life*, in Roman Britain near the
limits of its geographical and symbolic range, becomes mixed with the
idea of the *Sacred Vessel* out of which the Tree grows, seen as a chalice,
container of Christ's precious Blood; this complicated belief is fully
explored in its British instances by Sonia Chadwick Hawkes.[80] The
representative Romano–British occurrences are shown in fig. 8.

The third and last class of art concerns Christian depictions in human
form; and here, as Toynbee remind us,[81] Fathers of the Church from

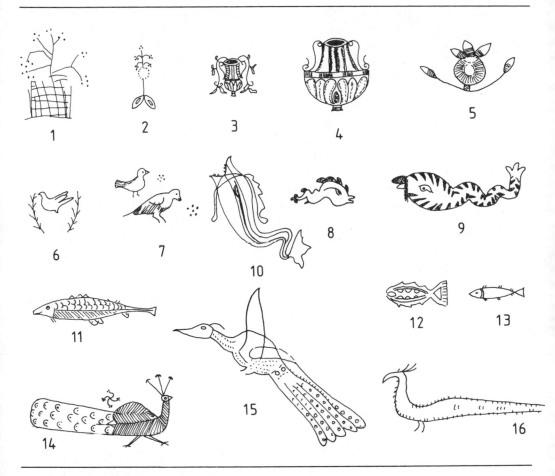

8 Christian symbols in Late Romano–British art
   Tree of Life: 1 Rivenhall tag   2 Tripontium buckle   *Cantharus (chalice)*: 3 Littlecote
   Park mosaic (with vines?)   4 Fifehead Neville mosaic   *Pomegranate*: 5 Hinton St
   Mary mosaic   *Doves*: 6 Fifehead Neville finger-ring (with (?) olives)   7 Lullingstone
   wall-plaster (with berries)   *Dolphins*: 8 Frampton mosaic   9 Fifehead Neville
   mosaic   10 Littlecote Park mosaic   *Fishes*: 11 Beadlam tag   12 Appleshaw pewter
   dish   13 Dorchester silver spoon   *Peacocks*: 14 Tripontium buckle   15 Isle of Ely
   bowl   16 Orton Longueville tag

Tertullian onward would have been outraged and horrified, their
revulsion reaching new peaks at the spectacle of the Hinton St Mary
pavement Head of Christ. The British examples are fourth-century. In
reiterating one's impression that Romano–British Christian practice was
already strongly idiosyncratic one seeks to explain, not canonically to
excuse, such illustrations. Nor is it necessarily clear what lies behind

these depictions. The figure-scene painted on a wall inside one of the Poundbury mausolea seems to be secular,[82] and if the men are local Christians, they are grouped in some local official context that need not be an ecclesiastical one – the Durotrigan *ordo* has been suggested.

The individuals in the Lullingstone frieze, whose setting is described later (p. 180), are entirely Christian; their posture, with the arms out, the forearms slanting upwards, palms to the front, constitutes the primitive Christian stance of submissive prayer. They are 'Orants' or *orantes*. Such figures are quite widely known, nearly always in funerary settings. Fig. 9 shows one of the Lullingstone figures, simplified for comparison, with three taken from funerary contexts in the fourth or early fifth centuries within other peripheral parts of the empire – Egypt, Tunisia and Spain. Fig. 9.2 is a simplified outline of a woman from a Lullingstone-like row of *orantes* on the strangely beautiful Tarragona sarcophagus, the flat but intensively sensitive work of which recalls, even more strangely, Eric Gill's masterpieces.[83] Does this imply a similar meaning for the Lullingstone frieze? This is uncertain (p. 181). There is even a British post-Roman example – an apparent, uninscribed *orans* tombstone from southern Scotland at Overkirkhope, Selkirk;[84] though this is not likely to be earlier than the sixth, perhaps later sixth, century.

9 *Orantes* in 4th–5th-cent. Christian art
  1 Tombstone of Chairemon – Egypt, 4th(?) cent. Limestone, Brooklyn Museum   2 Detail from the 'Sarcophagus of the Orantes', Tarragona, Spain, early 5th cent. Marble, Museo de la Necropolis de Francoli, Tarragona   3 Figure from frieze, wall-painting – Lullingstone, 4th cent. British Museum   4 Funerary mosaic, tesserae – Sfax, Tunisia, 4th–5th cent. Bardo Museum, Tunis

The Hinton St Mary head must be treated on its own (p. 105). For the other figures, and indeed all that has been examined in this section, we can say that if Romano–British Christian art rarely warrants the use of superlatives, it is none the less of interest, and regionally important. It is largely symbolic; and it is also largely derivative, in the sense that few Britons would be in any position to know, personally, what a peacock, palm, pomegranate or even a dolphin looked like. Models and exemplars must be postulated. That high proportion of glass and silverware, non-British in origin and widespread in well-to-do fourth-century circles, played a part in this. To continue by adducing richly-decorated and widely displayed Christian manuscripts would be to flout all the evidence; there were none. But we can just envisage small paintings on wooden tablets, as implied by a letter from Constantine's sister Constantia written to Eusebius;[85] and for the period these are more likely as a source than Christian-ornamented textiles. Any mosaic, and more important any publicly-shown wall painting, would form a potential source of inspiration in its immediate locality. But at the lowest social levels, of the Church among the poorer classes, we come back to the simplest kinds of graffiti – the Fish, the curled and crossed chi-rho; symbols that any one Christian could, after all, draw for another Christian with his finger in the dust.

CHAPTER FOUR

The Material Evidence
– First Part

The data of archaeology cannot be fully used until they are
located as accurately as possible in both time and space. The
time-aspect demands a chronological system, and the space-
aspect a series of distribution maps.
The archaeologist and historian who has not disciplined his
thought so that he thinks in terms of these two fundamental
dimensions will never really understand his subject. I could
quote amusing instances of lapses that, though trivial, reveal
undisciplined thinking. An account was published in
Archaeologia of the excavation of a Roman villa, but the
writer forgot to say where it was . . ..
O.G.S. Crawford *Archaeology in the Field* (1953)

We must accept that it is probably not possible to map a religion – any
religion – in the sense that a two-dimensional annotated diagram
showing selected items within a given space is no more than an aide-
memoire. But this assertion does not mean that the distribution-map, or
any further diagram designed to heighten or to intensify patterns demonstrably abstracted from such a map, is entirely useless; nor that
certain conclusions may not with care be drawn from the outcome of
these exercises. The marked clarification of a great deal of British
prehistory in the 1930s came from the increased use of such maps. It was
no accident that archaeologists who were also geographers or had been
exposed to geographical processes (Crawford, Fox, Phillips and Grimes)
both induced and refined these methods of presentation.

Maps which show the spatial occurrence of phenomena which we take
to belong to any religion, or belief, are however not quite the same as the
maps that present the distributions of hill-forts internally larger than 15
hectares, or of sugar-beet cultivation in England in 1900. The sugar-beet
map cannot tell us which beet-farmers went to agricultural colleges,
voted Liberal or Conservative, fiddled their tax returns, or individually
suffered from rheumatism. A 1980 map of the present distribution of
churches or temples built in Britain by the Mormons or Latter Day Saints
bears witness[1] to a remarkable evangelical campaign. The student of
religion in society would presumably far sooner know the un-mappable
aspects, such as comparative loss-figures suffered by other churches in

each area, and the degrees of ease and speed in getting planning consents.

Though in both cases (sugar-beet production and Mormon temples) it would in theory be possible with prolonged research to obtain, and to present in enlarged map form, much of this second-order data, the necessary fieldwork would proceed in conventional ways – the analysis of documented records, and presentation of controlled questionnaires to appropriate informants. If we travel back in time, the second method is pointless after about a half-century, and the first reaches invalidity as we get to periods for which records no longer exist, or had not begun to exist. Neither method has any relevance to Roman times. The analysis of documents in the making of distribution-maps of religious activity becomes worthwhile only by the full medieval period (e.g., spatial patterns and dependent territories of churches in European medieval cities).[2]

These restrictions have never discouraged the production of entire atlases, accompanied by prodigious (even illustrated) texts, devoted to the first-order mapping of Christianity. It is fair to state that these do present cartographically and summarily a mass of detail that it would otherwise be tedious and difficult to assemble. The *World Missionary Atlas* of 1925, for instance, remains in all its might an unexploited or under-exploited source.[3] For early Christian times there are compilations of equal status, the *Atlas zur Kirchengeschichte*,[4] *Atlas of the Early Christian World*,[5] and others. With reservations, then, there are precedents and guidance in applying these techniques to Christianity in Roman Britain.

The obvious parallel will be the mapping of non-Christian, pagan, religions and cults in Britain at the same broad period. This has been attempted. In her *Pagan Celtic Britain* Dr Anne Ross offers us distribution-maps that display such manifestations.[6] Two of these (Map *V*, votive shafts and wells; Map *VII*, sanctuaries, *loca*, and selected temples) must rest on the same methodology and type of source-material that one would look to for, say, a map of supposed Romano–British churches. They bring together visible and identified remains, and archaeological discoveries, sharing a particular significance, and known at the time of compilation. Dr Lewis' 1966 map of all known pagan temples in Roman Britain[7] is also illuminating. It shows south of the Hadrian's Wall zone certain linear emphases which perhaps reflect, not so much the historical reality of temple-building, but a very much more recent factor – rescue archaeology in post-War Britain, beginning in a tentative fashion when the Great North Road (A1) was doubled.

Dr Ross' Map *IX* (of gods most frequently invoked in North Britain) shows, along, behind and in front of Hadrian's Wall, symbols which stand for five deities. Four certainly, and one probably, are of wholly native, pre- and non-Roman origin. The interest here is that these deities seem to have been proper to North Britain; their emergence or creation as standardised concepts both before and during the initial Roman occupation is in some fashion bound up with the native tribes of the same region. But, inevitably, the map is constructed from (*a*) inscriptions that contain any of the names of these five, like DEO MARTI BELATUCADRO (RIB 970 at Netherby); and (*b*) depictions of these gods in guises, or with special attributes and accessories, distinctive enough to amount to a firm identification. Since the evidence of type (*a*) almost invariably, and of type (*b*) largely, comes from Roman as opposed to native contexts – like votive altars at temples or wells in the vicinities of military stations – the overall spatial pattern is heavily dictated by the line of the Wall itself, and the major stations behind and south of it. We realise that it is not possible to map all, nor perhaps any, of the remote rural shrines far away from forts and roads where (say) the native Carvetii chose to commemorate hierophanies of Belatucadros. We are not even sure, and can only make guesses by analogies drawn from the work of Tacitus and others, whether such particular sacred localities existed or, if they did, how they were made plain.

In Dr Miranda Green's treatment[8] of the religions of Roman civilian Britain, mostly south of a line drawn from the rivers Dee (at Chester) to Humber and excluding finds from military sites, the emphasis is divided between the three categories here mentioned in Chapter I: purely native cults; what she describes as 'God-forms with recognisable origins in the classical pantheon'; and the Oriental mystery religions. She rightly points at once to the inherent bias of any distribution-map; this exists because classically-influenced art forms were, by definition, a Roman introduction, and because epigraphy (inscriptions that mention gods by name) was a Roman concept foreign to the British. Nevertheless she offers[9] a summary, divided spatially under the headings of the main British tribes and later *civitates*, of apparent distinctions in religious distributions as between town and country; though again the data surely represent archaeological discoveries rather than total patterns. Seventeen distribution-maps display this evidence, derived from inscriptions, religious sites with specific ascriptions, and a range of portabilia.[10]

What these maps actually show is something open to discussion. Given a clearly and fairly described framework, one's impression is that the worship of major classical deities in Roman or interpreted forms by civilians throughout the most Romanised part of Britain was more or less uniform (maps 5 to 12). In contrast, the *Genii Cucullati*, a triple Being usually shown as three hooded (female) figures, are distributionally linked to the Dobunni and the Cotswold area, apart from a detached appearance in the northern frontier zone.[11]

Dr Green's map (no. 3) of the evidence for Christianity so confusingly appears to match that for Jupiter worshipped in classical guise that it must merit a little dissection. What is being mapped? What *can* be mapped? The convention employed to show density is normal, a small dot standing for one, or two, separate finds at one and the same place, a larger dot marking three (or more) such finds. Thus for Christian worship, the detailed evidence being included in her *Gazetteer*,[12] only four places – Silchester, London, Colchester and Canterbury – qualify for the larger (3 or more finds) symbol. But this is open to argument. In the case of London, *Londinium* as a Roman civil settlement, in fact the capital, one could argue that only the Copthall Court chi-rho incised bowl (p. 124) really counts. The literary allusion to a bishop in AD 314 (p. 197) is possibly not germane to any map of *things*; and the eight pewter ingots from the Thames with chi-rho stamps are generally regarded, rightly, as post-Roman imports. A fresh attempt to map this kind of evidence must be prefaced by fuller explanation.

The major division followed in this and the next chapter is between *fixed* evidence and *portable* evidence. It was foreshadowed, in a very preliminary way, by the present writer in 1971,[13] and more recent studies do at least show that the point was grasped.[14] It is neither a matter of size, nor of quantity. It follows from the contentions already advanced in the first chapter that evidence for adherence to any cult or religion will be at its most persuasive when it flows from *fixed* discoveries, anchoring some manifestation to some definite place; and conversely at its weakest when the material discovered is by its nature most likely to have suffered removal from the original place of manufacture, commission, or ornamentation.

A church, a baptistery, or an ornamented mosaic pavement, is by such tokens obviously fixed. It can probably be accepted that things commercially worthless, in effect rubbish, possessing decorations or graffiti with inherent significance also fall into the same class, simply because one cannot conceive there would have been very much point in removing them afar. On the other hand, small objects of attractiveness and value, especially if like finger-rings they are worn on the person, are bound to begin their travels from the moment they leave the craftsman's bench.

New distribution-maps, then, might take into account a spectrum of evidential (or inferential) weighting; at one end the suite of rooms at the Lullingstone villa-house, at the other the Christian finger-rings of gold or silver. Precisely where within this spectrum one places hoards, or things which if relatively ordinary are well above the 'rubbish' category, is a matter of individual judgement, though the judgements will have to be justified.

Three different numbers represent different weightings involved in accepting anything as signifying Romano–British Christianity; and on the maps presented below, these will be shown simply as dots or circles of decreasing size (figs. 14, 15) or, when totalled numerically for another form of presentation, by differential shading (fig. 16). While the allocation of a particular weighting or number in each case can represent only the writer's considered judgement, not some self-evident fact or truth, it is also true that if such allocations rest not upon whim but on a set of reasoned arguments, anyone else choosing to undertake the same task and guided by similar principles would be likely to produce very similar results.

The numbers (3 to 1 only; a wider series would, on the maps, lead to a loss of visual clarity) represent approximately, in words, (3) the near certainty or high probability; (2) on balance, a reasonable probability; and (1) the possibility only, that Christians in groups or individually were present at the places so indicated during a period roughly between AD 275 and AD 425. The three categories can be explained and to some extent justified, as follows.

Christian presence nearly certain (3)

This will include structures argued in Chapters 6 and 7 argued as having been *churches*, some of which also had *baptisteries* (Chap. 8); those few decorated pavements or *mosaics* indicating Christianity; and any *building-stones* with appropriate decoration, together with part of a *tombstone*. (The Christian wall-paintings at Lullingstone form part of an accepted church and are not shown by a separate dot.) Certain *cemeteries* with what seem to be Christian components are included. Among small finds, *tiles* and *bricks* with Christian ornament will pass, since such it is far more likely that such was added locally, than that such humdrum objects were carted around from place to place. The same thinking justifies inclusion of fragments or sherds of *pottery* and *glass* with similar graffiti, as having been broken in situ.

Despite their inherent value as possessions, *hoards* of metal objects, one or more of whose components shows Christian ornament, are perhaps preferably to be referred to the places where found, as places of their ultimate deposition of concealment, than to any other, unknown, spot. These hoards are confined to silver, silver-and-gilt, and pewter. Finally, large *lead tanks* of the Icklingham type that have Christian ornament should probably be given this same weighting.

Christian presence reasonably probable (2)

Criteria for inclusion here follow from arguments that, on balance, relatively portable objects which could be claimed to have possessed *relative* (as opposed to outstanding) value and interest to people at the time, especially to Christians, are more likely to be relevant to their find-spots than to any other places.

This would include entire *vessels* (not just sherds or detached pieces) with Christian graffiti, in pottery or pewter; various *objects* in bone, or base metals like bronze, pewter and lead (seals, boxes and caskets, appliqués, etc.); and along with them, justified by analogy only, *lead tanks* of the Icklingham type which are undecorated.

A secondary criterion must be that, while certain discoveries probably do indicate Christianity, this assertion still remains only probable and is not a matter of near-certainty. Such would include the so-called *plaster* or *gypsum* burials – deposition of skeletons in coffins filled with gypsum (plaster of Paris, hydrous calcium sulphate) or lime (calcium oxide derived from limestone). It also includes a small group of *tombstones* where the significance of the wording is ambiguous; and a few of the objects mentioned in the previous paragraph, where the Christian nature of ornament or inscription is constructed only by analogy, not directly perceived.

Christian presence no more than possible (1)
The third and lowest weighting is attached to sites or remains, which may represent those of Christian churches but where the evidence cannot be more highly represented at the moment.

For the rest of this group, the common factors are those of relatively high value, attractiveness and portability. Christian ornament or meaning is usually clear or can be analogously attached. There is seldom any clue as to the place of manufacture (some objects are in fact known now to be imports); and in many cases it is a matter of luck, the chance find of a much earlier chance loss, that we know of these items at all. They include, of course, all *finger-rings*, individual objects of *silver* (as opposed to pieces in hoards), and an interesting small group of late decorative bronze-work which can be exemplified by the *Rivenhall* strap-tag; also decorated imported glass of both the *Wint Hill* and so-called 'Fish and Palm-branch' varieties.

Unrepresented on the maps here, but appropriately to be considered now, are other finds (some listed in Toynbee's earlier catalogue)[15] which have to be mentioned. If one continued the system of weighting these would have to make up a class called '*O – Christian presence chronologically irrelevant or dubious*'. We begin, obviously, with the famous word-square discovered in 1868 at Cirencester, incised on a piece of red- and black-painted wall plaster.

Five lines in small capitals read ROTAS OPERA TENET AREPO SATOR.[16] If this is to be translated, word for word and literally, it ought to mean

'Wheels/by-way-of-effort/he holds,/Arepo/the-sower', as if it referred to some conscientious ploughman. The point is however that this is a true square or palindrome, reading the same horizontally as it does vertically. In the 1920s, various scholars showed that the letters could be re-arranged to read PATERNOSTER, twice, set out in cross fashion and sharing the central N; with A A and O O (alpha and omega, twice) left over.

Since 1868, other examples of this word-square have turned up, widely in space and time. Not all are demonstrably in Christian contexts; if PATERNOSTER A A O O is admittedly Christian in appearance, it is not the only arrangement than anagrammatic ingenuity has been able to produce. There appears to be some evidence that the 1868 Cirencester find was a second century one, and this pre-Constantinian estimate is certainly strengthened by another discovery in 1978: a fair-sized sherd from the shoulder of an amphora (Pl. 1) with most of the first three lines of the wording was found at Manchester, in a rubbish-pit within the vicus area north of the Roman fort (*Mamucio*), assigned to the late second century AD.[17] In their sensible summary, Hassall and Tomlin[18] conclude that it seems possible that this word-square was adopted by Christians before the fourth century, but it is unlikely that they devised it, or were its exclusive users. 'It should not be seen in isolation as evidence of Christianity in second-century Manchester.' Nor, despite its likely nature as a Christian focus at a later date, in second-century Cirencester either.

At the other end of the time-scale, we have to exclude the eight pewter ingots (six of which survive in the British Museum) bearing impressed stamps with the name SYAGRI(US), and encircled chi-rho with SPES IN DEO.[19] Found in the Thames between Battersea and Wandsworth, a stretch about 5 miles (8 km) upstream from the Roman London riverside frontage, these presumably fell from a trader's barge or ford-swimming pack animal and have little or no locational value; they are also probably to be seen as post-Roman imports.[20]

Lastly here, there are certain specialised and famous hoards of bullion, items within which are Christian in design or inscription or ornament, which we have to set aside. That found during work in 1919 within the native hillfort of Traprain Law, some 20 miles (32 km) east of Edinburgh,[21] contained about 110 pieces mainly of Gaulish origin, six at least with Christian symbols. Most of the pieces had been hammered flat or partially dismembered, the traditional way of sharing out loot among a large body of participants; it cannot even be said for sure that this treasure was seized in North Britain, and the event itself could lie rather widely in the late fourth or fifth century.[22]

Approximately parallel are the cases of the similar, if non-Christian, 'pirate hoards' of silver from early fifth-century Ireland, the Ballinrees (or 'Coleraine') hoard, and the Balline hoard,[23] which belong not so much to the story of late Roman Britain as to that of her enemies on the western flank (*cf.* p. 320 below).

Far and away the most spectacular hoard, a true national treasure, is the one found about 1942 near Mildenhall in Suffolk, acquired by the British Museum in 1946.[24] Kenneth Painter has argued with ingenuity and *brio* that this hoard, deposited intact with no signs of rough handling, can be dated to a little before *c*.360, and that one historical context at least can explain its deposition. It may have been part of the household or personal property of Lupicinus, a Christian general, who in 360, year of a major attack by the Irish Scotti and the Picts upon the northern frontier of Roman Britain, was serving as *magister equitum* in Gaul. At the same time, Julian (this is Julian the Apostate, 332–363) was Caesar in Gaul within the tetrarchy, the late Roman system that divided control of the empire, East and West, between two senior (*Augusti*) emperors and two inferiors (the Caesars). Lupicinus was despatched to Britain with a field force. While this experienced general was overseas, Julian was illegally proclaimed Augustus, the legitimate figure (Constantius II) being still in power. Julian's apostasy, which was to take the form of deliberate frenzied promotion of paganism coupled with anti-Christian policies during his brief period as the sole emperor (from Constantius' death, November 361, to his own in the summer of 363), was now apparent. Lupicinus, as a Christian, still under the ultimate control of Constantius II and with an effective army at his side, was an unknown force; as a precaution he was recalled to Gaul, and arrested at Boulogne.

His family and personal entourage, if they had planned to follow him back to Gaul, would now have had some reason – quite apart from any more immediate worries as to whether any part of the field army might declare openly for Julian – to conceal the general's treasure; and the Mildenhall treasure is probably just the type of collection one would attribute to a Christian of his personal standing and background at this period. It should be noticed that, though minor flaws in this exciting reconstruction have been pointed out, no one has yet offered any other explanation remotely as persuasive. Unhappily for us, Painter's thesis removed the Mildenhall Treasure from the scope of this volume.

When one turns to discuss the material previously grouped – the class given a weighting value of 3 in this chapter, those of 2 and 1 in Chapter 5 – it is difficult to steer a course on the reader's behalf between unnecessarily long, specialist accounts of every single find, and a cursory list in tabular form which would have to be relegated to an appendix. The course adopted has been to give short descriptions, and references only to reliable modern sources or, where anything has been the subject of informed debate, all relevant sources. Reference should be made to the earlier shorter catalogue of Professor Jocelyn Toynbee,[25] many aspects of which she later developed with enlightening scholarship and with illustrations in her major essays.[26] It would however be pedantic, pointless and tedious to include all Victorian and earlier references (save in the few cases where these are the only ones), because they are often stark records of discovery, comment and interpretation having been surplanted by later research.

Objects which form part of larger intrinsic groups – for instance, inscriptions on stone – are cited by the relevant corpora (as RIB). Certain finds (such as supposed churches) fully discussed in later chapters are merely listed here, so that the information can be at hand to accompany the distribution-maps.

MATERIAL WITH A VALUE OF '3'

Among the churches (Chaps. 6 and 7) we include here the sites at *Canterbury* (two: St Pancras phase I, and Holy Saviour), *Icklingham*, *Lullingstone*, *St Albans* (two: the present Abbey or Cathedral site, and that in Verulam Hills Field), *Silchester* and *Richborough*. Certain associated baptisteries are indicated by the same symbols, though that at *Witham* in Essex (Chap. 8) is separately marked.

The inclusion of certain decorated mosaic pavements is mainly a question of interpretation of individual cases. All are associated with villas, and where they occur in rooms whose exact functions can be debated it still has not been shown that these are *not* parts of villa-house complexes. Three mosaics only, from *Frampton*, *Fifehead Neville* and *Hinton St Mary*, all in Dorset, can be regarded as Christian; the first and last show Chistian symbolism, and the second is highly probable. It displays four dolphins concentrically around seven fishes, a central cantharus, and in two of the four spandrels what appear to be pomegranates.[27]

Of some nine or ten other mosaics, some of which were produced by the identified firms or workshops responsible for any of the three Christian examples,[28] the motifs which they show certainly come within the broad description of being 'mythological';[29] but in specific terms they are better described as Dionysiac or Gnostic. As we saw earlier, there were bodies of belief containing facets which ran parallel to contemporary Christian ideas. It is then just possible to suppose that possessors of such pavements, while for any reason reluctant to publicise their adherence to Christianity, hinted at it by commissioning designs – outwardly pagan, and in the high fashion of the day – able to bear rather more subtle and cryptic interpretations. The idea is a tempting one. It cannot be dismissed out of hand; it is clear (to take one area of potential syncretism alone) that early, pre-Constantinian Christian art could have a definite Gnostic element.[30] It is also clear that in fourth-century Britain Christianity was neither the sole, nor in every district the principal, fount of intellectual spiritual belief. Other cults which could be dignified by the label of 'religions', as we say, co-existed. One could then enquire, At what stage does the overt display, on the floor of a rich man's home, of a mosaic featuring scenes with Orpheus or Dionysus, become more likely to betray a lateral support for Christianity, and less likely to mean just an insouciant (or even direct) interest in matters Orphic or Bacchic? How can we possibly tell? And there is another factor of straight coincidence that cannot be ignored. If the favourite motif of the Four Seasons, or anything used to personify them, happens to occur in the same numerical division as the Four Evangelists, so too do the spandrels on a mosaic floor (the four corner-spaces left to be filled when a circle is contained within a square). For these reasons, the Gnostic and Dionysiac pavements[31] have to be omitted from this category.

The actual settings of both the Frampton and Hinton St Mary pavements are examined later, when we discuss estate churches. The Frampton mosaic[32] has a prominently-placed encircled ☧ (fig. 4), central in a row of seven roundels along the base of the apsidal portion. There is a cantharus or chalice-like vessel in a panel within the apse, and twenty-four rather dolphin-like fishes arranged clockwise, 6, 8, 6 and 4, around the borders of the main square area.[33] The Fifehead Neville pavement is independently interesting because two finger-rings with Christian devices come from the same establishment.

The Hinton St Mary mosaic, the most recently found, is also far and away the most striking; both before and since its fortunate acquisition by, and now admirable public display within, the British Museum, it has attracted some important literature.[34] It floored a space 19 by 28 ft overall (6 by 9 m), in a room that probably formed part of a fourth-century villa-house. Short cross-walls divided the room into two unequal parts, the larger being almost square, the smaller, rectangular. Within the larger part the design has a central roundel within four registers of geometric ornament; this shows a head and shoulders bust of a young male figure, fair-haired, beardless, and with emphatic dark eyes. Behind the head is an extended ☧ (fig. 4), the central crossing of which would lie behind the upper point of the skull. On each side, asymetrically within the side-arms of the 'X', is a pomegranate. (The remaining ornament on the mosaic is described in the references given above; and see Pl. 5.)

The unique aspect rests on one central assumption: that the portrait bust shows the youthful Christ. While this is not of course explicitly stated – unless the backing symbol is veritably to be read as Chi, Rho, and the explicitness resides in that proposal – prolonged discussion has given reasons for believing in this identification. If this is true, this is the only such depiction in Roman Britain. It is among the earliest, perhaps *the* earliest, in the western empire; and it now raises the peculiar problem of its being the only direct portrait of Christ – face, head and shoulders; not even partly allegorical – so placed that it could be trodden upon.

Jocelyn Toynbee has discussed the further matter of whether other motifs on the mosaic could be interpreted in a Christian light.[35] Bellerophon on Pegasus, slaying the snake-tailed Chimaera, may be the Divine Hero overcoming death and evil. A spreading tree, in a lunette below the central roundel, might be a Tree of Life. Four persons shown as busts in the spandrels, if they are the Four Winds, could signify the Evangelists. It has to be said that, devoid of the central roundel, the mosaic would fall into line with others and the force of any such interpretations would be correspondingly diminished. The problem *is* very much one of interpretation. Doubt (for example) has recently been expressed as to whether Bellerophon images ever carried a Christ-like connotation.[36]

More to the point may be the reconstitution of the frame of mind that produced such art-forms. John Chandler has expressed this clearly.[37] Either the villa-owner's understanding of Christianity was syncretic – he was prepared to embrace Christianity without renouncing his pagan heritage – or he was a cautious man, not convinced that Christianity would eventually win the day (and one recalls the two-year apostasy under Julian, 361–3). He therefore chose to decorate his home with motifs that would appear Christian to the Christian, and pagan to the pagan. Chandler goes on to draw attention to this, as a possible case of 'nominal Christianity' among the rural aristocrats of Roman Britain; men who tolerated, even professed Christianity, whether to impress or to conform, and without offering that degree of personal commitment which until 313 would have been essential for membership. This is persuasive; but at least at Hinton St Mary we are entitled, with Jocelyn Toynbee, to see Christian art in a Christian context.

The few building-stones come from widely-separated places. That found at *Catterick*, Yorkshire, during excavation of the Roman settlement very largely destroyed by the Catterick-Bridge by-pass,[38] was a small sandstone block some 11 by 18 cm, built into the external face of the cold plunge-bath in the bath-house. It was on its side, re-used from some setting earlier than the bath building (deserted in the early fourth century); roughly incised was an elongated ☧ (fig. 5.11).[39]

The curious little 'fish' at the West Park villa, *Rockbourne*, Hampshire (fig. 5.12), has already been mentioned. The large slabs which formed part of the formal surround of the natural spring (and Nymphaeum) at the rear of the villa-house, *Chedworth*, Gloucestershire, included ones incised carefully with ☧ symbols (figs.4.7; 5.13), have been illustrated from time to time,[40] and are discussed again in Chapter 8 with the idea that for a time they formed part of a baptismal arrangement.

From the Roman fort and settlement at *Maryport*, the Roman *Alauna*, on the Cumberland coast – where Roman occupation seems to have continued until late in the fourth century at least – there is a record of a lost, and apparently irretrievably lost despite intense modern search, fragment of a larger carved stone. It is known from a 1794 drawing by J. Lowes, Hutchinson's draughtsman (RIB 856); if this is accurate, as it seems to be,[41] it may be of the top (viewer's) left corner of a Roman tombstone, showing the summit of a side-column whose capital bears a row of XXX, and just the spring of a triangular pediment. It does not seem likely to be part of an altar: RIB labels it, cautiously, as 'a plaque, presumably sepulchral', and the Christian nature of the ☧ (fig. 4.1) is clear enough.

Among various building fragments, a tegula or tile found at *Wickford*, Essex,[42] had been incised before firing with a rare alpha-omega device, the 'A' being contained within a larger form of the actual Greek capital (fig. 5.7). It came from an area of scattered late fourth-century debris, overlain by traces of some sub-Roman timber structure; though the tile probably formed part of an original roof, where this form of the sacred monogram may have been displayed as 'a protection to the building', it had since becoming detached been broken down and rubbed smooth around the inscribed portion and was perhaps serving as a portable good-luck object. The tile has to be seen as a purely local, later fourth-century, product.

The second tile, from *York*, is also a standard local product, incised before firing in whatever *Eburacum* tuilierie produced it, in this case with a conventional attempt at ☧ (fig. 5.6). It was found in 1968[43] below the east end of York Minster nave, in Roman terms north of the *principia*, on whose roof it had no doubt served (as at Wickford) as an intended, if unofficial, Christian antefix. The form of the design is comparable to one on coins of Constantine I from the Antioch mint, 336–7, suggesting here a mid fourth century date (so R.P. Wright).

Surprisingly, in view of the millions unearthed over the years in Romano–British excavations, there is only one brick; a broken one, again with a pre-firing graffito, from south of the south range of forum buildings at *Ratae*, Leicester. The rho is crossed just below the loop by a single diagonal line, and on the left is an inverted 'V', a rustic capital A (for alpha?); the brick is not more closely dated.[44]

Allied in social contexts to these building-material fragments are the scattered instances of inscribed sherds. These surely reveal among the same broad class of urban artisans both a familiarity with the general lines of the commonest Christian symbol – one familiar to the literate and illiterate alike – and some need to bring into existence a visible representation of that symbol. As a sherd with a chi-rho scratched on it is something easily produced anywhere and any time that a hand, a sharp point, and a broken pot coincide, these sherds are about the last things that anyone would bother to take from place to place, and their distribution-map value is necessarily high.

An instance from *Canterbury* (fig. 5.3) illustrates the point that it is the date of the graffito, not its matrix, that matters. This is a piece[45] of a second-century samian bowl of form 31, broken and chipped but mended in antiquity. A later owner scratched his ☧ deeply on the underside within the foot-ring; and two scratched letters on the outer wall must be read as D N (the N reversed), and (as mentioned earlier) may perhaps imply *Dominus Noster*. This was found, possibly having been deposited as grave-goods, in a cemetery not further described, within 400 m of St Martin's Church, east of Canterbury (see fig. 23, below). From *Exeter* there is a sherd of a coarse black ware known from Late Roman contexts in that city.[46] It has a similar ☧ scratched on the exterior (fig. 5.2), the relevant sherd having probably been selectively preserved. This came from a domestic area off South Street, Exeter (see fig. 25, below).

At *Gatcombe* in Somerset, a rural walled settlement[47] which was either a small Roman town or the anomalous centre of some great estate, a sherd from the rim of a red-ware beaker, on which another and similar symbol (fig. 5.4) had been – as with all these sherds – scratched or incised after firing, came from 'Building 19', perhaps an out-house, one generally abandoned *c*.380. There is a record, *per* W.H.C. Frend,[48] of a fourth such sherd from Roman St Albans, *Verulamium*, said to be in the British Museum's collection (but unfortunately neither it, nor any such record, can be found).[49] Lastly, to these we can add a single example involving not pottery but glass; a fragment, found unstratified, in the 1959 season of excavation at *Catterick*.[50] On a broken portion of the rectangular base of a glass bottle, a chi-rho – again with single cross-bar, ☧ – had been scratched, reversed or retrograde on the exterior, so that it could have been read or seen correctly, the right way around, by looking down through the interior of the bottle.

The various hoards with Christian significance (excluding, for the separate reasons explained, those from Traprain Law and Mildenhall) all possess the common factor that they were the properties of well-to-do families in settled households – in one case, rather more probably a Christian community than a family. The concealment of these goods is to be viewed, not as the outcome of any selective persecution of Christians, but as one aspect of a widely-demonstrated habit of hiding personal wealth at times of disorder and imagined risk. In the absence of any system of safe-deposits or vaults (and, as the more recent social history of

10 Location of major 4th-cent. hoards mentioned in text (1 silver: 2 pewter)
A Appleshaw   B Biddulph   Ca Canterbury   Co Corbridge   D Dorchester
(Dorset)   (Do) Dorchester-on-Thames (Oxfordshire)   (G) Great Horwood   I
Icklingham   (M) Mildenhall   S? Sutton. Letters bracketed indicate no certain
Christian object(s) included

France suggests, even in their presence) a deeply rooted human instinct
seems to emerge, as a response to crisis; hurriedly-wrapped valuables are
stuffed inside hollow trees, interred below floors and walls, or taken out
into the grounds and buried X paces from this and Y paces from that. We
must remind ourselves that all the hoards found by archaeologists, or
now by contemporary looters, are only that unknown proportion of such
hoards *not* re-located and recovered by their provident owners and their
heirs.

A surprisingly common element in these late Romano–British bullion
hoards is the spoon. Typologically, these spoons lie within the known

range of Roman silver used by the well-off in precisely our own fashion; but 'Christian spoons' are those on the bowl of which a particular symbol of inscription has been, professionally or informally, added. Continued associations show that one sentiment, usually in the form X VIVAS – 'O (name), may you have Life (Eternal?)' – something also seen on other objects, could be, though perhaps was not invariably, an index of Christian thought. Precisely what these spoons imply in terms of social activity remains uncertain. There is a small hoard of five ornamental silver spoons, deposited after *c.*395 and found at Dorchester (Oxfordshire),[51] which has no Christian element at all. It would be a gross over-simplification to label all the supposedly Christian spoons as 'christening-spoons'; though the possibility that at least some were formal presents given after Christian baptism (adult, rather than infant, Chap. 8) must be allowed. But we must also reckon with gifts of such spoons simply between friends – spoons suitably inscribed and designed to convey, within a specifically Christian milieu, good wishes or messages of well-being. Nor can one rule out liturgical use (the Communion; various feasts of the early Church), or the straight addition of Christian insignia to anyone's existing table-silver. Painter has pointed out[52] that the attribution of any individual spoon to a particular use – and any spoon could have had a multiplicity of uses, similtaneously or successively – is impossible unless circumstances and associations of discovery are unusually informative. There are, for example, eight silver spoons or ladles in the Mildenhall Treasure, three purely decorative, three with double-line A/☧/W motifs stamped inside their bowls, and two more lettered PASCENTIA VIVAS and PAPITTEDO VIVAS.[53] It is not self-evident that these are Christian, or share in the Christian element in the treasure, though it is likely. The name Pascentia is conceivable as belonging to a member of Lupicinus' family, if this is Lupicinus' plate; that of Papittedo, suggesting at the most a Greek serving as a physician or tutor or *notarius*, is not; but one cannot be sure that either name had anything to do with the late fourth-century owner, whoever he may have been.

There are two (possibly three, if there was a 'Sutton Hoard' containing the Isle of Ely bowl, p. 124) hoards involving pewter-ware; and five which are mainly or entirely silver-ware. On balance, a sixth from Great Horwood, Bucks., must be omitted; it contains[54] a silver spoon inscribed VENERIA VIVAS but there is no other hint of Christianity present. The map, fig. 10, shows the location of all the hoards so far mentioned, including those not further discussed.

The pewter hoard from *Appleshaw*, near Andover (Hampshire), was found in the last century,[55] when thirty-two pewter vessels were unearthed from a metre-deep pit cut through the cement floor of a villa-house that was apparently abandoned in the later fourth century. There is no reason to follow Shimon Applebaum[56] in supposing that this 'presumably belonged to an estate church' or in taking the name VICTRICI scratched on one of the, otherwise unremarkable, pieces as having anything to do with Victricius, bishop of Rouen (p. 50). The hoard is the tableware of a comfortable household and we can only speculate why it was all so carefully buried. One walled and flanged pewter bowl bears, incised on the base,[57] a large linear ⚒. An oval dish, which proved to be nearly pure tin, is engraved – this is original ornamentation – with a conventional fish inside a pointed-oval border of double lines and running scroll (fig. 8.12).

At *Icklingham*, Suffolk, a site which will occupy us considerably, there is a find of pewter whose inclusion in this category of evidence could be justified by one particular piece and further by the plentiful evidence for Roman Christianity in the same locality. The discovery[58] took place, accidentally and by an R.A.F. bomb-disposal unit, in 1956. Nine pewter vessels with oddments of iron, bone, and Roman pottery were found some 75 cm below ground in an unreported context. The composition (cups, bowls and a large dish) points to conventional domestic ware. The fragmentary oval dish, originally about 22 cm long and flat-rimmed, had stamped or incised a drawing of a fish occupying most of the internal area;[59] as a fish, it may be detailed but is still conventionalised, the task of generic identification having defied the skills of the Cambridge Zoology department. One need not press this too far, but a fish-decorated dish of Christian import is at least possible (the find-spot is 2½ miles, or about 4 km, NNE of the main site at Icklingham discussed in later chapters). This, and the Appleshaw dish, might be tentatively seen against the rectangular silver *lanx* with its worm-swallowing fish from the Kaiseraugst (Switzerland) treasure.[60]

The third, potential, hoard from Sutton, Isle of Ely, cannot safely be included because it can only be suspected that the Isle of Ely Christian-ornamented bowl (p. 124) came from it; we pass to the silver.

The small hoard from *Biddulph*, Staffordshire, has only recently been sorted out and explained. Its nature has been complicated by an unexpected element – the presence of most skilfully-made (and dispersed) high-grade copies of one of the objects. This has led to a certain measure of published investigations;[61] and one isolated piece that might entrap future workers in this field, the spoon vaguely described as 'from Monmouthshire',[62] can be jettisoned. David Sherlock's meticulous note gives as much clarification as is now possible. The original find was inside an area of dispersed Roman settlement. A hoard of fourth-century gold jewellery found some five miles away in 1874 × 1879 may reflect the same period of insecurity. All that can now be said is that (probably) four silver spoons were ploughed up in a field about 1885. One[63] has within its bowl, engraved in double-line technique, an A/⳨/W device (fig. 6.5). The style and technique point to the Eastern empire in the earlier fourth century. After 1886, at least four copies (now at British Museum, Berlin, New York and Cardiff) of this spoon were made; but the other three spoons in the hoard were probably plain.

The *Canterbury* hoard, found in 1962 and now in the Royal Museum, Canterbury, is of wider composition, and interest. It was deposited probably not much before *c*.400 just outside the late Roman city wall on the south-west side (*cf*. fig. 23) and was found during excavations for a new bridge over the river Stour at this point.

Eight coins (AD 354–423) were not certainly associated, and must be disregarded. The hoard itself contained two small silver ingots, eleven silver spoons, a silver implement (described below), silver glass-headed pin, a gold ring and a gold hook-and-eye. Some at least of this material is clearly Christian; Painter[64] commented that 'as part of an expensive table service they may be recognized as the property of (Christian) adherents who were both educated and influential'. He also suggests AD 406 – the year in which the usurper Constantius III drained Britain of its garrison for his Gaulish venture – as a possible date.

One spoon, no. 4 (enumerations as in Painter's list), had a ⳨ in the centre of its bowl; another, no. 12, the bowl inscribed VIRIBONISM and the graffiti numerals IV and XII; and the silver implement, on each face of the flattened disc that terminated its handle, showed ⳨ within a circle, executed (except for the incised curve of the rho) in tiny punch-marks. This object, no. 14, has a twisted square-section 'stem' or handle, one end being a small spoon-bowl, and the other the flattened chi-rho ornamented disc just mentioned, continued as a prong. No particular name has been evolved for this, and similar objects, mainly because (below) the function is not clear. Various explanations have been put forward. In the case of those examples with Christian ornamentation, like this one, or one from the Kaiseraugst hoard,[65] or a later one from a post-Roman context at St Ninian's Isle (Shetland) actually recovered from below the floor of a church,[66] it has been suggested that the objects are of liturgical use – intended to divide, and by using the prong or point to lift, portions of the Host. Other possibilities – for eating shell-fish or edible snails; even for use as genteel toothpicks – have been aired. It is perhaps safest to continue seeing them as domestic and utilitarian like the spoons; the few examples with Christian ornament are thus just toothpicks or winkle-pickers, or whatever they are, so decorated.

The hoard from *Dorchester*, Dorset (the Roman *Durnovaria*; the Romano–British name of Dorchester (-on-Thames), Oxfordshire, has not survived)[67] was found, within the Roman walled town, in 1898–99 (fig. 24). There were at least 50 coins (of 360 to 400), recovered in association with five silver spoons and another silver, undecorated, pronged 'toothpick' object. Dalton, in the initial publication,[68] wondered if such a *ligula* (to use a permissible Roman term) was perhaps a manicure-knife. Confusingly, these spoons are not unlike some in the Dorchester-on-Thames find.[69] The hoard, hidden in town premises by a well-to-do Durnovarian, very probably a Christian in view of the proximity of the Poundbury site (Chap. 9), before 400, has one spoon with AVGVSTINE VIVAS inscribed on the bowl, and another, now broken and decayed (these are in the County Museum, Dorchester), with a stylised little fish swimming away from the handle-junction (fig. 8.13).

What is usually called the *Corbridge* find[70] is dispersed, insofar as it survives, and its status as a hoard is inferential; though it remains a perfectly reasonable guess that some extremely valuable silver treasure was concealed, late in the fourth century, outside the Roman station at *Corstopitum*. This first came to light in 1735 when normal ripuarian erosion of the south bank of the Tyne, a half-mile south of Roman Corbridge, probably began to expose a hidden cache. The most celebrated piece is the large silver tray or dish, the 'Corbridge Lanx', now at Alnwick Castle.[71] A small silver flat-rimmed bowl some 10cm high is now known only from drawings; its rim bore an outer beading ring and within this, around the flange, a zone of slender foliate scroll, interrupted by six instances of a linear ☧ within a square (fig. 13.6). As far as can now be made out these are original decorative elements. A further silver object, a small (10cm high) beaker, with DESIDERE VIVAS inscribed around its rim, probably came from the same source – it was found in 1760 floating on the Tyne 5 miles (8 km) downstream.

The common feature of all the hoards so far mentioned is straightforward: they comprise objects of value, within a range corresponding to the wealth and social status of their owners, hidden during the all-too-frequent alarums and excursions of the fourth century. Though fig. 10 is a location map, not intended as a full distribution-map, it is obvious that most of the locations are in the zone where most of late Roman Britain's wealth lay and that threatened incursions from a northerly direction (for example, in the 360s) would produce some such pattern. The particular hoards distinguished above contain items giving some indication that Christianity was known, to some extent advertised, and perhaps even strenuously upheld, by the proprietors in question. But the items, whether pewter or silver, are first and foremost in groups of domestic vessels and utensils, of things which lie within the known repertoire of the material culture of this region and period.

The last and most recently discovered hoard is of quite another character. It is spectacular, to the point where its importance becomes international rather than British and where it may well be Early Christian in a special sense – in that it could actually represent the communal property of an *ecclesia* or Christian community.

The *Water Newton* hoard was found early in 1975, in a cultivated field within the Roman town of *Durobrivae*, near Chesterton, Huntingdon-shire. It is to be regretted that the circumstances of the discovery, which involved an amateur treasure-hunter, excluded for ever any proper information about the precise context; the initial Press reports were not all mutually consistent.[72] In September 1975 a coroner's jury declared the hoard to be Treasure Trove. It passed to the British Museum, where with laudable promptness the objects were cleaned, accorded preliminary publication, and put on display.

The whole assemblage is of prime importance in any study of Romano–British Christianity, and only slightly less so in the whole field of the earliest Christian applied art within the empire. It should be noted that, though sentiment might have led to a preference for *Durobrivae* as a label, 'Water Newton' (this is the correct form, as against 'Water-newton') is now established; the *Britannia* entries, in referring to the find as 'Chesterton, Hunts.' merely follow their journal's long-standing rule, also employed in RIB, of using parish/county labels, and are not thus intentionally obscurantist.

The first announcement[73] was followed by a preliminary assessment in an international publication[74] and then another in the appropriate local journal,[75] *Durobrivae*. The first British Museum guide-catalogue[76] followed, setting out item-numbers which are used here; as did a commentary to accompany a set of colour-slides.[77] The treasure was, fortunately, cleaned and conserved[78] in time to be included in an internationally-based exhibition,[79] where it could be both seen and discussed in a properly broad framework. The inscriptions on the various objects were separately noted in *Britannia*.[80] Areas which now invite further analysis include the most likely date of the deposition (early to mid-fourth century seems indicated, but refinement may be possible); the precise meaning of all the inscriptions; the, so far unique, nature of certain items; and the general significance of the hoard in early British Christianity.

The find-spot, as far as can be determined, lies within the south-east angle of the enclosed area of *Durobrivae*, probably some 100 m inside the rounded corner.[81] The whole area has unhappily long been subjected to the depredations of greedy and unprincipled looters armed with metal-detectors. A smaller fourth-century hoard involving a bronze bowl, two silver scraps, a leather-and-fabric purse and 30 gold coins, all inside a larger lidded pottery bowl, was found in February 1974 in much the same area (cautiously described as 'some 200 metres from the A1 road at Waternewton').[82] The gold coins, *solidi*, allowed the estimate that this was concealed around AD 350 or shortly afterwards; a date relevant also to the major hoard (and indeed, as will be seen below, preferred for it by the present writer) in that it offers some indication of a common apprehension of loss at a fixed time. One cannot now pursue, on the strength of academic rumour alone, the disquieting idea that there may in recent years have been *other* improperly-exhumed and profitably dispersed finds of the same calibre as the two known hoards.

Painter has given a descriptive inventory of the treasure[83] and a summary is given here, using his numbers. The hoard is made up of: a plain silver bowl (1); mouth and neck of a silver spouted jug (2); large flat-based deep silver dish (3), interior centre with a very finely-incised ☧/W (no alpha) within a double circle (fig. 6.4); most of a thin sheet-silver facetted bowl (4); a largely-complete silver decorated jug (5); silver handled cup of cantharus form, 12.5 cm high (6); silver cup or beaker with double-line incised inscription around the neck zone (8), preluded by the very remarkable and beautiful chi-rho design reproduced here (fig. 6.3); another squat silver inscribed bowl (9), with inscription around the rim including an A/☧/W and a single word inscribed on the underside base; and (7) a silver strainer, the bowl with patterned piercing, long narrow (repaired) handle terminating in a disc with engraved A/☧/W (here, fig. 6.6) in a circle of punched dots. This object[84] is about 20 cm long.

There are then at least eighteen plaques, whole, partial or damaged, on average some 3 in (7 cm) long, roughly leaf-shaped or formed as elongated triangles with flat or slightly-curved tops. These (10–27) are in silver sheet, with relief ribs or raised lines giving them something of the appearance of a stylised palm-frond, or a feather seen in detail. Various silver fragments (28), some perhaps from further plaques, some from other objects, complete the list.

Of the plaques or parts thereof, 11 is a sheet-gold appliqué disc with A/☧/W. 10 and 14 may have been gilded over silver. Eight plaques (10, 13, 14, 16, 18, 19, 21 and 22) bear chi-rho motifs, with or without A W, and on 18 this appears as a gilt medallion on the plaque. In some cases the Christian symbol is to be read when the plaque, viewed as a triangular shape, points downwards; on 21 and 22 when it points upward.

Plaque 12 is damaged, has a repoussé inverted-W/☧/A in a circle (fig. 7.2) and just below the shallowly-curving top of the triangle, two lines of inscription. Most of the plaques show one or two small holes, indicating a means of attachment to some background.

The unquestionable Christian emphasis exhibiting, as this does, no less than fifteen examples of the Constantinian ☧ (with or without A and W) among twenty-seven objects, lends a particular interest to the inscriptions. Here, any problems are those of precise meaning, not of legibility. Concurrent words being written out separately, the presently-agreed versions of these inscriptions can be taken one by one, and fully discussed.

Cup or beaker (6)
One line, defective, letters in rustic capitals, double-outline, on band below rim.

(A/☧/W) INNOCENTIA ET VIVENTIA?? . . . RVNT

The NN of the first name is ligatured; the second vowel in the second name is a thin one, either an E[85] or less attractively an I.[86] Only a trace of the next few letters survives; LIB(ENTES) is a guess. The final verb might well be DEDERVNT, DEDICAVERVNT, or OFFERVNT. The sense is clearly 'Innocentia and Viventia, being (?), have (made, given, offered or performed something)'. The legend would then record a dedication or ascription of the vessel.

Small cup or bowl (9)
One line, complete, small neat rustic capitals, just below rim. (A/☧/W) SANCTVM ALTARE TVVM D (A/☧/W) OMINE SVBNIXVS HONORO. On the base, in a widely-spaced circle, PVBLIANVS.

All this is clear and in terms of verse composition the line could be accepted as a formulaic hexameter, 'Sanctum altare tuum, Domine, subnixus honoro'. There is no reason to deny 'Publianus' the rôle of first person singular in this sentiment: 'I *subnixus* honour your holy *altare*, O Lord'. Of the two Latin words, *subnixus* is an obscure past-participial adjective qualifying the 'I', and is not really translatable by any single English word. In this context its area of meaning is 'dependent-on-Thee', 'having-put-my-faith-in-Thee', or 'having-cast-myself-beneath-Thee'. The word *altare*, discussed further below (p. 149), is to be translated 'church' rather than 'altar'.

Fragmentary plaque (12)
Two-line inscription, rather irregular rustic capitals in relief, between the top of the plaque and the encircled (m/☧/A). Here the words are separated and some ligatures in the upper line omitted.

I)AMCILLA VOTVM QVOD / PROMISIT CONPLEVIT

The reading of the first word, a personal name, as *Iamcilla* (so R.P. Wright)[87] replaces the first reading as *Anicilla*; Iamcilla is presumably British, Anicilla standing closer to Latin *ancilla* 'female servant, handmaid' (cf. Patrick, *Epistola*, 10 – *servos et ancillas domus patris mei*). The sense is 'Iamcilla has fulfilled that vow that she promised'. This is a different formula from the common V S L M, but at once it must recall the (fourth century?) small bronze gable-topped plaque from the great pagan temple at Lydney, Gloucestershire.[88] This announces (fig. 11) that 'Pexillus gave to the God, Nodens Mars, the vowed-object which he promised'; it uses *votum quod promisit* in precisely the same way. (In the Water Newton inscription, *conplevit*, the rustic capital N actually written reversed is a graph, and has no linguistic significance.)

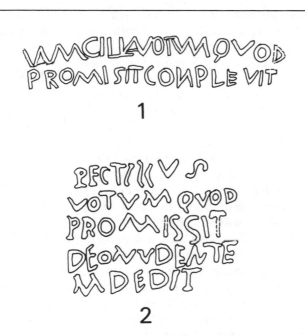

11 Use of *promisit* in Christian and pagan votive inscriptions
 1 Water Newton *Iamcilla* plaque (after P. Compton)   2 Lydney, RIB 307 (after R.P. Wright)

The meaning of the Water Newton treasure is a topic that will continue to merit discussion, beyond the limited comments offered here. The conjunction of all the pieces, presumably found in a contemporary hole or pit and certainly together, obliges us to begin by considering the hoard as unified, heterogeneous and Christian. It has all the characteristics one would attach to the more portable and more valuable possessions of a fourth-century Christian flock. A flock, a community; not an individual Christian and/or his family; and four distinct personal names – Innocentia, Viventia and Iamcilla (female) and Publianus (male) – underline this. In short, is this a collection of church plate?

The two jugs, strainer (for wine), medium-large dish and various cups or bowls can be seen against the predominantly domestic content of the silver-ware hoards earlier discussed. One could remark, at Water Newton, on the absence of any spoons, or an instance of the ligula object; and the presence of the jug-and-strainer wine service element. Since we are in no position to do more than hint at the liturgical accessories likely to have been found in Roman Britain, we must cautiously sketch the possibilities; the large dish with its prominent chi-rho as a communion plate, the two jugs and strainer for the Eucharistic wine, even the facetted ornamented bowl (4) which was reconstituted from fragments and perhaps[89] originally suspended by chains from rim-rings so that it could be viewed from below as a fore-runner of hanging-bowls employed in ecclesiastical ways (e.g., as a floating-wick lamp). Of the four individual cups or bowls (1, 6, 8, 9) all much the same size and capacity, two bear inscriptions hinting at devotional gifts, and 6, with its two handles and cantharus shape, is in one of the typological series leading to conventional post-Roman chalices.

If this *is* the plate of a well-off fourth-century British church, what of the plaques? These have two, diametrically-opposed, sets of characteristics. On one hand, they are typologically leaf-shaped ribbed 'feather' plaques of sheet-metal, affixed by tacks or pins to some background surface, presumably within a shrine by satisfied devotees. One bears an actual statement to this effect. These aspects the plaques share entirely with pagan votive plaques, found in pagan temples and shrines. On the other hand, all the plaques are in silver and the series includes gold and silver-gilding – there are no bronze examples; most of them bear chi-rho designs; and in this alone, apart from the fact that there are so many of them (for the fragments may represent even further ones), the Water Newton objects are without parallel.

It might be tempting to argue that the combination of these two sets of characteristics should refer, chronologically, to an era when Christianity was fresh and new; when rustic Romano–British converts and neophytes, not entirely able to unravel mentally the nice distinctions between the powers of the Christian God and those of Jupiter or the imperial *numen*, were understandably confused as to the outward trivia of correct worship. To them, might it not have appeared logical that promises fulfilled by a God should be commemorated in a time-hallowed way, but using a Christian symbol?

If this argument (which the present author does not favour) points to any particular date, for example shortly after AD 313, there are objections on temporal grounds. The Water Newton plaques are not all identical. One would be just as inclined to think that their manufacture covered several decades, as several years. Even if some of the tiny central holes were 'constructional',[90] holding a plaque to a board while it was marked out and tooled, others were for affixing or suspension; and it looks as if the plaques in the hoard were removed, to be concealed with the larger objects, from whatever they were hung from, or pinned upon – by pulling them down, or prising the tacks out. The sheet-metal is not always pure; not all the plaques are in the same state of preservation, and the fragments might include bits of plaques which, having been exposed longest or made earliest, had decayed and were more liable to get broken in a hurried removal. There is a band of time, not a narrow date, involved

here. The various chi-rho forms, including as they do a most sophisticated and developed one (fig. 6.3) and most of the possible variations of A
and W, point to a phase of established usage. They could perhaps further
point to a mass unpinning or gathering-up, nearer to a date like AD 350-
plus, the date when the *solidi* hoard was hidden, than to the Peace of the
Church in 313.

Painter's own provisional, stylistic and typological, conclusions that
the latest pieces in the hoard are not later than the fourth century and that
known parallels for certain items cluster around the earlier fourth
century do not of course rule out the idea of the continued use in, say,
325 × 350 of vessels, most of which were made and acquired before *c.*325.
One might argue that dedication of plate to any Christian church is
something likely to lead to much handling and prolonged use. The
handle of the strainer (7) was, we noted, broken, and then mended with
three rivets. A jug-handle had come loose; was it already weakened
through long wear when the treasure was hurriedly bundled up? The
surfaces of this same jug were 'rather worn, as the result of cleaning or
handling, giving a rather softened appearance to the detail'.[91]

As for the find-spot, it was rightly noticed that Durobrivae in the late
Roman period lay astride the major north route from London and
Colchester, to Lincoln, York and the Wall. There could be an implication
that a band of Christians, from some other town, when travelling north
or south paused at Durobrivae, and were then overtaken by circum
stances obliging them to conceal their portable wealth within its walls. But
economy of hypotheses – and perhaps the suggestion of Nene Valley
Christianity at Orton Longueville and Ashton, in a rich, by no means
entirely rustic, farming belt (fig. 12) – could just as well ascribe the
deposition of the treasure to Christians within the town itself. From
recent air photographs we can guess that Durobrivae was a complex and
fairly important place, set in a district that in terms of material wealth
was probably above-average.[92] Whether a treasure of this calibre implies
a community of episcopal status, and if so whether that bears upon the
idea that in the fourth century Durobrivae might have ranked as a civitas
capital, are separate questions.

The author, if given a free hand and unlimited resources to pursue the
entire problem, would be looking very closely within the 44-acre interior
of Durobrivae[93] for signs of conventionally-planned urban temples.
Speculation alone costs nothing, and here is some. One such temple (it
might be hinted) fell into disuse in the early fourth century, or before. It
was not necessarily demolished; the site may have been a prime one, in
the area of 'C' on Mackreth's plan – not in that underdeveloped south-
east quarter, apparently containing larger buildings in isolation, of the
town-house-and-grounds kind, where the treasure was found. One
would not wish to go as far as suggesting that the idiosyncratic nature of

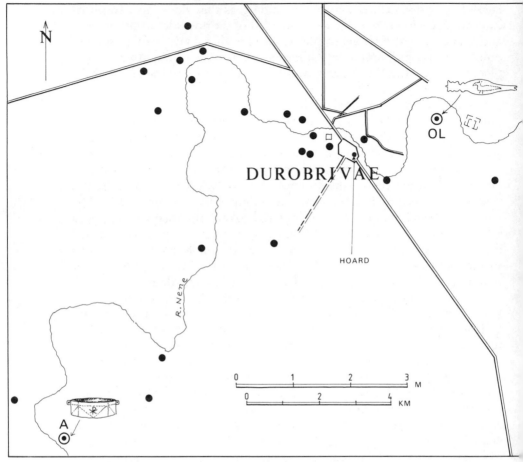

12 Late Roman Christianity in the area of *Durobrivae* and the Nene valley. Black circles mark villas or large farms
A Ashton (lead tank) OL Orton Longueville tag or nail-cleaner (*cf.* fig. 8, *16*). Approximate find-spot of Water Newton treasure is indicated ('Hoard')

the town plan itself reflected a certain independence of outlook and behaviour among its late Roman inhabitants, but we are forced in this direction *faute de mieux*. There is almost no evidence as to the cults favoured in pre-Christian Durobrivae; RIB 232, an old find from the fort, not the civilian settlement, is part of a stone inscription to Mars. Some faint indication of what could have preceded the Christian plaques is given by the elaborate silver votive plaques found at Barkway, Herts., 40 miles (64km) southward down Ermine Street (RIB 218–220).[94] Two of these are also to Mars, as *Mars Alator* and *Mars Toutatis*, the third to Vulcan. They belong to a class best known from the 1789 Stony Stratford

(Bucks.) plaques, discussed and figured by Toynbee;[95] but there are some bronze feather-shaped votive plaques a little closer to Durobrivae, at Godmanchester[96] 12 miles (20 km) south, one of which also figures an attached roundel – inscribed to the local and allegedly long-persisting town god of the place (*Abandinus*).

Is it, among the least improbable of the explanations that have been and doubtless will be advanced, possible that a former Durobrivae temple, whose interior had seen votive plaques to Mars and others – plaques in stylised feathered shapes, in bronze and silver, even in silver with mounted roundels – became the property of local Christians; and that the members of this comfortably-placed, perhaps isolated and certainly sadly aberrant *ecclesia* continued to affix or suspend silver and gold votive plaques, made Christian with prominent chi-rho devices, to the interior of their *altare* (no one having specifically prohibited them to do so)? If so, then far being regarded as indices of a trifling aberration in Christian practice, the plaques so very clearly partook of the special values attached to the church property that they were hastily removed, placed with, and at some stage in the mid-fourth century concealed alongside the Communion and liturgical vessels, one would guess in the garden belonging to a substantial member of the Christian flock.

This may sound like an explanation of the incredible by having recourse to the improbable. As John Chandler has commented,[97] the very existence of these objects suggests a notion of Christianity current in Britain which would have horrified the Church leaders on the Continent. But would their horror have been greater than that inspired by a picture of Christ's Head on a mosaic floor, in a place where (worshippers apart) house-servants with brooms and mops could hardly avoid the act of sweeping and rinsing Our Lord's image? We have to admit that religious phenomenology, let alone straight anthropology, provides many an instance where a divinity, introduced from one culture to a second, undergoes some degree of particular transmogrification – particularly when all the ancillary aspects of the hierophanies have not been fully assimilated. Exhortations to pray to God, whose priests would hardly extol as less potent than Mars and Jupiter, may in certain minds, their owners anxious to express public gratitude for answered prayers, have been interpreted as part of a system permitting, if not requiring, public acknowledgement in the usual fashion. If the cup gratefully supplied by Innocentia and Viventia represents one way of doing this, might not less polished persons see a silver ex-voto plaque merely as an alternative?

The question of Christian *cemeteries*, which in virtually all Continental studies of Christianity at this period constitute the mainstay of distribution-maps and church locations alike, takes on a different aspect in Romano–British research. It must be admitted that, despite a century of work in the field, we know comparatively little about this topic, in contrast to the position in other areas of the western empire. At the moment, and as far as the maps (figs. 15, 16) are concerned, the only entries can be *Poundbury*, Dorset, and (with some reservation) *Lankhills*, Winchester; more will be said of this in Chapter 9.

The remaining items under this category of evidence are the large lead tanks or cisterns, once known as 'Wiggonholt' type after a specimen found about 1943 at Lickford, near Wiggonholt, Sussex.[98] In view of the much greater significance of the group now known to come from another site in Suffolk, *'Icklingham* type' is preferred as a label. A full study of all these tanks is about to appear,[99] and the many references to individual discoveries therefore can be omitted. In view of what will be suggested below (Chap. 8) when the matter of baptism in Roman Britain is considered, it is assumed that the find-spots of these tanks, in this particular context those which bear Christian ornament, are not fortuitous; and that, whatever they were used for, it is more than likely that they served the needs of local Christians at the localities where they have subsequently been found.

The phrase 'Christian ornament' must be taken strictly, as meaning a chi-rho, with or without flanking ornaments of A and W. On the Wiggonholt tank itself,[100] the raised cast chi-rho was formed by rough cable-pattern lines – a 25-toothed wooden pattern was impressed into the casting mould to make these lines – with the relatively small rho loop being a U-shaped curve drawn into the mould with a blunt point. This design (fig. 13.2) lies within a square cable-pattern panel and the flanking panels around the exterior wall of the tank (one survives) would have repeated the 'X' of the chi-rho by itself. This use of XXX, or chevrons or triangles, is found on some of the other lead tanks, but to regard it as having any particular meaning would be unjustified; it seems to be merely ornamental. In the wider study of the production of sheet-lead coffins, ossuaria, etc., in late Roman Britain[101] this falls into line with a range of simple decoration.

An adequate list of these tanks has appeared,[102] to which should be added a fresh one from Icklingham;[103] from Ashton[104] there is now another. Jocelyn Toynbee has briefly discussed them.[105] Chi-rho motifs, partly moulded by impressing short lengths of wood, are shown in figs. 4.4 (Walesby) and 4.5 (Ashton). The tanks included here on the distribution-maps with a value of '3' are those from *Icklingham*, Suffolk; *Ashton*, Northants.; *Wiggonholt*, Sussex, and the very remarkable if incomplete example from *Walesby*, Lincs., whose figure-scene is examined at length in Chapter 8.

CHAPTER FIVE

The Material Evidence
– Second Part

The class of objects, items and discoveries accorded an evidential weighting of '2' in the previous chapter, implying 'Christian presence reasonably probable', is itself divided; into all those finds which may very well be or clearly are Christian but bear less direct relevance to their find-spots than the material just catalogued and, secondly, material where it is the Christian significance itself that has still to be assessed or agreed.

MATERIAL WITH A VALUE OF '2'

We begin with isolated entire vessels bearing any forms of Christian graffiti, vessels which are slightly more likely to have been moved from place to place than mere sherds with similar graffiti because, being entire, presumably they still possessed limited attraction. Under this heading come both those items where the Christian ornament appears to be an original element and those where it was added.

The sole bronze object is a small sheet-metal bowl with fluted sides and a footring, about 9 cm in diameter, found in 1922, exhibited and fortunately photographed in 1924 and since lost. It came to light during excavations at *Wall*, the Roman settlement of *Letocetum* near Lichfield, Staffs.,[1] possibly within a cemetery area. On the underside within the footring, a ⚹ with a small chi and disproportionately large rho loop was 'very distinctly embossed'; if this statement implies that the motif was worked in reverse from the inner surface, it might have been an original feature (fig. 13.1).

The pewter begins with a (mid-fourth century) bowl found in 1906, in rooms 17 or 20 of House VII N, opposite the north-east corner of the forum basilica at *Caerwent*, Monmouthshire (*Isca Silurum*). The graffito ornament (fig. 5.9) was more recently noticed[2] and takes the form of a rather spindly ⚹ with an extra stroke scratched on the basal underside; the context suggests 'the last third or so of the fourth century' (so Boon).

A flat-bottomed pewter bowl or dish, external rim diameter 22 cm, was found in the bed of the Old Welney River near *Welney*, Cambridge, and reported in 1948 in a catalogue note.[3] On its underside there is a scratched ⚹, the rho loop having been rather uncertainly made. There seems to be an attempt (fig. 5.8) to portray an omega beside it, in a rounded two-curve W form. From within the City of London, now in the Museum of London, there is another simple pewter bowl[4] from Copthall Court, which topographically lies in the central Walbrook 'valley' – see fig. 27, where the spot is marked as 5. On the underside an angular and poorly-constructed ☧ has been scratched (fig. 5.5).

In rather a different category is the Isle of Ely Bowl, a handsome little piece found some time ago at Sutton, Isle of Ely, around which hovers the suspicion that it really belongs to a known hoard of pewterware, the Sutton hoard (location, fig. 10); and that if this could be demonstrated[5] the hoard itself would be placed alongside Appleshaw. The bowl[6] is 10 cm high, with an octagonal rim, each rim-section being incurved; a known late Roman type. The rim flange bears ornament finely incised all around it, including a prominent double-line ☧ flanked by linear A and W (fig. 6.2); other motifs include peacocks (cf. fig. 8.15), Nereids and an owl.

On the underside of the rim of this bowl, scratched carefully in a neat, rather elegant cursive hand, there is a partly legible line of inscription, which was discussed by F.C. Burkitt.[7] He suggested that what can be seen

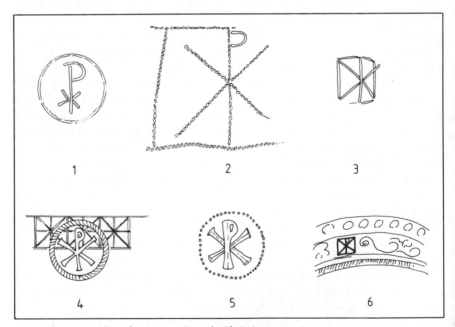

13 Further examples of Romano–British Christian art
  1 Bronze bowl (lost), Wall or *Letocetum*   2 Wiggonholt lead tank   3 Lankhills, base of pottery bowl, grave 250   4 East Stoke lead casket   5 Brentwood gold finger-ring (impression)   6 Corbridge, rim of silver bowl (lost), from Cay's original drawing

could be read as

SIIP..T...EPICL...Q..

and that, cautiously, this might be expanded to read *supectili epi(scopi) clerique*; taking the first word to represent a colloquial or contracted dative *suppelectili*, linked to *supellex* 'household utensil, furnishing, object'. The sense would then be 'For the furnishings of the bishop and clergy'. *Clerus*, as a collective term for 'clergy', is known from Tertullian's writings. If Burkitt's very reasonable version is accepted, this may be our earliest allusion in Roman Britain to the canonical orders.

The only complete pottery vessel was found in 1931 inside the shore-fort at *Richborough*, Kent (*Rutupiae*) during what was recorded as 'surface cleaning, south-west area'.[8] This is a small footed bowl, Oxford colour-coated ware of the late third or fourth centuries; the simple inverted ⚓ graffito (fig. 5.1) was recently noticed by Kevin Greene. The item goes with other evidence for fourth-century Christianity at Richborough.

Among the miscellaneous objects in this category are three caskets or containers in lead, all from the central part of Roman Britain; pottery lamps; and a small number of miscellaneous finds. The lead casket from *Caistor* in Lincolnshire[9] was unearthed in 1863, probably within the western end of the Roman walled town. When complete, it would have been a medium-size square-based casket or coffer, with its four outwardly splayed side-panels each bearing floral and figures ornament and the legend CVNOBARRVS FECIT VIVAS (?'C. made this: may *you* (its owner) have life'). The Caistor casket is generally regarded as fourth-century, which increases the chance that VIVAS implies a Christian sentiment.

In another example, from *Ad Pontem* (East Stoke, Nottinghamshire), only the upper part of one side of a similar casket was ploughed up in 1954.[10] The ornament, fortunately included on this fragment, is moulded in relief. It includes a circular medallion or roundel with ☧ in relief, interrupting an upper band of geometric ornament (fig. 13.4); and below between cables a widely-spaced line of lettering, of which VTEREEELIX can be read, placed between flat female-figure representations. The central E of the three together is a moulding-error for an F – *utere felix*, a sentiment that might be equated roughly with French *Bonne Chance!*, though perhaps allowing *felix* = 'fortunate' in a Christian sense.

The inclusion of the word *felix* links this with a third vessel of lead, a larger and composite octagonal object whose eight sides, about 45 cm wide and 35 cm high, were fitted around the base by double-flanged lead collars. Parts of it were ploughed up in 1946 and 1955 near Bishop Norton, Lincolnshire.[11] Jocelyn Toynbee would prefer to view this[12] as 'just conceivably, a large ornamental casket'. On one of the panels above

a band of floral scrollwork is part of an inscription, moulded, that reads
. . . D O E E C I T E E L I X. The first and third E's are really F's inverted and
reversed, giving the reading . . . *do fecit felix*, '. . . *do*[name] made this.
Fortunate (be its owner)!'

Roman pottery lamps make up a vast and long-lived group of
artefacts; they occur as plain objects, with basic ornament, in phallic,
pagan, grotesque and comic shapes, and (increasingly during the fourth
century and later) with Christian symbols and designs. Commonplace as
handy marketable souvenirs over the whole Mediterranean and North
African region – and just as commonly still being unobtrusively made for
the tourist market! – nearly all the late Roman, Christian-motif pottery
lamps in British museums must be suspect as genuine early finds. Only
two examples will be considered here. One of them[13] found at *Margate*,
Kent, in 1902 bears a plain relief ⨺ in a circle, and could date from around
400; this is a known period of Christian activity at the relatively nearby
Richborough shore-fort. The other, which is perhaps early fifth century,
is listed with some reserve. It was discovered earlier this century,[14] and
appears to represent a genuine find – the lamp itself is lost – made in
cultivating isolated grounds near *Tidworth*, Wiltshire. This lamp bore 'a
cross potent in relief', probably a cross of Latin form with expanded
terminals; almost certainly an import, it could have reached Britain by
c.425.

The remaining items make up a miscellaneous group. There is a (lost)
bronze spoon from *Colchester*, a Victorian find, which had AETERNVS
VIVAS on its bowl.[15] Then there are various forms of seals or sealings; at
the *Chedworth* villa, where there is independent evidence of Christianity
(Chap. 8), a 'metal stamp' (? probably bronze) bearing some form of chi-
rho impression was found before 1869, but has also been lost.[16] The finds
from *Silchester*, the Roman *Calleva*, include a lead seal from the forum
basilica[17] (indicated in fig. 24) one face of which has A to the left of ⨺, the
other a similar ⨺ with Greek capital omega to its right.

In worked bone, a material used instead of metal or wood to make up
open-work ornament and lettering for application to the surface of a
larger object, there are two relevant finds. A stone coffin with grave-
goods and the skeleton of a woman was found in 1901 at Sycamore
Terrace, *York* (fig. 29.1). It also contained a three-line open-work bone
mounting, reading S.ROR AVE/VIVAS/IN DEO ('O Sister, hail! May you have
life in God!').[18] Along with this must be considered a smaller incomplete
plaque from *Richborough*[19] with a name ending in . . S, and the word
VIVAS.

Very much on its own is the 'Wroxeter Letter', a missive stylus-
inscribed on both faces of a thin lead tablet 45 by 90 mm, found in 1880 at
Bath, the Roman *Aquae Sulis*, 'about 15 feet below the former level of the
King's Bath'. The letter is written in cursive and seems to have been from

Vinisius (a man) to Nigra (a married woman), sent by the hand of (?) Apulicus. The Latin is obscure, with contractions, and the hand not very clear. If the late E.W.B. Nicholson's reading and translation were approximately correct – and Celticists will raise their eyebrows at the mention of the author of *Keltic Researches, etc.* (1904) as an epigrapher – the sense is still not wholly clear. The text is full of contractions like *ihcv*, *xti*, *xpm* and *xps* (for instance, line 1.2, read as 'gratia dni IHCV Xti 7 tuis'). The general sense is that Vinisius writes from Viriconium (*Viroconium*, Roman Wroxeter) with moral exhortations and a more specific warning about the arrival – at Bath? – of Bilonicus, described as *canem Arii*; presumably less likely a named domestic dog, than an allusion to a follower of the Eastern heresiarch Arius, *c.*250–336.[20] In terms of actual evidence this must of course be linked to *Wroxeter* rather than to Bath.

We pass on to consider various finds where the Christian nature is either still under discussion, or can only be adduced by analogy. Here, as a start, we could include all those large lead tanks or cisterns of the Icklingham type which, if typologically related to the few mentioned in the previous chapter, do not bear any Christian ornament. Excluding a tank or vat found in 1943 at Low Ireby, in Westmorland,[21] which is probably not within this group at all, we are then left – the references given earlier cover these – with tanks (two) from *Bourton-on-the-Water*, Gloucs., and four from the area around *Cambridge*. These come from Willingham, north of Cambridge; Burwell, to the north-east; from the river Ouse near Huntingdon; and lastly one with only the provenance of 'from near Cambridge'.

The inscribed stone fragment with ⚹ from Maryport, regarded as sepulchral or funerary, was mentioned in the last chapter. At various times, other late Romano–British tombstones have been considered as possibly those of Christians. One of them (RIB 137) can be dismissed. It came from an extra-mural cemetery at *Abonae*, now Sea Mills near Bristol, and shows a bust of a girl(?) flanked by a dog and cockerel, above the legend SPES G(AI) SENTI. In the apex is a small design, in 1874 portrayed as chi-rho, albeit a six-ray unlooped one (in which it could have resembled the Lankhills motif, fig. 13). But this, *fide* R.P. Wright (RIB), must be ruled out. There is no loop, not even an uppermost sixth stroke.

The other three all come from the North (Brougham, Carlisle and York) and the Christian aspect, which in each case is just supportable, resides in details of the inscriptions. The stone from *Brocavum* or the modern Brougham, RIB 787, was centuries ago trimmed and built into a passage-ceiling in the medieval castle there. It commemorates (through trimming, the stone is defective) TITTUS M . . ., whose name is followed by the phrase, expanded, VIXIT ANNIS PLVS MINVS XXXII, 'he lived *more or less* for 32 years'. Though one must agree with Toynbee[22] that the argument is 'not quite conclusive', this publicly-advertised indifference to earthly age may hint at a Christian view of life eternal. The *Carlisle* stone (RIB 955) was found in 1892 in the extra-mural Gallows Hill or London Road cemetery.[23] It commemorates Flavius Antigonus Papias who, as his cognomen implies and as the legend states (*civis Grecus*) was a Greek citizen. He also VIXIT ANNOS PLVS MINVS LX and precisely the same comments apply as were made in connection with the Brougham stone.[24]

The stone coffin from *York* (RIB 690) bears a moving epitaph for a ten-months-old child, Simplicia Florentia, daughter of Felicius Simplex of Legio VI Victrix. It describes her as *anime innocentissimae*, words that taken with the known late Roman Christian regard for the nomina Simplicia, Simplicius (hers presumably formed from her father's cognomen),[25] and the fact that this was a gypsum burial, certainly warrants inclusion as potentially Christian.

Late Roman inhumation burials in wooden or stone coffins, where the bodies were contained and set within a poured plaster filling made of gypsum or prepared lime, have been briefly mentioned. A very full discussion which covers the European background has recently appeared;[26] taken with an earlier catalogue of recorded *plaster burials*, as they can be called, in Roman Britain,[27] it renders further exposition here unnecessary. The aim was probably to preserve the interred body in an associated form, the reason being belief in the Resurrection as imminent and in some sense a physical process. The obvious inference is that such a practice would particularly appeal to Christians.

The incidence of plaster burials is indicated on some of the detailed maps (e.g., figs. 27, 29; London and York). Ramm's 1971 list must now be supplemented by the Poundbury burials[28] but has otherwise been used to provide locations for symbols on the map (fig. 15). There is no exclusively plaster-burial cemetery in Roman Britain (or as far as we know anywhere) and the most that can be claimed is that it is indeed reasonably probable that some of these are Christian burials. The probability is heightened if other and independent evidence of Roman Christianity is known from the same localities.

MATERIAL WITH A VALUE OF '1'

Our third class of evidence, with the lowest weighting, goes with the implication that though most of the objects within it seem outwardly to be Christian (by direct statement or ornament, or because of some sound analogy) they are nearly all portable, in most cases also intrinsically valuable. Their value as locational indicators of Christianity is low because they could so readily have been lost or stolen or (if worn on the person) have travelled with their possessors.

The finger-rings, many of which are overtly Christian, make up a complex group and will be considered last. Other individual objects include a small silver hooked-handled spoon from *Sunderland*, Durham, its bowl inscribed (BE)NE VIVAS;[29] a small bronze medallion possibly worn as a pendant, showing a cloaked figure (Magnentius?) with a chi-rho, from *Richborough*;[30] and least persuasive, two pewter spoons now in the Museum of London. One from the Bucklersbury House site, near the London Mithraeum, bears an ornamentation of three fishes; the other, from nearby Princes Street, a chalice-shaped object below a bird (?parrot).[31]

What can be called the 'Rivenhall strap-tag' group, after a small find from *Rivenhall*, Essex,[32] has now been examined by Sonia Chadwick Hawkes, in the context of her discussion of the latest addition, a handsome buckle from Cave's Inn (*Tripontium*), Warwicks.[33] These are all small Late Roman functional bronzes and as such they also belong to a much larger class, discussion of which would involve the accoutrements of assorted soldiery in fourth- and early fifth-century Britain – Romano–British versions of a militia, Germanic federates, and assorted units from north-west Europe. The common factor is the style of ornament, one including motifs already discussed as having Christian meaning – the peacock, Tree of Life, fish, etc.

The Rivenhall bronze, like others from the Roman villa site at *Beadlam*, Yorkshire,[34] and (most recently) from *Orton Longueville* (fig. 12) just east of *Durobrivae* or Water Newton,[35] is a small flat-shaped object, either a strap-tag or a nail-cleaner. All three should be late in the fourth century. That from Rivenhall has a design showing a peacock facing a gryphon-like creature, and between them a Tree of Life in a cross-hatched container (fig. 13.1). On the Orton Longueville piece there is a single, dot-outline peacock (fig. 13.16); and the Beadlam one, a naturalistic fish (fig. 13.11). The Tripontium buckle has two peacocks facing another version of the Tree of Life (fig. 13.2; 13.14) and like a rather similar one from *Stanwick*, Yorkshire, it is an example of Mrs Hawkes' Type IB buckles of British origin and later fourth-century date.[36] The chances that the motifs used are deployed in a Christian sense seem reasonable and are discussed at length by Mrs Hawkes.

Decorated glass pieces, most if not all of which when found in late Romano–British settings are Continental imports (from such centres of glass-working as the Rhineland), are seldom found in complete form because of their fragility. There are two types with an ornamental range that includes Christian scenes and sentiments. The so-called 'Wint Hill' shallow bowls,[37] named after one found at Wint Hill, Somerset, have scenes of hunting, mythological topics, or Biblical episodes, and they can also bear legends in mixed Latin and Greek. The Wint Hill bowl itself[38] has a hunting-scene surrounded with VIVAS CUM TUIS ('May you and yours

have Life') and the Graeco–Latin PIE Z (see below). None of the handsome
and purely Biblical-scene forms of these Cologne-made bowls has yet been
found in Roman Britain, however.

The other group, sometimes called from their ornament the 'Fish and
Motto' or 'Fish and Palm-branch' cups, apparently third-century
imports from north-west Europe, show engraved horizontal fishes
separated by slender palm-fronds, with short inscriptions. These cups are
distinctive enough to be recognised from appropriate fragments. The
British distribution[39] includes *Caerleon, Chesters, Colchester, Corbridge*
and *Silchester*, and probably *Springhead* (Kent) and *Verulamium*. The
engraved ornament was not necessarily added at the place of manufacture; it is possible that, given the motifs, such glasses had a special
attraction for Christians.

In the same general area of possible Christian significance only, we can
include, with the low weighting, four sites which may be churches of the
Late Roman period (see further in Chap. 7); at *Colchester*, the Denmark
Street and St Johns Abbey grounds sites, *Lincoln* (Flaxengate), and the
intra-mural site at *Verulamium*. With them can be put the possibility of a
baptismal site at *Chedworth*.

The finger-rings which concern us are in gold, silver, and other materials,
of many kinds, and within the range of Roman personal jewellery. Any
distinctively Christian character occurs as ornament, or an inscription,
or both. All are considered, as locational evidence, to have the same low
value, though some which were found in localities otherwise mentioned
(for example, at Richborough) may stand out a little from the rest.

The most helpful recent discussion of many of these rings in their
Romano–British Christian context is by John Wall.[40] One looks firstly
for inscriptions of the type VIVAS IN DEO; secondly, for appropriate
symbols or motifs known to be Christian, and thirdly for any examples
which might be regarded as Christian by analogy.

Gold 'open-work' rings, probably Alexandrian in origin and of the
later fourth century, include two from *Corbridge*. These elaborate rings,
which are inscribed, have the lettering reserved, with the background to
each individual letter in its tiny panel punched out; they have been fully
discussed[41] and Wall has given reasons to suppose that on balance the
entire series is Christian.[42] Of the Corbridge rings, one shows the legend
AEMILIA ZESES, where this second word (as on the Wint Hill glass bowl,
above) is a latinisation for Greek *zēseias*, equivalent to the Latin *vivas*.
The other has (in Greek) *Polemiou philtron* ('The love-token of
Polemios') and may be a betrothal ring. An alleged third such find, from
Stonham Aspel in Suffolk, must be treated with great reserve.

Of other gold rings, there is one, an old find, from English Street,
Carlisle.[43] This had a flat bezel engraved with a palm-brach and AMA ME,

'Love Me', the palm rather than the sentiment suggesting Christianity. Another similar ring with two confronted heads in intaglio on the bezel was found in 1829 in the shore-fort at *Brancaster*, Norfolk (*Brano-dunum*).[44] The legend, above and below the design, VIVAS/IN DEO, would on impression be reversed; Toynbee wonders if this inscription was added on presentation to a Christian. A third gold ring was found in 1948 at *Brentwood*, Essex; it has a circular bezel[45] bearing an expanded terminal ☧ within a circle of punched dots (fig. 13.5).

The short formulae found on these, and other, rings are of some interest, not least in reminding us of the strong Greek element in primitive Christianity – we must not forget that it was in *Greek* that the Christian message was brought, from its cradle in Palestine, to the western Gentiles, making its first converts among the Greek-speaking residents of the great Mediterranean cities.[46] The growing number of converts who had no Greek, only Latin – what Palmer calls 'the simple folk of the back streets' – were presented with Greek words for notions, things, even sentiments that, in addition being largely foreign to the pagan world, had no Latin equivalents. *Angelus, baptizo, clerus* and *diaconus* are simply transliterations. A phrase like *pie zeses* survives from this same early background.

The *Vivas in Deo* formula, unequivocally Christian, is also found on the most famous ring – the so-called 'Vyne Ring' – found at or near *Silchester* in 1786.[47] The secondary engraving on its hoop reads SENICIANE VIVAS IIN DE, the blundered double 'I' leaving no room for the final -O. This has been plausibly linked to a lead *defixio* or tablet recording a votary's curse found at Lydney,[48] RIB 306, in which one Silvianus claims to have lost a ring, and adds the prayer to Nodens that 'among those who are called Senicianus, do not allow health until he brings it to the temple of Nodens'. Strange coincidence; perhaps a genuine link.

Of rings in silver, there are two found at the Roman villa site[49] of *Fifehead Neville*, Dorset, their bezels engraved respectively with the Constantinian ☧, and with the later form ☧ below a dove and two fronds of vegetation (*cf*. fig. 8.6). Two other late Roman silver ring bezels from *Silchester* again[50] might just be regarded as Christian on the strength of the reported inscriptions, VIVAS, and IVL BELLATOR VIVAS. There is a report of two more silver rings discovered early in the last century during the exposure of the villa at *Thruxton*, Hampshire,[51] said in 1823 still to be in the agricultural tenant's possession, one ring being 'inscribed with the chi-rho'.

The gold ring from the Canterbury hoard[52] has despite its context no intrinsic Christian character. Among the rings from *Richborough* is a bronze one, now lost, but known from a drawing.[53] The bezel displayed a rather muddled device (fig. 7.3), another instance of the confusion of A and W seen entirely as *symbols* in the later fourth century; the eight-panelled hoop read IV ST IN EV IVA SI ND EO (*Iustine, vivas in Deo*). Unlike the Brancaster and Vyne rings, where the inscriptions are secondary additions, this is a case of a ring wholly and originally Christian.

The dove is also known from a bronze ring (unpublished) from the *Moor Park* villa site, Hertfordshire;[54] the engraved bezel shows doves flanking a palm-branch. From the north of Roman Britain, 'a curious ring bearing the Christian monogram' was found in the river-bed below the Roman fort at *Brough-under-Stainmore*;[55] this is lost. Finally, John Wall has drawn attention[56] to a ring of jet, in the site-museum at *Cilurnum*, on Hadrian's Wall (*Chesters*), very probably found there or nearby. The bezel has a curious motif which, despite its form, one would agree is intended to be a chi-rho; and the simple but moving legend QVIS SEPA(.) MEVM ET TVVM DVRANTE VITA. *Pace* Wall's version, this is better read as 'Who shall separate my (heart) and thine, while Life endures ?'. In this intensely human trifle, seen across the mute centuries, personal and Christian devotion are combined.

It would be a rash person who would choose to put forward the foregoing catalogue as complete. Enormous quantities of small finds from the larger excavated sites of Roman Britain either still await, or have only begun to be fed into, the slow complex machinery of cleaning, conservation, re-examination and selective publication. In his corpus of engraved gemstones, Martin Henig discusses examples whose possible significances hover between Christianity and, often, Gnosticism. It is inconceivable that there are not many more graffiti to be noticed. The writer has been assured (for instance) by a site-assistant who handled it that another chi-rho graffito sherd turned up in the York (Church Street sewer) excavations; in due course this will presumably surface. An alarming proportion of the smaller or more valuable finds reported above, it will have been noticed, has either been permanently mislaid or has gone the way of the Witham Bowl and the Sark Hoard; though the odd object may survive, externally unrecognised, in private hands. All that can be safely claimed is that, the factors of chance being just about equally-distributed if we take excavated Romano–British material and its fate as a whole, the distributions that represent what has been listed (corrected to early 1980) ought neither to be distorted, or avoidably misleading. One can only work from what is known.

If we look at the problems in another light, all that has been so far discussed could be described as *material* and *positive* evidence – the information derived, often inferentially, from things which can be or have been seen and handled, and which exist or existed. But there are two other forms of evidence to be considered, separately, though not at any great length; the *literary* and the *negative* evidence for Christianity in Roman Britain.

These are plotted together in fig. 14, whose emphasis is designedly a geographical one. If Roman Britain is poorly provided with named, located martyrs, we can at least pinpoint *Verulamium* in connection with St Albanus (Chap. 2); and though the link is less positive, the connection of Aaron and Julius with *Caerleon* is probably real, and may have given rise to an independent local tradition which preserved their names in this setting.

To this can be added, foreshadowing a discussion of the limited evidence for bishops and their supposed dioceses in Roman Britain (p. 197), the few place-names that are extractable, for AD 314. These are recognisable as *civitas Eboracensis* (York), *civitas Londiniensis* (London), and with the most obvious emendation *civitas colonia Lindensium* (Lincoln). Argument allows us to add provisionally a fourth place; *Corinium* (Cirencester).

If one is allotting evidential values again, places of martyrdoms and fourth-century bishops must be allowed a weight of '2'; no more. This will simplify discussion of the value to be attached to the *negative* evidence, where a general and lower weighting of '1' can be applied.

The negative side of our enquiry consists of the assumptions that observed traces of fourth-century destruction of non-Christian temples and shrines suggest this was undertaken by Christians; or was inspired by the active presence and popular support of Christianity; or even took place under some provincial or central directive, at particular times when these actions were thought socially and spiritually justifiable. This is by no means the same as the situation supposed to have taken place in the seventh century – imperfectly assessed and not very widely explored (or explorable) – after Pope Gregory's letter of 601/2 to Mellitus[57] recommending the conversion to Christian ends, and not the destruction, of pagan places of worship. It is of course just possible that destruction in the fourth century of certain heathen temples was followed by the on-site construction of Christian churches; this has been most tentatively hypothesised for Water Newton and it may eventually prove to be the case at West Hill, Uley,[58] but it remains an area of great uncertainty.

The usually quoted cases of such destruction by Christians concern the temples of the exclusivist cult of Mithras, the *Mithraea*. The many superficial resemblances between Mithraism and Christianity – male hero-god, a Trinitarian aspect, the dualistic opposition of good and evil or light and darkness, the grading of initiates and officials and the employment of symbols that included birds and animals – have been seen as particular reasons for this cult having been an authorised target for

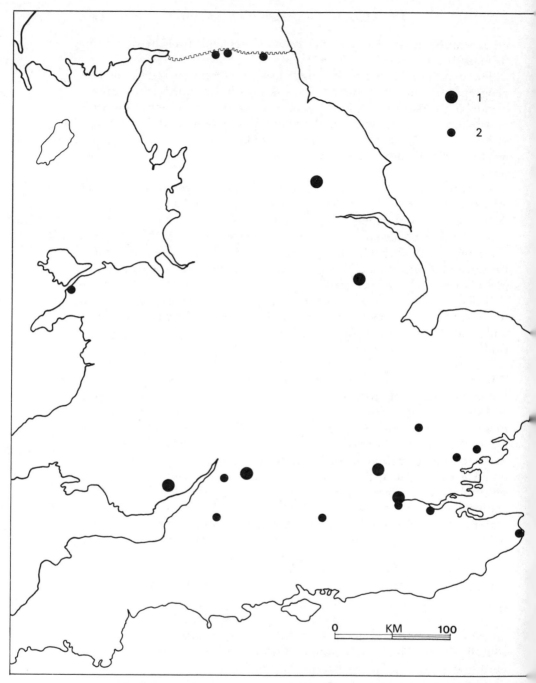

14 Distribution map, literary and 'negative' evidence of Christianity in late Roman Britain

1 Bishoprics, assumed from 314 list, and martyrdoms   2 Destructions, assumed by Christians, of Mithraea and other 4th-cent. pagan temples

Christian indignation. If the appeal of Mithraism leant in the directions of what we would now describe as Army officers, senior civil servants and successful businessmen, that of Christianity lay of course in its general accessibility and its attraction of a very different and wider social class.

These explanations have been brought forward following the discoveries of what do seem to be deliberately-destroyed Mithraea. Boon saw[59] the ruining of the one at *Segontium*, Caernarvon, in this light; the post-Roman history of north-west Wales, which makes it markedly likely that this was a district where Christianity was continuous from Late Roman times, lends some support to the idea. On the other hand, given the much more cosmopolitan nature of fourth-century London, Grimes' account[60] of what happened to the Walbrook Mithraeum is bound to involve us in more elaborate ideas. Here, the sculptures of Mithras, Minerva and Mercury are of a quality appropriate to the capital of a civil diocese; the temple itself, a long aisled rectangle with a shallow western apse, was not stinted in design or construction. The associated minor finds, like the famous silver casket from some Eastern source,[61] point to a rich and probably influential body of adherents.

If the dismantling of this temple, when the major cult marbles were buried below the floor of the nave, was really an event that stemmed from Christian opposition,[62] it could be argued that nothing of lesser moment than Constantine's publicly-announced conversion and from 313 the Imperial elevation of Christianity to a new status could explain this particular Mithraic loss. An unsolved puzzle is the subsequent history of the site itself. The building was re-floored and was used again during the fourth century, before 337 having a stone altar-base added to the centre of the apsidal chord. There is not much guidance in choosing between two courses that have been suggested; either that the Mithraeum became one of the (otherwise so signally unidentified) Christian churches of later fourth-century *Londinium*, or as Merrifield argues in an important re-assessment[63] that it was used by some other non-Christian cult, being consolidated in this rôle during Julian's short-lived apostatic reign (361–3).

The other Mithraea lay on the northern frontier, at Carrawburgh (*Brocolitia*), Housesteads (*Vercovicium*) and Rudchester (*Vindobala*).[64] The late Sir Ian Richmond, who provided in five pages a most elegant and pointed short account of Mithraism itself,[65] showed with John Gillam that the small and constantly-rebuilt Carrawburgh shrine, which stood on most insecure underlying ground, was eventually subjected to 'vindictively selective destruction', probably early in Constantine's reign. This destruction, which was concentrated solely that imagery which made Mithras himself manifest, and which it is suggested was ordered by a Christian commandant of the garrison, is firmly imputed to 'the wrath of the Church militant'.

At the Housesteads Mithraeum, excavated first in 1834, there is the same tale of smashing and wrecking, focussed upon the principal Mithraic sculptures, with signs that the temple itself may have been set on fire. At Rudchester, where the surviving remnants were examined in 1953,[66] the (rebuilt) Mithraeum was desecrated in the same fashion, with action concentrated upon the diagnostic images. These three sites raise the suggestion that a single wave of Christian enthusiasm, early in the fourth century, was responsible.

Alongside this must be considered the widely scattered hints of the purposeful spoliation of other temples, and shrines of general paganism. This is not easy to summarise; we must confine ourselves to consideration of those few sites sufficiently fully excavated to allow us to see any detail. There is also the complication that during the fourth century, if some temples were being destroyed, others were probably being reconstructed or even built anew.

Michael Lewis[67] picked out some possible examples. Subsequent researches might allow us to add to his list. *Uley* in Gloucestershire and – at the moment, apparently worth mentioning – *Witham* in Essex (p. 219) will be joined to *Colchester 2* (using Lewis's enumerations), *Great Chesterford*, *Silchester 3* and *Springhead 1*. There is also Bath, whose latest excavator[68] agrees that the fourth-century inscription, RIB 152, on an altar dedicated by the centurion C. Severius Emeritus probably alludes to sectarian temple-wrecking by local Christians after 313. It refers pointedly to *locum religiosum per insolentiam erutum ... et ... repurgatum*, 'a holy place, wrecked by insolent hands and cleansed afresh'. Since he dedicates the altar to the Imperial *numen*, the perpetrators of the *insolentia* may well have been upstart local Christians. The evidence from *Icklingham* (p. 175) points to the likelihood that some shrine was destroyed before the supposed church was built; and finally one is inclined on balance to suspect (with Frend) that the later fourth-century end of the *Richborough* temples forms another instance.[69] The distribution-map (fig. 14) brings together the locations of the literary clues and of all these cases of the destruction, presumably by local Christians, of pagan sites.

So much, then, for the various kinds of evidence for the existence of Christianity in Roman Britain. Is it yet possible to draw any further conclusions from presenting them locationally? Fig. 14 presents the literary and negative evidence, its temporal dimension being (if we suppose the martyrdoms to have occurred in the mid-third century) between a century and a century-and-a-half in extent. Fig. 15 is a display of all the positive, material evidence, the size of the symbols corresponding to the three categories of weighting earlier discussed; and again this probably covers some 150 years, centred on the period approximately AD

275 to AD425 (as was made clear, it omits the odd earlier trifles like the *Arepo* word-squares).

This larger map is more complicated than, say, Miranda Green's, not only because the evidence itself has been graded, but because there is more of it. To a limited extent it is also a map of Late Roman Britain, indicating the occurrence of a given activity in the setting of the principal urban settlements linked by major roads; but it is also significant in that it shows clusters of finds, for example at Dorchester, Silchester, London, Canterbury, Richborough, Verulamium, and in the further north, York, Catterick and Corbridge. These are important. Individually, any object for which a Christian meaning is claimed, firmly or tentatively, and which occurs at such a place, takes on slightly higher shades of probability simply because of the independent evidence for Christianity at the same location.

Fig. 16 is a less conventional form of map. It contains, factually, no more than the previous two drawings (figs. 14, 15), on which it is founded, but the presentation is designed to aid the eye. The geographical base, most of England and Wales in Roman times, has been first gridded into 50 × 50km squares by quartering the (United Kingdom) National Grid 100-km² squares. Within each 50 km square, values of the dots on fig. 14 (values of 2 or 1), and those on fig. 15 (values of 3, 2 and 1), were totalled; divisions of the range of such totals, which run from 0 to 24, were selected by plotting totals against occurrences and noting the numerical peaks; and the four divisions are then represented by hatchings of increasing intensity, the filled squares being rounded off to increase the general resemblance to contours.

Some of the gaps in fig. 16, areas of nil evidence, may be explicable if they correspond to late Roman zones of sparse settlement; the Northumbrian coast, the Wash, part of East Anglia, and the Wealden forest. Others (the top of the Cotswold ? part of the old Midlands forest ? the Peak ?) are not so easily interpreted; certain areas may, for instance, produce no signs of Christianity because they remained strongholds of paganism, or even because they have been archaeologically neglected.

What must be underlined is that, on the strength of what has been discussed in the last two chapters and after looking at the maps, it is quite unsafe to claim that Christianity in fourth-century Britain was either predominantly urban, or predominantly rural, in its emphasis. There have been in recent years far too many generalisations and sweeping statements, unsupported by proper analysis, on this score, in particular by the proponents of an 'urban centres and large villas only' model of Christianity. If on fig. 15 one were to strike out all those dots that represent finds in major towns (London, the civitas capitals, the coloniae, etc.), sufficient would be left to make up an impressive scatter concerned with a small-town, vicus and rural settlement presence. On the other

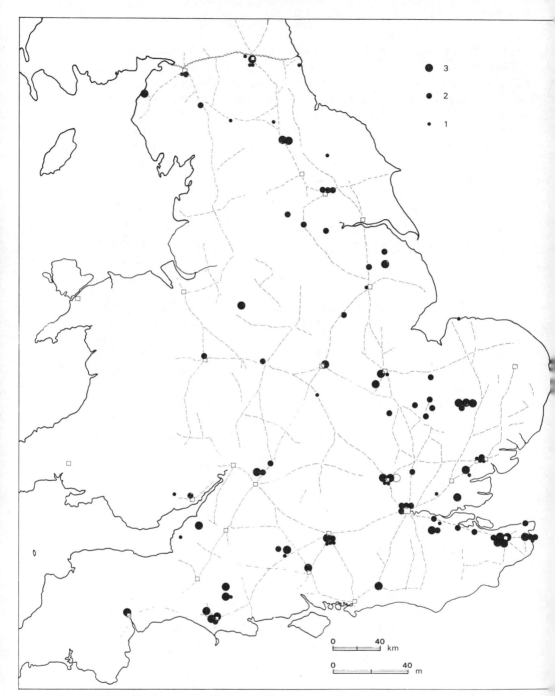

15 Distribution map, evidences of Christianity in late Roman Britain: 3, 2, 1, evidential weightings (explained in text)

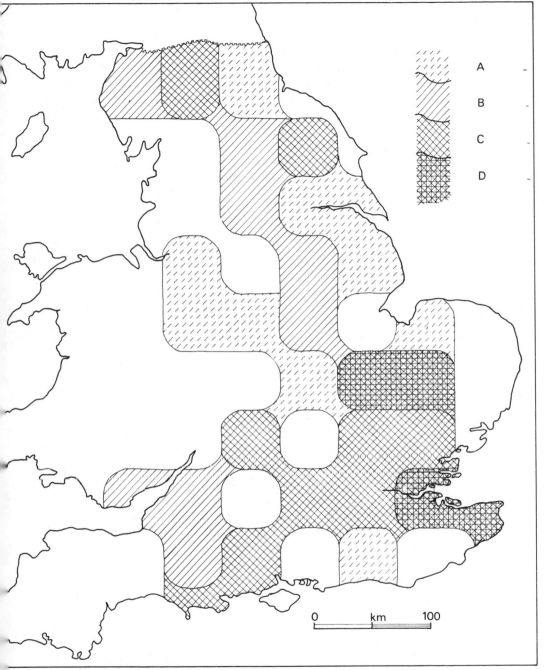

16 Contoured density map, all evidence for Christianity in late Roman Britain (based on figs. 14, 15). Totalled evidential weightings by 50 km squares; totals   A 1–3   B 4–7   C 9–12   D 13–24

hand, it would be ridiculous to deny that in Britain, as elsewhere in the Roman empire, innovations were primarily *urban* and the innovation of Christian worship in organised bands, using appropriate buildings, was certainly an urban one in Roman Britain. Here, again, our current knowledge to some extent reflects the uneven quality of archaeological attention; but it is worth putting forward another map (fig. 17) in which thirty of the most important urban centres are shown. The evidential values of the Christian finds have been totalled for each, and differentially indicated; and two-thirds of these towns or cities show some sign of Late Roman Christianity. There is little point in dissecting each case and suggesting practical reasons, but the ten with nil returns include places whose Roman archaeology is among the lesser-known aspects of their histories.

If we look at figs. 15 and 16, the heaviest concentration is, perhaps predictably, in the south-eastern third of Roman Britain: a region that underwent prolonged and effective Romanisation, that contained the administrative capital, and that because of its proximity to Gaul was the first to share in most forms of imports, ideas among them. Yet here the distribution is not uniform. If fifth- and sixth-century studies now tend to emphasise the strength of sub-Roman life, perhaps of sub-Roman Christianity, in (say) northern Kent, from London through Rochester and Canterbury to Richborough, the strong concentration in East Anglia is unexpected, and this does not entirely arise from the two main sites of Icklingham and Durobrivae; there is a rural scatter.

From this south-eastern focus, there seems to run two great arms, like the arms of a reversed capital L. One goes west to the villa-estates of Dorset, shading off northwards to Gloucester, Cirencester and south-east Wales. Its ending stresses the now-patent observation that, with the minor exception of Exeter (the only town of any size or status west of what later became Wessex), the whole of the great south-western peninsula was probably quite un-Christian in late Roman times. Indeed, when signs of Christianity do appear (and marginally; for example, on the north coast of west Cornwall, on the island of Lundy, and among Irish settlers in east Cornwall and west Devon) we are well into the fifth century, and the Faith may have been introduced from more than one direction. On the other hand, the Severn Basin and south-east Wales figure very well (Chap. 10) as areas that can claim to have perpetuated Christianity from Roman times.

The northern 'arm' follows the line of the major road-systems which prefer the eastern flank of the north-south spine of Britain. Again, with the very minor exception of north-west Wales, a district whose Christian importance is again a fifth-century phenomenon, most of Wales is blank, as is the Lancashire coastal plain. The stress is rather on the route past Lincoln to York, Catterick and Corbridge and, west of the Vale of York,

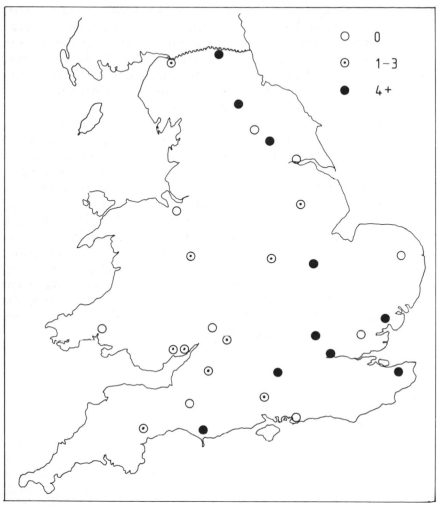

17 Evidence of late Roman Christianity in major towns and cities (1980). Total evidential weightings (as indicated) are taken from fig. 16

on that higher but often still fertile region that became the surely Christian principality we know as Elmet. In the hinterland of Hadrian's Wall, the uneven extent of our evidence is slightly weighted towards the western end, possibly relevant to the story of fifth-century Christianity in south-west Scotland (Chap. 11).

It will, the writer hopes, later prove instructive to match fig. 16 with other and similarly-constructed 'contoured density' maps, as we come to consider the sub-Roman fifth century. At this stage, one can round off this discussion with a single pointer. Transfer in the mind's eye the bold line shown elsewhere (e.g., in figs. 47 and 49) to figs. 15 and 16: the line which marks the approximate limit of English settlement attained early in the sixth century. All the land to the east of that line, occupied by pagan incomers, could be sponged clean of any traces of Roman Christianity, or (to go back) colloquial Vulgar Latin. What then lies *west* of the same line – in the whole Severn basin, in the west Midlands, north-central Britain and the north-west – makes up still a substantial tract of post-400 Britannia, even post-450 Britain. It is a tract containing at least some evidence of areas that could have been won over to Christianity, alongside paganism and total indifference, before AD 400; and by *c.*500 the same tract contained in part or in whole various native states and kingdoms that, in all the sources we possess, are presented to us as being officially, nominally, and perhaps historically Christian ones. Many of these areas, outside the direct of indirect control, after 500, of the Germanic-speaking settlers and their own nascent kingdoms, are also those in which a fresh generation of students – onomasticists, archaeologists, settlement-historians and specialists in the combined disciplines now involved in protohistory – continue to demonstrate, in secular and material aspects, a remarkable and most persuasively presented element of continuity from earlier centuries. Are we to suppose that, during the intervening fifth century, the progress and fate of late Roman British Christianity was so markedly different?

CHAPTER SIX

Churches in Late Roman Britain—the Background

A church is essentially a place for *doing*, for corporate *action*
in which all are participants and each has his appropriate
function to perform; it is not a sort of jewelled cave in which
the solitary individual may find some kind of worship
experience, and where his emotions may be kindled by the
contemplation of a remote spectacle.
Peter Hammond *Towards a Church Architecture* (1962)

No direct, contemporary reference to any late Roman church in Britain is known; either from history or from surviving inscriptions. This does not make a search for any such churches pointless, but it requires a most careful analysis of post-Roman written sources, and an investigation of linguistic and place-name elements, as well as a conventional archaeological summary.[1] Recourse to analogies taken from other and better-documented regions of the late Roman empire must also be made, as long as it is made clear that these are only analogies and only permit cautious inferences. Though this may not at this stage seem quite so relevant a comment, it has to be pointed out that, increasingly, the whole tenor of what we find out about Christianity in Roman Britain seems to imply that in this regard, as in others, Britannia could go its own peculiar way.

In the absence of documented evidence for the nature and physical character of any such late Roman churches, we are obliged to turn to sources that date between the fifth and eighth centuries, and to see if anything bearing upon problems of the fourth can be extracted.

BUILDING TRADITIONS

There are traces of later indigenous beliefs about Romano–British building and constructional methods, covering both secular and religious buildings – beliefs which after about 700 were largely common to Anglo-Saxons and Britons alike. Some of the sources involved have already been touched on, for other purposes, earlier in this book; but we can return to them for the present topic. Gildas, who was publishing his work in 545 × 549,[2] and who must have seen something of what was left of

Roman Britain, knew that some towns had boasted proper masonry houses with sturdily-built roofs.[3] He thought that after the Diocletianic persecutions – by which (Chap. 2) he may really have implied the Decian ones – the British Christians *renovant ecclesias* 'rebuilt churches' that had been razed to the ground; also that after the persecutions they laid out, built, and completed 'basilicas' for the martyrs of that time.[4] During the fifth century, as one result of fighting that broke out after the mid-century as the Saxon settlements impinged upon their hosts, there had been a widespread destruction of towns, high walls, towers and holy altars;[5] events that were centred on an actual region just possibly identifiable through Gildas' unspecific rhetoric, though whether this was the southern half of the old *Britannia Prima*[6] or from east to west across what is now the North of England[7] is a matter to be taken up later (Chap. 10). This destruction proved to be irremediable. We are told that the towns, wherever they really were, *desertae dirutaeque hactenus squalent* 'deserted and ruinous, lie filthy and neglected up to this very day'.[8] That churches of some kind or other, *ecclesiae domus*,[9] were visible in Gildas' time is entirely apparent from what he says, but he gives us no further descriptions.

When nearly two centuries later Bede set out to reproduce something of this view of Roman and sub-Roman Britain, he may have had rather more to draw upon. His use of Gildas apart, there was the library at Jarrow-Monkwearmouth,[10] and such individual works as Constantius' Life of Germanus, and the version of the *Passio Albani* (Chap. 2) that he used. But Bede's comment on, or extracts from, these and other writings have no *independent* value as to the nature and existence of Romano–British church buildings. On the other hand, when he describes the conversion of the Northumbrians, or events in Kent where his sources are known,[11] we can prefer him as a partial authority.

Bede saw no conflict with accepted fact, or with any observations that appropriate readers of his *Historia* might themselves make at first-hand, in saying that after 313 an *ecclesia . . . mirandi operis*[12] – a church of wonderful workmanship (and these seem to be his own words) – was built to mark Alban's martyrdom; or in linking this with whatever Constantius claimed that Germanus and Lupus had visited in 429; or in adding that up to the time of writing sick persons were still experiencing cures *in quo videlicet loco* 'in this very same place'. This martyrial church was, after all, a fully *Roman* phenomenon. Again, and we shall come back to dissect the details, Bede's story of the Kentish mission introduces rapidly a church outside Canterbury *facta dum adhuc Romani Brittaniam incolerent* 'built while the Romans were still inhabiting Britain'.[13] So sound, indeed, was this church that little or no restoration was required. Other Roman-style churches successively appear in the narrative. Augustine and his party receive permission to build or to *restore* (*vel restaurandi*)[14] churches in and around the same city. Within Canterbury itself, or so Bede was told by those who believed that Augustine was so informed at the time, stood yet another church *antiquo Romanorum fidelium opere factam fuisse*, 'built in olden days by the work of Roman believers'. It may not have stood alone; later (619 × 624) a fire in Canterbury caused much damage, but failed to destroy a, presumably similar masonry, church of the Four Crowned Martyrs.

The recital of this conventional, European-style Romano–British building tradition is then, as every student of Bede knows, extended northwards. After Edwin of Deira's conversion (*c.*627), 'a greater and more magnificent basilican church of stone . . . square in plan' was built at York, perhaps somewhere south of the Minster;[15] and not long afterwards Paulinus, moving to Lincoln, there made another stone church 'of outstanding workmanship',[16] conceivably represented by the recently-uncovered phase I of St Paul-in-the-Bail.[17]

Bede's emphasis (which can hardly have been totally unconscious, given the drift of the *Historia*) on this string of purely Roman churches, seen as some index of the continuity from that pure fount of doctrine springing from the Eternal City, a doctrine notably revived through Gregory and Augustine, only partly overshadows his rapportage in his capacity as a true historian of an entirely different architectural world. In this, churches were far less permanent, august, egregious, wonderful, or Roman-inspired. They were hammered together in the old secular tradition of wood (and/or wattle); they were constantly being burnt down, or collapsing, or needing large-scale renewal. From Constantius, Bede borrowed[18] the tale of the 'Alleluia victory', where the British army, exhorted by the visiting bishops, ran up some sort of field-church *frondibus contexta* 'woven from leafy boughs' in which to celebrate Easter before the battle. Even among his own Northumbrian ancestors, as Bede well knew, only very slightly more substantial affairs had been the norm up to a half-century before his birth. Edwin as a catechumen under Paulinus in the winter of 626–7 had built a small church *de ligno . . . opere citato* 'of wood and of hasty workmanship'.[19] Other churches on the various royal estates, where such hasty workmanship need not have been imperative at all, were not much grander. That at *Campodonum* was burnt down in a heathen raid, only its (stone) altar surviving.[20] At another place, not named[21] but possibly *Maelmin*, Millfield, where Aidan died in 651, the whole *vicus*, with the bishop's lodging and the church, was shortly to be burnt by the Mercians. Nor need we now rely entirely upon Bede's words; from *Ad Gefrin*, Yeavering, thanks to Brian Hope-Taylor, we can not only see what the church rather vaguely described by Bede looked like, but see it in a wider context of Northumbrian timber building-style.[22]

Bede was of course aware that the native British (whom his writings fully distinguished from the Romans proper) were, when left to their own devices, no more technologically advanced than his own English forbears. In this respect, Britons and Anglo-Saxons were at one with the contemporary Irish (*Scotti*). *Their* first impact upon the mainland constructional scene, Iona apart, was Finan's episcopal church at Lindisfarne[23] – this is around 651 – put up 'after the Irish manner, not of stone, but of 'hewn oak' (*robore secto*) '. . . thatched with reed'. This was a relevant point; these non-Roman ways served to emphasise what had taken place, rather closer to 400 in his eyes, at Whithorn in south-west Scotland, *Ad Candidam Casam*.[24] The really remarkable fact about the church here, built by or in the time of the British bishop *Nynia* ('Ninian'), was that it had been built in *stone*; remarkable because this was *insolito Brettonibus more*, 'in a manner to which the British were unaccustomed'.

One need not cite from other and later writers the instances of churches said to have been built in wood, or from planks or boughs. Zimmerman has usefully catalogued[25] most of the hagiographical references in early Western European literature. If we take Bede's death (25 May 735)[26] as the cut-off point, then in the period before this and back to the fifth century what all these varied references tell us is that, in the British Isles, persons who thought at all about churches in the near and distant past were aware of a dual tradition. There had been, in various places, substantial masonry churches of Roman character built in the last century or so of Roman Britain. A very few (in the south-east) may have survived the technological and in this case architectural run-down of the fifth century; but the expertise required to repair them, or to make fresh examples in the same general mould, did not return to England until shortly before 600. Nevertheless, alongside these, there had been churches in Britain – just as there were bishops and clergy – during the fifth and sixth centuries, and by the seventh century in regions that never knew the former imprint of Rome. During the fifth century, Patrick alone could be credited with churches in Ireland. All these non-Roman churches, built in wood, wattle and reed, must have been broadly like the various other constructions raised by the English – until their post-Conversion tutors introduced the use of masonry, lead, glass and similar refinements. To the author of the Life of Bishop Wilfrid, writing in 710 × 720, the churches of the native north Britons (probably in Elmet) were just *loca sancta*.[27]

It is not of itself an overwhelmingly sound inference that there *were* churches in the last century of Roman Britain, simply because Gildas and after him Bede thought, and said, that there had been. It is a presumption. The tradition may have been factual, if slender. In later literature, particularly hagiographical writings, much depends upon the weight one chooses to attach to the reality of incidental references, as opposed to direct statements about saints and religious heroes.[28] Before addressing ourselves to the question of what particular Roman models could have given rise to any such fourth-century churches, and what in the way of settings and incidence the contemporary Continental evidence might indicate, we must look at the literature again from another angle – that of the Latin vocabulary used to name all such buildings and features.

DESCRIPTIVE TERMS

We cannot be sure what Latin speakers in Roman Britain called their church buildings. We can infer that they called such novelties of the Roman period as a framed window *fenestra*, a school in a town run by some enterprising grammarian *scola*, and (as we saw in Chap. 3) a composite Roman-style bridge *pons* (*pont-em*); simply because the Welsh words *ffenestr*, *ysgol* and *pont* must derive from these Latin forms (however actually spoken or, if written, spelled), as also must the Cornish *fenester*, *scol* and *pont*. If we think in terms of material innovation and the impact of one culture upon another, as opposed to purely linguistic mechanisms, inferences drawn from the existence of Latin loans into 'lower' languages can offer a precise guide to matters otherwise revealed only by the chance successes of archaeology.[29]

However, granted that Welsh *egluys* and Cornish *eglos* both meant by the time of the Norman conquest at least 'parish church' or 'substantial church building', it remains considerably less certain that their common ancestor *ecclesia* necessarily meant this in the fourth century. It is fair to suggest that a minor semantic confusion (which exists now) could have been encountered in the Roman period, particularly in colloquial speech. When we say 'the Church' (or write *the Church*, *the church*) we may mean: a particular Christian place of worship that we and our listeners have in mind; a religious society or flock usually attached to some such specific building ('I know him; he belongs to our church'); the concept of whatever *branch* of Christianity is being mentioned ('The Methodist Church supports co-education in its own schools'); or, lastly, the totality of Christianity as the Church Universal ('the Church's views on events in Africa'). It is arguable that three of these four meanings could have been found in Roman Christianity.

This point has to be pursued, if only because recent work on the place-name type, *Eccles-* (simple and compound), seems to be in danger of hardening into the idea that any locations so named do represent the sites of actual church buildings in the fourth and later centuries (*cf.* Chap. 10). The evidence we have to look at is very largely linguistic, and it is not conclusive. In St Paul's Epistles, in their early Latin form – either as the Vetus Latina or Jerome's Vulgate – the Greek word *ekklésia*, 'assembly of those called-out; a popular assembly', was one of those words directly transliterated[30] into early Christian Latin, as *ecclesia*, to mean 'a body of Christians', at first of course local, later universally so. It has in the early Roman period no other meaning; and it is not really relevant to say that, for Paul, it could hardly have meant 'a church building' before any such constructions came into being.

Presumably this confined use of *ecclesia* arrived in Britain in the late second or third centuries. Still by the fifth century, for the Briton Patrick, *ecclesia* meant only 'the Church Universal', in his sense confined to Ireland, Britain, Gaul and Rome. (Patrick's writings may, as we shall see, hint at one Latin word for 'church building', but not this one.) Two generations later, Gildas, who possessed both a wider vocabulary and a more florid style, and certainly had had access to rather more Latin literature than Patrick ever saw or remembered, expressed the idea of the Church Universal both by *ecclesia*[31] and the minor expansion *mater ecclesia*.[32] Even by his time, in early sixth-century Britain, it can be inferred that no single Latin term to describe 'a church building' had become fixed in conventional writing nor presumably in spoken use. Gildas rings the changes on *ecclesia*, *basilica* and *ecclesiae domus*. These remarks refer, of course, to Britain, and to an increasingly isolated British Christian Latinity. It may have been different elsewhere. Egeria, the enthusiastic lady-traveller of the late fourth century whom we met in Chapter 2 (p. 52), her Latin reflecting the home usage in western Gaul or northern Spain, did seem to know the words *martyrium* and also *monasterium* (= an individual ascetic's cell), unless she acquired these as 'correct' on her pilgrimage. But each and every church that she saw she referred to as *aecclesia*, *ecclesia*. She may have known, but thought it inappropriate to use, the word *basilica*. It is doubtful whether by her day a full and distinctive vocabulary, in Vulgar Latin, for *types* of churches had evolved (and Egeria's world very probably could have shown rather more Late Roman church buildings than did Britain). *Basilica* had become primarily an architectural term used to connote major works of the basilican ground-plan. It is doubtful that any truly basilican church was ever built in Britain up to *c*.425, let alone afterwards, and when this word appears in Gildas' writings the addition presumably came from a literary source.

There is some evidence for the use of other terms. The Latin word *dominicus* 'belonging to a master, or lord', taken as alluding to Our Lord – perhaps as with the supposed *Dominus Noster* graffiti (p. 90) – had appeared in a Christian sense around 200. Tertullian referred to *dominica dies*, 'Sunday', and this usage was irregularly continued. Easter Sunday was *dies resurrectionis dominicae* to Constantius of Lyon, *c*.480, and was copied by Bede in the appropriate passage.[33] Daughter-languages of Latin perpetuate this (*Dimanche, Dominica*, etc.). The form *dominica*, qualifying the noun *domus* 'house, building', may have been used in fourth-century Roman Britain to mean 'the Lord's House, the building used for Sunday meetings, church'. The British VL form appears to have been borrowed into Irish (*cf.* p. 303), at a very early stage, to mean both 'church building' and 'Sunday' (OIr. *domnach*). It occurs as an Irish place-name element – Hogan listed several hundred examples in his *Onomasticon*[34] – and the circumstances support the idea of antiquity.[35] In his *Confessio*, Patrick made use of what seems to be a further derivative adjective, *dominicatus*, apparently to mean 'churchman, cleric' (*cf.* p. 339).

If *dominica* tends to weaken the simple, exclusive equation, *ecclesia* = church building, there is also the word *altare*. This is found, though rarely, in pre-Christian or non-Christian Latin (e.g., *altaria*, 'burnt offerings on a pagan altar'), but it became the normal word for a Christian altar as the focal point of any church, contrasted with the pagan *ara* (as in RIB 235). In Chapter 4, in the discussion of the Water Newton hoard, the inscription *Sanctum altare tuum, Domine, subnixus honoro*, was noted. If the use of the part for the whole, 'altar' for 'church', is implied, this is echoed (as Painter notices) in the phrase *introibo ad altare Dei* which occurs in the medieval Tridentine Mass;[36] here, *altare* stands for the entire sanctuary. Much closer to Roman Britain again, Patrick wrote[37] of certain well-born Irish lady converts, who *super altare iactabant ex ornamentis suis* 'flung down some of their jewellery upon the *altare*.' Is this a rather similar usage? Though Gildas naturally knew of stone altars as such – he accused oath-breakers of treating them as *lutulentia saxa* 'just dirty old stones' – he could also express the idea of 'holy churches' (as buildings) by the periphrasis *sacra altaria*.[38] Old Welsh, as in the *Gododdin* poem,[39] seems to have used the loanword *allawr* in just this way.

The conclusion must be that, until at least the fifth century, British Latin exhibited a certain looseness in finding any one specific word to mean 'a Christian church building'. The range of terms used very probably did include *ecclesia* (though we have no early example);[40] but the assumption that *ecclesia* necessarily and exclusively meant 'a church building' rather than that it could and did also mean 'a Christian congregation', is unsound. This is important when we come to consider the Eccles- place-names. There is also, perhaps, some indication that churches were not common, even by 400; and that the lexical uncertainty reflects their comparative uncommonness.

THE ARGUMENT FROM LATER INSULAR CHURCHES

We are left, after a perusal of the literary sources, with a firm presumption that church buildings did exist in Britain and Ireland during the fifth, sixth and seventh centuries, even if we cannot find them and dig them up as preludes to convincing reconstructions of their forms. Because, within the methodology of archaeological research, one tends to suppose that every artefact possesses a cause, a function and an origin – nothing is made without a theoretically-detectable reason nor lacks some theoretically-detectable use – there may be a temptation to pose a question: What models were followed for constructing churches in the fifth to seventh centuries AD? and to seek a partial answer retrospectively from the oldest dated Insular churches (probably of late seventh-century date).

There is a typology of Irish churches, up to the so-called 'Irish Romanesque' phase.[41] In the light of what was said earlier, about post-Roman traditions of two contrasting building styles, it is confusing to discover that the Irish churches generally regarded as the earliest ones are, actually, built in *stone*. They appear as small rectilinear churches or so-called 'oratories', the type-site being one at Gallarus (or Gallerus) in Co. Kerry. Often not much bigger than a modern gardening shed (e.g., internally some 10 by 15 ft; 3 by 4.5 m), these little buildings can stand within cemetery-enclosures.[42] The approximate starting-date, if seldom explored or justified in detail, is usually taken as being c.700.

Harold Leask was at pains to collect and to set out the many clues making it clear that, however early the archaeologists supposed these little churches to be, to him as a practising historical architect they possessed features which clearly indicated timber or wooden fore-runners. These features are what are called *skeuomorphs*; artefacts or parts thereof which were originally functional in one medium, but which are then copied or imitated non-functionally in another. They include flat projecting gable-end buttresses carefully built in shaped stone, which imitate squared upright corner-timbers – projecting, because plank walls would have been slotted into them or fixed to their inner faces; carved stones ('gable finials') at each end of a stone roof-ridge, imitating at some remove the decorated crossings of wooden gable-beams; and so-called 'trabeate' door surrounds with large single horizontal lintels, imitative of doors framed in substantial wooden beams. Peculiar too in this Irish style are the internal proportions, in the width-to-length ratio of 2 to 3 (this seems to arise from older secular rule-of-thumb markings of initial lay-outs); and also a preference for a doorway in the west gable end – again possibly derived from timber construction, where it would be less desirable to break the line of a longer side wall.

Harbison questioned the age of the whole Gallarus class, incidentally making a good case[43] for seeing the type-specimen church as a consciously archaic production of the tenth to twelfth centuries. He suggested, with some force, that these cannot be the first churches in Ireland; they may not even typify the first *stone* churches. As to Harbison's first point, which takes up the observations made earlier by

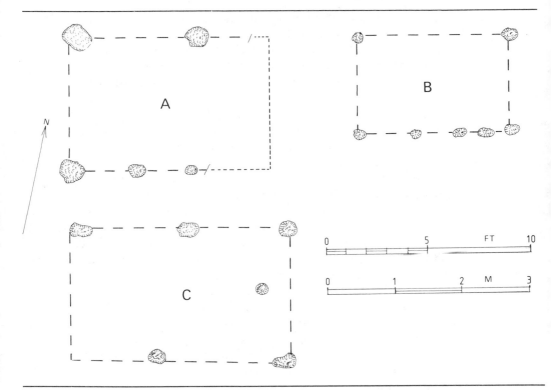

18 Plans, extended from post-holes, of three small wooden churches of Irish type
A Church Island, co. Kerry, late 7th cent. (after O'Kelly) B Carnsore, co. Wexford,
mid-late 7th cent. (after O'Kelly) C Ardwall Isle, Kirkcudbrightshire, *c.*700 (after
Thomas)

Leask, we do now have traces of small timber churches (archaeologically, expressed by post-holes for the corner and median uprights).
These have been found under, and therefore must be immediately earlier
and older than, stone churches of the Gallarus class. There are examples
from Ireland itself – from Church Island, Co. Kerry;[44] from Carnsore,
Co. Wexford, where there is a C-14 date of AD 660;[45] and from Ardwall
Isle, in an early Irish-settled part of south-west Scotland.[46] These belong
to the end of the seventh century, and at the moment are the best
claimants as the earliest known churches, of any type, within Insular
post-Roman Christianity (fig. 18).

The shift from wood to stone is found in other monumental groups, as
well as churches; for example in free-standing crosses.[47] In both Ireland
and western Britain ('Atlantic Britain'), the general shift occurred
between the late seventh and early ninth centuries. Mere technical and
craft challenges aside, there may well have been a direct stimulus, as

Radford suggests,[48] from what was taking place in Anglo-Saxon England – much the most likely source, by the way, for the appearance in eighth-century Ireland of conventional mortared masonry.

But what now seems increasingly likely is that these admittedly interesting tiny stone churches (and perhaps a smaller and similar group, of a slightly different tradition, in south-west Britain)[49] cannot possibly be the sole representatives of an older, Roman Europe, tradition of the congregational church. One comes to this conclusion on the grounds of their restricted capacity, sitings, particular contexts, and indeed comparatively late appearance in the archaeologically-dated record. Even their postulated (and now actual) timber predecessors need not be older than the mid- to late seventh century.

One possible answer is that they are the Insular versions of an originally non-Insular idea: the *memoriae* or *martyria*, cult-shrines erected alongside or above the graves of noteworthy local Christians. With related aspects of the whole cemetery-based cult of the martyrial dead, this would have been introduced to Ireland and to parts of Atlantic Britain, not before the sixth century, and probably *via* Spain from North Africa and the Mediterranean. This cannot be expanded here – it is a topic that belongs to a later volume altogether – but collation of certain published distribution-maps, for example Harbison's of the Gallarus group of churches,[50] and the present author's of relevant Mediterranean pottery imports[51] and certain classes of stone shrines,[52] would very well demonstrate such an assertion (*cf.* fig. 60).

There is, nevertheless, evidence from early Ireland of another and quite separate series of larger wooden churches. None survives, structurally. Recovery would in any case be hampered by the suspicion, or fact, that most of them probably underlie later stone churches on the same sites.[53]

Dr A.T. Lucas has brought together[54] an impressive collection of Irish annalistic entries which relate to the plundering and burning of wooden churches and monasteries, from the seventh to the sixteenth centuries. If the point-in-time, after which such allusions stand any good chance of representing near-contemporary records of events, is probably only the end of the sixth century,[55] Lucas was able to notice thirty-three such episodes between AD 612, and 795 (the first Norse or 'Viking' raid). Some of the churches involved were clearly extensive ones. At Trevet, Co. Meath, a church subject to a *combustio* in 849 contained an unhappy 260 persons. Another at Rahan, Co. Offaly, described in 747 as a 'jointed edifice', needed no less than a thousand planks for its construction.[56] Now these can hardly have been in the 10 by 15 ft (3 by 4.5 m) class; and Irish hagiography supplies us (in varying degrees of credibility) with further examples. We find them in the mid-seventh century Life of Brigid of Kildare;[57] and later in that century in Tirechan's Memoir of Patrick[58] and Adamnan's Life of Columba[59] – in the last-named, with plentiful allusions to large-scale timber construction. In the Old Irish language, quite apart from any introduced words like *dominica* > *domnach*, the rich vocabulary of visible Christianity contains two separate words of native origin which, at least as early as the eighth century, were used to express the idea 'a church'. These are *dairtech* and *daimliacc*. The former word is, literally 'oak-house', an interesting echo of the *robore secto* said by Bede to have been used by the Irish monks at Lindisfarne. The latter means 'house-of-stone', *daim* being cognate with Latin *domus*. Their co-existence is yet another symbol of that period of medial and constructional change-over mentioned earlier.

Radford has now put forward [60] his reconstruction of the only large wooden church described in any detail; that at Kildare, probably as it existed around AD 600. The dimensions which he prefers to follow are, for reasons he sets out, taken from those deduced for a tenth-century phase of the cathedral church at Clonmacnoise, assuming such to be an archaic Irish mode – internally, 28 by 62 ft (8.5 by 19 m). This is a minor point. Cogitosus's own description, in his Life of Brigid of Kildare,[61] makes it clear that some church of this order did exist there; the present author has already found reason to defend its authenticity on other grounds;[62] and with only minor reservations Radford's reconstruction is entirely supportable.

If we can explain away the Gallarus class of small stone churches, and their immediate wooden predecessors, as sixth–seventh century introductions, what are we to make of these very much larger and surely 'congregational' churches? Some kind of evidence for them, albeit slender, appears to exist from Patrick's days onwards; and there is no reason to suppose that similar constructions were not also known in contemporary mainland Britain.

For their appearance in fifth-century Ireland, possibly accompanied by lexical elements (borrowed from British Latin) to describe them in everyday life (p. 303), we have to look to sub-Roman Britain. These wooden churches may well provide us, inferentially, with some idea, and at the moment our only idea, of what were built by Christians to serve as churches in the earlier fifth century and indeed possibly in the very late fourth century too. If one supposes that, as with both the use of the basilican ground-plan, and in what we know of early Ireland, there was a direct architectural relationship between secular and religious structures, there is perhaps some further British evidence here. It concerns large timber halls in post-Roman Britain, halls which are wholly divorced from anything known or used or built by the incoming Anglo-Saxons.[63] Precisely where this originated, in terms of models, is also not clear, though one would think of timber-framed superstructures resting on masonry bases in late Roman British towns; of the surprising range of non-domestic Romano–British buildings, particularly the larger ones for agricultural use;[64] and, if one wants western Britain in the fifth century in particular, the evidence from Wroxeter.[65]

For post-Roman Britain, examples are known. At Castle Dore in mid-Cornwall, where some local kinglet re-occupied an Iron Age hillfort, the post-holes found in pre-War excavations helped to define two such large rectangular halls[66] – one about 40 by 90 ft, the smaller some 35 by 65 ft. The latter is closely matched by the fifth–sixth century excavated traces of another hall, at South Cadbury, Somerset,[67] which measured about 34 by 63 ft and possessed internal roof-supports.

If churches of only half these dimensions had been built before 400 in Romano–British towns – all in timber, or with timber superstructures on masonry foundations (as probably at *Richborough*: see below) – then, as we find ourselves removed in distance from Romanised south-east England, in time from the late fourth century, and in available technology from the resources of Roman workshops and yards, churches of the general Kildare type are precisely what one might expect to find; in the home-districts of Patrick and Gildas as a start, in the north and west of Britain during the fifth century and afterwards. As churches, these may well have been the norm; and one that the first literate Englishmen (who, in a secular idiom, shared very much this norm) both knew and reported. Some model along these lines can only have been what Patrick and his circle would have been able to introduce to Ireland. That our difficulties in proving the one-time existence of any such churches may be apparent, not absolute, and may have followed from earlier weaknesses in excavational and field techniques, is now implied by Philip Barker's lengthy campaign at Wroxeter. When he shows, as he has done, a town-centre reconstruction appropriate to some sub-Roman *tyrannus*, using timber-framed buildings on rubble foundations and moreover using, when appropriate, essentially classical models, this has aroused understandable interest.[68]

The approximate correspondence in size, between the Castle Dore and South Cadbury halls and the reconstructions of the Kildare Church, becomes more acceptable if we realise that these and similar buildings were obviously intended to accommodate, if for rather different ends, a hundred or more people. (As it happens, the three examples mentioned could all have been built in the same generation.) When one postulates, using these observations as guide-lines, that fifth-century and even very late fourth-century churches in Britain could have been earlier and smaller manifestations of such constructional techniques, one goes as far as argument permits; and the supposed examples, to be discussed below, must be considered again in this particular light.

CHAPTER SEVEN

Churches in Late Roman Britain – Analogies, Examples and Conclusions

It has long been clear, from specific references discussed later in the context of distributions and numbers, that there were bishops in the fourth-century British Church. It does not automatically follow, however, that because there were bishops there must also have been church buildings (as opposed to mere meeting-places). By 313, the structure of Christianity throughout the empire was uniform. It was one of groups or congregations, usually to be found in large or small towns, or exceptionally as in the north African provinces attached to villages, directed in all ecclesiastical matters by a clerical hierarchy with bishops at its upper end. Slender though the record is, there is no reason to suppose that Roman Britain was any different. But this is not an argument for the existence of archaeologically-recognised churches. Apart from the high probability that the Christian church as a definite architectural type had not fully emerged by the middle of the fourth century[1] – certainly not in remote Britannia – the picture of contemporary Gaul that can be derived from the (later) writings of authors like Gregory of Tours[2] offers an instructive guide.

At Tours, for instance, the first Christians, having had to meet outside the Roman city *per cryptas et latibula*[3] (a *latibulum* was 'a hidey-hole'), put up with this inconvenient concealment for half a century, under their first-recorded bishop (c.250–96). After a gap of thirty-seven years, the second known bishop was a local man and was able to provide them with a base by converting part of a senator's house – this is about AD 333. No further provision appears to have been made until soon after 397, when a real church, a 'small basilica', was raised over the tomb of St Martin. At Bourges following the Decian persecution in the mid-third century the first bishop, Ursinus, was able to build up a Christian congregation. There were however only 'small resources for building' and in the end these Christians and their bishop managed to persuade a rich sympathiser to let them have the use of his own home, against a nominal rent. By Gregory's own time, this had become a proper church; the site is probably represented by the Cathedral (St Étienne), but the conversion from town-house to church was relatively late.[4] Historical comment of this kind is supplemented by likely inferences from archaeology, as we look around northern Gaul and the great valleys of the Rhine and the Mosel; a good many churches known to begin in the early fifth century apparently originated in such acquisitions and conversions. In her thorough study of Roman Trier, Edith Wightman points out that several of the first suburban churches (*cf.* fig. 19: the sites marked 7 and 8 apply here) stand over Roman buildings and 'could have started as private chapels';[5] or, just as possibly, as the extra-mural meeting-places of Christians.

EXPECTED CATEGORIES OF CHURCHES

A better guide to any search through the remains of Roman Britain is also taken from the analogous instances of the Gaulish provinces, but in this case is mainly topographical in character. We can begin with the questions: How did a church-building first arise, and in the setting of a western, late Roman city precisely where could we expect to find such?

In the last few decades, most of the researches directed to these questions have been influenced by long, complex and generally successful demonstrations of links between martyrial tombs and a series of superimposed structures leading eventually to great hall-like churches of basilican ground-plan. The martyrs' tombs were those traditionally believed to contain the bodies of Christians who had perished in the major eras of persecution (this need not in all cases have been historical), though later much the same veneration was paid to tombs of early bishops, saintly clerics, and even outstanding local Christians. It was immediately around, often immediately *over*, these graves that the first churches could be built. This superimposition affords a most intimate connection between the foundation-grave, and any altar within a church placed above it; and hence between a named *sanctus*, celebration of the Christian mysteries and, in post-Constantinian times, all public worship.

This central thesis has drawn its strength from years of work at such sites as Salona, on the Adriatic coast.[6] It underlies most of the influential writings on this general theme,[7] which tend however to be centred on Christianity in Mediterranean lands. The significance of the 'martyrial cult' in the architectural history and development of churches cannot be understated; but – especially in the further west – it may not constitute the whole story, as we shall see. In looking at the evidence for the first Christian buildings within towns and cities whose status fell a good way below those of Salona, or Rome, or Milan, or Trier, other elements and other explanations may be detectable.

The lessons to be derived from post-War archaeology, particularly in the bombed cities of northern Germany and the Rhineland, battle-scarred centres in other western countries, and also from fresh work in

Switzerland, southern France and the somewhat art-centred researches in Spain, can be speedily summarised. They include: the very high value to be placed on *continuity* – or working backwards in time from the known to the unknown – raised by those demonstrations of modern and medieval cities as direct successors of their Roman ancestors;[8] the crucial role played by Roman *extra-mural cemeteries* in helping to determine patterns of the sitings of post-Roman churches (and hence, to some extent, of urban growth in both medieval and modern inner-city zones); and the parts played in the development of *church architecture* by models rather more humble than the Roman civil or judicial basilica. We could add, also, growing evidence of some use of pagan cult and funerary structures, both for actual sites and possibly partly as models; and the considerable aid to further archaeological enquiry to be gained from the early Christian literature of the West.

If most of these lessons still await reflection in popular and educational writings (in English), it is fortunately clear that they have made some impact in Britain already. It is also a legitimate comment that this seems to be due, less to Roman studies as such, than to their propagation through conferences and various publications inspired by the Council for British Archaeology's pioneering Urban Research, and Churches, Committees.

For Roman Britain, we can now expect to find churches (if we can find them at all) on sites of several, clearly-differentiated kinds. Apart from being described by implication in the prolix writings of Gregory of Tours, and less directly in other early Gaulish literature, these locational categories have been distinguished in the field elsewhere, in largely analogous settings. Theoretically, the task cannot be outside the present scope of Romano–British archaeology. Three such categories can be distinguished, and then illustrated with some examples from European topography and literature.

The first arises from the notion, already aired above, that Christian urban groups, *ecclesiae*, aimed to obtain formal meeting-places, ideally and after 313 practicably within their towns and cities; places for formal worship, liturgical use, general and baptismal instruction, and – also ideally – with episcopal or clerical domestic quarters attached. In an earlier chapter we saw how, moments of active persecution apart, Christian churches as *collegia*[9] could enjoy the necessary property-rights. In most cases, delay appears to have stemmed from the lack of funds one would associate with a poor, back-street congregation. These sites within the city bounds, intra-mural sites, we can call *congregational churches*. As long as, and where, Roman law or subsequently custom with the force of law was followed, obviously no late Roman inhumation cemetery would be attached to such a site (Chap. 9).

The second group comprises those churches which began, mainly after

313 – and here we see Grabar's central thesis provincially mirrored – as successive structural enlargements, right up to facilities for full congregational use, of what began as martyrial or episcopal tombs. These would be found in conventional Roman cemeteries outside any town or city bounds – extra-mural cemeteries – and presumably they would particularly occur in parts of cemeteries set aside, mainly in the fourth century, for Christian use. We can distinguish these as the sites of *extra-mural* or *cemetery churches*.

The third group is one of churches built through private initiative on rural estates, or possibly attached to *vici*, for private or household or estate or village or otherwise limited use. This of course postulates the existence of sympathetically-minded and wealthy Christian landlords. Such sites might come into being through the conversion of existing parts of a large house (Lullingstone, Ligugé; we shall look at likely cases) not entirely unlike the domestic oratories of our own Middle Ages; or, under certain circumstances, as entirely fresh constructions. These can all conveniently be called *estate churches*. We must keep them apart from a smaller and specialised class, the so-called *tituli* churches (the word *titulus* meant both a formal label or ascription, and a title or appellation implying some honour). The *tituli* churches, which played a very particular part in the ecclesiastical development of a few major cities like intra-mural Rome[10] where effectively they became the internal parish churches, were built and financed by prominent bishops, whose own clerical staffs served them, from endowments derived from wealthy donors or even (at Rome) the emperor Constantine. In such, mainly Mediterranean, settings the *tituli* churches enjoyed a special position[11] and were distinguished from others, *parochiae* or *dioceses*, which had been built and were maintained by the efforts of their own supporting congregations (*ecclesiae*). Small-town and rural churches for congregational use would all be *parochiae*. It is virtually certain, in this writer's view, that (the unknown and remotely possible case of Roman London apart) the *titulus* church did not exist in Roman Britain and was probably not a common distinction in most of the Gaulish provinces either. 'Private chapels' or estate churches represent another level of activity, for which other evidence does exist in both countries.

These three classes offer a valid base for our investigations. Immediately, from previously-existing literature on the subject, we ought to be able to see that in Roman Britain potential instances of each class could be brought forward. These would be respectively the so-called 'Silchester church'; the site (or traditional site) of Alban's martyrdom and burial, now St Albans Cathedral; and the Christian rooms in the Lullingstone villa-house. It is then reasonable to suppose that late Roman Western Europe offers more, and parallel, examples of all three.

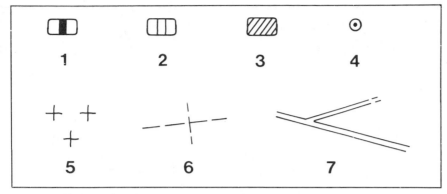

Key to symbols used in figs. 19, 20, 23–27 and 29
1 Church foundations of Late Roman date   2 Church foundations of sub-Roman or uncertain (but early) date   3 Saxon or medieval foundations   4 Significant Christian finds (see individual captions)   5 Late Roman inhumation burials and cemetries   6 Intra-mural streets   7 Roman roads

The European analogies are so numerous that, in a book mainly devoted to Britain, a cross-section by way of illustration has to suffice. This can be drawn from both archaeological discoveries and literature, and is materially aided by Mâle's account of the earliest Christianity in Gaul.[12]

For the intra-mural congregational churches, the cases of Tours and Bourges, as recorded by Gregory, have already been cited. There are much grander examples. At Reims, Jovinus, the *equitum peditumque magister* (as his dedicatory inscription described him),[13] is credited with a substantial basilican church, built before his consulate in 367, within the south-east quarter of the city (the site is now represented by St Nicaise). On the grandest scale, the first cathedral church at Trier, *Augusta Treverorum*, consecrated at the time of Valentinian I (364–75), was converted from part of the precincts of the Imperial palace, and this impressive double-church may have begun, with that part now below the present Liebfrauenkirche, not long after 326 (see fig. 19.1).[14]

The circumstances under which various churches began are not usually now recoverable. In the much more remote *Lugdunum Convenarum*, for instance, the Roman town on level ground below St Bertrand de Comminges (Haute-Garonne), a large elongated church was constructed south of the forum and civil basilica, apparently before 347.[15] In Switzerland, at Geneva (*Genava*, sometimes later *Ienuva*), where there was a fourth-century episcopate, an area around the praetorium bath-complex, south of the subsequent Cathedral, appears to have been converted into a church perhaps around 400 – the site itself is a rather complicated one[16] – with the original cathedral (St Pierre), its baptistery, and the adjoining Notre Dame la Neuve (see figs. 20.3; 20.4) being next to the mid-fifth century Burgundian palace; they represent sixth-

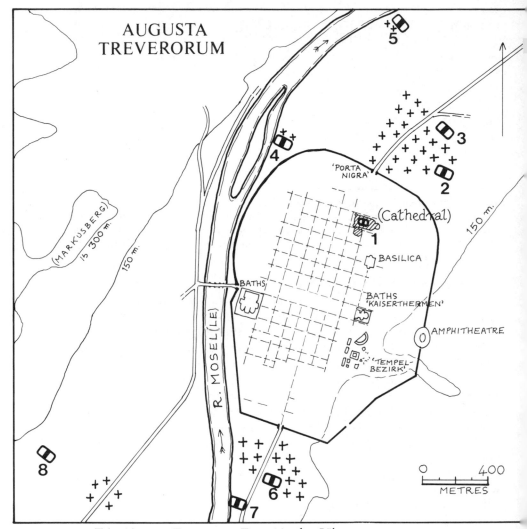

19 Trier (*Augusta Treverorum, Treveris*), after Böhner
  1 Cathedral and adjoining Liebfrauenkirche, over 4th-cent. double basilica   2 St
  Maximin   3 St Paulin(us)   4 St Martin (site; Martinsufer)   5 St Maria-ad-Martyres
  (site; Peter-Lambertstrasse)   6 St Matthias   7 St Medard (site; Medardstrasse)   8 St
  Helen(a), Euren

century elaborations of the original Christian complex. In the same city,
another intra-mural site, now represented by St Germain (fig. 20.2),
appears to overlie a primitive fourth-century church.

    We can expand this to consider examples of churches attached to
extra-mural cemeteries, since this, from the fourth century, is fairly well
documented and carries so many implications for later patterns of urban

growth. Reverting to Trier (fig. 19), often adduced as a classic instance, and publicised by Kurt Böhner's thorough study of Trier and its region,[17] most of the known late Roman churches are associated with the extra-mural inhumation cemeteries of the period – Sts Maximin, Paulinus, Martin, and Maria-ad-Martyres on the north (nos. 2–5), and certainly St Matthias (6) by the main road south. Trier's bishops commenced in the late third century; as a city with an Imperial residence, it was visited by Martin of Tours. The ascriptions of the various churches reflect Trier's history. Various early bishops were buried in the large late Roman inhumation cemetery by St Matthias, named for its medieval possession of a relic of the Apostle Matthew – it was earlier 'St Eucharius', after one of the first bishops. Other bishops were buried on the north side, like Maximinus (St Maximin, 2), and the anti-Arian mid-fourth-century Paulinus (St Paulin(us), 3) who died in Phrygia in 358, his body being later brought back to Trier. St Medard (7) and, across the Mosel, St Helen(a) at Euren (8), may be the sub-urban equivalent of private or estate churches.[18]

Literature and archaeology combine to shed light on other towns. At Bordeaux, *Burdigala*, the first Christians had a little church, later named for its possessing a relic of the protomartyr Stephen, by a cemetery alongside the main road to the west. Severinus, a popular bishop, was buried here. A second church then developed from the *memoria* or *martyrium*, the above-ground element erected over his grave. Both sites, now St Étienne and St Seurin (fig. 20.1), though now well inside the vast spread of modern Bordeaux, lie outside and west of *Burdigala*; the later cathedral (St André, 2) overlies a Roman temple. At Geneva again, *Genava*, the present extra-mural site of La Madeleine (fig. 20.1) seems to go back to a late Roman funerary church over a fourth-century inhumation cemetery,[19] near the waterfront of the period.

At Mainz, *Moguntiacum*, there is another classic demonstration,[20] with its scatter of extra-mural cemetery churches of late Roman origin. St Alban, the *Albanskirche*, in the area called *Albansberg* just south-east of the Roman city (fig. 20.4), is one of several whose burial-grounds have produced Christian memorial inscriptions from the fourth century onwards (see again below). Another frequently-cited case is that of Cologne, which need not be yet once more illustrated.[21] The site of St Severin lies about 1km south of the Roman city, *Colonia (Agrippinensis)*, in an extensive cemetery by the main southward road. Third-century Christian graves, including those of local martyrs, were enriched by an early fourth-century *memoria* and given added distinction with the burial, *c*.400, of Severinus, a local bishop. A continuous succession of churches then grew up around them. Very similar circumstances have been noticed at Xanten, on the west bank of the Rhine (*Colonia Ulpia Traiana*; the name is from a popular replacement, *Ad Sanctos*) – where

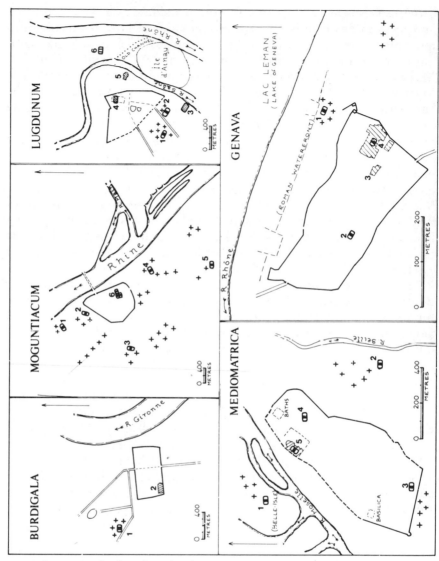

20 Bordeaux (*Burdigala*), after Blanchet. 1 St Seurin   2 Cathedral
   Mainz (*Moguntiacum*), after Weidemann. 1 St Theomast   2 St Peter   3 St Aureus (in
   city cemetery)   4 St Alban (Albanskirche, Albansberg)   5 Heilig-Kreuz   6 Cathedral
   complex
   Lyon (*Lugdunum*), after Wuilleumier. 1 St Irenée   2 St Just   3 St Laurent de
Choulans   4 Basilique de Notre Dame de Fourvière (over forum)   5 Cathedral (St
Jean)   6 St Nixier
   Metz (*Mediomatrica*), after Weidemann. 1 Site at Belle-Isle   2 Site at rue Mazelle   3
Ste-Croix (SW)   4 Ste-Croix (NE)   5 Cathedral (St Etienne)
   Geneva (*Genava*), after Bonnet. 1 La Madeleine   2 St Germain   3 Burgundian palace
(mid-5th cent.)   4 Cathedral (St Pierre) and Notre Dame la Neuve (early 6th cent.)

two martyrs, traditionally St Viktor and another, were commemorated by a fourth-century *memoria* which through successive churches became the present cathedral.[22]

In what is now France, we can note a very clear correspondence at Metz (*Mediomatrica*; fig. 20) between two late Roman churches and extra-mural cemeteries – this is visible on a wider scale in the maps provided by Weidemann[23] – apart from intra-mural churches and the complex partly beneath the magnificent Gothic cathedral of St Étienne (fig. 20.5). The circumstances at Lyon or Lyons, *Lugdunum*, are rather more complicated. The primary figure here was bishop Irenaeus, 'St Irenée', who died in 202 and was buried on a slight hillock, his tomb lying over the apse of a small pagan mausoleum. This much-venerated spot (fig. 20.1) was eventually covered by a church, possibly one of several attributed to the efforts of a later fifth-century bishop, Patiens. Close by, and also extra-mural, a 'basilica of the Maccabees' had arisen; after another bishop, Justus, who died in the Thebaid in 390, had been brought back to Lyon for patriotic burial, it was re-named after him – St Just (2). Probably another resplendent church, described by Sidonius Apollinaris,[24] was erected by Patiens to replace the older one. Across the Saône was another fifth-century church, St Nizier (6); and south of Lugdunum, near the river, the early sixth-century church of St Laurent de Choulans (3),[25] over a very late Roman cemetery which continued in use, was recently uncovered in the construction of a fly-over road. Intra-murally, Notre Dame de Fourvière stands on the site of the Roman forum (4).

The consistency of all this material – which could be expanded by reference to other provinces not mentioned, though necessarily further from Roman Britain – stresses the validity of the distinction between intra-mural congregational and extra-mural cemetery churches and the possibilities of our still making that distinction, not only by recourse to such writings as Gregory's, but through archaeology and detailed topographical reconstruction, notably of the sort carried out by Böhner, Weidemann and others. Before we consider the evidence for 'estate churches', and turn to Roman Britain once more, it is worth underlining the notion that general analogies, given the period, should be pursued and do shed guiding light.

The Roman cities and towns of the Mosel(le) and Middle Rhineland regions, now in north-east France and north-west Germany, survived in Christian terms both a considerable revival of paganism in the late Roman period[26] and the settlement of the Franks. One index of this, closely allied to the various sites previously mentioned, is the continuing use of inscribed memorial tombstones. Christian examples of these begin during the fourth century and there are local sequences, with later stones exhibiting Germanic personal-names and greatly-devolved forms of capital scripts, taking us to the seventh and eighth centuries. They show very clearly what we would have seen in Roman Britain, had the British Romans been more firmly wedded to urban life and more able to withstand the various events of the fifth century. The oldest of these Rhenish stones have motifs which recall the Romano–British Christian 'art', if it can be called that, shown here in figs. 4, 6–8 and 13; and later ones exhibit a pronounced regional development. This cannot be paralleled from Roman Britain, because the use of any such fourth-century Christian tombstones is lacking, as part of a general late Roman desuetude of such things. Where it *can* be partly matched is in the later fifth-century re-appearance, in what was earlier called 'Atlantic Britain', of Christian tombstones which occasionally display rather similar motifs, based on the chi-rho in its several guises. Where bird or animal motifs are involved, in their symbolic portent, it must be remembered that of all the material discussed in Chapters 4 and 5 under the general label of 'late Roman', some things at least are almost certainly early fifth century.

Fig. 21 therefore juxtaposes these two provincial art-forms; those from the Rhineland and adjacent areas, taken from the appropriate corpora,[27] have been given the dates favoured by those who have most recently studied them, and the British material generally the dates preferred by Kenneth Jackson, as indicated in LHEB. The illustration is intended to do no more than point to roughly parallel developments in two separate regions, proceeding from earlier common roots, and over much the same period. There is no closer connection, and as will be discussed later (Chap. 10) the stimulus that led to the re-appearance, or appearance, of the British inscribed memorial stones was unconnected with the Middle Rhine; the stones themselves however remain a native response. Though, too, the great cities of Gaul were, by their size, wealth and larger populations, able to respond to late Roman Christianity on a scale that we would not necessarily expect to find in Britain, they were still outside the Italian peninsula; the difference is perhaps one of degree. The forms assumed by fourth- and fifth-century churches, notably the sites employed, should provide by analogy a firm guide in any search directed to Britannia.

The third category is that of the *estate church*. Any example must be carefully distinguished from purely private arrangements made for personal worship. Ausonius, who had retired in old age, around 383, to a quiet life in his native *Burdigala* – a life delightfully pictured in his verse-sequence *Ephemeris*, 'The Daily Round' – show us himself rising early, washing and dressing, and then ordering that his boy *pateatque fac sacrarium* 'makes sure that the *sacrarium* is opened up'. He then prays

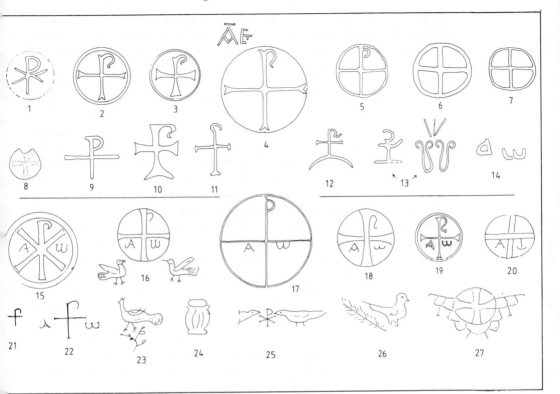

21 Parallel but unconnected developments in Christian funerary art: (above) Western Britain, 5th–7th cent. with CIIC numbers; (below) Middle Rhine and Mosel regions, with names of deceased (centuries AD in brackets)

1 Phillack, Cornwall (5)   2 Kirkmadrine 517 (5/6)   3 Kirkmadrine 518 (6)   4 Kirkmadrine 516 (5/6)   5 Drumaqueran, co. Antrim (after Hamlin, *Ulster J Archaeol 35* (1972), 23 (6/7)   6 Castell Dwyran 358 (mid-6)   7 Isle of Lundy (*Potiti*), *Thomas 1969a* (6/7)   8 The 'John Hewett' brooch, *Frend 1955*, 17 (5?)   9 Penmachno 394 (5)   10 St Endellion 478 (6)   11 St Just 483 (5/6)   12 Southill 486 (6/7)   13 Sourton 491 (6/7)   14 Boskenna, Cornwall (unpubl.) (6/7)   15 *Leoncia*, Mainz (4/5)   16 *Armentarius*, Boppard (5/6)   17 *Aiberga*, Bingen (5/6)   18 *Paulus*, Metz (4/5)   19 *Victor* Mainz (5/6)   20 *Ursus*, Mainz (5/6)   21 Linear: *Aetherius*, Bingen (5/6)   22 *Ingildo*, Wiesbaden (5/6)   23 *Pauta*, Worms (5/6)   24 *Remico*, Worms (5/6)   25 Mainz (Albanskirche) (5?)   26 *Rusticus*, Mainz (4/5)   27 Trier (St Maximin) (7?)

for a while in what we must call a priedieu or small personal oratory.[28] On the other hand, we know from the Letters of Paulinus of Nola that his friend, the historian Sulpicius Severus (*c.*360–420), had built some actual church, thereby replacing the family *lararium*, on his estate near Auch, dept. Gers – *Primulacium*, in the Pyrenean foothills. Somewhere else, in Aquitaine, he erected two more little churches, conjoined by a baptistery.[29] These rich and poetically-inclined Christian aristocrats – shrewdly yet affectionately described by Nora Chadwick[30] – producing verses to ornament their own, and each other's, churches, have no known counterpart in Romano–British life; but the occasional late Roman villa-proprietor may have approximated them in a desire to produce tasteful constructions for Christian worship.

The question of estate churches which are converted from, or in some way constructed within, parts of a larger standing complex remains uncertain and difficult – upper-floor examples, as we know from Lullingstone, would never be very easy to spot. The example of Ligugé, near Tours,[31] might be instructive. Whether or not this really has anything to do with St Martin's brief and miracle-working visit dated to 360–1, what can only be interpreted as a small church was built in the fourth or very early fifth century, inside the reduced but still-standing walls of a cement-floored, semi-subterranean basement granary. This appears to have been part of a wing of a notably large villa-house complex. All the later developments on this site (an added martyrium, if that is what it is; a sixth-century monastic foundation; and enlargements all the way up to the present abbatial church) do not affect this preliminary foundation. The little church, of conventional plan (fig. 22) – rectangular, with a small eastern apse – is of course of dimensions constrained by its setting within the older walls; but it need not be unique and this could have happened, on a smaller scale, in Britain.

Armed with this summary, then, we can turn to what is known from Roman Britain; for convenience, looking at the discoveries under these three putative categories of sites and origins.

The accounts that follow are not meant as substitutes for any interim or final reports giving site-plans and further details, to which appropriate reference is made, and which the interested reader should consult. The material will be considered under the three heads mentioned above, followed by special consideration of Stone-by-Faversham, Kent; by various analyses; and by an attempt, involving examination of the British evidence for bishops and their dioceses, to quantify potential totals. The italicised, bracketed number following each place-name entry is the evidential weighting used in Chapter 5 for the distribution-maps.

INTRA-MURAL CONGREGATIONAL CHURCHES

Caerwent, *Venta Silurum* (o)
A phase of supposed sub-Roman rebuilding over the bath-house south of the central forum involved a structure with a shallow flattened apse.[32] This has been claimed as a church but the evidence is inconclusive, and

---

22 Ground plan of 4th-cent. estate church in basement of villa-house(?), Ligugé, Vienne (after Coquet 1978, and site visit 1979)

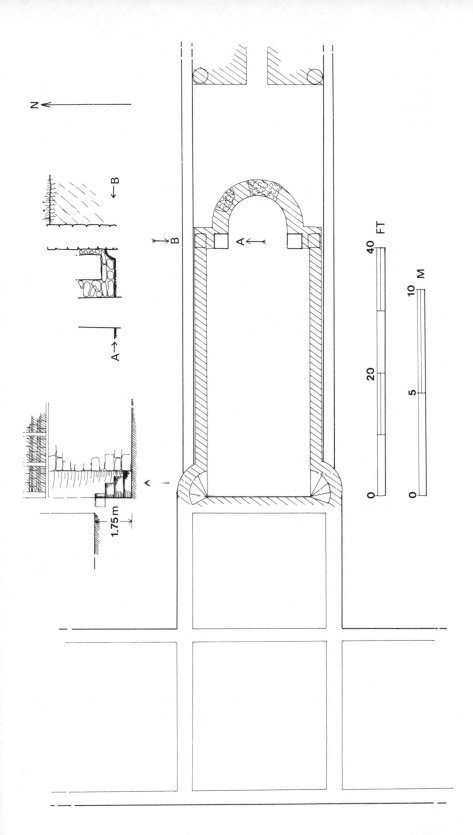

N

B

A→

A

1.75 m

A

B

FT
40

20

0

M
10

5

0

the identification cannot really stand. Objections were set out by Leslie Alcock,[33] and by George Boon[34] who also refers to his hope to show elsewhere that 'House XXII North embodied a church'. Christianity at Caerwent, apart from the evidence already given, may be inferentially implied by something in Insula XI, the so-called 'Shrine of the Head.[35] This adjoined a block of servants' or workers' quarters and was 'as far as possible from the main dwelling' (= House VIII S, enlarged in the fourth century); its clearly-isolated paganism might, Boon though, be '. . . an index of the proprietor's Christianity'.

Canterbury, *Durovernum Cantiacorum* (3), fig. 23
The special circumstances of London excepted, this is the most likely of all Romano–British cities to possess some history of continued use. The clue to an intra-mural church is strong, and concerns that site within the city said to be restored by Augustine (p. 171), dedicated, as Bede tells us[36] to the Holy Saviour. This is generally agreed to be represented by the present Cathedral[37], though the post-1067 reconstruction will have removed all traces.

Colchester, *Camulodunum* (0), fig. 24
In an appraisal of Colchester's ecclesiastical history, Warwick Rodwell[38] raises the possibility that St Martin's may occupy the site of a late Roman church. It stands in Insula XI, in the north-west quarter; the west end of any Roman structure would have been aligned on the frontage of a subsidiary north-south street. Reported churchyard finds of 'Anglo-Saxon burials' and at least four complete Roman pots (accompanying fifth-century graves?) underline 'the potential archaeological importance of this church'.

Exeter, *Isca Dumnoniorum* (0), fig. 25
The first of the major Roman Exeter reports draws attention[39] to six unaccompanied oriented burials, probably of Christians (two with C-14 dates of 420 and 409)[40] cut through the basilica floor in period 3b. Their NW–SE alignment, the excavator suggests, could conceivably follow some element of the post-400 town plan here. One might look to a building in the area of the forum courtyard, or as part of a town house south-east of the forum.

Lincoln, *Lindum* (*Colonia*) (1), figs. 24 and 37
Excavations in the Flaxengate area, in the extended or lower colonia, produced traces of a substantial fourth-century building, lying east-west, with an eastern apse, and a porticus or footed aisle on the north side (only the NE corner was available).[41] There were quantities of decorated wall-plaster and from the central area disturbed mosaic tesserae in black, red

and white (*cf*. Silchester, below). The function of the building is cautiously described as 'enigmatic'. It is at the moment the best candidate for an intra-mural church.

Richborough, *Rutupiae* (3), fig. 26

The presence of fourth-century Christianity here has already been strongly suggested by various finds mentioned earlier – not all now necessarily locatable but certainly within the area of the fort. Brown, in a persuasive essay,[42] has interpreted previously-found masonry foundation blocks in the north-east quarter as the footings of a rectangular church, aligned east-west, probably with an eastern apse, and (from what direct evidence remains) with some kind of timber superstructure (*cf*. p. 216). Its likely dimensions are discussed below, as are the remains of a probable baptistery (Chap. 8).

Silchester, *Calleva Atrebatum* (3), figs. 24, 40

This, the best-known Romano–British example, was re-excavated by the late Sir Ian Richmond in 1961, and subsequently reported by Frere.[43] It stood within a small insula south of the central forum, in a little area which may previously have lain open and perhaps have been used as a stock-yard, or the like. Silchester, which has produced other signs of Christianity, can be assumed to have been occupied well into the fifth century.[44] The building itself, which has been described in such confident terms as 'the first undoubted Romano–British "church" to be explored',[45] has a rectangular central area with side-chambers or porticus flanking this nave; a cross-room or narthex, possibly serving as a porticoed entrance (?); and a small western apse. On unfortunately rather slight evidence, it appears to be a fourth-century construction, used probably in the fifth, though eventually subject to squatter occupation. Outside, and close to, the east end is the foundation of what will here (Chap. 8) be argued to have been a baptistery. There were no burials in this plot and no convincing signs of its contemporary use for any non-religious purpose.

St Albans, *Verulamium* (1), fig. 23

The Roman city, west of the present town, is known mainly from the 1936 report by the Wheelers,[46] reports on subsequent excavations being awaited, following Frere's 1972 volume.[47] Lurking within the pre-War report is 'a small basilical building in the southern quarter of the town',[48] discovered inside the southern angle of the wall and west of the London Gate during the preparation of park gardens in 1934. The building, aligned ENE–WSW, was rectangular with full-length side-chamber footings, and with square projections at each end, that on the WSW end being, in plan, the more regular. It was considered that the character of the masonry pointed to a date late in the Roman period, when this intra-mural area despite its position seems to have remained undeveloped.

EXTRA-MURAL CEMETERY CHURCHES

Canterbury (3), fig. 23

This is a special and complex problem that requires full discussion. Bede, the quality of whose Canterbury sources must be properly regarded, is specific[49] that in 597 the Christian Kentish queen, who was a Frank, had for some unspecified time been accustomed to pray (*orare consuerat*) in a church *prope ipsam civitatem ad orientem* 'near that particular city on the east side'. This church, we learn, was built in ancient times while the Romans were still in Britain – i.e., the site and foundations at least were regarded in early eighth-century Canterbury as fully Roman. It was named – by that date, and possibly by 597, or 600, though of course not necessarily during the pre-400 era – in honour of St Martin of Tours, who died in 397. Martin was particularly venerated by the Frankish Christians. The church site at Canterbury known now, and so known since at least the Middle Ages, as 'St Martin' stands on rising ground 600 m due east of the nearest part of the Roman city walls, 100 m north of the main road leading west toward Richborough. The present St Martin's church has attracted a good deal of literature[50] and would be important even without Bede's comments.

So far, so good; these are factual statements which anyone can check. Nevertheless the present writer admits to a long-standing suspicion, subsequently found to have been shared by others in the past,[51] that this identification is in some way wrong and may have to be challenged. It is less likely that Bede misunderstood or muddled what he was told, than that during the course of time confusion had arisen at Canterbury. The implication is that St Martin's was not, or was certainly not the only, late Roman church outside and east of Canterbury; and that it may not even have been the church used by queen Bercta, bishop Liudhard (a Frank who served as her chaplain),[52] and their retinue from the mid-590s onward.

St Martin's is classed by the Taylors as 'period A 1'; that is, the present chancel is regarded as *c*.600-plus and might therefore represent – though without being visibly or actually anywhere near as old as *c*.400 – part of a church used by Bercta and Liudhard. The present *nave* however, added to the west of the older, truncated 'A 1' chancel, is later, and historically could be attributed to the general seventh-century restorations of the Augustinian mission. But Frank Jenkins has argued[53] for a rather different ground-plan. The effect of what he says is to suggest that the oldest, and only potentially Roman, part of the church would be a central near-square component (17.5 ft E–W, 14 ft N–S; 5.2 by 4.3 m) with stubby buttresses on its north and south sides.

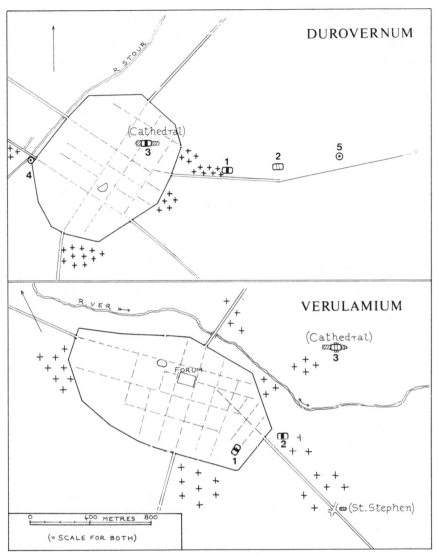

23 Canterbury (*Durovernum Cantiacorum*), after Wacher and Canterbury Archaeol. Trust maps. 1 St Pancras 2 St Martin 3 Holy Saviour (site below Cathedral) 4 Christian silver hoard 5 Pottery bowl with chi-rho graffito

(Roman) St Albans (*Verulamium*), after Frere. 1 Intra-mural church(?) of 1936–37 2 Verulam Hills Field church 3 Shrine and church of St Alban (below Cathedral)

This structure, if seen on its own as a separate Roman structure, most resembles (as various students have now pointed out) a square *cella* or mausoleum, not necessarily anything but pagan, and rather as was found at Stone-by-Faversham, in the same county (p. 183 below). As for the idea that St Martin's (if one follows Bede exactly), being so pointedly 'extra-mural', must have been a late or sub-Roman extra-mural cemetery church – and, as we saw above, topographically it would be hard to support any other conclusion – Jenkins raises further objections. This church is not associated with any known Roman occupation. It does not stand in an appropriate cemetery, either; there is an early cremation cemetery about 50 m south of it, but the principal, east-side late Roman inhumation cemetery lies over 300 m west, much nearer *Durovernum*.[54] There may have been occasional later burials nearer the St Martin's site – the chi-rho graffito sherd (p. 108) was supposedly found 'a quarter of a mile' from the church, possibly in the area of one of the older cremation cemeteries; and Brooks, who appears to accept the Bedan statement in its entirety, notes the finding 'in the graveyard to the south of St Martin's'[55] of Frankish objects presumably interred around or after 600. This does not negate Jenkins' point.

The implication so raised is that St Martin's is not a surviving Roman church (even if its core was a Roman mausoleum); the earliest post-Roman, Saxon addition, if indeed earlier than the landing of Augustine (597) *at all* (this is impossible to clarify now), might conceivably be the work of Frankish or Gaulish masons imported by Bercta for that end;[56] and it is not likely to have been ascribed to Martin of Tours at any time before Bercta and Liudhard, though in any post-597 reconstruction and enlargement such a dedication would be entirely likely.[57]

Where, then, was the church in question? There is an alternative, in the shape of the building known as 'St Pancras'. This also lies outside and east of Roman Canterbury, a little over 300 m from the walls, about 50 m north of the Roman road; and to its south-west is a large late Roman inhumation cemetery. St Pancras is in the grounds and enceinte of St Augustine's Abbey, the great extra-mural monastic complex whose nucleus was the Church of Sts Peter and Paul, founded by Augustine himself.[58] It was Albinus, abbot of this establishment, *c*.709–34, who supplied Bede's *Historia* with Canterbury information;[59] though the fact that Bede calls him *vir per omnia doctissimus* cannot hide the probability that Albinus sent only that information supported by contemporary tradition and belief.

The ground-plan of St Pancras[60] is of a rectangular nave with elongated apsidal chancel on the east, porticūs to north and south, and a protruding west porch. That it was certainly restored in Saxon times is agreed and the visible remains again led the Taylors to allot it to their period A1. But H.H. Howorth, in a very thorough review of this puzzle,[61] pointed out that by the period when Albinus was abbot, and was corresponding with Bede, St Pancras 'was no doubt quite overshadowed by the much larger church of the monastery' (the centre of the St Augustine's complex is 100 m due west) and that 'it would to any casual observer look merely like an unimportant and quite subordinate building forming part of the abbey'. Howorth thought that even as early as the eighth century, and this without prejudice to whatever reconstruction took place, confusion arose because of the general circumstances of the site. He also wondered whether St Pancras, since it was a good deal larger (as seen in 1913) than St Martin's and would thus have been more suitable for Augustine's party with their dependants and fresh converts, was not the more likely of the two to have been, both the church actually *used* by Augustine (if not also Bercta before him), and thus 'in fact, the first one built by the Roman missionaries in Britain' – i.e., the church mentioned by Bede.

The St Pancras site has now been examined by Frank Jenkins.[62] If we call the structure seen by Howorth and earlier writers, and also described and classified by the Taylors, as 'Phase II', a post-597 aspect, then Jenkins appears to have defined an earlier Phase I from excavation. This has shown a rectangular nave, about 26 by 42 ft (fig. 34), opening through a single arch into a small apsidal chancel, polygonal above ground. The Phase I structure, with re-used Roman bricks laid in *yellow* mortar or coursed, unmortared flint foundations, was floored with clay directly above 'a normal build-up of occupation soil' with pottery up to the third century. Close to the base of the outer face of the south wall was a coin of the House of Constantine (up to 337).

After a period, represented by a build-up of some 9 in (22 cm) of soil, this Phase I building, its walls now reduced in height either by temporal neglect or because they were 'deliberately demolished by the builders preparatory to carrying out the structural alterations', was somewhat re-modelled. Roman bricks, of which one assumes a plentiful supply was still to hand, were again used, this time set in a differentiated *white* mortar. The inner floor was raised about 6 in (14 cm) with a bed of concrete. Subsequently, burials were inserted in the chancel, and a cemetery with 'late seventh-century graves' appeared outside, to the south.

One should add here the peculiar Canterbury tradition, of now-unascertainable age and origin but known by the fourteenth century,[63] that St Pancras before 597 was in use as a heathen temple, containing an idol or image (*simulacrum*) of the Kentish monarch, and used for pagan gatherings by Aethelberht and his circle. After Aethelberht's conversion, Augustine was allowed to destroy this idol, purge the fane, and consecrate it in honour of Pancras, the Roman boy-martyr saint dear to the heart of Pope Gregory the Great.

This tale is not inconsistent with the evidence, though it can hardly be employed as an argument on its own. Some pre-597 pagan use of a decaying, but originally late fourth- or early fifth-century, church (Phase I) could be an inducement to include fresh work here in the general *restoratio* attributed to Augustine. It does not invalidate the idea that St

Pancras, Phase I, was built late in the Roman period, not too far from the Roman city and close to a late Roman cemetery, as a *church*. It may indeed, with its unicameral nave and apsidal chancel, have served a fresh purpose. As Howorth put it,[64] 'Those who argue for its having been a heathen temple [that is, and nothing else] must explain the fact of the temple of the heathen god being built after the fashion of a Christian church, and one so satisfying to the missioners from Rome, that they made it the model upon which their smaller churches were built.'

These arguments, taken with Jenkins' evidence (which has, at the time of writing, only seen preliminary publication), do permit the idea that St Pancras, Phase I, is an extra-mural cemetery church of late Roman date. This long excursus has been necessitated because this statement contravenes the generally-accepted view. If it is valid, it means that this is really the church said to have been built (and with justification) while the Romans were still in Britain. How, when and why Bede's informants came to confuse this with the smaller and more distant St Martin's, which also had at least a Roman core, and was probably built around that as part of the same initiative which produced St Pancras, Phase II, we cannot tell; but we can surely allow that confusion could have arisen. Nothing short of total excavation of St Martin's would begin to resolve this. It should be clear that Bede's remarks cannot be accepted without very great reservations, and the present writer favours the St Pancras identification.

Colchester (1 and 1), figs. 24, 28

Of three conceivable extra-mural church sites here,[65] two – both south of the Roman city, associated with cemeteries, and close to Roman roads – can be considered briefly. Site no. 6a (following Rodwell's list) is an apsidal building, now in Denmark Street, explored in 1935 and again in 1965. It was badly disturbed and can only be called 'probably late Roman', but is included because of its plan, the size of which may in one particular recall the Lincoln (Flaxengate) building (fig. 37). This was an east-west rectangle, about 16 ft 4 in × 67 ft 3 in (5 by 20.5 m), with a small eastern apse. It could, Rodwell adds,[66] just possibly represent a Jewish synagogue.

Site no. 10a, which was discovered in the grounds of St John's Abbey,[67] is within an interesting sequence detected over a large area, beginning with a late Roman cemetery. Over part of this, a square tower-like building, having a Roman grave exactly in its centre, was erected. Internally, it was about 19 ft (6 m) square, and aligned more or less to the compass-points. A stubby apsidal chancel was added to the east, and in a second phase a nave, of the same width as the central block, on the west. By the early Middle Ages, the building was demolished (it was unearthed during work on an overlying monastic burial-ground). Comment on the interpretation of this sequence, which at once echoes something of St Martin's, Canterbury, appears below in the discussion of Stone-by-Faversham.

Dorchester, Dorset (*Durnovaria*) (o), fig. 24

The very large extra-mural Christian cemetery at Poundbury is examined here in Chapter 9. It exhibits various phases of growth,[68] with internal divisions and enclosures; subtleties of alignments of graves (and groups of them) probably influenced by the positions of certain remarkable mausolea; and traces of buildings, probably post-Roman rather than late or sub-Roman. Mention is included because here surely, if anywhere, an extra-mural church might be expected. For the moment, Christopher Green wonders if any of the rectangular mausolea 'may have served as small churches'. It is not splitting hairs to say that, if this proved to be so, any such structures should be seen as Christian *martyria*, prevented by the circumstances of the later fifth (?) century from undergoing the development (into a full church) noted from various European sites.

Icklingham (Suffolk) (3), fig. 33

This is a case, and no doubt others will emerge, where a building with strong claims to be regarded as a church, associated closely with inhumations, forms an aspect of a Roman rural settlement whose status is unclear. Roman Icklingham may be a vicus or 'small town', rather than part of a large villa-estate; if so, the best parallels would be the fourth–fifth century rural-settlement churches known from parts of Germany, France, and Switzerland.[69]

Icklingham, as an unwalled Roman occupation-area of 37 acres, seems to possess peripheral cemeteries, that on the south-east side having now yielded what look like Christian burials. The site in question may not be, in the strict sense, 'extra-mural'; but it is within a cemetery, and evidence for Christianity here has already been given. The supposed church, identified from remains of foundation-trenches, was a small east-west rectangle (dimensions are shown in fig. 33); there is room for, and likely to have been, a little eastern apse. An inhumation cemetery of coffins and plain burials surrounds it. The stratification is considered more fully in Chapter 8, where what seems to be an associated baptistery is discussed; all that need be said now is that a date in the later fourth century is likely. A sealed pit contained debris, including material that could come from a dismantled pagan shrine (*cf.* p. 136 above).

London, *Londinium Augusta* (o), fig. 27

As it will have been noticed from earlier chapters, there are extraordinarily few signs and then mostly in the form of small objects of

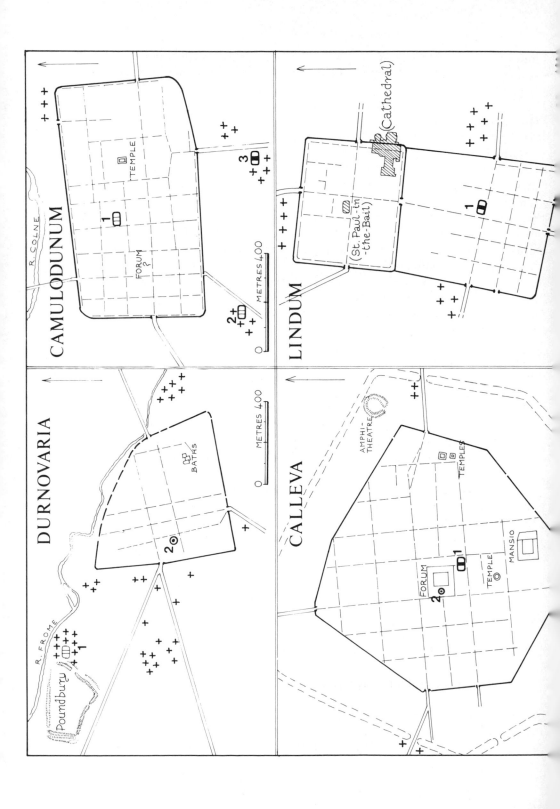

CAMULODUNUM

R. COLNE

FORUM?

TEMPLE

1

2

3

METRES 400

DURNOVARIA

R. FROME

Poundbury

1

BATHS

2

METRES 400

LINDUM

(Cathedral)

St. Paul-in-the-Bail

1

CALLEVA

AMPHI-THEATRE

FORUM

2

1

TEMPLE

TEMPLES

MANSIO

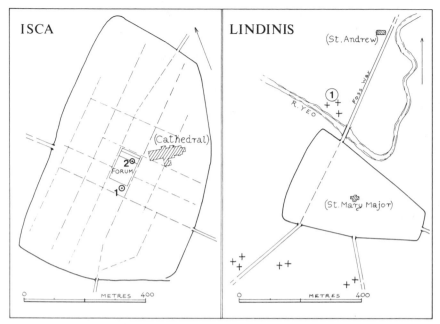

25 Exeter (*Isca Dumnoniorum*), after P. English (1979). 1 Chi-rho graffito sherd, South Street 2 5th-cent. Christian burials
Ilchester (*Lindinis*), after P. Leach. 1 Extra-mural cemetery with sarcophagi and lead coffins

low evidential weight, of Christianity from the capital of Roman Britain. What is more striking is that neither post-War salvage work, nor the current campaigns of purposeful excavation, produced any candidate for an (expected) intra-mural church. The earliest historical record would be Bede's mention of the first English episcopate (about 604: St Paul's). Reviewing what we do know of London between about 400 to 600, Martin Biddle[70] came to the conclusion that in the setting of continuing urban and commercial life within the city, dominated by a population of Roman (British) rather than English character, there is no reason to deny the likelihood of some Christian succession, similar to that in the Gaulish and Rhenish cities. Alas, no English Gregory provides us with a bishop-list, historical or traditional.

24 Dorchester, Dorset (*Durnovaria*), after Green. 1 Poundbury cemetery, with mausolea (?memoriae) 2 Silver hoard
Colchester (*Camulodunum*), after Crummy and Rodwell 1 St Martins (Rodwell no. 2) 2 Site at Denmark Street (Rodwell no. 6a) 3 St Johns Abbey grounds (Rodwell no. 10a)
Silchester (*Calleva Atrebatum*), after Boon 1 Late Roman church 2 Chi-rho seal
Lincoln (*Lindum*), after Colyer 1 Site at Flaxengate (*cf.* fig. 37)

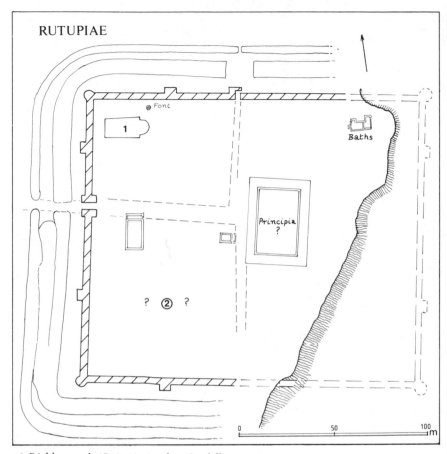

26 Richborough (*Rutupiae*), after Cunliffe
  1 Late Roman church and font   2 Area of findings, bowl with chi-rho graffito, and
  gold chi-rho ring

The probable sites for extra-mural churches (to Biddle in 1970, and
still in 1980) are those of certain suburban churches, especially with
Anglo-Saxon components, known to stand directly above Roman
buildings; as on a larger scale we noticed at Trier. Those associated
spatially with any evidence for Roman cemeteries must be emphasised;

27 London (*Londinium*), after Biddle, Hudson & Heighway
  1 St Bride, Fleet Street   2 St Andrew, Holborn   3 Bucklersbury spoon   4 Princes
  Street spoon   5 Bowl with chi-rho, Copthall Court   6 Minories cemetery. (Inset,
  lower left: key. A 5th-cent. imported Mediterranean pottery sherds   B find-spots of
  objects AD 400 to 800   C pre-800 church foundations, certain   D the same, possible
  only) Scale: 400 metres

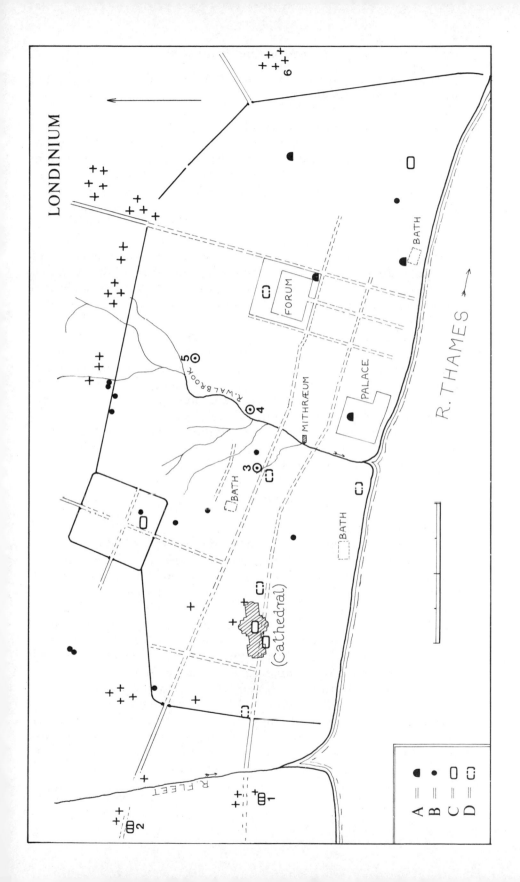

LONDINIUM

R. THAMES

FORUM

PALACE

BATH

BATH

BATH

MITHRÆUM

R. WALBROOK

R. FLEET

(Cathedral)

A =
B =
C =
D =

and both St Bede's, Fleet Street, and St Andrew's, Holborn (indicated in
fig. 27) can be mentioned.[71]

St Albans (3, and 3), figs. 23, 35, Pl. 4

If we allow that Albanus was martyred here, whatever the real date (*cf.* p.
50 above), the best identification for the spot, and for the martyrium
visited by Germanus and Lupus in 429, and for whatever subsequent
church Bede had in mind, lies on the hill-slope crowned by the present
abbey church, ranking as a cathedral. The graves from time to time
reported from this area either belong to an extra-mural inhumation
cemetery as such, or (if Alban was martyred under Decius or Valerian)
more probably a cemetery that developed around the traditional spot of
his martyrdom and burial (and we could remember Bordeaux, Lyon,
Cologne, Xanten, etc.). This is the strongest case in post-Roman Britain
for seeing a continuous sequence, and in any scheme of differentially-
weighted evidence one that for an extra-mural cemetry church of
martyrial origin must be given at '3' at once.

There are indications of a second extra-mural church,[72] found in the
early 1960s within Verulam Hills Field, not far from the external south-
east angle of the walls, and east of where Watling Street emerged from
the London Gate. A ditched Belgic cremation-cemetery gave way to a
Roman one, which later exhibited three phases of inhumation graves
from the late third century onward. Over the area of the Belgic cemetery,
a flint-walled building (fig. 35) was erected, aligned north-west to south-
east; reconstruction of a part of it sealed fourth-century pottery.

ESTATE CHURCHES

Lullingstone, Kent

The site is too well known[73] to require more than a summary. It is the
centre of a large and rich villa estate, the principal dwelling having been
expanded (or altered, or both) in the late second, late third and mid-
fourth centuries.[74] This great house stood against an east-facing slope,
and behind it were successively a second-century circular shrine and an
early fourth-century temple-cum-mausoleum. During most of the third
century, there was also a family *nymphaeum* in the 'Deep Room', a
basement within the house. At some stage in the second half of the fourth
century, the proprietors embraced Christianity. A suite of first-floor
rooms, in the north-west corner, were separated by blocking-off from the
rest of the floor, and probably had a new external access. The suite
included a porch, an outer room with wall-paintings of a wreathed chi-
rho, etc., and leading off from this, a rectangular inner room with similar
painted ornament on two of the walls. On the shorter west, or 'back'
wall, was the painted frieze with human figures, as *orantes* (fig. 9),

framed between columns and in some cases curtains. The meaning of this frieze is still a mystery; one can either join Jocelyn Toynbee in regarding it as depicting the Christian living and dead, presumably members of the extended villa-owning family, or given the more usual weight attached to *orantes* depictions at the period, as entirely funerary. We do not know. But this obviously Christian suite, whose two main rooms could functionally correspond to the narthex and sanctuary of a primitive, free-standing church – the distinction was liturgically important (*cf.* Chap. 8) – could have been in use after 380 (when the baths were dismantled); after 390, when some agricultural outbuildings were demolished; and up to whatever time in the early fifth century a final fire put an end to the establishment.[75]

Frampton & Hinton St Mary (Dorset); Littlecote (Wiltshire)

As was discussed in an earlier chapter, various late Roman villas in southern Britain contained mosaics which have indirectly or directly been taken to allude to Christian proprietorship. In the case of Frampton, where the apsidal portion of the mosaic featured a cantharus and the chord of the apse an encircled chi-rho, the question arises as to the nature, and possible functions, of the room thus floored.

The Frampton mosaic is for two rooms, divided by a wall with a 12 ft break (possibly arched). These continuous, two-room mosaics form a small class by themselves,[76] embracing Frampton, Hinton St Mary, Littlecote, and a fourth, Pitney in Somerset, whose mosaic (from the *Corinium* school)[77] does not lend itself to the same Christian weight as Frampton or Hinton. These are indications of a common, fourth-century, idea; a continuous floor to fit two interconnecting rooms, with a wide opening between them, and something not really part of a conventional winged corridor villa. David Smith has opined that, in the case of Frampton and Hinton St Mary, not only the same mosaicist but the same *architect* may have been at work.

The question naturally further arises as to what we know about the main buildings. At Frampton, Lysons in 1797 speculated that the site might have been a temple and not domestic at all. It is, as a visit makes clear, in a most unsuitable valley-bottom location. Farrar points out[78] that, insofar as an overall plan can be put together, it is also inconsistent with that of a winged corridor villa. The Frampton mosaic is more like a miniature and regular basilican plan, with apse, side-chamber and narthex, aligned north-south – in fact, rather like a small church.

What has brought the matter to attention yet again has been the revival of interest in the long-lost Littlecote Park mosaic, known from Vertue's careful engraving of *c.*1730.[79] The recent re-excavation[80] had cleared up several points. The mosaic is for a double room with opening, one part rectangular, the other presumably with triconchal apses (capped with half-domes?); it shows Orpheus and the Seasons in the apsed part, and the end-panels of the other rectangular portion have canthari between beasts, sea-monsters and dolphins (*cf.* fig. 8). Aspects at least thus suggest a knowledge of symbols within Christian art. The missing orientation is now revealed; the longer axis is WNW–ESE, the apsidal part at the WNW end. The structure housing this mosaic appears to have been virtually separate from the rest of the (?) villa-house complex. Isometric reconstructions,[81] the latest embodying the discovery that the apse footings are polygonal, not curved,[82] are bound to raise comparisons with plans of fourth-century churches. Smith based his drawing on that of a small church of the period from Turkey where (his words) 'the plan exactly suits that of the (Littlecote) mosaic and the dimensions are identical'.

This revives Kenneth Painter's point[83] about the *design* of the Hinton St Mary mosaic, which can hardly not be Christian. As we shall see shortly, none of the potential Romano–British churches seems to have been particularly elaborate or luxurious; even at Silchester, and perhaps at the Lincoln site, the mosaics and painted plaster were restrained. One contrasts this, both with the veritable parade of colour and *imagerie* at Lullingstone, and the high and lush standards of decoration reached in the richer villa-mansions.

With the substance of the double-room mosaics and their settings just described, one might air the possibility that, from the mid-fourth century, there may have stood somewhere in Roman Britain a small church of fairly advanced design – custom-built, or converted from part of a high official's residence; a private church (?) and if in the 'estate church' category, probably urban – which was based ultimately on a Mediterranean, rather than British/Gaulish, model. This is the kind of construction that might have inspired the Littlecote Park physical arrangements, aspects of Frampton and of Hinton St Mary, and (if Painter is right in regarding the mosaic design, with its central Christ roundel, as misplaced from ceiling to floor) the Hinton St Mary pavement itself – with Christ as the Son of God *Pantocrator* looking down from on high. It is, naturally, tempting to argue that London, as the administrative centre for the civil diocese, should before 400 have contained an intra-mural church of prestige; but one also remembers other towns and cities that could have been the capitals of fourth-century *provinciae*, the constituent provinces within Britannia, and seats of metropolitan bishops. Given the distances from Frampton, Hinton and Littlecote, Cirencester is one that must be envisaged.

The common elements one would deduce, for a hypothetical model (it goes too far to offer an actual drawing of such), include at one end a trichonchal (three-apsed) ground-plan, as at Littlecote, with over the central area between the apses a small but true dome resting upon a square. Painter,[84] having argued from the detailed design of the Hinton floor to an original ceiling pattern, shows that it would include a barrel-vaulted central nave 'in which the horizontal, flat ceiling was suspended from the interior of the curve of the vault'. Hence we produce something like a small basilican ground-plan, as Farrar argued from Frampton and Smith from Littlecote. The dimensions would suggest a nave perhaps 20 ft (6 m) long, a total external length of perhaps 40 ft (12 m) and a central dome at the apsidal end of just under 7 ft (2 m) diameter at its base. In Imperial terms, this would be an ornate and complex basilican church on a miniature scale; and one must allow for the chance that any copies, or derivative forms, were reduced from a larger original.

Finally, if such a church did exist, it need not have been in Britain. It has been argued in recent years[85] that some at least of the southern British villa estates were, by 300, in the hands of émigrés from Gaul or Germany, who would introduce Continental tastes. It is nonetheless worth having in mind, as we consider the few, and poor, instances of what can be put forward as Romano–British churches, that they do not all necessarily typify what could have existed. We remain to some degree in the dark about estate churches; and it is clear that Lullingstone is a different sort of church from anything represented by these Wessex villas. On the other hand, Frampton and Hinton, in particular, must for the moment remain as possible candidates for rooms within not wholly typical villa-houses that were, from time to time, used for Christian worship, and in that sense the term 'estate church' might justifiably be employed.

Stone-by-Faversham, Kent – *a special case (fig. 28)*
The ruined church of Stone lies just north of Watling Street, a little west of Ospringe, roughly midway on the Roman road between Rochester and Canterbury. Meticulous excavations in 1967–8 and 1971–2 produced the evidence,[86] despite the handicap of previous and unrecorded digging in 1827 and probably in 1926 as well.

A Roman settlement marks the immediate vicinity. There have been Roman small finds around the church. This church proved to have a central core standing on a rectangular raft of roughly-coursed mortared flints. This, with walls 3 ft (1 m) thick, looked at first like the central *cella* of some small Romano–Celtic temple. It was almost square – 14 ft 6 in (4.5 m) internally east-west, 13 ft (4 m) north-south – and originally it had three equally-spaced buttresses on the outer north and south walls. Materials and workmanship suggested a Roman date, refined by coins and pottery to the fourth century. There were signs of an inner *opus signinum* floor, with quarter-round moulding in the angles against the walls.

The Roman structure was later adapted to form the west part of the chancel of a small church. On the west side, a timber nave was added, probably in pre-Norman times, and replaced c.AD 1000 by a stone one. This last extension, at its west end, cut across the outer *east* wall of a *second* Roman masonry structure; but one quite separate from, and not aligned with, the central Roman block. The interpretation of this central block (which has a west doorway, and a footing centrally against its inner east wall) is as a free-standing mausoleum, or shrine and mausoleum combined; any burials would have taken place above floor-level, in coffins. From the coin evidence it could have been in use in this way until c.360. The next, clearly-dated, phase of activity, the timber nave, lies only between the seventh and eleventh centuries. There is thus a clear implication that the central mausoleum – a pretty solid construction – was still sufficiently serviceable, centuries after the Roman period, to form an obvious and attractive starting-point for an early Saxon church.

It would however be difficult to claim, either that during the late Roman period this seemingly-pagan affair had been accorded a fresh, direct Christian meaning (for instance, as a *martyrium*); or that it was converted into a church at any time before Augustine's mission turned its attention to the Kentish countryside (mid-seventh century?). In brief, this was a Saxon church; it cannot be claimed for Roman Christianity. It does however illuminate a wider scene. Small rectangular mausolea cannot have been too uncommon in late Romano–British cemeteries and, because such solid masonry had a good survival rate, a subsequent incorporation in a Christian church is perfectly possible. The cases noted earlier – St Martin's at Canterbury[87] and the St John's Abbey grounds site, Colchester[88] – are both, like Stone, in south-east Britain. All three mausolea are oriented, and all of the same order of size (fig. 28).

The missing link if any real evidence of a late or sub-Roman use of these structures to house a Christian burial. (The central pit at Stone was neither demonstrably for a grave, or necessarily earlier than Anglo-Saxon times.) We must accept they are probably pagan. The cases are not the same as the reputed burial of St Irenaeus at *Lugdunum* inside a pagan funerary shrine (p. 163); in fact, the closest parallel comes from Switzerland, the little church at Mett, 4 km ENE of Biel (Berne).[89] Here, a late Roman masonry mausoleum, overlying earlier inhumations in a wood-lined pit, and containing three (possibly Christian?) graves, was incorporated as a chancel into a small seventh-century church. But precisely this sequence cannot yet be demonstrated in Britain.

SUMMARY

Common to quite a lot of the sites or foundations just discussed is their discovery in relatively recent years, mainly through expanded post-War excavations, or the essential re-assessments of remains unearthed in the

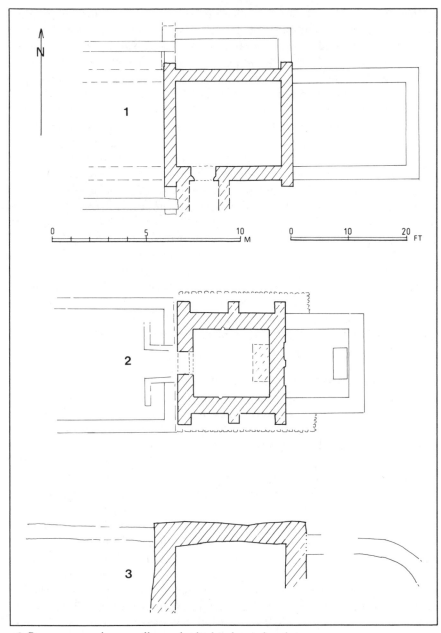

28 Roman mausolea or cellae embodied in later churches
  1 St Martins, Canterbury (after Jenkins)   2 Stone-by-Faversham (after Fletcher and
  Meates)   3 Colchester, St Johns Abbey grounds (after Crummy)

earlier part of this century. It now seems a trifle alarming that in his survey of internal elements and reflections of liturgy in early Christian churches, published as recently as 1969, C.J.A.C. Peeters had to dismiss the British Isles with the short statement that 'Concerning Britain, there is little to deal with, in regard to our topic', and a solitary reference to Fox's 1892 Silchester report![90] If the distributions implied by figs. 14–16 are any kind of guide, we could expect eventual signs of other potential churches from other Romano–British towns – particularly when small finds of Christian character go along with evidence of Theodosian refortification, indications of post-400 urban life, and any degree of place-name retention. This point will be taken up briefly below.

Of the churches examined in the previous sections of this chapter, there is just sufficient to allow a short discussion, treating the remains as a simple architectural group. Our discussion must concern itself with looking for common features, and attempts to relate such features to the general *probability* – for this is all that seems to be permissible – that these were actually churches. The chapter can then conclude with comments on actual and potential numbers and their geographical distribution. Plans exist, at the moment, for St Pancras phase 1 (Canterbury), Icklingham, Richborough, Silchester, and the two known Verulamium sites. Icklingham, as being by far the smallest, stands out somewhat from the other five.

The argument from internal areas

The concept of the congregational church has already been explored; and if the arguments are accepted, even provisionally, it follows that in late fourth-century Britain one major characteristic of anything claimed to be an intra-mural congregational church should be its capacity (unlike the later Gallarus-type churches in Ireland, and any British counterparts) to accommodate a reasonably-estimated group of Christians for regular worship. At the outside, we can begin to think of things like the Lincoln (Flaxengate) site which, if a church, could have been of basilican plan with a nave of dimensions up to 50ft (14m) wide and (allowing for a narthex and external portico) 100ft (28m) long (fig. 37). This is not impossible, and scant remains of a similar building of very much the same size were reported from York in 1967–8.[91] However, we cannot be sure these were churches. The ones we have selected are on a smaller scale. Some other broad idea, quantitatively, of what might be expected in terms of capacity could be afforded by dimensions of late Roman pagan temples, other than those of cella-and-ambulatory plan; except that as we know different considerations governed the size and nature of their congregations.

Excluding for the moment Icklingham, whose nave as reconstructed in fig. 33 measures only some 12 by 21ft (3.6 by 6.5 m) or the area of a

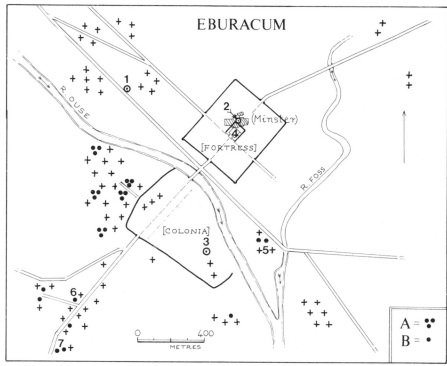

29 York (*Eboracum*), after RCHM, Ramm, and Phillips
  1 Sycamore terrace burial   2 Tile with chi-rho   3 Bishophill (possible churches?)   4
  Principia complex, partly below Minster   5 Castle Yard cemetery   6 The Mount
  cemetery   7 Trentholme Drive cemetery. (Inset, lower right: key. A, groups of plaster
  of gypsum burials (after Ramm)   B, single plaster or gypsum burials)

modern living-room, one can examine the remaining five in terms of
what will be called 'the congregational area'. This implies the main
internal unit, produced when any apses, porches or other rectilinear
outshots are subtracted from the overall ground-plan. Internal side- and
end-divisions, corresponding to the formal *porticus* and *narthex*, are
included, because it will not always be clear how these were physically
divided from the 'nave' – i.e., whether the relevant internal foundations
bore walls, screens, spaced uprights or simple arcading.

  What we then have left is the internal area theoretically available for
congregational use – the congregational area. We have to assume for the
moment that this envisages Christian groups of full members, *ecclesiae*,
numbered in dozens rather than in hundreds.

  Fig. 30 shows the dimensions so plotted. Even with so limited a sample
one can detect a kind of average, or mean, constituting signs of a
common response to a shared function rather than any true module,
about 30 by 42 ft (9.1 by 12.8 m), implying a floor area of 1260 sq.ft

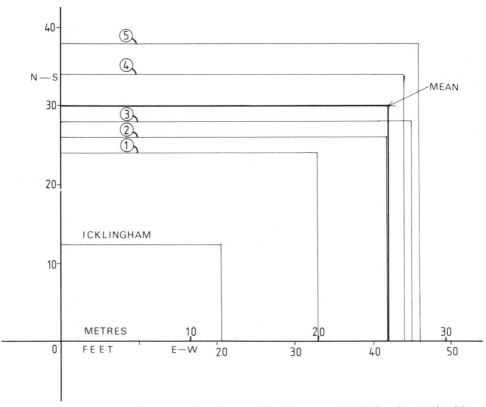

30 Dimensions of congregational areas of five Romano–British churches (with Icklingham church, inset)
    1 Silchester   2 St Pancras phase I, Canterbury   3 Verulam Hills Field   4 Rich-
borough   5 Verulamium, internal SE quarter

(116 m²). The significance of this figure appears to be that, when the same
exercise is applied to seven of the earliest church plans from east and
south-east England in the early seventh century,[92] an appropriate figure
also emerges. This (fig. 31) is of the order of just over 25 feet by just under
44 (7.7 by 13.4 m), giving a floor area on this mean of 1100 sq.ft (102 m²) –
since these first-period Saxon churches are all slightly narrower, the
differences are relatively insignificant. It should also be noted that, as
may have been the case in late Roman Britain taking Icklingham as
representing another type of church, a smaller model was also current.
The mean of St Martins, Canterbury, and the contentious first phase at
Bradford on Avon is about 13 by 27.5 ft (4.2 by 8.4 m), which is nearer to
the Icklingham figure estimated at some 12 by 21 ft.
    Without exploring the notoriously difficult and often subjective topic
of mensuration, it can also be suggested that a third mean, of the same

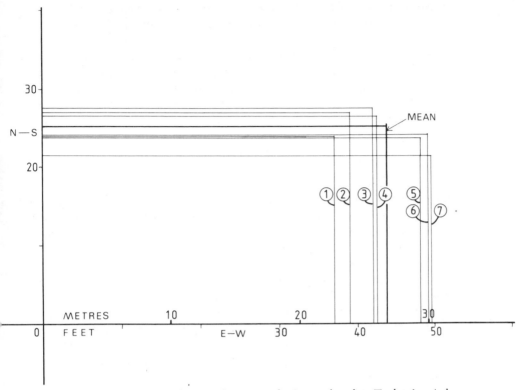

31 Dimensions of congregational areas of seven Anglo-Saxon churches, Taylors' period
A (7th cent.)
   1 Reculver   2 SS Peter & Paul, Canterbury   3 Rochester   4 St Pancras phase II,
Canterbury   5 St Mary, Canterbury   6 St Paul-in-the-Bail, Lincoln   7 Bradwell on
Sea

general order, results from looking at a sample of twelve European
churches (published as being either late fourth or fifth century), where a
figure of 29ft by 42ft 5in (8.8 by 13.0m) can be extracted; this is close to
the Romano–British figure. There is a further possibility, which the
present writer, content to leave future work in other hands, believes now
may be real, that ground-plans of the supposed British churches were
initially pegged out in Roman feet – using the *pes monetalis* of 11.6in
(29.6cm) – and that churches, as public buildings, were liable to be
accorded publicly-used modules. An external nave length of 50 *pedes*
(about 48.5ft, or 14.8m) would, allowing for end-wall thicknesses, or
end foundation-trench widths, produce the observed mean internal
length. (In the case of Icklingham, fig. 33 shows how the inevitable
imprecision of the foundation-trenches, all that it would now be possible
to recover in a modern scientific excavation, does not of itself rule out a

regular or even modular (ratio of 2:3) piece of Romano–British building, the external nave of which could well have been pegged out as 16 by 24 *pedes*.)

All that can be, and all that is, claimed here is that these potential churches from late fourth or very early fifth-century Roman Britain are of the same *order of size* (fig. 32) as those of other buildings, known to have served as congregational churches, in the western parts of the late Roman empire and its successor states. It is also clear that they are *not* of the same order of size as the earliest known (post-Roman) Irish and British churches, discussed in the previous chapter (p. 150 and fig. 18).

Stylistic comments (*cf.* figs. 33–35)

Five of the six buildings could have possessed apses – truly semi-circular or polygonally so – and three actually produced them. At Silchester and probably both the Verulamium buildings the end which corresponds to a sanctuary or chancel is at the *west* (or nearer to west than to east). At so early a period, such placing does not rule out Christian use. The (extramural) church of St Severin, Cologne,[93] is similarly aligned; and Frere has provided a useful discussion in the setting of Silchester.[94]

No particular model need be indicated for such relatively humble buildings. Any details of the Richborough reconstruction, where the addition of a (hypothetical) apse is entirely justified on grounds of analogy, have been given by Brown.[95] The Silchester church, the most complicated one, is examined rather more fully in the next chapter (p. 214) because of what seems to have been a conjoined baptistery, and remarks on the Icklingham stratification appear in the same place (p. 218). There are however aspects of the group, seen particularly in the internal arrangements at the Silchester church, where Sheppard Frere has voiced caution against any over-stressing of parallels and analogies seen at Rome, or places even further eastward, until we have a larger corpus of plans from Gaul and the Rhineland. Simple side-chambers are found, for instance, at St George, Cologne, which appears to be an early church,[96] where they are only partly dictated by the underlying pre-400 pagan temple walls; and also at some early Swiss sites.

The basic ground-plan of the British churches is one of a rectangular chamber, the nave, joined to a constricted terminal outshot, which can be apsidal or rectilinear. With the sole exception of Silchester we simply have no evidence of (for example) the placing of the altar, except for a general indication that it would be likely to stand within that end of the nave nearest to the apse or equivalent. The currency of this ground-plan in the oldest, and most simple, churches over so much of the late Roman world (*cf.* here Ligugé, fig. 22) makes it most unlikely that its source should necessarily be sought in Roman Britain. However, if one wants to revive earlier controversies about the origin of the earliest, non-basilican,

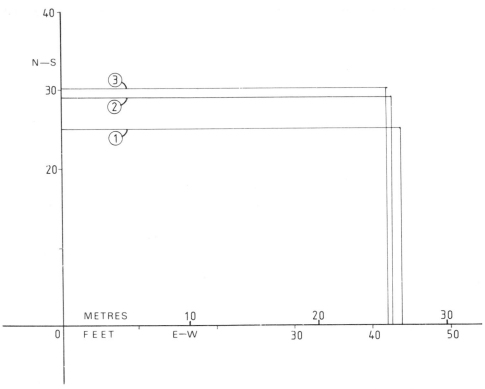

32 Comparison of means of congregational areas
1 Seven Anglo-Saxon churches (fig. 31)   2 Twelve 4th–5th cent. European
churches   3 Five Romano–British churches (fig. 30)

church plans,[97] it can be hinted (for Britain) that there were partial
models to hand in several categories of third- and fourth-century temples
– for example, Mithraea.[98] Plans of these, involving a simple, aligned lay-
out with rectangular body and apsidal termination, perhaps even with
builders' traditional measures of length and width suitable to urban
insulae, could well have provided ideas for Christian temples.

Potential totals, bishops, and distributions
It is on the face of it unlikely that the churches listed here could be all the
potential examples. There are other Romano–British towns where, given
existing finds and the towns' histories, we could expect further churches.
A very rough guide can be offered, by taking the map shown earlier as fig.
17, and distinguished such extra aspects as the presence of Theodosian
fortifications, evidence for the survival (whole or part) of the place-name,
and whether any town is included in those called *civitas* by Bede.[99] The
result (fig. 36) is only a pointer. But it suggests instantly that Carlisle,

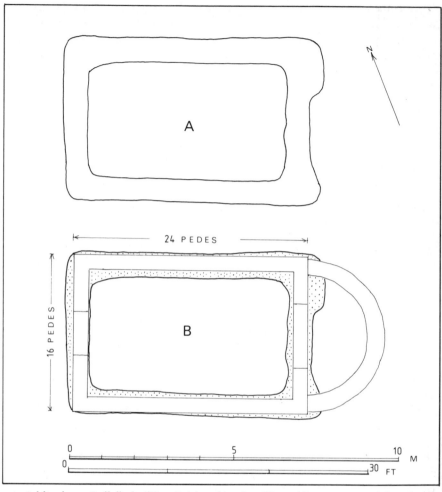

33 Icklingham, Suffolk: building B (church), after West. *Above*, excavated foundation-trenches. *Below*, reconstruction of a late 4th-cent. apsidal church, employing the late Roman *pes* (*monetalis*) as unit

York, Lincoln and London, to which one could perhaps add Corbridge, Catterick, Wroxeter, Cirencester and Winchester, are places to be watched in this light. Ilchester, Exeter and Durobrivae have been mentioned in previous chapters. We have very little idea of what we may be looking for; it is quite possible that York, Lincoln and London each possessed a very much larger intra-mural church in the late fourth century. The York sites that have from time to time been mentioned, both at Bishophill in the south-east part of the colonia (*cf.* fig. 29), include the Roman building with fourth-century pottery underlying St Mary Bishophill Senior church,[100] and in ground adjoining the nearby St Mary

Bishophill Junior church[101] a larger apsidal building closer in size to that at Lincoln, Flaxengate. The cautious interim report on the last-named[102] gives part of a plan which, if hypothetically expanded (as in fig. 37) becomes that of a conventional medium-sized basilica; the disturbed floor had black, red and white tesserae bedded on *opus signinum* (*cf.* Silchester) and there were remains of 'quantities of highly decorated wall-plaster and a fragment of Italian marble'; while the non-domestic nature of this building may be stressed by the total absence, among thousands of tiles excavated there, of any hypocaust tile.

The other guide, to potential *totals*, arises from consideration of the existence of bishops in the early British church. If before 313, as was discussed earlier, the mere existence of a local bishop does not necessarily mean the contemporary presence of any building archaeologically recognisable as a church, it is on the other hand very much more likely that, nearer 400, any city or town in Roman Britain having its own bishop possessed, at the minimum, an intra-mural church. The likely unit of episcopacy would, on analogy, have been any place acting as the centre, focus, or capital of a civitas, an administrative division of the civil diocese of Britannia; to which we have to add London, and the coloniae. Nor does this rule out the possibility that late Roman settlements of different status (Catterick, Corbridge) or those which may have been, even if we cannot show this, equivalent to civitas capitals in the later fourth century (Durobrivae, Chelmsford) were similarly distinguished; and to this, estate churches apart, churches of the kind seen at Icklingham must be added. The potential total is therefore minimally of the order of at least thirty, possibly more, such churches, a high proportion of which ought to be recognisable as such.

Again, as a rough check, we can look to better-documented areas of the late empire.[103] We are presumably dealing, in Britain, with a church hierarchy related as elsewhere to the spatial divisions and sub-divisions of the Roman empire. We have no idea of the true extent of the late fourth-century British population – though it is now clear that it must have been larger than was previously thought[104] – nor what percentage of that population, urban-based in the last decades before 400, was nominally Christian. It can be no more than a guess that in the later Roman period the *urban* population of Britain (at around five per cent of the total population) was about 200,000.[105] On the further assumption that organised *ecclesiae* would tend to be more numerous in the towns, where any form of communal activity would be both eased and heightened, even a mere five per cent of this figure gives us 10,000 urban Christians, devout or nominal; and individual town numbers might range from several thousand in London to a few hundreds in somewhere like Lincoln.[106] Even a hundred Christians probably implies a bishop.

In north Africa, the province of Numidia in the granary belt had some

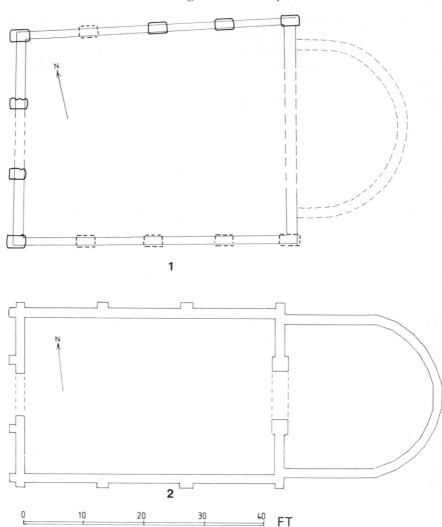

34 Ground-plans of churches, Roman Britain
  1 Richborough, after Brown   2 St Pancras, phase I, Canterbury, after Jenkins

50 bishoprics in 411, roughly one per 1200km². In the Nile, from Latopolis down to the Delta, the figure is one per 2300km². We know that all the North Africa provinces were over-provided with bishops, churches, and separate flocks; and we could look to Hispania, Spain and

35 Ground-plans of churches, Roman Britain
  3 Verulam Hills Field, St Albans, after Anthony   4 Silchester, after Frere and Richmond   5 Verulamium, internal SE quarter, after Wheeler & Wheeler

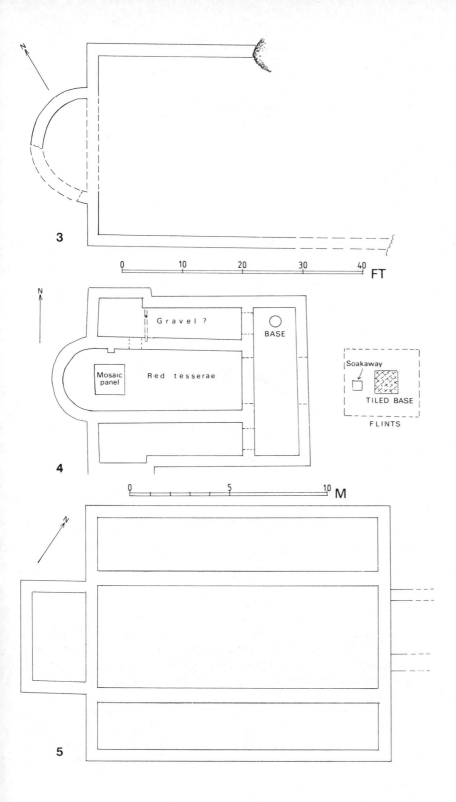

3

0   10   20   30   40   FT

N

Gravel ?

BASE

Mosaic
panel

Red tesserae

Soakaway

TILED BASE

FLINTS

4

0   5   10   M

N

5

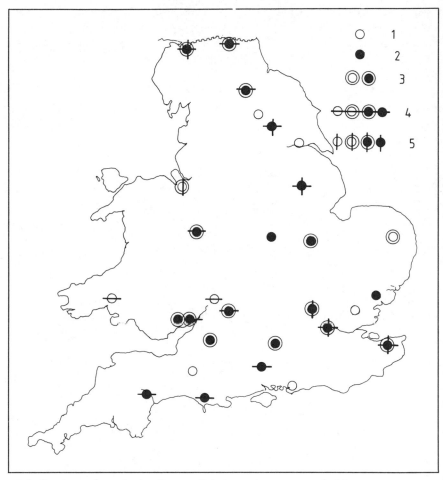

36 Indications of continuity, Roman Britain, major towns and cities
    1 Absence, and 2 presence (1980), of Christian evidences   3 Signs of Theodosian re-
    fortification (after Frere 1978)   4 Place-name survival (*cf.* fig. 44)   5 Place described
    as *civitas* by Bede (Campbell 1979)

Portugal, a diocese whose subsequent Christian history is often instruct-
ively rather like our own in some respects. Spain had complications of
maintained native languages – the people who are now the Basques were
numerous, appear to have resisted Latinity, and were largely pagan to a
late date; but overall the late Roman figure is 96 bishoprics, giving a
density of one per 5300 km².

Britannia is smaller than Hispania, but if one allowed (say) a late
fourth-century picture of 25 bishoprics, this would give a density of one
per 5400 km², in a landscape which *mutatis mutandis* (our forests and
fens standing for the Spanish plateaux and sierras) might just be regarded

as a scaled-down version of Spain. We are guided to the same conclusions; and can allow, with John Mann, that if 'it is impossible to gauge what proportion of the population of Roman Britain became Christian', then '. . . the small number of surviving monuments of the faith is certainly no guide'.

The documented evidence for the British bishops, the later part of which is considered in Chapter 10, begins with the *acta* or proceedings of the Council held at Arles in the south of France in 314.[107] Three British bishops are named – *Eborius* from *civitate Eboricensi*, or York; *Restitutus* from *civitate Londenensi*, or London; and *Adelfius* from *civitate Colonia Londinensium* (or *Lindensium*, if one amends the textual versions – 'the city, Colonia of the people of Lindum = Lincoln'). (Colchester, *Camulodunum*, is not entirely a supportable reading.) There are then two other names, *Sacerdus presbyter* and *Arminius diaconus*; leaving aside any question of whether this is really *sacerdos* 'a bishop', rather than a name, if these two represent a fourth delegation it is from an unnamed place.

The question of 'four delegations' arises because, shortly before this time, the old division of Britain into *Britannia Superior* and *Britannia Inferior*, roughly the southern and northern halves, had given way to a system of four *provinciae* or 'provinces' in the civil diocese. *Inferior* appears to have become *Britannia Secunda* and *Flavia Caesariensis*, the provincial capitals being respectively at Lincoln and York, with their governors of slightly different rank – a *praeses* at Lincoln, a more senior *consularis* at the more important York.[108] In the south, the old *Superior* ('superior' in the sense of being nearer to Rome itself), the division was between *Britannia Prima* and *Maxima Caesariensis*; the latter being known to include London, the former must have embraced some of the west midlands, Wales and the south-west. (After 367, a fifth province, *Valentia*, was created, in the context of Theodosius' reorganisation of the entire defensive system of north Britain in particular; Mark Hassall has suggested[109] that *Valentia*, centred on York, replaced *Flavia Caesariensis*, the name of the latter being kept for a small, new fifth province at the west end of the Wall centred on Carlisle.) The sketch-map (fig. 38) will clarify this. The divisions between the provinces are not ascertainable in any detail; but the Arles list, beginning as it does with London, York and Lincoln, might be thought to include in some guise – perhaps through persons representing an unavailable fourth bishop – a party from the fourth provincial centre. Of the possibilities for this, Cirencester (*Corinium*) is strongest.

British bishops were probably present, though the western episcopal delegates are not named individually, at other councils; Nice in 325, Sardica in 347.[110] At a Council at *Ariminium*, Rimini, in 359, there was a much-cited episode when, of the many bishops present, *tres tantum ex*

Britannia ('three only from Britain') used imperial funds, the publicly-financed system of travel and lodging, because of the poverty of their own resources. Hanson, whose analysis of this anecdote from Sulpicius Severus must command special attention, makes the point that there must have been many more than these three poverty-stricken British bishops in the whole delegation from Britain and that these three constituted an exception – object of comment and discussion – even among their own compatriots.[111] Again we come to the idea that, in the second half of the fourth century, the total of bishops in Britannia may have been in double figures. As we shall see in Chapter 10, the evidence from the fifth and sixth centuries, even in a Britain increasingly confined to its western and northern parts, implies a state of affairs that would hardly be credible unless before 400 there had been a widespread episcopacy. In dealing with Patrick and his times, we shall revert to a related subject; that of the inferences that *metropolitan* bishops, each based on the metropolis or centre of a *provincia* and having authority over other bishops within that *provincia*, probably existed. It would be too early to postulate this for AD 314, but the germ of the system lies within the evidence from that date.

In conclusion, then, we may well be glimpsing a picture of Britain in the last few decades of the fourth century, where Christianity had made sufficient headway, particularly in the major towns, to produce something very close to that state of affairs exhibited in other civil dioceses of the empire in the West. There were urban churches, under bishops, whose dioceses if not fully territorial or all-embracing would have covered the towns or cities and immediately-dependent areas.

We may postulate twenty or more such bishops with intra-mural churches mainly in the known civitas capitals, though only at Silchester and (presumably) Canterbury is it clear that we yet know of these; in coloniae, thinking particularly of the Lincoln site; and with Richborough (in a shore-fort) and Icklingham (a rural settlement) we have examples of other settings. If we wish to look back to history, it must be clear that a synod of such bishops and senior clergy, probably in some numbers, and meeting regularly in some major centre, contacted the Church in Gaul shortly before AD 429; and earlier, when Victricius of Rouen came to Britain, probably in 396, he was able to write that his delay in reaching Rouen to welcome the arrival of holy relics from Milan '. . . is pardonable, and you will forgive me for it; if I have gone to Britain, if I have stayed there, it is to carry out your own orders. The bishops, my brothers in the priesthood, called on me to make peace there. Could I, your soldier, have refused them?'[112] Precisely what dissensions required

---

37 Lincoln, Flaxengate Street site: hypothetical reconstruction of large basilican building (church?), from excavated portion, top right – after Colyer & Jones 1979

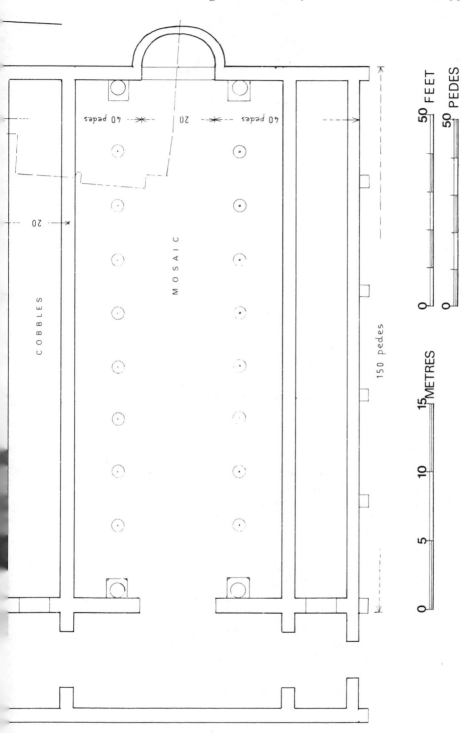

COBBLES

MOSAIC

40 pedes — 20 — 40 pedes

20

150 pedes

50 FEET

50 PEDES

METRES

0 5 10 15

38 The post-367 *provinciae* of Britannia
   Provincial capitals (triple circles) are: *Ca*rlisle, *York*, *Lin*coln, *Cir*encester, and
   *Lon*don. Scheme of names after Mark Hassall; boundaries only schematic

Victricius' presence as an arbitrator or mediator we are not told; but the
clear implication of a British episcopate, sufficiently numerous both to
form opposing parties and to require a Gaulish metropolitan's prolonged
visit, carries us to an equally clear implication of an established Christian
presence – and a corresponding range of actual churches. The examples
we have discussed tell us a certain amount. The analysis of what they
imply may be even more useful, as a guide to the search for, and the
identification of, the missing buildings; some of which in the course of
time, and continued archaeological exploration, cannot fail to emerge.

(*Note*: In *Temples, Churches and Religion in Roman Britain*, ed. Warwick Rodwell (BAR 77, Oxford 1980), which appeared after this book was finished, Philip Crummy argues (264 ff.) that the Butt Road, Colchester, site – just south of '6a' on the map, Rodwell (1977) fig. 9 – may be a Christian martyrium; and Ann Ellison (305–320) suggests that the post-temple, 5th century 'Structure VII' at West Hill, Uley, may be a small Christian church – if so, with timber(?) nave of about 2.4 by 4.8 metres (8 by 16 ft) and north-west apsidal extension.)

CHAPTER EIGHT

Baptism and Baptisteries

Beneath the Water Peeple drown'd,
Yet with another Hev'n crown'd,
In spacious Regions seem'd to go
As freely moving to and fro:
In bright and open Space
I saw their very face;
Eyes, Hands, and Feet they had like mine;
Another Sun did with them shine.
Thomas Traherne (*c*.1637–74) *Felicities*

Christian baptism has from its beginnings been a sacrament replete with mystery. Traherne's poem ('Shadows in the Water') makes the lake surface, on and through which he sees reflections and fantasies, represent a boundary between worlds. The water is both a barrier and a gate. It is in this light that we can also view baptism, as a rite of initiation — in outward terms, to membership of the Church; spiritually, to a new life in Christ. The origins of this *initiatio Christiana* have been continuously sought, in customs of earlier Eastern religions whose followers practised forms of ritual bathing, or lustrations. But the primacy of baptism within the Church's own history, stemming as it does from John the Baptist's own ministry in the river Jordan, makes it unnecessary here to consider it other than in its Christian guise. As J.G. Davies puts it, too, 'It is indeed the richness of meaning with which the rite was invested that distinguishes Christian baptism . . . from the use of water for the purpose of religious purification which is common to so many faiths.'

Both the history [1] and archaeology[2] of baptism reveal much of a ritual which, by the fourth century, had not only come to possess a complicated ceremonial structure, each stage of which had evolved its special vocabulary and meaning, but could also be portrayed in visible symbols drawn from a growing stock of appropriate motifs (*cf*. p. 92). Entry into the water, whether total or token, marked that divide between the old, pre-Christian life, and the new. It was thus a ritual death followed by a re-birth in Christ; and so the soul might be pictured as having been born in the water, like a fish. The baptistery (or 'baptistry' — the former spelling is used here), that is the building designed to house the font or cistern, could appropriately be made to bear a resemblance to a mausoleum, since one of its rôles was to be 'the baptismal tomb wherein the Christian died and rose again with his Lord' (Davies). Any ornament, in mosaic, wall-paintings or relief sculpture, might embody ideas underlining these interpretations; fishes, or the hart (from the favourite baptismal psalm, now no. 42, *Quemadmodum cervus* – 'As the hart panteth after the water brooks, So panteth my soul after thee, O God'); or perhaps Christ as the Good Shepherd; or, in later centuries, some form of the Cross to signify the gift of eternal redemption.

When considering baptism as a rite that may have left detectable traces associated with churches of the fourth and fifth centuries, it is important to understand (and here *adult* baptism is almost entirely implied) how this fitted into the sequence of the Christian life. Those who had decided, or had been persuaded, to seek membership of the local ecclesia did not just turn up one Sunday, so as to speak, clasp hands with the *seniores*, and immediately become full partakers of the Life Eternal. Already by the time of Constantine, an elaborate system of entry had been refined. Persons who sought to become Christians normally started as *catechumens*, and would have to be instructed by scriptural readings, homilies, and some practical training in the rites and duties of the Church. After 313, in a settled urban church, this training-period or *catechesis* may well have been prolonged; and if any of it took place in a church building, we can suppose that it did so at times removed from those of the various major services.

A special 'Hall of the Catechumens' is, as the evidence considered in the last chapter probably makes clear, rather too elaborate a notion for Roman Britain; but catechumens, along with penitents, would on formal occasions be allowed only to stand in a narthex, or some division of the church distinct from the central congregational area holding the altar-table (*cf.* figs. 34, 37).

At an appropriate time, shortly before one of the feasts set aside for baptism (Easter or Pentecost or, in sub-Roman Britain, possibly the Epiphany too), those seeking to be baptised became known as *competentes*, persons by now 'sufficiently prepared' to discard the old life and to be born again. The actual baptism, which in Roman Britain would most probably have been personally supervised by a bishop, may have been preceded by exorcism, during which one of the lower grades of clergy, *exorcista*, expelled any lingering evil spirits with prayers and set formulae. For the baptism proper, the *competentes*, assembled in or by the baptistery, with the bishop, clergy, and their own sponsors, would remove their worldly clothing, and be conducted to the receptacle of water, where the central part of the sacrament would take place. Of the Latin words used to name this receptacle, it is the symbolic *fons*, 'fount (of the new Life)', that has given us our 'font'.

THE METHODS OF BAPTISING

J.G. Davies has carefully set these out;[3] and because they are relevant to an archaeological enquiry, we must distinguish them with the same care. The four principal modes are:

1. *Submersion*; or total immersion, where the candidate goes briefly but entirely below the water, on the model of those baptised by John in the river Jordan.
2. *Immersion*; where the head, as the prime seat of Man's rational and spiritual being, is in some way submerged, with or without the candidate having to stand in the same container of water.
3. *Affusion*; where water, in some quantity, is poured (usually from a container held above it) over the head, and streams down the body – convenience would probably dictate that a candidate stood unclothed within some cistern while this took place.
4. *Aspersion*; where water is merely sprinkled on the head, much as in the present Anglican baptism of infants.

Representations in art of any of these methods are surprisingly rare; but the baptism by affusion of a small boy called Innocens is shown on his late fourth-century tombstone from Aquileia (fig. 39)[4] There is limited evidence for the use of curtains or hanging-screens to enclose the font, and to limit the number of those who would see the candidates in their nudity.[5] The existence of such, dependent from a very simple frame, might also be inferred from discovery of any traces of wooden uprights (e.g., as post-holes) around a receptacle. More positive evidence is provided by nails around the base or edge of a ciborium, a kind of internal roof or ceiling, sometimes dome-shaped, carried on pillars around a font; but this will not apply to Roman Britain. Rarely, too, a second and much smaller basin, beside the font, could be taken as pointing to the subsidiary right of *pedilavium*; the washing of the feet (as Christ washed the feet of the disciples) on leaving the baptismal water. This will be mentioned below.

Baptism had the effect of introducing a person into the body of the Church. Those who had just been baptised were known as *neophytes* (from Greek words meaning 'newly planted'), and as *neofitus, -a*, the term was probably current widely by the fourth century. Several of the Christian gravestones from Trier, notably in the 'southern grave-field' attached to St Matthias (fig. 19), appear to include *neofita* among the wording of their inscriptions.[6] This introduction was, logically, followed by confirmation, as the outward and public ceremony of acceptance. Indeed, until the Middle Ages baptism and confirmation formed a single concept. In some of the earliest churches of the Mediterranean lands, churches more complex in their lay-outs than those of Britain or Gaul, it

1 The Manchester *Rotas Opera Tenet* sherd, shown life-size (*Dept. of Archaeology, Univ. of Manchester*)

2 Emperor Constantine I: the 'York' head, local stone and perhaps executed at York in AD 306 (*Yorkshire Museum*)

3 Constantine I: small onyx (?) head, from Egypt (*Royal Scottish Museum, Edinburgh*)

4 St Albans Abbey, Aerial view from south (*National Monuments Record*)

5 Hinton St Mary, Dorset, mosaic: central roundel with head of Christ (*National Monuments Record*)

Opposite
6 The Walesby (Lincolns.) lead tank: part of frieze with figure scene (*Lincolnshire Museums; City and County Museum, Lincoln*)

7 Ruins of Whithorn Priory Church, aerial view from north – small stone oratory below E end indicated by arrow (*Prof. G.D.B. Jones, Manchester*)

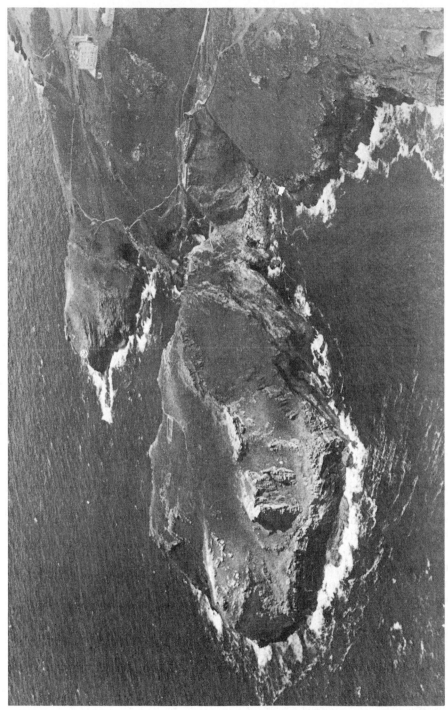

8 The next phase – Tintagel headland, Cornwall, first (?) of the post-Roman Insular monasteries: aerial view from west (*Prof. G.D.B. Jones, Manchester*)

39 Detail from the tombstone of Innocens, Aquileia (4th cent.); water descends on the child from the Holy Ghost as a dove

is possible to argue for the existence within a cluster of ecclesiastical buildings of, not only the church with its narthex or hall for catechumens, but also rooms particularly linked to the baptistery. These might include a final antechamber (*catechumenon* or *exorcisterium*) entered as an immediate preliminary to the baptism; and after the ceremony, perhaps another room (*chrismarion*, *chrismarium*) where the neophytes were then confirmed, the entire rite being completed by the imposition of the bishop's hands and the unction or anointing with *chrism*, a sacred oil.

In the mundane world of archaeological interpretation, we are obliged at any given site to try to decide which particular *form* of baptism may have been used; and, if possible, eventually to argue for the predominance of particular forms within given regions and provinces. It will be clear that total immersion or *submersion* can only take place – apart from such natural settings as a deep river or the sea – in a receptacle of sufficiently large dimensions. Anything more shallow will tend to imply one of the other methods. In western Europe, baptismal cisterns in contexts dated to the fourth and fifth centuries are not infrequently found to have been sunk into the ground (this continues the analogy with the tomb), and to have internal steps. Considerations of the infirmities of elderly competentes apart, this setting would place the celebrant standing slightly higher than the baptismal candidate. These are but some of the clues that might suggest *affusion*.

The predominance of affusion over submersion in the western empire was one conclusion reached, on wider grounds, by Davies, having made a full review of the archaeological remains, most of which were usefully catalogued by Khatchatrian.[7] In early churches in Greece, to name only one area, 'there does not exist a single baptistery of which the font was deep enough to allow the submersion of the candidate'; and this proves generally true, also, of Syria, Palestine, Egypt and North Africa, and of the very few sites in France now supportable as being really early.[8]

Many years ago, Clement Rogers, in what was then a near-exhaustive review of all the archaeological material,[9] concluded that despite the continuous documentary allusions to the desirability of submersion[10] it had in fact been rare, and hardly ever followed. J.G. Davies now believes that, while submersion cannot entirely be ruled out in a very restricted number of early fonts, the general practice would seem to have been either for the candidate to stand in the font and have his head dipped in the water (= *immersion*; it must be said that, in the cases of many such cisterns, this would involve a spectacular feat of gymnastics), or for the water to be poured over his head (*affusion*). In the last case (*cf*. fig. 39), Davies stresses again that where the font was large enough for a candidate to stand wholly within it, the water would flow down over the body.

NUMERICAL SYMBOLISM

The baptistery, whether as rooms or a room within a church, or a quite separate construction, could exhibit in ground-plan (as opposed to ornamentation) another distinct range of symbolism linked to early Christian belief – one involving certain prime numbers and geometric shapes. The ground-plan might, just as a normal architectural convention, be square; but it could also be (truly, or polygonally) a circle, again suggesting ideas of mausolea or circular tombs, and it might also have been planned overall as a hexagon or octagon. Within, the cistern, font, or *lavacrum* could be a circular bowl or tank; but it could equally well be cruciform in plan, or quadrilobate, or else be contained within a hexagonal or octagonal surround.

If the circle takes us back to the idea of the *tomb*, then other plans with their emphasis on the number *four* – square, and especially cruciform or quadrilobate – point to the Cross, and to Christ's death and resurrection.[11] The significance of the numbers *six* and *eight* is also specific. The sixth day (Friday) was that of the Crucifixion, and burial; the eighth, of the Resurrection. A combination, such as a hexagonal cistern within an octagonal baptistery building, places these events against their reflection in the structure of the actual baptism. Study of the corpus of surviving remains[12] shows the probability of different preferences and emphases in different regions. It is worth noting that the octagonal plan seems to have been popular in early Christian Gaul; and both the octagon and hexagon generally in the western parts of the late empire.

The evidence from Roman Britain comes from discoveries made in the field, mostly of recent date, and has not been brought together. It also comes from a limited number of historical or documentary sources; this form of evidence, like that for the types of church construction (Chap. 6), is largely retrospective, but must nevertheless be examined. Certain provisional conclusions about the nature of baptism in Roman Britain do emerge, and they will be summarised at the end of this chapter.

HISTORICAL ALLUSIONS FROM POST-ROMAN BRITAIN

Patrick's writings
If, as will be claimed below, St Patrick's own experience of sacramental and liturgical usages stemmed directly from fifth-century Britain, it is important here that his writings contain a number of allusions to baptism. Looking back over his years in Ireland, he explains (*Conf.* 40) that, as one might have expected in the circumstances of a pioneer church and episcopal mission, he followed Gospel precepts in baptising as many converts as he could make, and as quickly as was possible. Patrick did so to ensure that during and after his own lifetime *ubique essent clerici qui baptizareni et exhortarent populum indigentem* 'that there might be, everywhere, clergy who could baptise and exhort a needy people'. He gives however no indication that during his bishopric anyone save himself had administered baptism. This is only negative evidence; positively, he mentions an Irish lady of noble birth *quem ego baptizi* 'whom I myself baptized' (*Conf.* 42); and in defending himself (*Conf.* 50) against certain base rumours, Patrick asks rhetorically whether, when he had baptised so many people altogether, it could really be said that he had ever done so in the hope of reward.

More specific are passages in the *Epistola*. The core of this letter (Chap. 14) concerns Patrick's reactions to the enslavement of some of his recent Irish converts. These appear to have been notably and perhaps predominantly feminine. They are called, variously, *ancillas Christi baptizatas* (*Ep.* 7) 'the baptised handmaidens of Christ'; *mulierculas baptizatas* (*Ep.* 19) 'poor weak baptised women'; and *captivatas baptizatas* (*Ep.* 21) 'baptised women who have been enslaved'. However, *creduli baptizati* (*Ep.* 17) shows that male converts were also involved.

The assault which had preceded this enslavement took place so soon after a baptismal occasion that those who had taken part in it could be called (*Ep. 3*) *neophyti in veste candida* 'neophytes, (still clad) in the white garment'; and as *crismati* 'persons having been anointed with the chrism', which *flagrabat in fronte ipsorum* 'was still fresh and fragrant upon their very foreheads'. It is also clear (*Ep. 2*) that Patrick, as the officiating bishop, had confirmed (*confirmavi*) these people. (Ludwig Bieler makes the point[13] that the verb *chrismare* (to apply chrism; hence, to complete a baptism) is here used by Patrick at least a century before any other Western writer – for instance, Gregory of Tours.)

The various sacramental aspects indicated here are: baptism, undertaken by a bishop, and culminating in confirmation; the anointing with chrism; use of the correct term 'neophyte'[14] for persons newly instructed and just baptised; and a mention of the white baptismal garment, assumed after the baptism as a symbol of the purity now attending spiritual re-birth. Technically, the adoption of the white robe came after the sacrament, when it was worn for some time; the rather loosely-used term 'candidate' recalls the older, secular Latin *candidatus*, applied to any person standing for a formal office who had made his toga white (*candida*) to indicate his intention.

Whatever practice was followed in fifth-century Ireland, and presumably in contemporary Britain, we have very little to add to Patrick's hints from any source older than about 600. But one particular matter may reside in what Patrick seems to imply in *Confessio* 40. This concerns any extension of the right to baptise, to clerics below the grade of a bishop, particularly in regions where the Church was still thinly spread and communications were difficult. The *acta* of the so-called 'First Synod of Patrick' constitute a document whose date, if clearly later than Patrick's own day, is a matter of some contention.[15]

Sections 24 and 27 have the effect of circumscribing the powers of a *novus ingressor*, a cleric who arrives as a newcomer in a diocese or monastic community or area administered by a given church. They state that he must not administer baptism, until he has received permission from the bishop, on pain of excommunication. These rules appear to depict a sixth-century world in which clerics as well as bishops could undertake baptism. The oldest of the Irish Penitentials, that ascribed to St Finnian or Vinnianus,[16] shows some concern about the provisions for *infant* baptism, the history of which goes far back in the Church[17] – particularly where sick or moribund children were involved. In this Penitential, we find that clerics do indeed have a duty to baptise by this period (sect. 48) – though mere monastic brethren are forbidden to do so (sect. 50); and the canonical ability to baptise forms one of the distinctions of the offices of both priests and deacons (sect. 49).

The only indication in such sources of what were considered as the appropriate times of year for general baptism occurs in the 'Second Synod of St Patrick'.[18] Here, the solemn feasts of Easter, Pentecost and the Epiphany are named, but this compilation may be no older than the seventh century.[19]

Augustine and the British Bishops

These hints from early Ireland are apposite to Bede's account of an event that took place about 600.[20] Augustine, on Pope Gregory's instruction, had arranged a meeting with the bishops of the British; and we learn that this was believed to have taken place at Augustine's Oak, somewhere that has been traditionally identified as Aust-on-Severn but is probably a now-untraceable locality presumably in the west of England.[21] At this meeting, disagreement soon arose, mainly on the score of liturgical custom and practice. A second meeting was arranged; and at this, the British party, depicted as mainly from Wales, were told that their practices were in sorry contrast to those generally followed in the Church, notably in regard to reckoning the correct dates at which to celebrate Easter (p. 334), and the performance of baptism.

Exactly what British divergence gave rise to this second charge is not made clear. If Bede knew it, he nowhere explains it; and this has been much discussed.[22] It might have arisen, as Hugh Williams supposed, simply because the British adhered to some older usage. The most likely explanation is that, while the British and probably the Irish followed all the liturgical stages of baptism, the concluding imposition of hands, anointing of the neophyte's forehead with chrism, and the confirmation – those parts of the sacrament which confirmed full membership of the Church – could on occasions be performed, not by a bishop, but by priests and even deacons.

If Augustine had become aware of this, he would have seen it as an uncanonical departure from the norm – the kind of thing otherwise to be linked with heretical churches, or such equally archaic regions as rural Spain. Since the fifth century, it had been constantly held that confirmation at the conclusion of baptism could only be performed by a bishop.[23] Baptism undertaken by the late sixth-century British Church might therefore be called partly invalid. Bede, who from his knowledge of the limited contact between Christian Northumbria and the British Christians to their west, may have had some inkling of this, makes Augustine urge the British bishops *ut . . . conpleatis* 'that you may *complete* the ministry of baptism according to the manner of the Holy Roman Apostolic Church'.

The death of Kentigern

An unexpected glimpse of what may well have been a baptismal ceremony in sub-Roman North Britain was brought to light, with characteristic ingenuity, by the late Monsignor David McRoberts.[24] The central figure is Conthigirnus or 'Kentigern', first-recorded bishop of Strathclyde, and later the patron saint under both his name and the Anglicised hypocoristic 'Mungo' of the diocese of Glasgow. There is broad agreement that Kentigern was historical, a North British aristo-crat of the sixth century, who became a bishop and probably did die around the time of his recorded obit in AD 612.[25] The main source is a Life composed *c.*1180 by Jocelyn, a monk of Furness. Behind this must lie some older compilation; and this in its turn may have been drawn from oral tradition preserved around the saint's shrine (now Glasgow Cathedral), or even a hypothetical 'Oldest Life' – to Kenneth Jackson,[26] no older than *c.*1000, to MacQueen however[27] a production of the seventh century. That Jocelyn's account included material, and whole episodes, relating to Kentigern and his times, which Jocelyn simply did not understand because these tales embodied the customs and traditions of a very much earlier order of Christianity, is a contention separately advanced,[28] and one taken up again by McRoberts.

The episode that concerns us is the death of Kentigern, said to be extremely old (185 years) and now being prepared by an angel for a death of especial comfort, as a reward for his long and virtue-filled life. It is the Octave of the Feast of the Epiphany, a day long marked out by Kentigern for holding annual baptismal ceremonies. A warm bath is prepared. Kentigern, placed in this bath by his followers, falls asleep in the Lord; all his brethren who bathe themselves in the same water, while it is still warm, are similarly translated to glory. Kentigern's body is then interred on the right of the altar in his church, and the brethren in the external burial-ground.

In analysing this curious tale, exceptional in hagiography, McRoberts began with the date (13 January; this was later kept as the Feast of St Kentigern), associated as part of the Epiphany with baptism because of the tradition that it was earlier the day of Christ's baptism in the Jordan. The story might thus be seen, not as a death tale, but as a description, grossly distorted and garbled in transmission, of the last annual baptismal service carried out by Kentigern as bishop. The stone bed, or *lectulus*, from which Jocelyn makes the saint deliver his farewell speech represents the *cathedra*, the episcopal chair or throne, from which a bishop would deliver the final catechetical instruction to the group of catechumens who were about to be baptised. The bath – variously called *lavacrum*, *vasculum* and *balneum* – is not further described; but recalling, as McRoberts says, that 'mid-January is never very warm in Glasgow'(!) the provision of warmed water, when a frail old bishop would be obliged to stand in the cistern along with the candidates, is reasonable. McRoberts proposes that historically Kentigern may have collapsed during precisely such an Epiphany baptism – which he might well have preferred to hold on 6 January, the Epiphany feast proper – and to have died a week later, on the Octave. Jocelyn, partly from his own style, but mainly because of his failure to understand very much older source-material, built up his 'Bethesda-type miracle' out of what began as a straightforward description of Kentigern's last baptismal service.

The Life of Samson

The Kentigern story apart, there is little that can be regarded as illuminating here in the older stratum of the lives of British saints. A partial exception may be the Life of Samson (of Dol), a Breton composition of the seventh century that covers the career of one who had worked earlier in his native Wales, Cornwall and Armorica.[29] For all its crudity, this Life appears to hold a restricted core of historical matter. Two largely incidental passages, which refer to Britain in the sixth century, seem again to stress the rôle of the bishop in baptism.

In the first (I.50), Samson encounters a crowd of pagans worshipping a stone idol in North Cornwall, and reveals Divine power to them by reviving an apparently dead youth. The pagan chief – and here the Life telescopes what would have been a longer period of instruction and conversion – *omnes ad confirmanda eorum baptismata a sancte Samsone venire fecit*, a tortured piece of Latin translateable as 'made all his people undergo first baptism and then confirmation by saint Samson'. In the second passage (II.7), Samson is visiting Dubricius, a saintly bishop in south Wales; he attends to an unfortunate young deacon who belongs to Dubricius's spiritual family. In order to please his friend Dubricius, Samson *suum crisma . . . unde officium episcopatus adimplebat hilariter eidem diacono praecipit dari* 'saw to it that his chrism, through which he used to fulfil his office as a bishop, was with gladness given to this same deacon'. The verb *adimplere*, even in this setting, must carry the force of 'to do something properly; to fulfil an action entirely'. If this means no more than that the Breton author wished to portray his hero as canonically wholly regular, it perhaps implies also an awareness that not all baptisms in Britain at this period culminated in episcopal confirmations.

Other miscellaneous allusions

Very little light is shed on the actual modes of baptism, as they were defined earlier. In the Kentigern story, it is not made clear whether the saint and his catechumens would have stood ankle-deep, knee-deep or waist-deep in their *balneum*, nor precisely how baptism was effected. When the author of the eighth-century poem, *Miracula Nynie Episcopi*,[30] a composition that draws some elements from much earlier Whithorn tradition, claims that Nynia's Galloway converts *merguntur* 'were immersed' at their baptisms, this is hardly a factual guide. Rivers were certainly used, or were believed to have been used. In Constantius' Life of Germanus, subsequently given fresh currency by Bede,[31] the story of the battle between the British (led by the Gaulish bishops) and some Saxons begins with an assembly at a makeshift camp. Lent is being spent, with homilies, as a prelude to a mass baptism which takes place on Easter Day. There is a river, which is to prove deep enough to drown many of the fleeing pagan enemies. In its waters, the British militia was presumably baptised *en masse*. The British assembled *madidus baptismate* 'soaking wet from the baptism'; and they then celebrated Easter, after which they began the battle, many of them still *recens de lavacro* 'fresh from the font'. Though not strictly relevant to any consideration of British practice, we can recall Bede's account of Paulinus in Northumbria,[32] and how during six years or so Paulinus undertook similar mass baptisms of the Northumbrians ('he washed them in the waters of regeneration') in the rivers Glen at Yeavering and Swale at Catterick.

For Gaul in the sixth and seventh centuries, O.M. Dalton[33] brought together the many, if conventionalised, references in Gregory of Tours' *History of the Franks*. The baptisms singled out by Gregory – that of the Merovingian king Clovis is the best-known – may relate to Gaul in late antique times, but in general they are apposite to fifth-century Britain. As a bishop himself, and a traditionalist at heart, Gregory saw these occasions very much from an episcopal standpoint. This is notably so with regard to the application of confirmatory chrism at the conclusion of the sacrament. There is mention of the newly-baptised *in albis* 'in their white robes'[34] – these were traditionally made from linen, so as to be free from wool or any animal fibre. Insofar as Gregory is specific, his material permitted Dalton to conclude that 'the *immersion* of the ancient texts does not mean *submersion*; it means *affusion*'. The bishop normally stood at the side of the basin or cistern. As soon as the priest had performed his part, the bishop stepped down, received the newly-baptised, and applied the chrism; and Dalton points out that this must be the action meant by such phrases as *suscipere de sacro lavacro* 'to receive (a person) from the holy font', which Gregory frequently employs.

Summary
Baptisms in late Roman Britain, as far as this evidence takes us, were probably no different in their essence from baptisms anywhere else in the late empire. Where, after the fifth century, divergences began to appear and to give rise to comment, they may have done so because of the relative isolation of both Britain and Ireland, and the relative absence of major urban centres where norms could be maintained and followed. Though the use of seasons other than Easter and Pentecost were progressively condemned by Church councils in the fifth and sixth centuries, as inappropriate and out of step, it is possible that a local

preference for the Epiphany as well reflects a fourth-century fashion continued in Britain. As for the erosion of the bishop's particular rôle, this was a development not confined to Britain. By 398, the Council of Toledo recorded[35] that in some places and provinces – this may have been aimed at Spain, but Britain would be just as apposite – *presbyteres* were irregularly blessing the chrism, and even deacons were known to have been giving it to neophytes. It was decreed, obviously with some reluctance, that in the absence of any bishop presbyters might be allowed to give the chrism. If Gildas' picture of the state of the British episcopate in the early sixth century is only partly accurate, we begin to see how there could have been occasions when the entire ceremony – right up to the chrismation and the confirmation – would have to be entrusted to an isolated cleric below the episcopal order.

The textual guidance offered to the archaeologist may be sparse, but it contains particular hints and clues. By 400, and *a fortiori* after that stage, provisions for baptism in Britain need not always have been linked to urban churches, under their own bishops, of the sort examined in previous chapters. The special (and probably not very typical) instances of mass baptisms in rivers apart, we could expect isolated rural baptisteries to have made an appearance. There is a distinct probability that, whether or not the candidate had water applied to him only once, or thrice ('Trine Immersion') in the separated names of the Father, Son and Holy Spirit, total submersion was *not* the common practice. Affusion seems to have been by far the most likely mode of baptism, in Britain as in Gaul. In an archaeological or material sense, then, any search for the equivalents of our late or sub-Roman fonts and cisterns should bear this conclusion in mind.

Lastly, we might infer that baptism continued to be a major Christian event – this is just implicit in Patrick's *Epistola* – performed only at intervals, and among a scattered and predominantly rural populace. Baptisteries, or any structures specifically intended to house such fonts or cisterns, might then be expected to show characteristics less substantial than those of any contemporary churches.

THE ARCHAEOLOGY OF ROMANO–BRITISH BAPTISM

Among the various sites considered as those of churches, three – at Silchester, Richborough and Icklingham – can be claimed to possess baptisteries of a kind. Attention must also be drawn to the Roman villa-house complex at Chedworth in Gloucestershire, and to recent discoveries at Witham (Essex). The evidence of the growing class of lead tanks or cisterns of the 'Icklingham' type, some of which bear Christian symbols, must be assessed; and the implications of a small but very remarkable relief-scene on one of them, from Walesby in Lincolnshire, will be fully examined.

Silchester (figs. 35, 40)

The church within the Roman town of *Calleva*, Silchester, is a small aisled building aligned east-west, the western end terminating in a semi-circular apse, the eastern in a narrow north-south compartment internally some 7 by 25 ft (2.1 by 7.6 m) and having the appearance of a narthex, or ante-room (figs. 24, 35). If as Richmond and Frere both thought the largely-ruined circular foundation within the north end of this narthex was the base of a table for offerings, accessible to unbaptised, and no other special features were met with inside this narthex, it seems clear that there is no room for any internal provisions for baptism.

To the east of the church, on the same axis and only 6 ft (2 m) from the outer west wall, lies an enigmatic feature. This has been reconstructed as a rectangular platform (fig. 35) or setting of flint blocks, measuring just under 11 ft (3.3 m) north-south, and 14 ft (4.3 m) east-west, with on its centre a base of large tiles measuring some 4 ft (3.2 m) square. Immediately to the west of this base is a small pit, about 20 in (0.5 m) across and 3 ft (1 m) deep; carefully built with flints and tiles, clearly intended as some kind of soakaway, and forming, as Richmond said, an integral part of the larger structure.[36]

From the position, the formal lay-out, the proximity to the narthex, the provision of drainage, and the integration in the overall plan and style of the church, one may conclude – particularly in the absence of any alternative – that these remains present themselves in the light of a baptismal arrangement. This has not always been agreed. The excavators of 1892 were positive[37] that this was 'clearly the place of the *labrum* or laver, in which the faithful used to wash their hands and faces before entering the church, and the shallow pit in front was probably covered by a pierced stone, and served to carry off the waste water'.

Frere in his very full discussion sets out the objections to seeing these remains as those of a 'detached baptistery'. They comprise: (1) the unsuitability of the tiled base as a stand for any kind of baptismal cistern which, 'since the rite was by immersion', would have to have stood to such a height above this base that steps – of whose necessary substructure no trace was found – would have been placed beside it; (2) the general unconformity with baptismal basins of 'almost all late Roman churches', which are sunk into the ground, and down into which one had to step; (3) the absence of any traces of wooden sill-beams, implying some enclosing shed or building, around the edges of the flint platform; and (4), the observation that any such baptistery 'would have been inconveniently close to the main door of the church'. He therefore concluded that the alternative interpretations were either, as St John Hope suggested in 1892, the base of a *labrum* or laver; or 'an extremely unusual arrangement for apparently open-air baptisms of the most public kind on open ground close to the city centre'. This latter he rejected because of the sheer unlikelihood, voiced by Radford, of 'nude candidates for baptism thus climbing into an open-air, above-ground baptismal piscina'.[38] Few and distant as any parallels for such an external laver are, and then entirely from the east Mediterranean, Frere somewhat reluctantly accepted this as the explanation.

If one assumes, as has been done already, that the building is a Christian church, and that successive excavations have been sufficiently extensive to exclude anything else within reasonable proximity that might be seen as a baptistery, then perhaps one can look again – as George Boon suggested[39] – at Frere's particular reasons for rejecting the flint platform with its tiled base in this light.

We cannot, as a start, by any means be so positive that immersion was the normal mode of baptism in late Roman Britain, and the arguments set out earlier in this chapter point much more readily towards *affusion* as the most likely rite. Secondly, the argument that the Silchester remains do not conform to the expected would carry more weight, were it not that (as Frere himself points out) we know virtually nothing of what the Romano–British arrangements were, and very little of cases in contemporary Gaul.

Thirdly, as to any enclosing structure, one can envisage something fairly light, entirely in woodwork, that could have sufficed to give privacy; and could even have been put up (and then taken down and stored) only at the one or two times in a year when needed. Richmond himself is reported[40] as having assumed something on these lines. Boon considers that 'there can hardly be any other explanation to account for the preservation of a straight edge of flintwork' (this is around the rectangular platform: fig. 40) 'on the South and East at least'.[41] If such a shed had been used, the total weight distributed upon sill-beams, whether carried upon the edges of the flint platform, or immediately around them, would almost certainly have been insufficient to leave detectable traces for the excavators of 1961, still less those of 1892. Lastly, the objection that the remains are inconveniently near the church disappears, if one agrees with Boon[42] that this is precisely what so small a postulated structure must imply. If all that were needed was room enough for three or four to gather and to perform the sacrament with perfect seemliness, we can picture the candidates for baptism preparing for the ceremony in the narthex, and crossing the short intervening space, either under some cover, or bundled up in wraps.

The conclusion is not entirely satisfactory, and the matter of any actual font or cistern will occupy us again below; but the present writer is on balance inclined to regard these remains as those of a late fourth-century baptistery, virtually conjoined to the church.

Richborough (figs. 26, 40)

P.D.C. Brown's interpretation of old features here rested, not upon the re-exacavation, but on a skilled digest[43] of earlier records from a long period of investigations (*cf.* figs. 26 and 34). At a point centred about 25 ft (7.5 m) north-east of the external north-east angle of the church, Bushe-Fox found during his 1923 season a tile-built structure just below the surface. This was encountered in a long trial-trench taken diagonally across the north-west interior of the fort. The structure[44] comprised a thick stone and cobble foundation, on which tile-and-mortar walling had been raised to form a hexagon with six incurved faces; externally measuring 7 ft 6 in by 6 ft 6 in (2.3 by 2 m), and enclosing an elongated hexagonal cavity some 3 ft 2 in by 2 ft (1 m by 60 cm). The internal cavity floor and the inner and outer faces of the hexagonal surround had been coated with a hard pinkish plaster. On the eastern side, a later cut or gash made through the walling suggested a secondary removal of a (?) lead inlet or outlet pipe. The whole construction was obviously meant to hold water, and Bushe-Fox thought it might have been a garden tank, or a fountain. Two of the opposed, incurved, external faces of the hexagon had at some stage been blocked or filled to produce a straight external face, and also to thicken the walls at these points as if to carry some small superstructure. In 1923, in terms of the occupation-sequence at Richborough, this whole feature was considered as both 'high' and 'late'.

Brown's paper cites various and appropriate European parallels to show that this is most likely to have been a font or baptismal cistern. (The garden-tank hypothesis collapses when one sees that there is no evidence of houses with gardens anywhere inside the fort walls.) The reconstruction of the church proposed by Brown (fig. 34), in itself eminently reasonable, rests on the foundation-piers which, because they were masonry, were left standing by the earlier excavators.

As was suggested earlier, there is nothing objectionable to any such reconstruction which postulates a timber-work church of *c.*400 or later resting on these piers; but the piers remind us that during 1924 some three *feet* of mixed topsoil were removed, wholesale, from the northern half of Richborough's interior, as a preliminary to exposing deeper, earlier, and presumably more exciting levels. Only such masonry structures (devoid of context) were left upstanding, for more leisurely examination. One can conclude that the 'font' was of the same period as the church; and that if the church were in timber, the (probably) slighter requirements around the font, making an isolated baptistery, would also have been in wood, all and any traces having been unceremoniously shovelled away. As a font or baptismal cistern (fig. 40), this is quite acceptable, and Brown produces appropriate parallels to make the point.

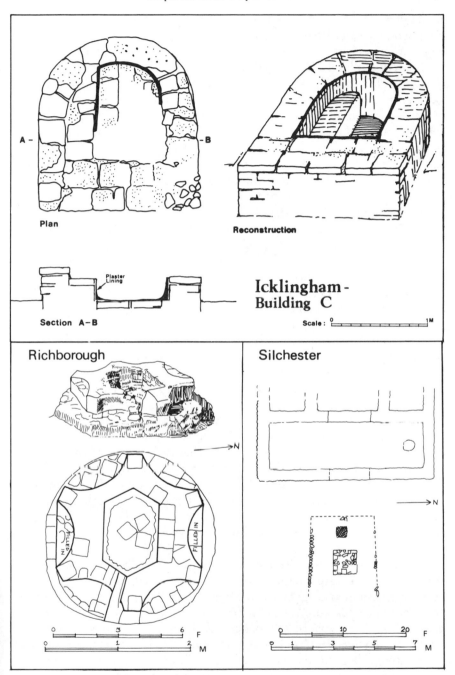

40 Fonts, cisterns or baptisteries, Roman Britain
  Icklingham, building C (Stanley West's drawing, 1976). Richborough, after T. May,
  1923. Silchester, after Richmond.

Icklingham

The sequence here can be briefly recapitulated from Stanley West's report.[45] The little building regarded as a church (fig. 33), and the associated, probably late fourth-century, graves, all lay above or were cut through a thin chalk layer. This layer sealed both an earlier secular occupation on the same site, and a large circular pit, containing finds, some of which might point to the destruction of a pagan shrine or similar monument. About 30 ft (9 m) due east of the church, and more or less on its east-west axis, was the structure marked as 'Building C'.[46] The linear or horizontal association is important; because this structure unfortunately lies beyond, and outside, the edge of the chalk layer, and therefore its contemporaneity with the church (West's 'Building B') has to be assumed.

Building C (fig. 40) can be described as a D-shaped cistern made of coursed tiles, which 'would appear to have been set in the ground'; i.e., was sunk. Internally, a third of its area was taken up by a shallow step, and the whole inner face showed traces of a white plaster lining. The cistern measured internally 5 ft 7 in (1.7 m) east-west, and 5 ft 3 in (1.6 m) north-south; as recovered, with some of its walling gone, it was only about a foot (30 cm) deep.

The excavators considered, from traces which they found immediately around it, that this cistern had originally been incorporated within a larger and more substantial building, which was 'probably to be associated with the fragmentary wall footings around it'; but it was not physically possible to recover enough for a convincing plan of any such enclosing construction. On the other hand, its nature, as timber-work on rough masonry footings, may be suggested by some of the miscellaneous finds recovered only about nine feet to the north-west, within the lead tank unearthed in 1971.[47] These finds included iron fittings – hinges, hinge-pins, iron nails, and a couple of small saw-blades – that could point to the dismantlement of a light wooden shed or something similar; which, from the state of the door-hinges, 'must have been burnt away to leave the ironwork in shape and nails in position'.

Taken together, these discoveries – in the most likely chronological order, from Silchester, Icklingham and Richborough – could very well represent formal arrangements for baptism, or baptisteries of a kind. At Icklingham and Richborough actual cisterns were found; at Silchester, the base for a (?) portable equivalent. At Icklingham and Silchester (the evidence having been destroyed in 1923 at Richborough) we can postulate timber baptistery sheds or buildings. We cannot tell how permanent these *tabernacula* were, or whether it was the custom to put them up and take them down again, once or twice a year.

Witham

The most recent discoveries are those initially reported[48] from Ivy Chimneys, Witham, Essex, a site still under excavation. It lies about 10 miles (16 km) north-east of Chelmsford, *Caesaromagus*, in an area of known Roman occupation close to the London–Colchester Roman road.

Within an irregular and perhaps trapezoidal ditched enclosure or *temenos*, comparable perhaps to that at Gosbecks in the same district,[49] traces of a complex structure about 40 ft (12 m) square and aligned approximately north-south may be those of a second-century Romano–Celtic temple (over an Iron Age predecessor). It had a double entrance, and faced NNE into the temenos enclosure towards a large, artificial sub-rectangular hollow or depression. This is explained as being a pond, constructed in the third century, floored with tiles, and fed by natural springs led in through gullies.

At some time in the fourth century, this pond was summarily filled up, using occupation debris, and including what could be votive offerings from the (now destroyed?) temple. North-west of the pond, and 60 ft (18 m) north of the front of the temple, there is a fairly large shallow depression, filled with gravel, and showing signs of much human use. In the centre of this, amid a complex of post-holes, what may be another baptismal cistern has now been found.

Its floor, made of Roman tiles set in *opus signinum* laid over clay, forms an octagon about 6 ft (2 m) across. The side-walls are of brick – two courses remained – making up an external octagonal shape as well, with an inner depth now some 2 ft (60 cm). The outer faces were supported against the general gravel surroundings within a square setting, having clay packed against this brick walling and a wooden box-like arrangement around the clay. There were traces of four post-holes, one at each corner of the clay-and-wood square.

In the wider context of the site, work during 1979 revealed, 100 ft (30 m) to the ENE across the filled-in pond, the extreme western end of a masonry building. Most of this building will lie further to the east, outside the area of current excavation; but the west end proves to be apsidal, and therefore raises the possibility that this may be another church, on the model of (say) Silchester. The whole setting, with its ill-defined secular occupation, signs of a pagan temple destroyed in the late Roman period, and hint of a detached baptistery involving a masonry cistern in a flimsy building, is bound to recall the shape of things at Icklingham. (For what it may be worth, Witham and Icklingham are about 38 miles, or 60 km, from each other.)

Chedworth

The slight evidence for late Roman Christianity at this substantial Cotswold villa estate has already been mentioned (pp. 106, 126). There is nothing within the excavated range of buildings to suggest an estate church of Lullingstone character; there was a small Romano–Celtic temple a short distance from the villa house,[50] and another structure, a small building north-west of the house found in 1864 and destroyed by a railway cutting in 1890,[51] produced a domed niche with internal scallop-shell canopy. It may have been ritual (a shrine?) but can hardly be claimed as Christian.

Immediately on the north-east side of the villa-house complex, however, set back into the hill slope there was (and is) a fine natural spring, feeding an octagonal basin set within a small apsidal building. The water was piped from here and fed through a junction-box into the house; it still supplied the custodian's lodging. Sir Ian Richmond felt clear that this was a little shrine: it 'must certainly have served as both a pleasaunce and a shrine' and in the latter capacity would have been a Nymphaeum, dedicated to a tutelary water-sprite.

Nevertheless, late in the fourth century, some of the stone slabs that originally formed the rim of this octagonal reservoir were decorated with small neat carved chi-rho symbols[52] (*cf.* figs. 4.7; 5.13). These were not subsequently left in situ. One was found in the steps leading to the west wing baths, and another in the north bath-suite; the third (unlocated) is now in the site museum. As Goodburn points out, it is a puzzle to know when (and one might add, why) these stones, having been so marked, were re-used; possibly the proprietor's family once Christianised their shrine, and successors eschewed the new religion. Chedworth is virtually within the western zone of revived paganism indicated in fig. 48.

There is still the implication that, at some late fourth-century phase, this Chedworth Nymphaeum – whose importance, housing and controlling the sole and extensive water-supply, can hardly have been less than that of the family *lararium* – was overtly made Christian. It is at least arguable that for a period it may have served as a ready-made baptismal cistern, perhaps upon the conversion of the household and the estate workers.

The lead tanks or cisterns

These objects, mentioned in earlier chapters, make up a class which if largely homogeneous has not been fully explained. Ignoring an atypical outlier (from Low Ireby, Cumberland),[53] most of them have been found in Roman contexts or as chance discoveries in south-east and eastern Britain, the greatest concentration being in East Anglia. Such a pattern happens to be something like that of the distribution of Roman lead coffins and caskets.[54] It must be irrelevant to the *source* of the lead, the most likely areas for the mining of which – with cupellation to extract any silver – would be the Mendips[55] and to a lesser extent the Peak District of Derbyshire.

Though lead was produced in considerable quantity for a variety of uses (including water-pipes) and in the later Roman period was much in demand as a component of pewter, it was not necessarily a cheap substance. The finds of these tanks in the predominantly Romanised parts of Lowland Britain may reflect the uneven emphasis of both purchasing-power and fashion. The tanks themselves are large circular objects, holding 25–45 imperial gallons (115–205 litres), are 2–3 ft (60 cm–1 m) in diameter, and with sides 1–2 ft (30–60 cm) in height. As far as is known, tanks in this form are peculiar to Roman Britain.

Many of them bear decoration, produced by impressing wooden stamps (*cf.* fig. 13.2) into the face of the sand-mould bed.[56] In this respect there is a link, particularly as regards the use of 'cable-moulding' and the linear arrangement of ornament, with the decoration seen on Romano–British lead coffins and ossuaria.[57] As was noted in an earlier chapter, four of the tanks exhibit the Constantinian chi-rho, in one case flanked with A and W; another, now lost, may have had a solitary alpha upon it; and a sixth, from Walesby, further discussed below, has a figured scene with what appears to be a baptism. Two of the chi-rho tanks were found at Icklingham, one of them so close to the church and supposed baptistery cistern as to suggest an immediate and intimate relationship.

No one, clear, obvious functional use suggests itself. The varying liquid capacities do not seem to fall into any graduated scale of volume measurement, or reveal any common module; nor does the often-repeated 'X' motif in the ornament seem to be numeration. If these tanks were to be viewed as commonplace commercial containers, then given the vast amount of material from Romano–British excavations there are still relatively few of them counting fragments, a minimum total of sixteen, so far. Further aspects of the tanks, as a group, will be explored in Christopher Guy's forthcoming paper.[58] The existence of the specifically Christian ornament, the context at Icklingham, and the lack of any functional explanation, all raise the supposition that these are ritual (non-functional, in the secular, domestic and industrial senses); and are linked to Christian use. What that use may be have been will be discussed below; but one particular tank requires examination.

The Walesby Tank (Pl. 6)

This, unhappily fragmentary, object was recovered in the course of ploughing – an activity which damaged the surviving part – at Walesby, near Market Rasen, Lincolnshire.[59] Entire, it would have been about 3 ft (1 m) across, and about 20 in (0.5 m) deep. What now survives is part of the side, or wall, with a linear chi-rho, probably equidistant between upright bands of double cable-moulding. Above the chi-rho, centred between the bands, and dependent from just below the rim, is a unique figure scene. This scene may originally have occupied three horizontal panels, all three being contained and recessed within a simple rectangular frame; these internal panels were contained and divided by representations of four architectural columns. The panel on the (viewer's) left is missing, and a gash made by a plough cuts diagonally across the lower part of the central panel.

The right-hand panel (fig. 41) shows three standing figures – men in cloaks and tunics. The central panel is less clear. Jocelyn Toynbee sees it as containing a naked woman, a robe slipping from her right shoulder, and standing between two other 'thickly veiled and draped' ladies (the hair-styles alone permit these to be identified as female). 'And was there a scene of the actual baptism in the left-hand portion of the frieze that is

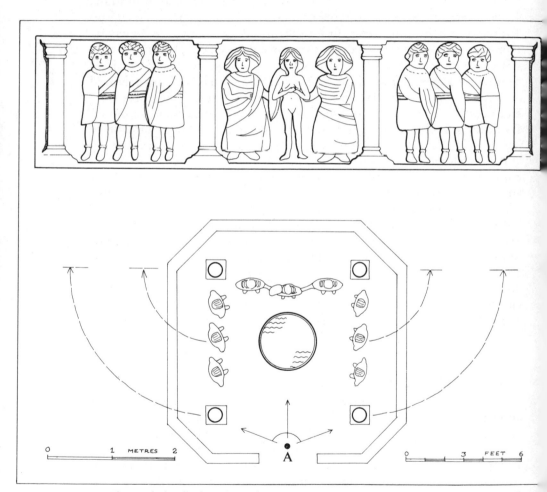

41 The Walesby lead tank – above, reconstruction of the frieze; below, plan of hypothetical baptistery involved (the viewer's standpoint is marked A)

lost?' she wondered;[60] suggesting that the columns indicate the interior of 'perhaps a church or baptistery'.

This is sound guidance. But it could also be suggested that what Toynbee describes as 'the naturalistic and wholly unbarbaric style', indicative of a 'competent and careful worker', might rather imply a symmetrical composition of the pattern A–B–A. The present writer regards the *central* panel as showing an actual baptism about to take place. The flanking figures, who may (as seen on the right) have been repeated on the missing left panel, are not necessarily either clerics or catechumens. They could represent the members of an *ecclesia*, attending this sacrament and forming an audience to support the baptism of a female *competens*, who is shown about to step into a lavacrum (it is not now possible to be sure about any of the detail at the level of the feet).

That the scene, here drawn out in fig. 41, does in some fashion represent (as Toynbee of course saw) the interior of a building is certain. It seems most probable that it shows the interior of a baptistery. This need not lie further afield than Roman Britain. The use of architectural columns to frame and to punctuate a frieze is a commonplace cliché in late Roman art – in British Christianity, we need think no further than of the Lullingstone *orantes* – but there is a more subtle convention involved here.

Presumably the nude competens, centrally, represents the centre of the baptistery itself, where the cistern or font would stand. The three-part frieze could therefore be a 'flat' version of an interior. The four columns, which have necessarily to be portrayed in a line, two-dimensionally, represent actual columns of stone or painted wood, at the four corners of an inner area, perhaps supporting an inner roof or ciborium over the font. The viewpoint (fig. 41, lower) is that of the officiating cleric or bishop, who stands immediately by the font, opposite the candidate he is about to receive into the water, from her sponsors. In each side-scene, we view members of the congregation in support, tidily but quite normally clothed – there is no suggestion that these are clergy. We see them, as it were, the way that the bishop or officiating priest would see them; between and slightly behind the side-pairs of the four upright corner columns.

This flattening-out of architectural subjects, a device to overcome the difficulty experienced in showing buildings – notably the interiors of large buildings – in perspective, isogonic or three-quarters view, has appropriate parallels, particularly when (as here) the technique has to be one involving low relief. Though Roman wall paintings were able to show complex buildings in good, often shaded, perspective of a kind, from an early period (an obvious example would be the Villa Boscoreale frescoes of the first century BC), carving in stone seldom managed to portray this. The flattened conventions were repeated in mosaics, and to

some extent in a later low-relief medium, the late classical schools of
ivory carving. *External* flattening, i.e., of a building's exterior, can be
seen on a well-known sarcophagus now in the Lateran Museum, Rome,
where a temple or mausoleum is so treated.[61] In Roman Britain, this
occurs on the surviving part of a third-century frieze from the Temple of
Jupiter Dolichenus at Corbridge[62] (fig. 42). *Internal* flattening is a little
more difficult to convey; but again there is a fourth-century sarcophagus
from Arles[63] showing the interior of a small basilica with apse and
arcades, which repeats on a much grander scale the triune convention
seen at Walesby. Christ as the Good Shepherd (centre, apse behind Him)
hands the scroll of the Law to Peter; the two side-panels each contain two
disciples, turning inwards. This interior convention is also seen on the
famous fifth-century mosaic from Tabarka (*Thabraca*, Tunis), reconstructable as a three-quarters interior view of a large aisled basilican
church.[64]

The reconstruction in fig. 41, then, if we allow the limitations of the
setting and the medium employed, shows how an anonymous
Romano–British artist produced his own version of this convention. The
lower part of the figure is simply a general idea of the model he may have
had in mind. The scene is good presumptive evidence for the existence of
a baptistery of this order of plan in late Roman Britain. Since it appears
on this tank, it supports the idea that the Walesby cistern in particular,
and therefore probably the whole class, is connected with the sacrament
of baptism.

There is also a broad correspondence in size, as far as width and depth
both go, between the dimensions of some of these tanks (taking only
those with Christian ornament) and the dimensions of the fixed cisterns

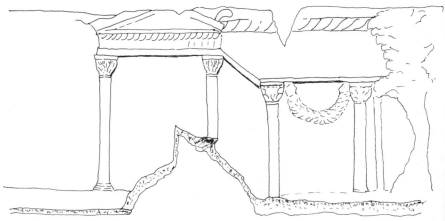

42 'Flattening' of structures in Romano–British art: part of frieze with Temple of Jupiter
Dolichenus, Corbridge (figures and animals omitted for clarity)

at Richborough, Icklingham and Witham. One might point out that any such tank could have been accommodated nicely by the central tiled base at Silchester. Clearly none of these containers would measure up to the 'plunge-bath' cisterns found in certain European baptisteries of the fifth and sixth centuries.[65] Against this, all the putative examples from Roman Britain, with an average depth of about 1ft 6in (0.5m), could easily accommodate one standing figure, perhaps two figures, the filled water-level being a little below knee-height.

Conclusions

Our comment on all these discoveries and remains can still be no more than provisional, and thus not entirely satisfactory. It would be unreasonable and against all analogy to deny that the Christians of fourth- and early fifth-century Britain possessed appropriate provisions for baptism, since their contemporary fellow-Christians throughout the western provinces were doing so, and have left us appropriate archaeological documents to that effect. We approach the position reportedly defined by Sherlock Holmes, when he remarked, 'When you have eliminated the impossible, whatever remains, however improbable, must be the truth'.[66] It is impossible that baptism did not occur in fourth-century Britain. The phenomena described above, however improbable they may appear to be in this light, make up the British versions of baptisteries and fonts.

The implications to be derived from their study are as follows. In those few cases where any sign of a baptistery has emerged, this is detached from the parent church. None of the buildings claimed as or construed as a church (in Chap. 7) contains an internal font or integrated baptistery. It may be a matter of regret that the physical circumstances at Silchester, Richborough and Icklingham removed the necessary evidence, and prevented modern archaeologists from detecting structures around the cisterns. The probability that there *were* structures, and that they were in wood, or timber on masonry footings, has been aired already.

At Silchester, 'detached' might be refined to 'semi-detached'; any shed around the flint platform would have been so close to the church that a linking passage, even a temporary one, is surely possible (fig. 40). The intervening distances at Richborough and Icklingham, about 30 and 25 ft (9 and 7.5 m) respectively, are not inordinately far. We might compare these with Hemmaberge in Austria,[67] where the southern of two fifth-century churches has a small octagonal baptistery with a hexagonal cistern, 50ft (15m) west of its outer west wall.

As for the method of baptism, our post-Roman literary material gave us no direct evidence of traditions of total immersion. All the indirect evidence, whether literary or archaeological, pointed to *affusion*; a mode where the competens or candidate, unrobed exactly as in the Walesby frieze, stepped into a receptacle full of water up to mid-calf, and then received the baptismal waters over the head, shoulder and body.

Since the British Romans, like the Romans anywhere else, had become fully accustomed to the whole social and domestic ritual of bathing, the water might very well have been warmed for baptisms taking place at an early Easter and at any Epiphany. There is no pressing need to look for any particular jug, patera or bowl in the context of affusion, but – recalling that this ablution was only a minor and ritual one – a spouted jug of the sort encountered in the Water Newton hoard might well have figured commonly among a church's possessions.

We have of course to explain the lead tanks, peculiar to Roman Britain; a group that may have emerged only in the fourth century (none is securely dated). They ought to reflect some particular and regional liturgical need or custom. Leaving aside suggestions of secular use (like brewing, steeping, dyeing, fulling, etc.), it has been proposed that in a Christian context they were meant, not for baptism, but for some other kind of ritual washing. Are they indeed lavers for the faithful to wash their hands and faces before they entered the *domus ecclesiae*? Are they for the obscure rite of *pedilavium*, and is it really credible that this was a feature of worship in fourth-century Icklingham?

A fresh objection to their interpretation as fonts is bound to arise from the Icklingham discoveries. Here, one has to explain away the co-existence of a fixed cistern (interpreted as a baptismal cistern within an insubstantial baptistery building) and the recently-found third lead tank close by; with the strong probability[68] that tank no. 2 (found in 1939) and tank no. 1 (found about 1726, since lost) both came from the same field that held the excavated site.

It is impossible to offer any full explanation, save that these lead cisterns did form some sort of alternative to fixed, constructed ones. They were the property of a Christian community, as the ornament on the Icklingham tanks makes clear. Were they just what they might seem to be – *portable* fonts or baptismal cisterns? Some of them have lugs or pierced handles of stout design, which would facilitate their being lifted into a cart. Such a font might, for a day or so, be placed within the appropriate room in one of the villas marked out earlier, or upon a tiled base like that at Silchester. If this sounds like yet one more eccentricity of Christian practice in Roman Britain, we have to admit that the very existence of these tanks could attest some such idiosyncratic custom.

It is a reminder only, not a true parallel or proleptic analogy, to point out that by the seventh century we have Irish, British, Northumbrian and probably Kentish churches of episcopal standing where, as well as the main, fixed, consecrated altar, we can envisage portable altars for use by a bishop visiting outlying and newly-converted settlements within his diocese.[69] In the case of St Cuthbert at Lindisfarne, we not only know this to be true; his enshrined portable altar survives among his relics kept at Durham. In fourth-century Britain, especially perhaps within the sprawling and often relatively well populated farmlands of what is now East Anglia, the population was at best partially Christian. One can imagine circumstances when it would have been both easier, and canonically preferable, to take the provisions for baptism out to some distant flock (by taking a portable font, normally kept at a church), rather than to insist upon personal attendance at one ecclesiastical centre of converts whose catechetical instruction might be suspect, or at best not under a bishop's immediate supervision. We cannot be sure to what extent heresy was a factor in church life in Britain in the fourth century. It may in fact be unnecessary to raise this particular spectre; but one could also argue that a bishop might well choose to keep the increasingly-conventional instruments of baptism – a portable, Christian-ornamented font, and chrism in particular – under his immediate control and at his own church, rather than to see any risk of irregular baptisms and irregular confirmations taking place in his absence.

This is verging on speculation. But it is speculation forced on us largely because of the lack of suitable and specific evidence; and other explanations might seem even less plausible. The conclusions, until there is fresh reason to change them and to offer new and alternative hypotheses, are that arrangements for fixed baptism, and what we have to call portable baptism or baptism-at-a-distance, both existed in late Roman Britain. These arrangements are, admittedly rather imperfectly, represented by the various discoveries mentioned. All such material that we have points to *affusion*, the pouring of baptismal water over the head of an unclothed candidate standing in some kind of font or cistern, as the most likely method of baptism in Britain, both in late Roman and sub-Roman times.

CHAPTER NINE

Burials and Cemeteries

Ecce mysterium vobis dico: Omnes quidem resurgemus, sed
non omnes immutabimur. In momento, in icto oculi, in
novissima tuba (canet enim tuba) et mortui resurgent
incorrupti; et nos immutabimur.
Vulgate, I Corinthians, xv

These words, from the Tract on the Resurrection in Paul's first epistle to
the Corinthians, will (in English) be familiar enough to anyone who has
recently attended a conventional funeral service, and to all those who
have the libretto of Handel's *Messiah* off by heart. They are quoted here
in St Jerome's sonorous Latin, the Vulgate New Testament of the late
Roman period, because that proclamation that 'the dead shall be raised
incorruptible' is one that millions of people at that time would have
taken in the most literal sense. It bore reference to a cosmic event, the
Second Coming and the general Resurrection of the Dead, that to them
might truly occur, sounding trumpets and all, at any moment.

Though faith requires Christians to view the dead body as a mere shell,
of no import at all in itself, and reconstitutable instantly and wholly by
Divine power from whatever gross decay time could have wrought, we
can sympathise with the notion that a corpse neatly laid out and decently
preserved in a stout container, so disposed as to minimise risks of
impious displacement and possibly with external indices of name and
status in society, would, in the nature of things, perhaps experience more
speedy resurrection than a handful of scattered fragments housed within
an insignificant urn and buried in a negligible pit. If such ideas were not
the major reasons why, in the late second and early third centuries AD,
inhumation replaced cremation as the commoner burial-rite in the
Roman empire, they were certainly among the reasons why inhumation
remained the custom, above all in Christian circles.

The concept of some form of afterlife, which in its Christian sense is
defined and promised by the New Testament and has been expanded by
commentators since the Church's earliest days, was not exclusive to the
followers of the Christian God. We may have only a very sketchy idea,
and then painstakingly derived from much later legend and literature, of
how the native, Celtic-speaking British saw the next world. The Druidic
idea of 'literal personal immortality'[1] must be taken as no more than the
philosophical pinnacle of a great body of belief, at the base of which only

muddled peasant ideas of afterworld carnality need be supposed. On the other hand, the Mediterranean civilisations did possess highly-evolved conceptions of the afterlife, common in essentials to the major aspects of paganism elsewhere in Europe, and fully explored for us by the Greek philosophers. It is scarcely necessary to remind ourselves that virtually all the facets of Christian thought in this direction had previously been foreshadowed by one, or other, of the many pre-Christian cults.[2]

Within the Roman empire, and particularly in the Italian peninsula, North Africa and the major cities of the Gaulish prefecture, the treatment of the dead eventually rose to a level of architectural complexity which (should one want to be unkind to Rome) could be said to recall the vulgarities of bourgeois Victorian Britain. Nor, in the richest of the western provinces, was Christianity exempted from such funerary fashions. Roman Britain however, its severance from the mainstream of very late Roman developments having impoverished it in so much outward detail (for example, as in the absence of any notable late Roman Christian basilicas), shows us a relatively commonplace history of burials, tombs, and cemeteries. One cannot help remarking how infrequently in Jocelyn Toynbee's concise and masterly account[3] of Roman death and burial her narrative – strongly Mediterranean-centred – has any recourse to Britannia for illustrative material.

Where one *can* find room for comment, when in linking Britannia with death and burial in the Roman world, is in the surprisingly low emphasis that has been accorded in Romano–British studies to the cemeteries, in particular the urban extra-mural cemeteries seen as discrete phenomena worthy of special and selective attention. With few if honourable exceptions, such as Trentholme Drive at York,[4] Lankhills at Winchester,[5] and Poundbury at Dorchester,[6] we find the details of these late Roman inhumation cemeteries (among which every indication and analogy warn us to look for the graves of Christians) occupying subordinate parts of narratives, concerned rather with urban life and its multifarious debris. This is in growing contrast to post-War work in Europe, and indeed to Anglo-Saxon studies in Britain; when the tale is taken into the post-Roman centuries, the cemetery, as a source of direct archaeological evidence and half-a-dozen repositories for skilled inference, is seen to be central rather than marginal in any kind of progressive research. Such research, moreover, has notoriously attracted among the most able and advanced minds.

This is no place to explore at length the reasons for our national shortcoming here, even if one could set them down with precision. It is true that the circumstances of post-War Europe offered many chances, mostly grasped with commendable speed, to explore extra-mural cemeteries in the course of reconstructing the penumbrae of major Roman cities; and it is also true that forms of State-backed excavation on the required scale began in several European countries about a decade before such became feasible, given our own climate of social and legal thought, in Britain. Yet – and possibly fig. 27 will underline this – even in Londinium, capital of the civil diocese and a place at the top of any list of British urban centres potentially occupied without a break since Roman times, we have almost no clear picture of what must have been many, and extensive, extra-mural cemeteries, beyond the sporadic records of those graves exposed by chance and also subject to the chance observation of appropriate workers. It must rank high among the scandalous, if now tardily rectified, attitudes to the ascertainable past of our national capital that the opportunities to explore any such cemeteries – and to yield a picture approaching that known for Trier (fig. 19) – have been lost, probably for ever.[7] A limited acceptance of the new demographic estimates for Roman Britain, argued by M.E. Jones,[8] forces us to realise that during the fourth century alone London would have produced nearly a hundred thousand dead, most if not all of whom would have been given inhumation burials.

It still remains true, however, that the task of identifying any *Christian* cemetery – that is, a cemetery of persons whose Christian allegiance necessarily resided in their minds, not their cadavers – is a formidable one. Radford, in numerous papers,[9] has hammered home the point that Christian identifications attached in such areas as the Rhineland to the remains of late Roman buildings and to closely-defined cemetery areas actually rest more on the continuity of Christian tradition than upon any direct archaeological display. The tradition he has in mind involves the continuity of names, dedications, records of proprietorship, and physically the avoidance of disturbances by later secular building. Leaving aside the problematical affair of St Martins and St Pancras at Canterbury, St Albans Abbey is probably the one British spot that could be put forward with any confidence in this light.

If Jocelyn Toynbee set the wider scene in studying death and burial over the whole Roman empire,[10] the best short summary where Roman Britain is concerned remains a nine-page one, written by or revised by Sir Ian Richmond.[11] There is of course a continuous, if sometimes slender, interest displayed. In a recent symposium report[12] four out of nine papers relate, varyingly, to Romano–British burial and cemeteries; and virtually all works dealing with either the larger[13] or smaller settlements[14] set out what they can about the known urban cemeteries. The coffins, and ossuaria or containers for cremated bones, have been separately studied as a class of lead artefacts;[15] where the housing of remains in these or any other kind of container rises, as it rarely does, to accompanying art, it is the latter aspect that merits comment.[16] But Britain never possessed, as did Aquitaine, Provence and Spain from the fourth century, its tradition of the ornamented stone sarcophagus; the British tale is very much one of 'dirt archaeology'. A major dissertation which linked all such detail with a full topographical study, publishable with some such title as Death and Burial in Roman Britain, remains as unrealised as it would be both timely and desirable.

One popular conception of an early Christian cemetery is that it might be composed entirely of extended inhumations – bodies, wrapped or unwrapped, laid full-length in the ground in trenches or in coffins of lead, wood or stone – with these graves being *oriented* (or, to use a later and now commoner form, *orientated*), that is laid with the axis of the body and the longer axis of the grave on a line approximately or precisely east-west. A corresponding popular aetiology has long since grown around this picture. When the skeleton is orientated, the head is normally expected in Christian usage to be at the western end so that, at the moment of the Resurrection, when as Jerome puts it *canet tuba*, 'the Last Trump shall sound', the risen dead will be facing in the appropriate direction. They would face east, since the event in question has for many centuries been linked to the Holy Land. There are of course no grave-goods with the Christian dead. Apart from specific pagan connotations (the coin for the Ferryman, food and drink to pacify earth-fast ghosts, etc.) any such trinkets are redundant if the spirit, not the mortal shell, is to enjoy Paradise.

These are firmly-entrenched beliefs, which occasionally surface in literature at all levels. Few Christian parents would feel total confidence in having to satisfy an intelligent small child as to whether Christian graves in India or Australia – regions where the Holy Land lies decidedly to the *west* – contain burials with the head at the other end. (The answer, incidentally, is, not within the history of post-medieval European Christian colonisation.)

It has gradually been realised that if these simple criteria used to mark Christian burials be applied to late Roman Britain, or many other provinces, they can be picked off one by one, leaving us as uncertain as we were at the start of the enquiry. The absence of coffins, shrouds and containers or of any accompanying offerings substantial enough to be archaeologically detected is as likely to mirror the sheer poverty of the communities so buried as any rigid interpretation of Scriptural doctrines. Christians may since late Roman times have favoured inhumation, as more seeming within a cult that contains ideas about the Resurrection; but, fashions and fads aside, inhumation involves no more than a shallow trench, whereas the adequate cremation of an adult corpse is a rather more exacting task[17] and requires much more in the way of materials and experience. Orientation is so complex a subject that, in discussing it now, one could well start by pointing to some wholly non-religious factors. If all the graves in a cemetery are orientated, they can also be described as *aligned*. But any inhumation cemetery with serried rows of graves, the commonest axis being more or less east-west, is aligned; and alignment may be a feature not connected with orientation. In such a cemetery, the earlier graves, being shallow, probably grass-grown after a year or so, and not necessarily marked permanently at surface-level, could subsequently be (and demonstrably were in most cases) partly or wholly disturbed by the digging of later graves. In theory, archaeology can sort out such a sequence, since the principles of stratigraphy apply; in practice this is not universally successful. Nevertheless, there is now growing evidence that rows of inhumation graves, the rows being defined by the short-axis direction of the graves, were somehow marked (by stones? by posts?), that rows began and ended within regular bounds and confines, and that one can suggest that late Roman cemeteries in Britain were often *managed*.

Given the administrative machinery of a large Romano–British town, its extra-mural cemeteries usually arranged alongside the approach roads where, in Richmond's words, 'the dead might be gratified by the notice of the living', and given too the pressure upon the authorities to accommodate burials of citizens in a world of short lives passed among crowded disease-prone conditions, it would not be credible to suppose otherwise. 'Management' implies initial choices of sites, allocation of plots, and a degree of small-minded fussiness about order, arrangement and alignment. Chance alone would tend to make a fair proportion of the predominant alignments in such cemeteries fall into the east-west, as opposed to north-south, arc; would bring a proportion of these into an axis near to true east-west; and, other things being equal, any orientated skeleton stands an equal chance of having its head to the west or head to the east. All this is seen against a late Roman Britain, whose population of three to four million would mean a rapid demographic turn-over. It is now inescapable that we think of urban cemeteries, known or unknown to us, as containing many hundreds or several thousands of inhumations – not as clusters of 50 or 150 graves at the outside. It has also become an inescapable conclusion that crude, simplistic criteria as to what could constitute and define a late Roman Christian cemetery must, fortuitously, have been constantly reproduced in entirely pagan cemeteries of the same date.

Orientation, for long the sheet-anchor in discussions of this topic, is something that since the eighteenth century has attracted as much in the way of literature as it has in the way of enthusiasm. The pitfalls will be obvious. In the absence of modern aids to surveying, and given our notorious British climate where even the approximate points of sunrise and sunset are usually shrouded in some type of obscurity, what was meant by 'East', and how was it located? How great a variation from correct east-west can be allowed, when significant orientation is alleged to have been found at a site? It would be a waste of time to recapitulate all the debates, in any case more relevant to medieval ecclesiology than to the Roman era, about east-west axes linked immediately to the point of sunrise on the birthday, or feast, or day of martyrdom, of a patronal saint. That pathway, long beloved of mathematically-inclined vicars and retired nautical persons, leads, alas, generally to the excessive and irrational claims that continue to impede astro-archaeology.

Philip Rahtz, whose own personal study of large and meticulously-explored cemeteries entitles him to a particular hearing, concludes a recent summary[18] with his view that 'the interpretation of *orientation* patterns as Christian is only one of several explanations', and he reminds us that 'in west-east graves, solar orientation is clearly a major factor'. This important point, behind which hovers an area of early Christian syncretism, is also raised by J.L. Macdonald in the Lankhills, Winchester, report[19] – particularly appropriate, since this is a cemetery where we are offered persuasive evidence[20] that 'the cemetery was far more organised than one might have expected' and that, taking into account the overall plans, one could agree that (using the previously-cited term) it was *managed*. Macdonald assigns the appearance of orientated alignment in the Lankhills burials to the period *c.*300–20; since, and the whole tenor of the present volume to this point supports him, it is most dubious that at that date the Church was necessarily strong enough to influence the lay-out of a cemetery like Lankhills in which pagans were (and would continue to be) buried, one can look for alternative causes. If Christianity, even after 313, did not yet possess a sufficiently powerful status in Britain to bring about orientation, 'it is certainly possible that an imperial sun-cult did'. Given the early fourth-century date, which is an archaeological one, we are reminded of the sun-cult, the worship of the conflated concepts of Apollo and *Sol invictus*, that characterised the family of Constantine the Great and (for Britain) had a particular meaning through the person of his father Constantius, whose recovery of Britain after Carausius and Allectus took place in 296. He concludes that 'it is easy to see how a west-east alignment could have been adopted later by Christianity, when one considers Christianity's early and close associations with this sun-cult which preceded it in imperial religious policy'.[21] The particular obstacle, in British studies, is that (sites like Lankhills apart) we possess so little firm evidence as to early cases of orientated inhumations, pagan or Christian; we can thus only speculate whether pioneer immigrant Christians from the eastern provinces in late second(?)- or early third(?)-century Britain had themselves been influenced by oriented burials, which in the Levant occur sporadically among early non-Christian communities, and whether (this seems most improbable) any such tradition survived to be absorbed by Romano–British fourth-century Christian inhumationists. What can we recover from this debate? Macdonald is realistic: 'it is thus difficult to accept that all graveyards with this characteristic [orientation, heads to west] were necessarily Christian, even if they contained no grave-goods' and the lesson from Lankhills is that 'the pattern in particular localities may have been set by Christianity's predecessor, without being affected at a later date by Christianity itself'.

It would, of course, be remarkable if one ever found in an overt public setting related to the life of a Romano–British town a recognisable and exclusively Christian inhumation-cemetery *before* 313. The most we might expect would be a 'crypto-Christian' component, possibly in the form of a private (family or guild) burial-plot. But here again, since absolute dates are mentioned, we come up against a paradox. Such a hypothetical Christian cemetery, in most cases, would have certain temporal limits set by historical probability – after *c*.313, and before the likely abandonment accompanying the disintegration of town manage-ment in the fifth century. The very notions which are supposed to constitute Christianity would require us to picture inhumations, pre-sumably orientated, but devoid of those grave-goods that might allow estimates of date and sequence through *archaeology*, and if one entertains further pictures of the poorest and most numerous citizens being so inhumed, a further absence of those organic remains (wooden coffins, fibrous shrouds, etc.) from which scientific as opposed to typological estimates of date could be won. In short, the more Christian a cemetery, the less chance of according it any sort of detailed internal chronology. This reminds us once more of Lankhills, where it is rightly suggested that the most promising step towards the solution of orientation/Christianity in any such cemetery 'is clearly to determine the exact date at which burial with the head to the west began on a regular and systematic basis'.[22]

This dilemma becomes all too apparent when one turns to a group of very large rural cemeteries, such as Cannington in Somerset, whose beginnings fall well within the Roman period but where use continued long into post-Roman times.[23] It is becoming clear that the major hope of progress in studying these sites lies in a fairly complicated operation. This involves prolonged, and difficult, analysis (if necessary, computer-aided) of the internal sequence of burials, probably cluster by cluster rather than grave by grave, in search of an ideal construct, the overall *relative* grave-sequence; and then the attachment to such a sequence at casual points of *absolute* dates, won by any means possible (e.g., the radio-carbon dating of skeletons, organic traces of all kinds, and materials displaced by grave-construction). It is also possible, as Rahtz has shown – though this exercise is decidedly not for the untried hands – that minor shifts in alignment and orientation can be translated into sequential terms.

What has encouraged this approach is the fact that we possess a growing list of such cemeteries, outwardly suggesting a link with rural life in Roman Britain, and often not attached in any way to churches of later (though pre-Norman) foundation; cemeteries, in fact, which can be loosely thought of as 'sub-Roman'. It is at least possible, given the historical setting, that some of these are predominantly Christian; and though they fall outside the usual urban extra-mural positionings it is also likely, where no clear contrary evidence has been found, that some of them go back to the fourth century. Not all are truly rural. Some seem to reflect a continued interest in the, presumably much-altered, locations of small towns, villa estates, or former military installations. Others are (not wholly explicably) linked to late Roman pagan temples and their precincts. In a brave attempt to face this muddle, Rahtz recently went so far[24] as to propose classificatory divisions – 'sub-Roman secular: sub-Roman religious', etc.

These cemeteries are in the present writer's view more germane to the setting of Chapter 10, and often to centuries beyond the scope of this volume, than to late Roman times. It is perhaps allowable – reverting momentarily to the maps, figs. 14–17 above – to see a rather general relationship with those areas of Roman Britain for which evidence of any kind for pre-425 Christianity is known, and over which the Anglo-Saxon settlement did not run until the first half of the sixth century. Rahtz has paid special attention to the Dorset, Somerset, Gloucester and south-east Wales region.[25] On a lesser scale altogether, recent studies[26] point to something of the same kind in the western hinterland (Cumbria, the Lancashire coastal plain) of Hadrian's Wall. For Northumbria and Yorkshire, one could adduce the important fieldwork and analyses of Margaret Faull.[27] In some fashion related are the so-called 'long cist' cemeteries, with their strong and earlier native component, of the Borders and southern Scotland,[28] a subject partly revisited now in Hope-Taylor's essay devoted to early Bernicia.[29] Much of this concerns 'Highland Britain' or the Highland Zone, and there is the inherent disadvantage that these areas include those whose acid soils, derived from older igneous rocks, are the least favourable to the preservation of skeletons and organic materials. Nonetheless, somewhere within this whole, large, sprawling category there should be, and on historical grounds there have to be, Christian graves and very probably all-Christian cemeteries. As Rahtz has commented,[30] 'The class is neither obviously Roman nor clearly related to the English settlement . . .', and

in any future overall consideration one would have to add occurrences, in
Roman settings, of sporadic but obviously post-Roman inhumation-
groups, as now found within Roman Exeter (p. 168 above) or long known
from the Lantwit villa in south Wales,[31] to select merely a couple. Again,
it is in the nature of things that even when such cemeteries occur on sites
identified as Christian they may not always necessarily be part of them,
nor yield direct and conclusive evidence that those so buried had been
Christian in life or were buried by fellow-Christians. The present writer's
pioneer efforts[32] to isolate, as the primary field-monuments of fifth-
century (and later) Insular Christianity, those phenomena labelled as
'enclosed' or 'unenclosed (or undeveloped)' cemeteries, have come in for
some heavy buffeting, notably from pragmatically-inclined colleagues
like Rahtz. This does not affect the validity of such models in the later
sixth and seventh centuries, where 'development' of certain burial-
grounds in the form of additions of the first churches, *c.*700 or later, is
increasingly demonstrable. For the earlier phase, backwards from the
early sixth to later fourth centuries, the hypothesis is admittedly shaky.
The evidence may well be there, and in quantity. At the moment, because
of the uncertainties and obstacles outlined above, the correct elucidation
is still beyond our corporate capacity.

At the other end of the inferential spectrum, what particular clues might
betray late Romano–British graves of Christians? Ideally, a tombstone
inscribed in unmistakeably Christian terms, found directly attached to its
original grave, would be a starting-point. As we saw earlier, RIB nos.
690, 787 and 955 cannot fill this bill. The same rigorous approach that
has now been accorded to the Lankhills cemetery has tended to expunge
an earlier candidate for Christian status – the late Roman inhumation
cemetery at Ancaster, Lincolnshire. This site[33] lies west of the town, has
already yielded some 300 burials, and probably began not before the
early fourth century. Of ninety-one burials examined up to 1966, 94 per
cent were extended and orientated (heads to west) inhumations. This is a,
surely typical, small-town cemetery, whose use must have coincided with
the steady growth of officially-recognised Christianity. It appears to have
been managed ('such order suggests a master plan for the graveyard')[34]
and as well as a few wood-coffined or plank-lined graves, there were at
least eleven burials contained within sarcophagi of the local limestone.
Wilson, understandably, thought the strict orientation alone suggested a
Christian element. By 1975, with more evidence to hand, Malcolm Todd
was 'sceptical of this and would prefer to leave the matter open', a view in
which the authors of the more recent Lankhills volume would presumably join him. Rahtz[35] saw Ancaster as a case where the religious
connotations must remain unproven; though this same comment was
extended to the burials at Icklingham, where it is difficult to see them

other than as Christian. Nevertheless, even if not susceptible to rigid proof, and therefore omitted from the distribution-map (fig. 15), one would suspect that Ancaster may well be as near as we can get to a fourth-century, Romano–British 'small town' cemetery of mainly Christian character.

The only two cases included on the map are Lankhills and Poundbury, and this paucity in itself must remind us of the strictures earlier voiced. At Lankhills, where most of the burials have to be seen as those of the pagan inhabitants of Roman Winchester, *Venta Belgarum*, an isolatable feature (Feature 6) was a gully enclosing an area 4.0 by 2.5 m, interpreted as the bedding-trench for a hedge.[36] Burials within this, and later interrupting the line of the gully, range (on finds evidence) from *c*.310 to *c*.370 at the latest – two human generations. The interpretation[37] is, on balance, that the group may be seen as representing use of the particular burial-plot by a Christian family. The feature was separated from other burials in the cemetery; some of the graves were very carefully prepared. Grave 250, that of a young woman, suggested perhaps as the mother of the infant in Grave 259, held among other items (outside the coffin) the platter with what may be an IX monogram (p. 90, and fig. 13.3). The associated grave-goods may, as Macdonald implies, point to syncretic or nominal Christianity; but given the date, the combination of evidence 'does make it conceivable that this family was Christian'.[38]

The incidence of gypsum burials – coffins where the corpse was preserved in some form of poured plaster – has already been mentioned (p. 128). When we turn to other civitas capitals or the coloniae, having in mind the implications expressed by fig. 36, there is very little hard evidence. York is, after all, a place where late Roman Christian burials might be expected; among the incidence of gypsum burials there, and the odd finds of Christian meaning, it is possible (as Frend reminds us)[39] a partial Christian burial-area existed in Castle Yard. The only fully-published cemetery, Trentholme Drive, offers no comfort; the excavator was in a position to state[40] that 'there was nothing whatever to indicate any Christian burials in the area excavated' and that 'all the evidence . . . implies a wholly pagan cemetery'.

Poundbury, outside and to the west of Roman Dorchester (Dorset), *Durnovaria*, is now the solitary example. It is an extensive extra-mural cemetery, closely attached to a civitas capital with signs of fourth-century Christianity, and in a region which might be called 'a villa belt' that contains the Frampton, Fifehead Neville and Hinton St Mary villas. The history of the site is complicated, and no summary can be a proper substitute for the excavator's own (forthcoming) report.[41] Poundbury, with a minimum of 1100 burials – and here we see a realistic figure, of the order argued above – shows signs of orderly lay-out and some degree of management. What is taken to be the fourth-century Christian burial-area has ditches as boundaries and is clearly divided from (say) a pagan area with burials not all orientated and in some cases accompanied by bird and animal reamins. Coffined and gypsum burials occurred; and in the Christian part, small rectangular mausolea were erected over particular graves. Two of these mausolea contained painted plaster, one with a scene involving men carrying staves – perhaps civic, rather than particularly Christian, notables.[42] The worn state of their floors, suggesting continuous visits, is appropriate to an interpretation as *memoriae*.

For reasons, and in circumstances, not yet clear, the cemetery seems to have come to an abrupt end around the close of the fourth century; and unusually a phase of purely agricultural settlement with timber build-ings, yards, corn-drying ovens and pits was, in sub-Roman (or perhaps early sixth century?) times, superimposed above the burial area. This sequence, effectively preventing, as the presumed collapse of town life in Dorchester itself would have done, any development of the mausolea into extra-mural cemetery churches on European lines, at the same time fossilised as it were the late Roman Christian cemetery. The breadth of the skeletal material, which as Green makes clear has already indicated (from bone analysis) an ingestion of lead (from water-pipes?) at an undesirably high and dangerous level, will give a very full picture of an urban population.

It is hardly possible that Poundbury constitutes something unique. The accidents of its placing – on the skirts of an old country town, up against a neighbouring hill-fort, on margin-land developed in recent years as an industrial estate – permitted a long campaign of purposeful and productive excavation. Corresponding cemetery sites attached to other civitas centres, now modern cities, long ago vanished into inaccessibility below Victorian suburbs and railway yards. We may have cause to be thankful that Poundbury could be examined at all.

This account of burials and cemeteries in Roman Britain has been both defective and unsatisfactory, because the material itself is so very fragmentary and dispersed. If one particular moral, in any way peculiar to the story of Christianity in Roman Britain, is to be drawn, it would be that the lack of *continuity* in the use of such burial-grounds virtually precludes firm identification of pre-400 burials (unless on the Poundbury scale) as Christian; and that this fact sets Britain very much apart from comparable European studies. One cannot entirely discount the chance that further, revelatory, cemeteries will be found; one can be fairly sure that, if this happens, it would provide more information than we stand to gain from continued assessment of what we have already. As Rahtz's work increasingly seems to imply, the most one can hope to construct is perhaps a scale of probability, 10 being a positive identification, with

Poundbury about 9 and Ancaster perhaps around 6 or 7. Continuity of Christian burial will be among matters raised in the next few chapters; but it has to be said that, in the long tale of British Christianity, it is by no means the most convincing, nor illuminating, facet of any such continuity.

CHAPTER TEN

Fifth-century Britain
and the British Church

*From then on victory went now to our/countrymen, now to
their enemies; so that in this people the/Lord could make trial
(as he tends to) of his latter-day Israel to see whether it loves
him or not. . . . But the cities of our land are not populated
even now as they once were; right to the present they are
deserted, in ruins and unkempt. External wars may have
stopped, but not civil ones.*
Gildas, *De Excidio Britanniae*, c.535
(trans. M. Winterbottom)

It could be said that British history begins only in the fifth century AD, and
that all that happened before this time was part of the history of Rome's
north-westerly component. If this is so, our history begins at just about
its most obscure stage. We may not share the particular views of Gildas,
priest, moral critic and historical innovator[1], about the God-directed
harrowings of what had once been a happy Roman land; its hills and flat
places rich with corn and flocks, and bedecked with flowers and shining
rivers.[2] To a very large extent, however, we share his ignorance of what
really occurred on a national scale between about 425 and 500.

Former literary and historical models (like J.R. Green's) of the end of
Roman Britain and the coming of the pagan Saxons, ones often derived
(alarmingly) from no more recent source than Bede's *Historia*, have been
progressively modified, even in large part replaced. This did not arise
from the discovery of new historical sources — there are none — but
through archaeological research, and in recent decades linguistic
analyses (notably onomastics and toponymy, the study of personal
names and place-names).

It may be helpful to sketch out a picture of what seems to be common
ground. This will hardly be a model in itself. One might better describe it
as some of the pieces of a great jigsaw puzzle, spilled upon a table-top,
and finally agreed by the players to be, at least, pieces of the *same* puzzle.

Roman Britain had by 410–11 undergone a series of events, and
political changes, that rendered it outside the control of the emperors of
the West.[3] Whoever may have written to whom, or may have complained
of assaults and fears and begged for aid, or whichever party succeeded
for any cause in replacing its predecessor as the *de facto* or *de jure* rulers

of part or all of Britannia, one fact at least stands out. There was internal dissension, and on a scale not experienced elsewhere in the West at that period. It was the start of a long period of what Gildas called *bella civilia*, civil wars; and he could, looking back from the sixth century, contrast this with *bella externa* – fighting against all the various non-Romans; the Picts, the Irish coming from Ireland, the Irish who had based themselves on the British mainland, and the ship-borne Germanic-speaking raiders we label corporately as 'Anglo-Saxons'.

This may not all have led to the total devastation of all the urban centres of Romanised England and Wales, centres which Gildas says amounted to twenty-eight cities *ac nonnullis castellis* 'and plenty of fortresses' – a good approximate total of the civitas capitals, London and the coloniae, and as the *castella* perhaps places such as Chester and Richborough.[4] As in our very much later seventeenth-century Civil War, between the King and Parliament, one that involved (by modern standards) tiny peripatetic armies encountering each other on rare occasions and which at a rural level bypassed most of the countryside and its annual cycles, it may have been that Romano–British town life continued in some if not most centres, under increasingly defensive guise. Archaeology indicates that this does seem to have been the case. But since the 360s there had been, particularly in East Anglia and northwards from the English Midlands, abundant cause to apprehend assault from barbarian raids, mounted by land, or sea, or both. One aspect of defence took the shape of increasingly large presences of what can only be interpreted as auxiliary, mercenary forces, residing within or hard by the towns they were particularly to defend. Their presences are betrayed by the records of archaeology.[5] Their equipment, and possibly the forms assumed by their burials – for these static militias required homes, land for their families, and provisions to dispose of their dead – imply that, as in the Roman army, many of them were being drawn from the German provinces and the Low Countries.

What happened next is, in its very broadest shape, apparent enough. Some of these non-British groups mutinied or revolted, were aided by subsequently-arriving reinforcements, and by the middle of the fifth century were in no sense under any Roman British control. *Why* this occurred, we do not know, since this question involves not the examination of material remains, but the elucidation from most defective sources of unrecoverable policies, motives and mistakes. We are guided, dimly, by Gildas, by Bede using Gildas[6] and other earlier writers, by native British chroniclers of later centuries, by versions of what came to be known as the Anglo-Saxon Chronicle,[7] even by the odd entry in European chronicles.[8] We are, naturally perhaps, prone to seek guidance in the balancing of probabilities. And here, it is highly probable that a partly-civilised nation whose components have begun to fight among each other, party against party, have-nots against the haves, will very rapidly lose control of imported heavily-armed mercenary regiments, whose members may have had plainer and more direct ambitions, practised other religions, and spoken incomprehensible tongues. Nor would Britannia find comfort in the realisation that her urban centres were starting, markedly, to suffer the withdrawal of means of technological renewal and maintenance, and her agrarian-centred economy beginning to collapse through inflation and money-shortage and the disappearance of marketing machinery.[9]

It is the 'Lowland Zone' of Roman Britain, the east, south-east and south central parts of what is now England, that forms the best background for such hypotheses. To the north-west, the south-west, and in Wales, regions where the hand and *mores* of Rome had lightest lain, there were older, never wholly submerged, patterns of society. There was the native British, Celtic-speaking background, with a social stratification that differed from the Roman one. Its higher levels, if they had supplied the *curiales* and *magistratūs* of the later Romano–British civitates, included men and entire family-networks who governed local affairs by immemorial and indigenous right. The glosses of Roman citizenship, Roman *praenomina* and *nomina*, and progressively more inappropriate (if jealously guarded) Roman titles, together with a century or more of Imperial recognition in their caste, can hardly have disposed them to do other than to continue ruling, in their own names; once, that is, circumstances no longer called upon them to do so in the name of any emperor, or his *vicarius* in London.

Precisely when these native states and principalities or, as we must call them, kingdoms (*cf.* fig. 49) arose is not made clear, by sources which are themselves not earlier than the sixth century. Implicitly, they were rooted in the last days of Roman Britain; the British kinglets tended to encourage construction of genealogies and king-lists[10] which derived their families from Magnus Maximus, or other suitable fourth-century figureheads. It certainly happened in the fifth century (Gildas is evidence that there were kings in the latter part of it), and perhaps earlier in some regions than in others.

The settlement of the eastern half of England by the Anglo-Saxons – Angles predominantly from East Anglia northwards, Saxons mainly south of them, Jutes in Kent, and smaller groups whose specific identities are lost to us – is charted in two main ways. It is hardly the fault of modern students that neither is wholly satisfactory.

Archaeologically, the incidence of graves – with cremations or inhumations, singly or as cemeteries, the burials accompanied by diagnostic pots and a mish-mash of iron weapons, often-elaborate jewellery, and other domestic trifles – dominates the distribution-maps.[11] It must do so, because until recently very little settlement-archaeology was known. The relative and absolute dates of these burials and cemeteries, which are of course progressively *later* as one moves westward across Britain, are won from typology, construction of internal sequences of objects found in graves and less commonly elsewhere, and analogies and parallels, the matching of these objects with dated counterparts on the Continent.

Linguistically, the vital and crucial aspect is that of place-names. We are indeed fortunate that the Anglo-Saxons spoke related dialects of a Germanic language (Primitive Anglo-Saxon, later Old English) so markedly separable from both Vulgar Latin and Late British; and that their relatively simple modes of allocating names to the places where they settled, to the features which they needed to distinguish, and even to their foci of religious and communal actions, began so early, and that these names have proved to have lasted so very extensively. Now that the debate as to which precise types, or strata, of these place-names indicate primary settlement appears to have reached useful conclusions, it is possible to classify and to map them.

The defects of both these approaches should be apparent. Cemetery-archaeology may, theoretically, be closely anchored in *time*, but it tells us little or nothing about the relations of the Anglo-Saxons to the British; only about their own relationship to their own ideas of death and afterlife. Place-names tend to lack even this aspect of contemporaneity. The oldest records, starting as a trickle in late seventh-century charters, and becoming a veritable flood by Domesday Book, must embody (if they continued to be spoken names, in general use) linguistic developments and changes through time. These have to be, painstakingly, reversed; by comparative methods, and by the application of rules or principles believed to govern the operation of Indo-European languages and their phonetics through time – in other words, historical linguistics in an extremely specialised field. It is a tribute to the thoroughness, the *élan*, and the maintained scholarship of modern British (or English) onomasticists that what emerges can be seen, pretty clearly, to confirm what might be seen on other and independent grounds.

A combination of these approaches, added by the most cautious use of historical material, does now permit us in making a working model to draw a great diagonal line across England (as in figs. 47, 49), and to state that – give or take 20km either way – this will do as an idea of a 'frontier', in the human generation centred around AD 500, between lands to the east where Anglo-Saxons had been or had settled, and lands north and west where they had not. In another, specialised branch of place-name study, hydronymics or the names of rivers and streams (these are the most resistant to ethnic changes, and the first to be adopted more or less unaltered – think of Australia, or the eastern United States), the line is also more or less the boundary on Kenneth Jackson's famous 'Map of British River Names'[12] of the easternmost Area I. Within it, British or Brittonic names, like *Thames* and *Trent*, are rare, and then confined to large or medium-sized rivers traversing long tracts. It marks the western confine of the most English part of England; one where, even now, many Welshmen, or westerners of ultimately British origin, feel uneasy at the absence of high ground and the total lack of familiar place-name elements.

But what none of this can tell us – and we come back again, to the core of the present book – is what happened, between AD 400 and 500, to that million or more British, descendants unto the third and fourth generations of the Latin-speaking, British-speaking Roman citizens of Britannia, living in this province, east of the line. We can allow that many perished in civil and external wars, as Gildas claims.[13] There may have been pestilences;[14] though modern epidemiology counsels us to be very chary of over-estimating the rate at which such plagues, transmitted by uncertain vectors, can run through scattered rural populations. There may have been famines, failures of distribution rather than harvests. There were emigrations, both to Armorica or Brittany[15] and to other regions of northern Gaul.[16] Even if all this reduced the population by fifty per cent – surely an outside guess – a very great many Roman Britons would be left, probably outnumbering their invaders many, many times.

We are bound to recall that other hypothesis, aired above in Chapter 3, where it formed part of the 'refugees and Gaulish missionaries' explanation for the presence of Christianity and spoken and written Latin in Atlantic, Highland Britain from the mid-fifth century. But even the most enthusiastic proponents would admit that it need not have involved more than what Jackson supposed were the native British squirearchy, their households and estate retainers. What now weighs heavily against it – apart from a growing suspicion that the spread of Christianity, northward and westward, took place earlier in the fifth century and for other reasons – is the evidence that, in certain specific zones and in some cities, the British did *not* leave Jackson's 'Area I', then, or at any subsequent period.

Before we examine the distribution-maps with which this chapter has to be provided, the reader may care to have summaries of the three most recent models concerning the Collapse of Britain.

One can preface the examination by drawing attention to certain named persons, familiar to generations of schoolchildren and now, through popularising works, to a very wide public indeed. They would include Ambrosius Aurelianus, whom Gildas tells us was descended from a family that ought to have worn the purple – that is, was (at a guess) from a family that had provided a usurping British emperor – and who rallied the British against the Saxons in the mid-fifth century.[17] We know his general date because Gildas implies his grandchildren were living in his own day. There was Vortigern, an arrogant British *tyrannus* or self-maintaining king;[18] he hastened the climax of the Saxon wars by actually inviting more Anglo-Saxons to enter Britain, in order to repel invaders from the North, Picts and *Scotti* (Irish). Vortigern is mentioned by Bede; it is not yet clear[19] if the earliest texts of Gildas gave his name as well. There were Hengist (Hengest, Hencgest) and Horsa, leaders of a particular group of ship-borne Saxons. There was Arthur, who led a mobile British army and defeated the Saxons and other barbarians in a series of battles, culminating in a victory at a place Gildas calls[20] *Mons Badonicus*, the Badonic mount, Mount Badon, around AD 500 or a little earlier; and the effect of this victory was to hold the line of the Saxon advance (as shown in fig. 47) for at least a half-century.

Now though these persons can all too easily dominate any model of a reconstructed British history in the fifth century, they are in fact *unnecessary*. Some may be historically more real than others; Ambrosius Aurelianus is credible, and was accorded wide treatment by John Morris.[21] Hengest and Horsa, great-great-grandsons of the god Woden or Odin,[22] are more like symbols than people. Gildas, as we have his text, merely *implies* Vortigern; Gildas does not even imply the existence of Arthur. Many will agree with Dr David Dumville's *cri de coeur*: 'The fact of the matter is that there is no historical evidence about Arthur; we must reject him from our histories and, above all, from the titles of our books.'[23] Any sane person would agree. These enticing Will-of-the-wisps have too long dominated, and deflected, useful advances in our study.[24] In strict historical terms, Voteporix, the Irish-descended king of *Demetia* or Dyfed, south-west Wales (*cf.* fig. 49) is more truly 'real' than any of these people. He is named by Gildas, who tells us quite a lot about him;[25] his mid-sixth century tombstone, with his name in both British and Irish spellings and in Latin and *ogham* survives, from Castell Dwyran in Carmarthenshire (fig. 43.3); he figures in various versions of an Irish saga about his ancestral tribe and their emigration to Britain, and in Welsh reflections of this, complete with regual-lists and pedigrees which, fairly calculated,[26] place him at the right period for Gildas' remarks.

It is possible – it may be preferable, and in the particular case of 'Arthur' it is *desirable* – to construct models of fifth-century Britain devoid of individual names altogether. A cynic might say that the fewer names that appear in any fresh hypothetical reconstructions the greater the chances that it offers something new for us to consider.

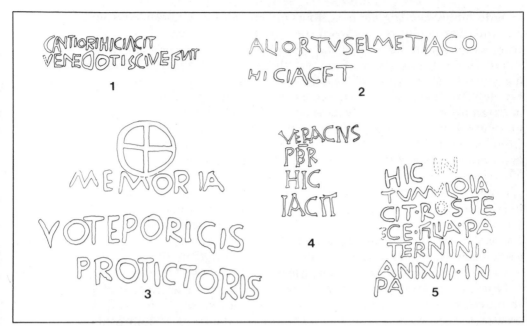

43 Significant inscriptions from memorial stones, Wales, 5th–7th cent.
1 CANTIORI HIC IACIT VENEDOTIS CIVE FUIT (CIIC 394, ECMW 103) 2 ALIORTUS ELMETIACO(S)HIC IACET (CIIC 381, ECMW87) 3 MEMORIA VOTEPORIGIS PROTICTORIS (CIIC 385, ECMW 138) 4 VERACIUS PBR (= PRESBYTER), HIC IACIT (CIIC 393, ECMW 77) 5 HIC (IN) TUMULO IACIT. ROSTE(E)CE. FILIA. PATERNINI. ANI XIII. IN PA(CE) (CIIC 421, ECMW 294)

The late Dr John Morris' views of fifth-century Britain are contained in his *The Age of Arthur* (1973). They have a multi-disciplinary origin, are studded with brilliantly original ideas and provocative assertions in equal measures, and where historical sources are used these are interpreted according to criteria and canons which the author set out elsewhere.[27] His is a mighty and rumbustious book, daily reminding us of what British scholarship lost with his death in 1977;[28] and if the present writer feels obliged to disagree with Morris on certain early Christian matters, this does not touch most of the secular, historical aspects, from which passages dealing with the British Church are largely excisable.

Since it would be impossible to summarise *The Age of Arthur*, it is fortunate that the author himself provided a fore-shadowing précis a few years earlier,[29] of a scheme much elaborated but not essentially changed in the major study. (Morris' own interpretation of the period 406–15 or thereabouts was earlier discussed, in the context of Pelagianism, p. 57.) It involves four distinct, detectable, and approximately-dated periods.

In the first, marked both by events inferred from 'Pelagian' sources and by the evidence of Germanic bands, federates or *laeti*, around the towns of lowland Roman Britain, Britannia continued in Roman ways, under its own Roman-style *potentiores*, until about 440. An anonymous Gallic chronicler is thought to have noted that Britain was subjugated by the Saxons in 441–2, and though this source has now been called into serious question,[30] somewhere in this decade it is probable that the first major Saxon revolt occurred, aftermath of Vortigern's ill-advised importation of fresh barbarians, Hengest and Horsa, and the plain fact of their being too many armed Saxons at large.

Prolonged fighting, the very last part of which is linked with the name of Ambrosius Aurelianus, led not only to mass emigrations to Gaul (about 457–60), but eventually to a successful campaign of the Britons. This reached a climax, in 495 or 500 or thereabouts, with the battle at Mount Badon. After that, a period of stability began; the Saxon advances were halted and this, Morris' third main period, lasted until about 570. There was then a *second*, general Anglo-Saxon rising, the red tide again flowed west and north, and for subsequent British history we can begin to look to increasingly specific and even reliably historical sources.

Morris considered that there was just sufficient evidence to give the approximate, and realistic, dates of the main events dividing the fifth and sixth centuries into his periods: I 410–440 II 440–495 III 495–570 IV 570–600 and after. Gildas lived, and wrote, in period III and was a source for his own time (before about 540) and some if not all of period II. The vital factors included the first Saxon revolt (dividing I from II) with the arrival of many more Saxons from the Continent, the minor invasion often known as the *adventus Saxonum*: and the chain of British triumphs leading to Mount Badon, which much later Britons were to use for some national epic, possibly circulated in Latin verse, featuring the Twelve Great Battles of Arthur.

The attractions of Gildas are manifold. He was interested, for stated reasons, in Britain's past and the Roman side of that past. He wrote in Latin, which may be florid and verbose and occasionally ambiguous, but is intelligible, even if certain cruces of precise meanings demand resolution still, and the text of DEB itself awaits a desirable new edition. The date at which he wrote is more or less agreed; DEB composed after about 535, and 'published', or widely-circulated and locally copied, between then and about 550.[31] His are the only allusions to more than purely local events for much of Morris' periods II and III.

It will not be impertinent, in either sense of this word, to point out that the other two models of fifth-century Britain have both come from persons who are ancient historians, with long interests in the historiographical specialities germane to this period, and who both regard Gildas as the primary source. Both, too, began with considerations of the shorter period around 390–410, where their interpretations[32] differed both from

John Morris' and each other's – let alone from the conventional views of purely Romano–British studies, which tend to die away, historically as well as in depth, at this time. There is another minor distinction, in that Dr Mollie Miller has been concerned mainly if not wholly with the north of Britain, Professor Edward Thompson (until recently) more with the south, and the adjacent Continental provinces.

Dr Miller, who has elsewhere examined Gildas simply as a historian,[33] is concerned with what Gildas has to say about Morris' first period (to the mid-fifth century) and about the first Saxon revolt. She would see, in the earlier chapters of DEB, where these deal with the material side of Britain's fate (as opposed to the moral lessons inherent in such events), a concealed historical narrative; and one that is presented in two, complementary sections.

The first, DEB 14–21 (chapter 21 being mainly a summarising passage), deals with the northern wars, British against Picts and *Scotti*; and Gildas is taken to be aware of earlier struggles on the northern frontier, about 383 × 390 and 398 × 400, the existence of which Dr Miller argued in another reconsideration of another source.[34] What Gildas described was a 'Third Pictish War', and one that had relatively little to do with matters in Britain's far south. The barbarians occupied the lands between Hadrian's and the Antonine Walls; attacked and overran the Hadrianic frontier from the *north*; and initiated a long age of massacre, famine and social collapse in the north of England. At an unspecified date – anywhere between 410 and 446? – native British resistance was successful. The Irish went home; some of the Picts settled between the Walls. It is implied that the British victory was however hard-won, and in reality short-lived, and that by Gildas' time the Irish raids and Pictish pillagings had long since recommenced, as perpetual irritants.

Gildas' twenty-second chapter begins with the word *Interea* 'Meanwhile . . .'. Dr Miller takes this to mark a chronological overlap, and that chapters 22–26 now deal with approximately the same period, and its outcome, but in the south of Britain. Much of what Gildas says is familiar, if only because of Bede's use of it – the threat of renewed Northern attacks, Vortigern, his council and their terrible decision, the importation of Saxons to repel Picts, and the three boat-loads (Hengest and Horsa? unnamed). More Saxons arrive; demand payments in kind; and though allegedly paid, and supposedly for a time fulfilling their hired duties, they mutiny. Fighting and devastation break out. Dr Miller points out that, without giving any place-names, Gildas and his readers must have known precisely which region(s) of Britain were affected. Certain tantalising details are given. The main area contained *coloniae* and *civitates*, and was west of an (east-coast?) area already settled by Saxons. It possessed 'at least one important ecclesiastical centre which also had stone towers'; hills (some fortified) and forests were within reach, as were sea-cliffs and 'at least one haven from which emigrants departed'. It contained the home-country of the Aureliani, the ruling family, of whose members only Ambrosius Aurelianus survived – to rally the British, and then to fight back. The area was not permanently occupied, since [35] 'after the passage of a certain time, when the most cruel plunderers had returned to their homes' (*scil.*, eastwards), the Britons gathered their survivors around Ambrosius, and their counter-campaigns led to Mount Badon and the end of the fifth century. A régime, possibly with Roman echoes, was re-established, and a generation later when Gildas writes it is the moral decay of the British, rather than external threat or actual attack, that poses the greater threat.

Though Dr Miller does not say so, there must be an implication that, if DEB 22–26 is separated from the previous account (which is northern), it must refer to the south, at least as far south as the Midlands. The hills, forests, cliffs, etc., suggest Somerset or Wales; the ecclesiastical centre, Cirencester (?); and one might toy with placing the *superbus tyrannus* and his circle no further north than Wroxeter, the Aureliani then being at Gloucester (a *colonia*) and the lower Severn (and, as will be discussed later, Gildas' contemporary Aurelius Caninus is most at home if located between the Severn and the Mersey).

Edward Thompson, providing now a third model,[36] proposes a radical difference. His interpretation also extracts a first, northern account from Gildas; but the reading must depend to some extent upon Gildas' own geographical standpoint, the place where Gildas was writing about 535, and 'somewhere in the Chester area' is hinted at as consistent with the evidence.[37]

The 'Third Pictish War' becomes a struggle in the years preceding 446, when certain Britons appealed to Aetius (in Gaul) during his third term as a consul, begging for Roman aid against the barbarian assaults; Gildas probably knew a version of this actual letter. But when the Picts and Scotti seized the whole of the north part of the land from its inhabitants, as far as the Wall (*muro tenus*, DEB 19), they were not coming down from the north; this they did from the *south*. The land (*terra*) is Britannia, the civil diocese, and thus by definition south of Hadrian's Wall anyhow. The *indigenes* are the British Romans, not any British-speakers living beyond this frontier. The Scotti from the north-west, the Picts from the north (= north-east), had come by sea, as Gildas makes very clear.

For Thompson, Gildas describes a war in northern England, which began perhaps about 440, and raged in Britannia north of the Mersey and the Humber. Massacres and famine followed, many British had to surrender or, worse, compound with the barbarians. Others, stouter of heart, fought back 'from the very mountains, from caverns and ravines, from entangled thorn-brakes' – this description 'hardly suits south-eastern Britain' (Thompson). As in Dr Miller's reading, the Irish returned home, and the Picts, repulsed, settled further north; the British guerilla drive had for the moment succeeded.

But the models diverge further now, in that Thompson would see the *Interea* of DEB 22 as continuing (after a short, moralising chap. 21) the purely northern story. This 'Meanwhile . . .' implies, not 'Meanwhile (while all this happened in the north), down in the South, etc.,' but merely that he is now resuming a single, unitary narrative. It is rumoured that the old enemies were again posing grave threats to the *regio* (not the *terra*; the *regio*, or region of north Britain, as it were the equivalent of the forgotten Valentia and/or Flavia Caesariensis provinces). It was now that the unnamed Vortigern invited Saxon allies – who, on this reading, must have been spear-headed by three boats *other* than those represented by Hengest and Horsa – who were joined by others from the same source and accorded the status of *foederati*. Their function would have been to defend the eastern coastlands of northern England against sea-raiding Picts. Their revolt, on whatever pretext, took them right across to the west coast (*de mari usque ad mare*); after this, they may have turned south, and pillaged some of the Midlands. Then they returned to their *domus*, perhaps Lindsey and the East Riding of Yorkshire – and so to Ambrosius, Mount Badon, and the recital of Our Present Discontents, which took Gildas beyond 500 and to the time of his own composition, in his *cellula* or *domunculus* at Chester, Bangor Is-Coed, or wherever he wrote DEB.

The unnamed *regio* – and if Thompson is right, it may for the first time be dimly seen, cartographically, in fig. 47 – suggests itself: the turretted ecclesiastical centre (York?), the *coloniae* (plural in Gildas: York and Lincoln?), the fastness of the Yorkshire dales and the Pennines, such former forests as the Lancashire Forests of Bowland and Rossendale, the navigable estuaries of Mersey and Ribble. But Thompson has other interesting points to make. Apart from the idea that the post-446 emigration, if it took Britons to Gaul – where, from about 460, they do indeed sparsely appear on the historical scene – may have taken others to *Ireland*. He stresses that the entire DEB narrative, unified, from chapters 14 to 26, may be localised in space as well as in time. Gildas may have had nothing to say about the far south-east, or Wessex, or in the other direction Cumbria, still less lands between the Walls, simply because he did not know and had no means of finding out what had gone on there. The main fury of the Saxons' northern revolt took place after the appeal to Aetius in 446; whatever happened in the Thames Valley or the south-east, even if the Gallic chronicle-entry of 441–2 (which Dr Miller would now expunge as 'a ghost-date, born in 1892 . . . originating in a marginale by Mommsen') is fortuitously about right, was another and separate Hengest-and-Horsa episode.

As far as the north of England, a very large *regio*, is concerned, perspective is urged on us. No more than one or two thousand Saxons need have been involved. The whole revolt, with its suppression, may have occupied some fifteen years. If renewed and occasional fighting did break out, this is of course not inconsistent with an isolated British victory at 'Mount Badon' (which may itself also have been, independently, a quite separate southern event) nearer to AD 500. One might add that, if anyone wishes to retain 'Arthur' as the symbol of British resistance, there is ample evidence to place Arthur and all or any of his battles in northern England and southern Scotland – in strong preference to (perhaps even to the exclusion of) a wider background stretching as far south as Somerset, with its mythical 'Camelot'.[38]

The end of urban life in Roman Britain, or that part of it about which Gildas was in a position to know, was not primarily the result of mid-fifth-century Saxon assaults, bitter as these may have been. Civil war continued, to the point where Gildas seems to say (in DEB 26) that it had become a standing reproof among *in circuitu nationes*, 'the surrounding nations' – the Irish? Gauls? the British in Armorica? As Thompson puts it, 'it was the action of the Saxons combined with the ensuing activities of the Britons themselves which put an end to urban life.' Or to *most* urban life; Gildas nowhere mentions the name, or the bare existence, of the former capital city, *Londinium*. Possibly he knew nothing of it; very probably he never went near it. His remarks cannot be taken to preclude the continued occupation of Roman towns in the later fifth century, let alone from 400 to 450, in regions of which he had no direct knowledge.

What Gildas tells us (in DEB 27–36) is that Britain had kings, even if they were tyrants; and he addresses himself to five of them. Three are known, independently of Gildas; Voteporix or Vortipor (of Dyfed) has been mentioned above, Constantine (of Dumnonia, the south-west) and Maglocunus or Maelgwn (of Venedos, Venedotia, or Gwynedd; north-west Wales),[39] occur in both the Lives of Saints and early Welsh pedigrees.

The five are addressed in obvious order; and assuming with Thompson that Gildas writes from Chester or Bangor, and is looking south in addressing them, Cuneglasus would be the ruler of an unnamed kingdom between Vortipor and Maglocunus (*cf.* fig. 49) – perhaps where Ceredigiaun, Cardigan, lay. The second king, between Dumnonia and Dyfed, is Aurelius Caninus. Since Gildas also implies that the grandson(s) of Ambrosius Aurelianus lived in his own day, and since (for Aurelius Caninus) Gildas cites the *iuuenilem inmaturamque mortem . . . patrum fratrumque tuorum* 'the youthful and untimely death(s) of your fathers and brothers', which must be the massacre of DEB 25, it is hard not to see Aurelius Caninus as a direct descendant of Ambrosius and other Aureliani. In fig. 49 he is, tentatively, placed in the region of Gloucester and Cirencester and Bath, towns captured by the brothers Ceawlin and Cuthwine with their West Saxons in 577, during the renewed Saxon advances of Morris's Period IV. These Saxons killed three kings, Conmail, Condidan and Farinmail, probably inflated from local *praefecti*, but perhaps also latter-day Aurelian descendants. Alternatively, the Aureliani may have been the rulers of Wroxeter, with its grandiose fifth-century town centre and half-timbered classical palace.[40] Where does this place Vortigern and his council? Where would be more suitable than *Eburacum*, York, provincial capital for nearly two centuries, and the only Roman city of any real importance to fit the geography of Thompson's reconstruction?

These five kings and their realms do not represent the only kingdoms. Later, though not very much later, Insular sources name others, which can be broadly located. Bernicia, earlier British **Bernaccia* 'Land of the Mountain-passes'(?),[41] was between the Tyne and the Tweed. Deira, whose centre can hardly have been other than York, lay in the Vale of York and the East Riding. West of Deira, in higher country, from Leeds to Sheffield and westwards (and including *Loidis*, the district of the modern Leeds city), was Elmet. An early sixth-century tombstone from north-west Wales (fig. 43.2) commemorates a native of Elmet, with the correct late British adjective, *elmetiacos*. This interest in a man's origin is echoed by another, contemporary stone (fig. 43.1) of a citizen of Gwynedd, described as *venedotis cive*.[42] In the north-west, a powerful realm of uncertain extent, homeland of those British *combrogi* who gave Cumbria its still-used name, was Rheged (various spellings exist).

It was large, its rulers mighty men of the sixth and seventh centuries in later Welsh verse and tradition, and H.M. Chadwick suggested that both Dunragit in Wigtonshire (south-west Scotland) and Rochdale in Lancashire contained its name; eastwards, it may have stretched thinly or notionally over to Catterick.

There were other, smaller kingdoms; for instance, in south Wales, figs. 49 and 51 pick out Ercing (or Ergyng), whose name looked back to the Roman town of *Ariconium*, and forward to the *Archen*field district of Herefordshire. Native kingdoms of southern Scotland, not all included in fig. 49, will be discussed in Chapter 11.

Where any direct information survives on this point, the rulers of all these principalities are shown as Christians – lapsed, steeped in sin, rarely devout, but Christian nonetheless. Like the fifth-century Coroticus whom we shall meet in Patrick's career, Gildas' five monarchs are Christians; and it is not impossible that Constantine of Dumnonia was young enough in 535 (early 20s?) and exceptionally lived long enough, to be that Constantine whose 'conversion to the Lord' was noted for the year 589 by the *Annales Cambriae* – as the spectacular, last-minute saving of an aged, royal and now penitent backslider.

Against the background of the three models for fifth-century British events earlier summarised, the problem of indicating the extent (or in distributional terms the density as well), the locations, and if possible the very nature of British survival within that zone settled by Saxons up to 500 is the greatest challenge facing anybody who studies this topic. It has long been recognised that place-names offer many and valuable clues. The names of the towns are important for a particular, British reason. In post-410 Britain, as Leslie Alcock pointed out,[43] any continuity from the Roman civil organisation of the fourth century was one of the *towns*, not of the *civitates*. In this respect, Britain differed from (say) Gaul; and nomenclature reflects this. Paris is named from *Lutetia Parisiorum*, and the tribal, civitas name has survived. But our *Venta Belgarum* became Winchester, our *Venta Silurum* Caerwent; in both English and Welsh, the town name mattered, the tribal, civitas label early disappeared.

This aside, it is not an accident that the Roman *Londinium* is perpetuated in 'London', a city which in some fashion has never been deserted since Roman times; or that, because the medieval city developed around and east of the cathedral, which was extra-mural to the Roman town, 'St Albans' as a name totally replaced *Verulamium*. Nothing of the name of *Isurium Brigantium* can be found in the modern 'Aldborough', the meaning of which could be translated as 'the old deserted walled town', this site having been abandoned at the end of the Roman period, and re-occupied at a very much later time.

Assuming that retention of the Roman name points either to continued occupation (however tenuous) long enough for the name to have social meaning, and to have been adopted by English speakers generally after 500, or to the use of such a name for an extra-mural settlement dominated by the Roman town, we can map the incidence of these cases. In fig. 44, a system of weighting has been used, near-whole survival (as *Londinium*, London) being given a value of '3'; and partial, usually with sound-changes and transmission through another language (as *Luguvalium*, Carlisle), a value of '2'.

But these are not all the relevant names. Margaret Gelling[44] has now suggested that, over much of south-east England – and it is implicit that this could have been in the later fifth century – English speakers coming into direct contact with Britons whose own place-name vocabulary (if not, indeed, everyday speech) still contained spoken *Latin* forms, adopted or borrowed certain elements which they now heard in this guise. Most significant would be *vic(us)*, the usual Roman term, both for

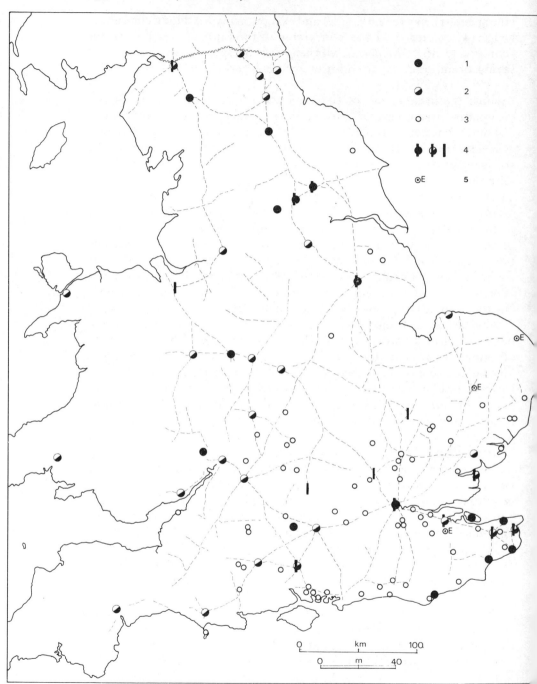

the smallest unit of civil administration, and it is thought colloquially for what we would now call 'village' or even '(small) town'. The Old English compound of *ūīc*, a direct loan of this word, and *hām*, 'village' (our 'home(stead)'), as *wīchām*, underlies many of the Wickhams, Wycombs or Wykehams today. A gratifying large number of the known instances, over half of them, either coincides with or is closely associated with Romano–British settlements.

With this can be placed other elements: *camp*, from Latin *campus* 'field', *port*, Latin *portus* 'harbour', and *funt*, either from Latin *fontana*, or the oblique stem (*font-em*) of Latin *fons* 'spring, fountain'. More specialised are rare, or sole, cases of *corte* (as Dovercourt, Essex), Latin *cohort-em* 'enclosed yard'; *croh* (as in Croydon, Surrey), from *crocus* 'saffron'; and *faefer*, Latin *faber* in the sense of 'master metal-worker' (i.e., maker of Saxon or sub-Roman jewellery).

The distribution of these elements[45] supports the general hypothesis that they belong to the most likely area for any such loans, and they have been added to the major settlement-names in fig. 44, with an evidential weighting value of '1'. A minor point of interest, shown on the same map by the upright-bar symbol, no. 4, is rather later in time – the use, by Bede, in the early eighth century of the word *civitas* in connection with certain Romano–British towns and fortified places. This is not casual. James Campbell,[46] in a discussion and analysis of Bede's usage, concludes that he had reason to distinguish such terms as *urbs* and *civitas*. These did not always represent translations of OE *burg* and *caestir* (now our '-bury' and '-chester'), and moreover '. . . all the identifiable places which Bede calls, or usually calls, *civitas* had a significant Roman past'. He also notes that Bede, and other early English writers in Latin, do not use *civitas* for any place which was *not* of Roman significance, and for which the OE term would be *caestir* (Canterbury and Carlisle, the former with OE *burg*, the latter a British name, are the only exceptions). The Bedan *civitas* label is therefore of some minor importance in fig. 44, as underlining the early knowledge of the status of towns across the north of Surrey and Kent – London, Rochester, Canterbury and Richborough.

When this map is converted to a contoured density form (fig. 45), the emphasis becomes clearer. The areas of greatest continuity in this respect are the lower Thames basin (the Essex coast, London, north Surrey and Kent); a region around Gloucester, Cirencester and the lower Severn; and in the north, a region involving the area of Elmet (*cf.* fig. 49), the Vale of

---

44 Distribution map, survival (after 400) of Romano–British place-names and certain Latin place-name elements (after Gelling, Hogg, Jackson, and Rivet & Smith)

1 Near-whole survival (as London), evidential weighting of '3'   2 Partial survival only (as Carlisle), weighting of '2'   3 Elements (after Gelling 1978), weighting of '1'   4 Places described as *civitas* by Bede (Campbell 1979) – no weighting   5 The Eccles – names in Norfolk and Kent

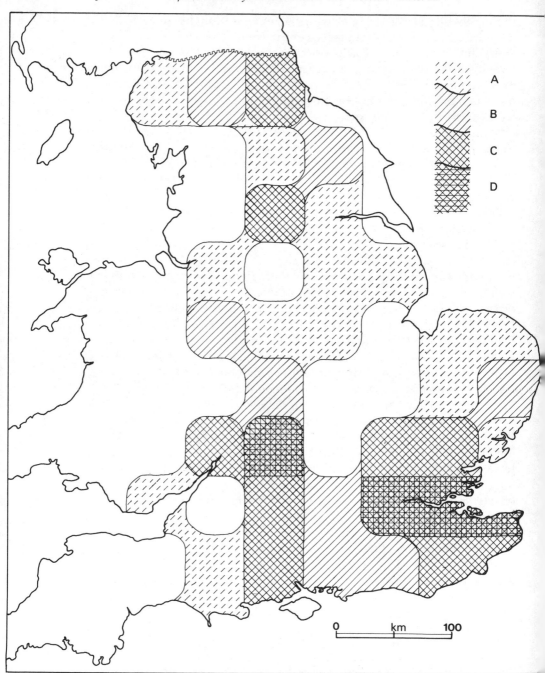

45 Contoured density map, survival (after 400) of Romano–British place-names and elements, derived from fig. 44. Totalled evidential weighting by 50km squares; totals, A 1–3 B 4–5 C 6–7 D 8–10

York, and the eastern hinterland of the Wall. There are large, and if they were early settled by Saxons, significantly blank areas, like the Yorkshire coast. But if this is taken as a simple index of whereabouts, unevenly through Britannia, names or name-elements of Roman (Latin) origin were used into the fifth and later centuries, it may begin to highlight those regions where British survival and continuity was at its most marked.

There is another way of approaching this; and that is through the names given by the English to places where Britons, or whole communities of the British, supposedly continued to live alongside them. Place-names of this class are specialised, and have been comparatively little explored on a wide scale, though it is known that the expected *Brettas* ('the British') forms, as in Brettenham, do not demonstrably occur before the ninth century.

The Anglo-Saxons called the British *walas* (plural), *walh* (singular) – a name they brought with them from the Continent, where originally it meant people speaking Celtic, or even Latin-speaking (Celtic) Gallo-Romans. *Walh* developed a second meaning, 'serf, slave', and so occurs (in its West Saxon form *wealh*) from the late seventh century in law codes; Margaret Faull has provided a full study of this.[47] Professor Kenneth Cameron has now assembled a wide range of place-names compounded with the element *walh*, either certainly, or with acceptable probability – names of the types Walcot, Walton, Walworth, etc. His article[48] provides the necessary long discussion; but it can be noted that a significant number of the names so listed are, again, directly or closely associated with Romano–British settlements of various kinds.

Another word used by the Anglo-Saxons was OE *cumbre*, itself a borrowing from the Primitive Welsh term meaning 'a Briton, a Welshman', seen now in contemporary Welsh *Cymro* 'Welshman', *Cymru* 'Wales', *Cymraeg* 'Welsh', etc. During the Roman period, and as the postulated British **combrogos*, plural **combrogi*, adjectival **combrogicā* – '(those) with (the same) border: fellow-countrymen' – this must have been a common intra-national name, or what the British of the Highland Zone in particular called themselves; it can be seen in Cumberland and Cumbria. OE *cumbre* occurs in various place-names of the Comber Mere and Cumberworth type.[49]

The second contoured density map (fig. 46) is constructed in the same way as fig. 45, allotting a weight value of '1' both to the *cumbre* names, and the *walh* names selected by Cameron. Those *walh* names whose sites appear to be linked to Romano–British settlements[50] have been given a value of '2', and the map shows the overall pattern.

The most obvious distinction between this map, and the previous one, is that while the bias is still southern rather than northern, the whole pattern has shifted some 50–100 km westward. This must reflect name-creation at a later date; and a moment's reflection will suggest that, if fig.

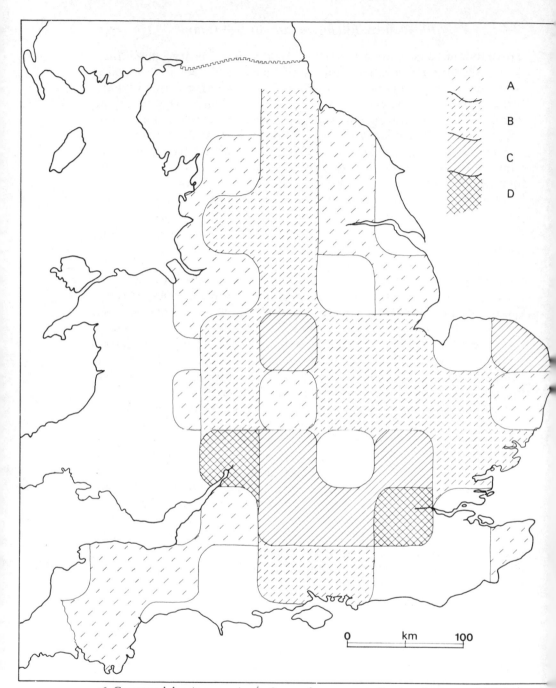

46 Contoured density map, Anglo-Saxon place-names indicative of contact with British communities or settlements: *Cumbre* names (after Gelling 1978), weighting of '1'; *walh* names (after Cameron 1980), weighting of '1'; the same if significantly close to Romano–British sites (Todd, in Cameron 1980), weighting of '2'. Totalled evidential weighting by 50km squares: totals, A 1–2   B 3–4   C 5–6   D 7+

45 is mainly concerned with the later fifth and sixth centuries, fig. 46 must involve Morris' period IV and later, the continued westward movement of Anglo-Saxons after about 570 into regions where one might well expect them to encounter long-standing British settlements. At the same time, and it would seem over much of East Anglia, the east Midlands, Wessex and the south, communities of both origins might be postulated in the same landscape.

As an experiment, these two maps have been combined (again by using the total weightings in each 50 km square) as fig. 47. This has been done partly because the *implication* in either case is much the same – a continuity of British population – and partly to bring out any common features.

Here, it is useful to add a little more information. The line across England marks what, on present evidence, is the approximate limit around AD 500 of Anglo-Saxon settlement. The major Roman towns and cities are also included, with a preliminary idea of which of them are thought – mainly on archaeological evidence – to have been occupied (as towns) after 400. This is not an easy aspect to map, since the information is far from readily available and must in some instances be derived from personal communications, or incomplete news of work still in progress. The black circles indicate towns where there is little doubt that occupation continued at least during the first half of the fifth century: London,[51] Canterbury,[52] Silchester,[53] Verulamium,[54] Gloucester,[55] Wroxeter,[56] Carlisle[57] and Chester[58] are included. There is fair agreement that (say) Aldborough, Brough and Durobrivae were abandoned at the end of the fourth century. In other cases, the evidence (or its interpretation) is still uncertain.

The striking correlation between areas of relatively high density derived from the two forms of place-names, and towns with post-400 occupation, suggest that again it is worth inserting cases of Bede's application of the term *civitas*; and though they are not major towns, Dorchester in Oxfordshire, and Rochester in Kent, are included. The former qualifies on several grounds.[59] Rochester, whose Roman name was another *Durobrivae*,[60] was known to Bede both as *civitas Dorubrevi* (Latin) and *Hrofæscæstræ* (OE).[61] As a site selected for a bishopric by Augustine's mission, it must be another strong potential instance of continuity.

But, viewed from further back, there are two other and wider impressions to be gained. One is a clear distinction between the north, and south, halves of the old Roman Britannia, the divide being a line roughly from the Mersey estuary (north of Chester) to the large inlet of the Wash (south-east of Lincoln). In the northern half, may one suppose, not that there were necessarily fewer British in the north of England, but that the northern wars described by Gildas – and placed here by Edward Thompson – took place between Catterick (on the north) and Lincoln-to-Chester (on the south), producing that disruption of continuity reflected in the paucity of appropriate place-names? Is this in fact a *visual* counterpart of what Gildas is talking about?

The other impression concerns the two blank areas. That which lies south-west of York seems to imply, since it largely coincides with sub-Roman Elmet,[62] not absence of sub-Roman British population, but the relative absence of intrusive *English* settlement that might have produced *cumbre* or *walh* names. In the south, the other blank, centred some 40 km west of Verulamium, is also significant, because it covers the northern half, and foot, of the Chiltern ridge, and the rising ground of north Buckinghamshire. This again, notably in the case of the Chilterns,[63] is a tract regarded as likely to have housed a continuing Romano–British population; and one in which the relatively few cemeteries of the post-Roman centuries are predominantly inhumation ones.

The area around London – the eastern part of the highest-weighted zone in fig. 47 – has attracted attention already in this context. Wheeler,[64] in what still remains a classic essay, offered a model of a 'sub-Roman triangle', taking in Colchester, Verulamium, London, Rochester, Canterbury and Richborough, in which at this period Anglo-Saxon cremation burials were virtually absent and the dominance of 'the Roman rite of inhumation' was but one mark of a continuing British presence – robust enough to influence the character of a mixed population. This triangle is indicated on the map. More recently, Martin Biddle[65] would agree that, in the special and not fully understood circumstances of sub-Roman London and its surrounding area, and allowing that later discoveries slightly modify Wheeler's ideas, we must envisage conditions closer to those in Gaul than in, say, the English Midlands. Contemporary studies on the Kentish side, which now bid fair to shed detailed light on the complex nature of this Saxon–British juxtaposition[66] – and it has the further dimension of a cross-Channel trade, long after 400[67] – tend towards similar conclusions. But the whole of this east-west belt across southern Britain, the heavily cross-hatched area in fig. 47, supposedly stressing continuity of the British in an increasingly Saxon-disrupted, Saxon-dominated fifth–sixth-century landscape begins to exhibit even more complexities. We now have Dr Tania Dickinson's demonstration[68]

---

47 Combined contoured density map, based on figs. 45 and 46. Broken line – approximate limit of Anglo-Saxon settlement, *c.*500. Major Romano–British towns and cities, evidence of post-400 occupation: 1 Not known 2 Known (to 1980) 3 Dubious 4 Places described as *civitas* by Bede. Totalled evidential weightings (from figs. 45 and 46) by 50 km squares: totals, A 1–3 B 4–6 C 7–9 D 10+. 'S-RT' = Wheeler's 'sub-Roman triangle' (Wheeler 1935)

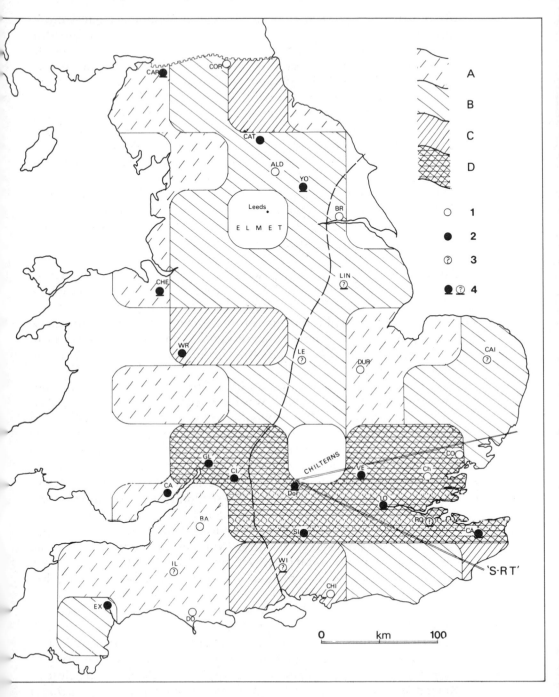

that Saxon graves of the period 450–550 can be securely recognised from certain grave-goods, even those of *c*.500–50; and that the distribution of the latter suggests a Saxon penetration westward along and around the Upper Thames valley-system, as far west as Cirencester, during the supposed pause after Mount Badon. Saxons may have been in Cirencester well before its capture by Ceawlin and his brother in 577.

If the cumulative effect of these maps – which are based on one main category of evidence alone, that of place-names – is to imply that certainly in the late fifth century, and to an appreciable degree up to AD 600 (or later), very substantial numbers of Roman-descended British continued to occupy the same areas and even, marginally, the towns which had been the homes of their pre-400 ancestors, it has to be allowed that some element of Christianity may also have been maintained. To claim that is one thing. To demonstrate it, by place-names, or any form of general and objective evidence, is another.

An element not hitherto mentioned is that seen in such place-names as Eccles, Eccleshall, Exley, etc. The whole *Eccles-* group was brought to modern notice by Professor Kenneth Cameron[69] who gave all the known examples, and plotted them against the Roman road system. Some few further instances have since come to light;[70] and notes on a number of papers dealing with Eccles names were included in a summary by Gillian Fellows Jensen.[71]

The ultimate source is Latin *ecclesia*, a word encountered in an earlier chapter of this book (p. 147). It was borrowed, in its British VL spoken form – and most of the Britons would have been pronouncing this word as *eglēsia*[72] – to give (with loss of the final unstressed syllable) primitive Welsh **eglēs*. Saxons who heard this word, in general not before the late sixth century, then borrowed it themselves from the British, as **eclēs*, substituting their *-cl-* for the British *-gl-* cluster. Later, the stress shifted to the first syllable (*écles*), and the older spellings of the recorded place-names show when this element is involved.

In modern Welsh, *eglwys* means 'a church'; and the history of Cornish *eglos* in place-names shows that from Norman times onward it was the conventional term for a full parish church with rights of burial. Kenneth Jackson, however, went no further than saying[73] that the English Eccles-place-names could imply 'the existence of some sort of British population-centre with Christian worship'. But in 1922 Eilert Ekwall[74] opined that these names actually indicated that there had been British churches in the place so called; and Cameron, agreeing that each such name 'no doubt denoted a British church', sought to show that many of them lie close to Roman roads and that a quarter of them are very close to Roman sites. Since 1968, fairly uncritical lay statements suggest that a number of writers assume a firm approbation, by leading onomasticists, of the idea that Eccles- place-names all define British churches of Roman origin – if not indeed Romano–British churches – and that all we need to do is to locate the sites on the ground.

As a start, we can say that these names are not quite all in the same group, and this is apart from the existence of simple (*Eccles*) and compound (*Eccleston*, Eccleshall) forms. In her discussion of those possible spoken Latin elements, like *camp*, *funt*, *port*, etc., borrowed to form early English place-names, Margaret Gelling[75] would include three Eccles- names which stand, geographically, well outside the general distribution. From their locations, these could be very early borrowings indeed; perhaps from fifth-century spoken VL forms, rather than from the later British derivative. All three are simple forms. Eccles, near Attleborough, and another Eccles near Hickling, are both in Norfolk. The Eccles in Kent (in 975, of *aecclesse*) lies 5 miles (8 km) SSW of Rochester and 12 miles (19 km) east of Lullingstone and there are known Roman remains immediately north of it. These three instances are distinguished (by the capital *E*) on the basic map (fig. 44).

The other Eccles- names are in northern and western Britain, and beyond the AD 500 Saxon limit. To Cameron's 1968 list, with its additions, it is desirable now to add a further group (several of which Cameron had noted) which lie north of Hadrian's Wall; these will be described shortly. But before exploring the significance of the distribution-pattern, we might look at possible meanings.

In Chapter 3, where the British Latin terms for various Christian ideas were examined, it was suggested that the commoner fourth-century meaning of *ecclesia* may have been 'a Christian society; Christian group', and though we have no examples any contemporary locative with *ecclesia* might have mean, primarily, 'a place where Christians live'. A most instructive pointer comes from Gregory of Tours' *Historia*; he tells us[76] about a *vicus* near Clermont (Ferrand), in an area where rural paganism persisted until the seventh century, *plerumque . . . quem Christianorum vocant* 'which they generally call Vicus Christianorum, the Village-of-the-Christians'. Now in fourth–fifth-century Kent and Norfolk, we cannot rule out the idea that a rather similar *vicus ecclesiae*, or *ecclesia*, was the name given to hamlets of sub-Roman British Christians (to be picked up by Saxons), and that such names were created, in spoken VL, by other Roman Britons in the immediate district who were not themselves necessarily Christian yet.

The pattern of all the other Eccles- names (fig. 49) is such that, beyond the Saxon line, most of them are within Jackson's Area II on his river-names map, in that general N-S zone affected by Anglo-Saxon advances after the late sixth century. English borrowing of the British form **eglēs* gives, however, no indication that the semantic root or the etymology of this word meant anything to English speakers; it would have been just another *Walas* word. It is a strange fact, as R.L. Thomson[77] reminded us, that for the idea of 'a church building', the Anglo-Saxons used, not anything taken from Latin *ecclesia*, and certainly not *ecles* (which does not occur as an OE noun at all), but *cirice*. This entirely different word (our 'church, kirk'), of Greek origin and semantically parallel to *dominic-us, -a*, is one that their Germanic forbears had acquired in the eastern, Greek-speaking parts of the Roman empire; it is also seen in, e.g., Old Icelandic *kirkja*.

Some of the places indicated by the north Eccles- names may prove to be archaeologically significant. Eaglesfield, near Cockermouth in Cumbria,[78] is associated with a possible Christian sub-Roman cemetery. Dr Margaret Faull, in fieldwork, has noted[79] certain remains in connection with an Eccles at Stanbury, near Haworth. Historically, Professor Geoffrey Barrow[80] gives us a further dimension, in the first place by adding a group of names from southern Scotland. In the past, there has been a slight reluctance to include these with the northern English Eccles-group, because the linguistic history of Scotland means that rather later introductions of the Scottish Gaelic *eaglais* (derived from Old Irish *eclais*, 'the Church Universal: a church building; a Christian community', and of course itself ultimately from Latin *ecclesia*) might be involved.

Barrow regards the Scottish examples shown in fig. 49 as true Eccles-names. They include *Egglesbrec(h)* (twelfth century), near or at the present Falkirk;[81] the ancient St Ninian's Church, formerly *Eggles, Egles, Eccles*, near Stirling Castle; *Ecclesmachan* in West Lothian; an 'Eccles Cairn' just east of Yetholm; and Eaglesham, formerly *Egglesham*, in the Mearns, south of Glasgow.

What many of these places have in common with some further south, notably in Lancashire, is that at a later, pre-Norman period, churches at these sites had the status of a *matrix ecclesia*, mother-church of a territorial division smaller than a modern county, and of a kind that can be traced over much of England and southern Scotland. This is also indicated in fig. 49. In Lancashire, for instance, the five 'hundreds' of South Lancashire (Amounderness, Blackburnshire, Leyland, Salford and West Derby) each possess just one Eccles-, three in the 'Eccleston' form of place-name.

This is a strong hint of antiquity, if nothing else. The present writer would be inclined to see most, perhaps all, of these Eccles- sites originating in sub-Roman British Christian communities of the sixth century AD, and if this is so, one cannot exclude the idea that a good many of them go back to the fifth century; they were merely recognised as such some time after the 570s. Whether the use of the word (as late British *eglēs(ia)*) in each case arose to distinguish a community of Christians – three or four of which could have met in a common, centrally-sited church, later the *matrix ecclesia* of the 'shire', thanage, or local royal

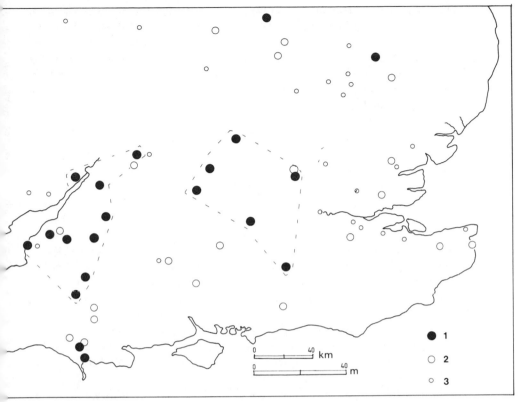

48 Indications of 4th-cent. revival of paganism in southern Britain
  1 Temples, on votive coin evidence (after Painter 1971a), with additions – Thistleton, Nettleton Shrub, Congresbury, South Cadbury, Bath and Uley 2 Christian evidence (fig. 15), weighting of '3' 3 The same, weightings of '2' or '1' only

estate – or whether a locally-notable large wooden church was always involved, we cannot determine. It may be that both uses were in operation, and that again the nomenclature arose, in British mouths, to describe Christians who were seen as distinct from their non-Christian neighbours. By 600, the very word may have been becoming a linguistic fossil. The national distribution *is* significant. The marked absence of Eccles- sites south of the Severn is, the writer suspects, due to the employment there, and in the south-west, of other terms altogether (like Primitive Cornish *lann*, alluding to a church standing in its enclosed cemetery).[82] In the north, the concentration of Eccles- sites in the area of Elmet must strengthen the belief that this principality was not only British but increasingly after 400 a *Christian* British state. Those *loca sancta*, of which Wilfrid and others knew in the seventh century, can hardly have failed to include the Elmet Eccles- sites.

The argument is now becoming clear. The British were not expunged or totally expelled by the Saxon settlements and wars in the second half of the fifth century; some, perhaps many, of these British were Christian heirs to Romano–British Christianity, something that encouraged the specialised retention of spoken VL alongside spoken British; and British Christianity continued, notably rather more to the west and north of Britain than in Roman times.

But this cannot be the whole religious picture, and the very suggestion that the homes of Christians could be onomastically distinguished implies that other Britons were not Christian. The strength of remnant paganism cannot be dismissed. The fourth century in Roman Britain saw, as did the late fourth and fifth in the Rhine provinces, something of a revival of the *prisca religio*.

The reasons for this are not clear; the apostasy of Julian in 361–3 may have given it a limited impetus, but this cannot be all. The evidence comes from archaeology,[83] and is summarised in fig. 48. These are dated instances of pagan temples being reconstituted, even constructed, in the fourth century, and marked by the quantities of coins interpreted as votive offerings found on such sites. The emphasis is mainly southern. The map, plotting these against (faint circles) the distribution of evidence for Christianity (taken from fig. 15), points to two principle areas. The eastern one again skirts the Chilterns, and the Berkshire Downs. to the west, there is the southern shore of the Severn Estuary, with Mendip and Cotswold, a zone containing such outstanding pagan centres as Lydney, Bath, and Uley.[84] It is noticeable that late Roman Christian evidence is relatively weak within either of the zones indicated. There is little point in pursuing this here, but a body of opinion (headed in this century by Dr Margaret Murray) has long held that paganism, from native British rather than Romanised cults, continued to form a concealed background to British religion throughout the first millenium AD, and surfaced briefly in the Middle Ages as an aspect of the various witch-cults.[85]

If one can make the following assertion without prejudice to *origins*, it would be difficult to dispute the notion that an organised Church of episcopal character existed in the south-west, Wales, the north of England, Cumbria and southern Scotland during the fifth and sixth centuries. What Gildas has to say is direct evidence[86] for this, back to the generation before 500; and implicit for the slightly longer stage back to about 425 where we left the archaeological evidence discussed in earlier chapters. The inscribed memorial stones, a series that begins in the late fifth century, can hardly be other than Christian. If few of the inscriptions are of the kind, or long enough, to state this directly, the entire tradition is a Christian one and those phrases or formulae which can be matched from Gaul, Iberia or North Africa have only Christian parallels.

The evidence that relates to southern Scotland, and to Ireland in the fourth and fifth centuries, will be examined in the following chapters. In Chapter 11, it will be suggested that sub-Roman Christianity in the south of Scotland was, after its own fashion, both episcopal and diocesan; a church under the leadership of bishops, who themselves controlled, spiritually, adjacent or contiguous areas. That this was probably true of England and Wales at the same period is not only a matter of analogous likelihood; it is indicated by various references.

The British Church's capacity to hold meetings (synods) and to communicate officially with the Church in Gaul was seen in the contexts of Victricius of Rouen, in the very late fourth century, and of Germanus and Lupus in 429. A second visit of Germanus will be mentioned, later. Unless we are prepared to suppose an otherwise inexplicable lacuna, this continuity of some form of church government must run, through the *seniores* and the *dominicati rhetorici* whom Patrick mentions (either as between 432 and 461 on the 'orthodox' dating, rather nearer 470 on the model postulated below), to the later fifth-century bishops implied in Gildas' writings, and indeed to the *sacerdotes* – almost certainly meaning 'bishops' as contrasted with *presbyteres*, 'priests' – on very late fifth-century or early sixth-century stones from south-west Scotland and north-west Wales (fig. 50). Together with allusions on similar inscribed stones to *presbyteres* (*cf.* fig. 43.4), and possibly – though the stones are now lost – to *episcopus* and *diaconus*[87] as descriptive titles, this must mean a church organisation not radically different from that assumed for late Roman Britain.

As for the territorial extent or definitions of any dioceses, in sub-Roman and sixth-century western and northern Britain, the pattern of the former *civitates* represented, episcopally, by their urban centres had disappeared. What presumably replaced them were the native kingdoms, some of which may themselves have possessed internal divisions reflecting dynastic arrangements. We get a hint of what a sixth-century diocese may have been. It is that of St Dubricius or Dyfrig,[88] in south-east Wales; a region where direct continuity between fourth-century Roman estates, and the post-Roman land-holdings, between Roman villas and native seats, is now strongly argued.[89] Was Dubricius really the 'territorial' bishop of Ercing (fig. 51)? A simple map, indicating the early churches under his patronage, suggests we may see the outlines of a native principality and a Christian diocese as coincident areas.

By 600, we have Gregory's correspondence with Augustine, and the Pope's allusion to *Brittaniarum . . . omnes episcopos* 'all the bishops of Britain'.[90] Slightly later, there was Augustine's meeting in the west[91] with *episcopos sive doctores proximae Brettonum provincae* 'the bishops and religious teachers of the neighbouring province of the

Britons'. Augustine's second meeting involved no less than seven of these *Brettonum episcopi*; and also many learned men, chiefly from *Bancornaburg*, Bangor on the Dee, near Chester. The bishops were not monastic bishops. Bede, only too well aware of the monastic custom whereby abbots ruling monasteries were in that respect superior to bishops, specifies that Bangor was then under *Dinoot abbas*, Abbot Dinoot. In 604, Augustine's successor, Laurence, wrote not only to the bishops and abbots throughout Ireland, but also, *cum coepiscopos suis* 'with his fellow-bishops' (a synod, in fact) to *Brettonum sacerdotibus* 'the bishops of the British'.[92]

One can omit, because the sources are very much later redactions, all the inferences possible from Insular hagiography, and select merely the tenth-century Life of St Paul Aurelian,[93] who like Samson (of Dol), David and Gildas himself was a pupil of Illtud at Llanilltud, or Lantwit, in wouth-east Wales. This Life may descend from a much older (seventh-century?) original. Paul, before leaving Cornwall for Brittany, is involved with the sixth-century Cornish king, Marcus Conomorus. He provides religious instruction at the royal seat, now claimed as the re-occupied hill-fort of Castle Dore near Fowey,[94] and because he is determined to go to Brittany, Paul has to refuse the king's invitation to accept *pontificatum suae regionis*, the office of bishop over his region or realm.

It is possible to argue that all these traces of episcopal Christianity in Britain, west of the Saxons, have nothing whatsoever to do with Roman Britain; that the extinction of the Romano–British church, in the south from about 440, and in the north during the period of fighting envisaged by Edward Thompson from Gildas' DEB, was total; and that all that had been described was the result of a massive re-implantation of the Faith from outside, probably from Gaul. Economy of hypotheses alone demands that we should at least explore the idea that direct continuity did exist. Where the post-Roman Church in Wales is concerned, it has been both assumed and argued, for so long and by so many students,[95] that this is directly and continuously derived from the fourth-century Romano–British church that, in Welsh eyes, the onus would lie upon the doubter to show otherwise.

Figure 49 is an attempt to bring much of this evidence together. The map has purposefully been left blank, within the area affected by Saxons up to around 500. West of this line, the different diagonal hatchings (symbols 6 and 7) show, from the earlier fig. 16, those regions of west and

---

49 Indications of sub-Roman Christianity in Britain
   1 Likely centres of Christianity (see text)   2 Towns whose place-names show near-whole or partial survival   3 *Eccles* place-name sites   4 The same with later *matrix ecclesia* status (after Barrow 1973)   5 Inscribed stones with S (*sacerdos*), P (*presbyter*), D? (*diaconus*) and E? (*episcopus*). Diagonal hatching (from fig. 16); Christian evidences, by 50 km squares   6 Weighted totals A and B;   7 Weighted total C

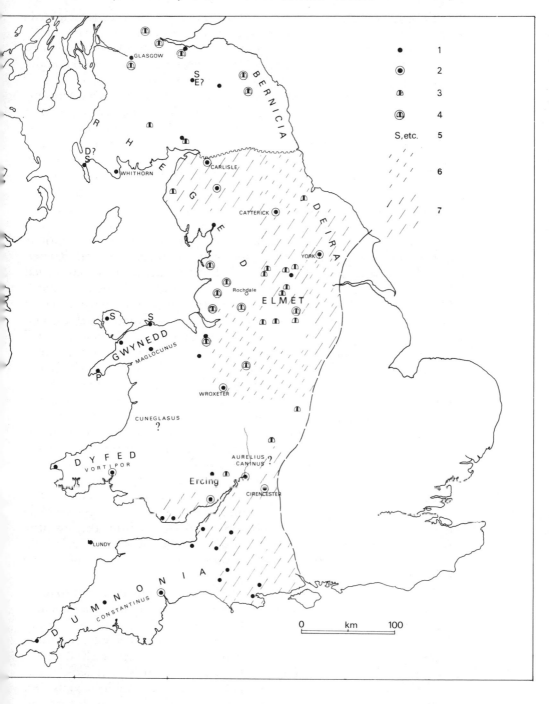

north Britannia – and they are still within *England* – where the weighted-
total densities of late Roman Christian evidence were, respectively, in the
lowest (fig. 16. A) and in the two intermediate (B and C) grades. They
indicate the potential existence of Christians, in the parts shaded, at the
end of the fourth century and the start of the fifth.

The most important native kingdoms are named, and where appropriate the names of the early sixth-century (Christian) rulers we have
from Gildas are added; as are the Eccles- place-names, further distinguished if they later attained *matrix ecclesia* importance. The
principal Roman towns, the symbols encircled where there is any whole
or partial retention of the place-name, have been indicated, because of
the possibility that some of these were still relevant to the native
kingdoms in the fifth century.

The small black dots show – and there has to be selection, and an
element of subjective preference, in this – places where, for various
reasons, one could suppose the existence of Christianity after the Roman
period, and before the arrival or the direct influence of the converted
English. The kind of site one might have in mind would be represented
(in Scotland) by Glasgow, because of Kentigern; Dumbarton Rock, if
this was the seat of Patrick's *Coroticus*; and Abercorn, Peebles, Old
Melrose, Kirkmadrine, Whitehorn and Hoddom, about which more will
be said in the next chapter. Leeds (*Loidis*) in Elmet, and to the south-
west, Chester and Bangor, have already appeared in this discussion. The
Welsh sites, of which only a handful is shown, are those (like Llanilltud)
where one has reason to suspect that the Christian importance antedates
the monastic vogue of the earlier sixth century. In the great south-west
peninsula, the sites include some whose history, in this respect, has
recently been argued by Susan Pearce;[96] they must include Wareham,
with its remarkable outlier group of inscribed stones dating from the
later seventh century,[97] and Sherborne, potentially among the most
intriguing cases of continuity of an urban/religious settlement; and
further west, such sites as Cannington, the Isle of Lundy, Lewannick in
east Cornwall (with, like Lundy, inscribed stones from the late fifth
century), and Phillack in west Cornwall, perhaps an isolated early fifth-
century Christian focus by a little commercial harbour (*cf.* its chi-rho
stone, fig. 21. 1).

As it stands – and it must be seen in the light of a first attempt to make
this point, in such a form – this distribution-map contains, over much of
the north of England from Shropshire-Cheshire-Staffordshire up to the
Wall, and in the south over a smaller area with Dorset-Somerset-Severn-
Cotswold, a degree of correlation. This is between regions (the diagonal
hatching) where by 400 some element of Christianity, archaeologically
detected, was present; where until after 570–600 the Anglo-Saxons were
simply not present in enough strength seriously to disrupt British life,

religious or secular; and where on a variety of grounds, from history, archaeology, place-names and inscriptions, Christianity was again present in the sixth century, and either demonstrably or inferentially in the fifth as well. The map is, given the limitations of the evidence that we can hope to recover, as near as one can get to a picture of the sub-Roman British Church, mainly in what became England.

What, then, of the Gaulish missionaries, or the chances that this Church sprang from an Atlantic re-kindling of the Faith? More will be said about this in the final chapter; but another map (fig. 50), its centre lying rather further to the west, provides the setting. This shows some of the relatively few ways in which archaeology is able to suggest contact between Ireland and Atlantic Britain, and (in general, Atlantic) Gaul, after 400. It includes the 1980 distribution of imported wheel-made vessels, distinctive varieties of pottery, known by their archaeological labels of Class D and Class E wares[98] – which, as far as can be ascertained, originate in Atlantic regions of Gaul from the fifth century onwards. Other related minor imports of glass, and minor metalwork, have been omitted; the pottery is by far the most abundant of such imports. What this pattern marks is something of the outcome of a long-lived straggling sea-trade, between on the one hand such ports as Bordeaux and the Garonne, La Rochelle, Nantes and the Loire, and perhaps Brest: and on the other, Shannon mouth, Cork harbour, Dublin Bay, Strangford Lough, the Clyde, and down around the myriad landing-places of the Welsh and Dumnonian coastlines. Small ships that could carry jars and mortaria and perhaps wine in little casks could of course carry people – people like Patrick in the fifth century, Columbanus in the sixth, let alone the merchants from the lands of the Gauls and the occasional Frankish mercenaries who brought their swords with them.

That Christians, in the early fifth century including pilgrims on their way to the Levant, could have travelled this way is certain; and it is in the highest degree probable, as has so often been suggested, that the revived custom of erecting inscribed Christian tombstones has a great deal to do with Gaulish (or Iberian, or even North African) models, either seen by Insular pilgrims or urged on British Christians by Continental visitors and refugees. What was imported was, of course, the *idea*. The technology, the methodology, if one can use such terms for the first, rather crude, horizontally-inscribed British instances was not entirely alien. In fig. 52, the two examples from west Cornwall (1 and 2) may be separated in time by the best part of two centuries; in space, they stood within half-a-dozen miles of each other, and those who put up no. 2[99] quite possibly trudged towards the cemetery in question along a dusty track where no. 1[100] still stood by the roadside. The re-used stone (3) is both a Roman milestone and a tombstone.[101]

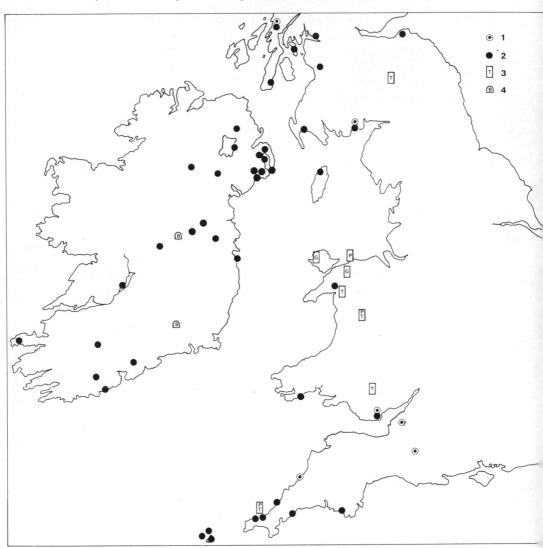

50 Gaulish contacts with sub-Roman Britain and Ireland, 5th–7th cent.
   1 Class D pottery   2 Class E pottery   3 Inscribed stones with T (*in hoc tumulo*, etc.),
   P (*in pace*), or G (direct Gaulish allusion)   4 Place-names *Bordgal* (*cf.* Thomas 1976)

The ideas would be expressed, also, in the wording; and fig. 50 takes merely a handful – those stones which use the formulae IN HOC TUMULO, or IN PACE, or both together; and two stones from Gwynedd[102] which have even closer Gaulish allusions – one mentions a Gaul, the other a Gaulish consular date equivalent to AD 540. It is possible that the scattered examples of the later, un-encircled chi-rho on some of these stones (*cf.*

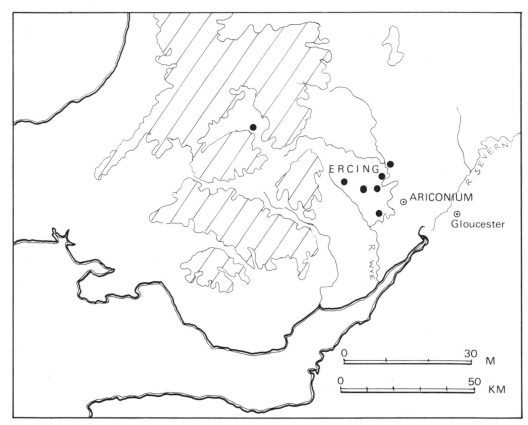

51 Sixth-cent. diocese in south-east Wales? Dubricius and Ercing; black circles, early church dedications to Dubricius (after Doble). Land over 800 ft (250 m) shaded

fig. 21, second row) are also of Gaulish or non-British inspiration. But the locations of these stones, and the incidence of the imported pottery finds, mapped as they are in fig. 50, emphasises the essentially Atlantic nature of this later fifth- and sixth-century contact. Its Gaulish emphasis is finally stressed in a most peculiar way by the occurrence, in early Ireland, of two place-names whose forms argue an original *Bordgal*;[103] this can only be a direct borrowing from the Gallo-Roman *Bordigala*, *Burdigala*, Bordeaux, the principal port and intellectual centre of Atlantic Gaul south of the Loire. The debt that may have resulted, if academic refugees from fifth-century Aquitaine really implanted cultural offshoots in distant Ireland, has its lighter side; *bordgal* also became, as in more recent centuries did the name of Waterloo, a pseudo-noun, meaning in Old Irish 'a famous resort, gathering, assembly'.[104]

But the map must imply that this limited post-Roman Insular contact with Gaul – and the Christian aspect is only a part, possibly a minor part,

52 Roman milestones, and sub-Roman inscribed memorial stones
   1 St Hilary, Cornwall (RIB 2233, after Wright)   2 St Erth, Cornwall (CIIC 479, but
   after Beckerlegge 1953)   3 Port Talbot, Glamorgan; front, RIB 2254 (after Wright),
   back, CIIC 407

of a wider range of contacts – cannot be adduced to explain the
phenomena implicit in the previous map (fig. 49). It gives at the most part
of the explanation for the memorial stones of the kind shown here in fig.
43. We are left once more to balance probabilities. The burden of this
chapter, summarised in the various maps, is to suggest that such a
balance comes down slowly but surely on one side; that of the probability
that, whatever the true course of Britain's history of *bella externa* and
bella civilia in the fifth and sixth centuries, neither the majority of the
Britons in the lowland half of Britannia, nor the Christian faith
increasingly practised, was expunged. In some fashion, Christianity
continued, and with it we have to suppose an element of spoken vulgar
Latin alongside spoken British, and even more, written Latin; the
continuity, and a degree of percolation or spreading outwards from the
old south-east, is most detectable in all those regions where the record is
not otherwise dominated by the evidence of Saxon presence. The present
writer has avoided too rigid a definition of the term 'sub-Roman', leaving
it mainly to carry the implication of 'events within a period where
continuity from Roman times is still implied or argued'. The subject of
this chapter has, in that sense, been the sub-Roman British and the sub-
Roman British Church. The following chapters will describe the
extension of both, though emphasising the latter, to southern Scotland;
and, mainly in the person of one outstanding sub-Roman Briton, Patrick,
in Ireland.

CHAPTER ELEVEN

St Ninian, and Christianity in Southern Scotland

The earliest and (if my understanding is right) one of the most
important currents of Christianity which flowed into what is
now Scotland was a direct offshoot from the Roman
occupation of Britain . . . . In an inquiry that deals with times
so remote and materials so diverse and obscure, there is
abundant room for conflict of judgment.
W. Douglas Simpson *The Celtic Church in Scotland* (1935)

If Saint Patrick has no real rival as the Apostle of Ireland, there have been
two claimants, north of Hadrian's Wall, to an equivalent title in respect
of Scotland – the man we know as 'Ninian', or more correctly *Nynia*, and
St Columba or Columcille. Nynia, who whatever his historical dates
must be viewed as a sub-Roman figure, is most imperfectly recorded, and
not at all before the time of Bede. Columba, on the other hand, probably
lived 521–597, is the subject of a partly-biographical Life[1] compiled
about a century after his death, and is independently named in other early
sources. Nynia's sphere of activity, south-west Scotland and perhaps
some wider region occupied during the fifth century by Picts, lies both
temporarily and spatially in sub-Roman North Britain, mostly Scotland
between the Walls. Columba, an Irishman of aristocratic origin, worked
from a monastery that he founded on the isle of Iona, just west of the
larger Scottish island of Mull. Columba was concerned with the spiritual
leadership of the *Scotti*, the Irish who had settled in Argyll, and
eventually with the northern Picts, who were centred near Inverness.

These differences are established, and not in dispute. More recent
writers have however produced diverging models of the Christian origins
of Scotland. These tend to contrast Nynia, as Apostle of the Picts, or less
confidently, 'of Scotland', with the better-recorded Columba, who is
accorded rather similar epithets.[2] On the strength of one, late, reference
by Bede, Nynia is seen as having been in some fashion Roman (i.e.,
Romano–British) and orthodox, while Columba as well as being Irish
can thus be anachronistically 'Catholic', and can stand for the
separatism of the Celtic Church. In the kaleidoscope of Scottish
sectarianism, ranging from the pre-Reformation Catholics to the

extremes of congregationalism, there has been ample opportunity for alignment and re-alignment on such matters.

At the end of the Roman period, however, we possess as yet no evidence for Christianity beyond the northern frontier marked by Hadrian's Wall (*cf.* fig. 15). Lowland, or southern, Scotland, that region between the two Walls, or between the Clyde-Forth and Solway-Tyne lines, is some 120 miles (190 km) east-west, and 60 miles (100 km) north-south. Much of it is, today, still wild and mountainous. A winter flight from, say, Carlisle to Glasgow will provide a minor revelation for anyone who thinks of this region as, literally, a *Lowland* one. Throughout history, settlement has been concentrated on the coastal lands, and up such large and branching valley-systems as that of the river Tweed.

Our knowledge of the native peoples of the region during the Roman period comes from the second-century geographer Ptolemy, and the much later compilation known as the Ravenna Cosmography.[3] The four principle tribes – Damnonii, Novantae, Selgovae or Selgoves, and Otadini (more usually written Votadini) – are important, because the situations of their homelands emphasise the principal areas of settlement. These are, respectively, from Ayshire and Renfrew across the Clyde valley (Strathclyde) into Dunbartonshire and Stirling; the south-west lowlands or Galloway (counties of Wigtown and Kirkcudbright); the upper Tweed basin; and the east coastal lands, from north of Hadrian's Wall up to the Forth estuary at Stirling (fig. 53).

Maxwell has argued[4] that, from the time of Agricola, the Romans regarded these peoples as ethnically distinct from the tribes who lived north of the Clyde-Forth line – some of which in late Roman times formed the historical *Picti*, or Picts – and that in very broad terms the east-west line of the Antonine Wall was an ethnic, as well as political and military, reflection of this view. The southern Scottish tribal names, the river-names, and the names of settlements recorded by Ptolemy and elsewhere, show that the predominant speech was British.[5] These peoples of southern Scotland, though living *extra limites*, were no more terrifying or alien to the Romans in Britain than their compatriots in Cumbria and Wales.

When we turn to the matter of their relations with Rome, and the degree of recognition (if any) accorded to their native rulers, we find several interpretations. If Maxwell's reasoned analysis is accepted, these North Britons in the third century AD showed if not yet a friendly attitude towards Rome, then at least a political stability; and hence 'the continuing survival of a political and cultural frontier on the Forth-Clyde isthmus'.[6] One must not make too much of recent distributional summaries of Roman material found at non-Roman native sites in Scotland;[7] these could in the main reflect trade, and tell us little of opinions. A state of cautious neutrality, even one lubricated by a trickle

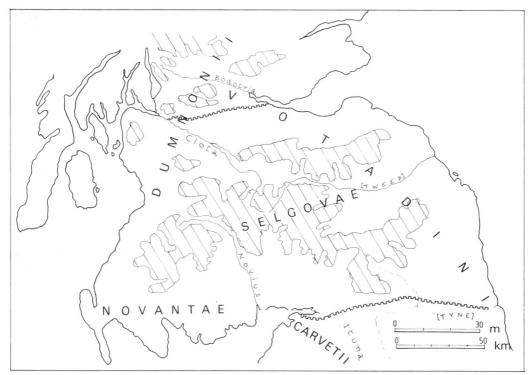

53 Native peoples of southern Scotland, from 2nd cent. AD (locations after Rivet & Smith 1979). Land over 800 ft (250 m) shaded

of luxury imports, beyond a military frontier is by no means the same as the enjoyment of officially-recognised self-government.

Our interest, where the spread of Christianity is involved, lies in the later fourth century onwards. Events in 367–9 drastically upset any former balance. Picts from the north, *Scotti* (the seaborne Irish raiders), and certain mysterious aboriginal groups called *Attacotti* – conjoined barbarians, some described by Ammianus Marcellinus as *per diversa vagantes* 'roaming about from all directions' – attacked the northern frontier. They overran, probably in part outflanked, and for the time overcame the garrisons of, Hadrian's Wall. When after 369 they had been expelled, and under Theodosius the defences of Britannia began to be reconstituted, Rome's influence and prestige where Scotland was concerned must have lessened considerably. John Mann goes so far as to suppose that all Rome could do in 369 was to regain control of the Wall itself.[8] 'She never again had any military or political authority beyond its line.' While these remarks leave aside the eventual history of the Wall itself, a frontier whose most recent historians[9] see as ending, when after

410 'all that happened was that the central government ceased paying the salaries of the civil service and the army', by the Wall garrisons (of mainly local origin) simply returning to the soil from which they sprung, there are particular archaeological observations. After 383, when Magnus Maximus seems to have withdrawn those of the garrison troops he needed for his Continental venture, it is not possible to detect wheel-made Roman pottery of later dates than this; coins do possibly take us, sparsely, to the decade 400 × 410, but that is all.

The late Sir Ian Richmond held the view[10] that certain of these North British tribes, in particular the Damnonii and the Votadini, respectively at the west and centre, and the east, parts of the Clyde-Forth isthmus, became during the late fourth century *foederati*, or formal treaty states. The period after 369, for Richmond, marked the moment when their tribal chiefs became recognised independent kings – 'that they would still be in treaty with Rome cannot be doubted'. The idea was not doubted by Frere, who saw these peoples, too, as having been granted 'more complete independence with client or federate status'.[11] It was a reasonable guess; but one that can be and has been doubted. Much of the 'client kingdom' or federate idea is derived from somewhat specialised evidence, or inference, currently open to question.

A large corpus of native tradition, probably not committed to writing before the late sixth or seventh centuries, was transmitted to early medieval Wales from southern Scotland and north Britain, and much of it concerned the king-lists and genealogies of these 'Men of the North'.[12] They include personal names of ruling figures which have been interpreted[13] as Late British or Primitive Welsh renderings of familiar Roman names – Clemens, Paternus, Quintillus or Quintilius, perhaps Urbanus, and (impossibly) Caelius. Much play has been made of the epithet *pesrut* 'Red-Tunic', attached to one *Padarn* (Paternus), and the supposition that this person as a chieftain of *foederati* had been invested with some official Roman robe as a visible mark of his status.

This is not firm ground. Kenneth Jackson, some time ago,[14] warned that the Latin, 'Roman', character of these names could be, as indeed it has been, uncritically exaggerated. The immediately post-Theodosian ancestors have been, without a shred of firm evidence, represented as Roman decuriones and praefecti, sent northwards to set up and govern 'protectorates' between the Walls. There is a proper suspicion that the pre-sixth-century portions of these transmitted genealogies may be no more than 'systematic pseudo-ancestries', hardly reliable for fifth-century reconstructions and totally unreliable for the fourth century.[15] Finally, John Mann would explain[16] such names, if really originating in the roman hierarchy, as perhaps having spread with the spread of Christianity; and Kenneth Jackson reminds us, simply, of 'the inevitable prestige of Rome among the barbarian tribes on its borders'.[17]

Our picture of Lowland Scotland and that part of Northumbria beyond the Wall after 369 should be one of lands beyond a still-manned frontier. South of it lay the vast civitas of the Brigantes, by now constituting the bulk of the re-named province of Valentia, the smaller civitas of the Carvetii with its centre at *Luguvalium*, Roman Carlisle, being correspondingly smaller and probably perpetuating the pre-367 province-name of Flavia Caesariensis.[18] We examined earlier (p. 197) the evidence that *Eburacum*, York, held a bishopric in the fourth century; and assuming that bishops would, if anywhere among the Roman towns and cities of Britain, be likely in the provincial capitals, Carlisle might be added to those indicated in figs. 14 and 38 above.

From such a fourth-century setting, could the knowledge of Christianity have reached either the Damnonii or the Votadini before 400? We certainly cannot safely argue this from the presence of silver objects with Christian devices in the Traprain Law hoard, which has all the appearance of barbarian plunder.[19] Our most important source for the first Christians north of the Wall is so very late: Bede's *Historia*, completed about 731.[20] The context can be determined. When Bede wrote, the Northumbrian Angles had extended their kingdom westward, both north and south of Hadrian's Wall, and by the later seventh century they reached Dumfries and Galloway. Ecclesiastical settlement – and the Northumbrians had been Christian since the 630s – followed on the heels of military victory and political conquest. At an uncertain date, possibly not much before 710, a good generation after south-west Scotland had been incorporated within Anglian Bernicia,[21] a new Northumbrian bishopric was established at Whithorn. The first bishop, whom Bede seems to have known, was Pecthelm.

During the previous two centuries, Whithorn, a site that cannot have lost its great religious prestige, may have expanded ecclesiastically to become a monastic centre, involving one or more churches, a resident community, school, and possibly agricultural ancillaries and its own immediate lands, under the stimulus of Christian Irish settlers in the Galloway coastlands.[22] Given such a history, and at such a time, it is almost certain that a shrine, glorifying the founder Nynia, would be publicly exhibited and venerated.[23]

We cannot be confident that we could discover the British name of Whithorn. Ptolemy attributed to the Novantae only two places, one of which is usually identified as Stranraer (Loch Ryan: *Rerigonium*), the other (*Lucopibia*) being unlocated. Whithorn was not, in Roman terms, an important settlement. The former ascription of a name *Rostat* or *Rosnat* (*Rosnant*) to Whithorn, or the Isle of Whithorn, has been called into doubt as well.[24] To Bede, it was (in Latin) *Ad Candidam Casam* '(At the) White House'; the Old English name, which meant the same, was

Hwit-ærn, and we even find an early Irish borrowing of this Northumbrian form as *Futerna*.[25]

Bede, whose informant (if not Pecthelm himself) presumably came from the Northumbrian Christians here, introduces this topic in a section first describing how the Picts and the Irish had received Christianity. He begins with Columba, priest and abbot from Ireland, coming to Iona in 565, and mentioned by Bede specifically as the man whose primary task was to convert the northern Picts.[26] In contrast, the *southern* Picts (*australes Picti*) did not require this service because they had, long before that time, been converted – or so Bede had been given to understand; *ut perhibent* 'as people hold' – by a most reverend bishop and holy man of the nation of the Britons, Nynia.

Bede has no further details to offer us about Nynia, and no dates. One can agree with Professor John MacQueen that, had Bede been able to supply such information, he would have done so.[27] We then learn that Nynia had been 'regularly instructed at Rome in the faith and mystery of the Truth'. The implication must be, less one of an actual visit to the city of Rome, than a background of Roman Christianity – presumably among the nation of the Britons, and in accord with orthodoxy (*regulariter*). What Bede writes is contrasted, and this must be intentionally so, with what he tells us about the less orthodox career of Columba. Columba was the product of a system in which a man might be both bishop and abbot, and in which a bishop might be, *ordine inusitato* 'contrary to the usual scheme of things' actually *inferior* to an abbot; the normal arrangement in a sixth-century Insular monastery.

We read next that Nynia's episcopal see is distinguished by a church named after St Martin the bishop (this is Martin of Tours), where his, Nynia's, body now rests, together with those of many other holy persons; and further that this place, now belonging to the kingdom of Bernicia, is commonly called 'At the White House', because there Nynia had built a church of stone, in a manner to which the Britons were not accustomed. (The architectural aspects of Bede's not wholly unambiguous passage were discussed earlier, p. 146.)

Some details of this bald recital are echoed in another and later, but still eighth-century source, a poem known as *Miracula Nynie Episcopi* 'The Miracles of Bishop Nynia'.[28] In grossly rhetorical and convoluted language, the poem nevertheless does contain references to Nynia's stone shrine, resting in his own church, which is clearly described as if it were part of a monastic establishment. The author of the poem, a former pupil of Alcuin of York, may have had access to a now-list and earlier source, for example a seventh-century Latin life, but it is not likely that this would have told us much more than we know from Bede.

When, then, may we suppose that Nynia lived? The reference to Martin of Tours, who died in November of 397, offers no help. Some cult of Martin had, in all probability, been established at Whithorn before Bede wrote – it is by no means unlikely that this cult was actually introduced by the Northumbrians, and a similar connection between Martin and the last days of Roman Christianity had been reported to Bede in the case of Canterbury, as we know. A likely occasion might have been the construction or alteration of a Whithorn church – possibly the one sketched, rather than properly described, in the *Miracula* poem – with an altar containing a representative relic brought from Martin's shrine at Tours. There is a famous cave not far from Whithorn, at a place called Physgyll, on the beach; as a religious retreat of a kind much favoured by post-Roman monastic Christianity, it may well have been seen as an echo of one of Martin's hermitages (such as one under a rock-face in a gorge near Tours) described by Sulpicius Severus.[29] This cave has been excavated; nothing found there suggests Christian use, however, before the later sixth century at the earliest.[30] The improbability of any *contemporary* connection between Nynia and Martin, and of an early fifth-century dedication of an unprecedented kind in Martin's honour at Whithorn, has been fully demonstrated by Professor Owen Chadwick.[31] There is really little warrant in Bede's scant words to assume that Nynia was a pioneer monk or that he reproduced Martin's prototype Gaulish monastery in south-west Scotland;[32] still less can one safely translate Bede's word *regulariter* as 'trained as a monk' on the assumption that it contains *regulus* 'monastic rule'.[33]

There is one straw, as we begin to drown in the chronological uncertainties, that has been clutched: a reference in both the *Miracula* poem, and in the late twelfth-century Life by Ailred of Rievaulx, who claims to have made use of a source in a language other than Latin (*sermo rusticus*, *sermo barbaricus*). This may have been a vernacular (Old English?) Life produced by Northumbrians in the generation(s) after they reached Whithorn, and it might be related to traditional material apparently underlying the *Miracula* poem. Both this poem, and Ailred's Life, mention a British king, Tuduvallus or Tudwalus, as an opponent and therefore a contemporary of Nynia.[34] Now in the transmitted genealogical milieu mentioned earlier, what seems to be the same name is attached to a person calculated to have lived in the fifth century, and indeed to have been alive in its fourth decade.[35] But perhaps the most one can safely say is that such an estimate is not in open conflict with estimates obtained in other ways.

As for the stone church itself, the remains now on view below the eastern end of the ruined, medieval Whithorn Priory church may be those of some small church that housed a relic connected with Martin, or even a shrine of Nynia. It cannot seriously be claimed that this, possibly a subsidiary building of the postulated seventh-century Irish monastery, more-probably a structure of the Anglian period, is of late Roman or sub-Roman age; still less that it is the eponymous *Candida Casa*. It is not quite correct to say that the outer faces of the surviving foundation-walls are 'daubed with white plaster'.[36] The excavator of recent times himself changed his assessment slightly between 1950–67,[37] eventually concluding only that it may have been an 'oratory . . . probably that within which St Ninian lay'. The late Nora Chadwick surely provided the answer, when she suggested that Bede's *candida* '. . . undoubtedly refers to the exceptional building technique of dressed stone, in contrast to the wooden buildings'; and she adduced the interesting parallel of Belgrade (Beograd), 'White City', named for the same reason.[38] Bede, at great remove, was retailing a tradition of a Roman building, with dressed ashlar, exceptional in its location at its time (the surviving oratory-remains are built of local stone which is anything but dressed) (Pl. 7).

The pointers, slight as they are, hint at the period around the end of Roman Britain. In terms of Christianity and the late Roman empire, the only conceivable explanation for the presence of a Romano–British, orthodox bishop, working and then dying in a place beyond the frontier – and in a tribal area that we cannot even claim was of federate status – would be the previous existence in that place of a community of Christians; and they could hardly have come from anywhere except within Britannia, south of Hadrian's Wall. This point was made with justifiable force by Edward Thompson.[39] As he says, nothing in the history of Roman Christianity warrants any other reading; and the nearest parallels, the cases of Palladius and then of Patrick, both in Ireland, are susceptible to similar explanations. In Thompson's words, 'No example is known of a man who was appointed bishop with the specific task of going beyond the frontier in order to convert the barbarians. A bishop with no Christian communities subject to his authority was an unknown phenomenon beyond the Imperial frontier.'

Whithorn, a little market-town or burgh, lies several miles inland, on a gentle rise, with natural harbours not far away. The coast of Galloway forms the northern reach of the (North) Irish Sea; this is often little more turbulent than a large lake, and the blunt peninsula, the Machars, that contains Whithorn is frequently intervisible with the north end of the Isle of Man. The establishment at Whithorn, or hard by it, of a small late Roman settlement – either for purposes of trade, or perhaps in connection with a fishery – originating in Roman Britain of the Solway Shore, or Carlisle, is not glaringly unlikely.

In the early 1960s, as-yet unpublished excavations below the east end of Whithorn Priory church, a monument in State care, shed a little light.[40] The excavations went right down, in the area of the small plastered-wall oratory, through levels of identifiably medieval burials, to others of the Northumbrian Anglian period. Below them, at a depth of 12 ft (3.7 m) below the surface, the bedrock, shelving down westwards, was encountered. Here lay a series of orientated inhumations, east-west burials; lower than, and earlier than, those assumed to be of Anglian date, and putatively Christian graves of pre-Anglian age. One of these oriented burials had disturbed a pre-existing cremation, fragments of burnt human bone and specks of carbonised wood being scattered; and there were some fragments of red wheel-made Roman pottery.

This sequence must suggest a cemetery, attached to a Roman or Romanised settlement; with cremation-graves, replaced in the later Roman period by inhumations orientated east-west, the cemetery itself continuing in use not only for Christian burials of the period after Northumbrian domination, but as a site for whatever succession of churches led up to the medieval Priory. It is a sequence we have explored in earlier chapters. If it implies a place where, perhaps not before 400, Christianity was established, then a community at such a distance from the nearest episcopal seat (presumably then at Carlisle) might well have felt itself numerous or important enough to warrant a request for its own bishop. The traditions about Nynia imply this request was met; we must be talking about a period when this was feasible. It follows, then, that we are more likely to be nearer the beginning, rather than the close, of the fifth century.

Bede tells us that Nynia was a Briton, and the name is a British one. In Latin, it may have been rendered Niniavus (for a British *Niniavos, or the like);[41] and the later 'Ninian' presumably came from various mis-readings of Niniauus as Ninianus in a pre-Norman script. The oldest Christian record from Whithorn is an inscribed tombstone[42] (fig. 54). It commemorates Latinus, aged thirty-five, and his unnamed daughter aged four, and seems to have been erected by an unnamed *nipus Barrovadi* – a grandson (*nepos*) of Barrovadus. Uniquely, the inscription open with *Te Dominum laudamus* 'We praise thee, O Lord' – an echo of Romano–British scripture. The horizontally-lined stone is not closely dateable, and estimates have ranged from the very early fifth to the mid-sixth centuries. But despite signs, not surprising at this geographically isolated outpost, of rusticity – *ic sinum* for *hic*(!) *signum*, *ficerut* for *fecerunt* (itself a plural for a singular verb) – the disposition of the lines, use of the *Te Deum* phrase, and the very prolixity, all favour an estimate, preferred by Radford, not later than the first half of the fifth century. Here is a man, Latinus, probably like Barrovadus and indeed Nynia himself a Briton, who has taken a Roman name, dies at about the average expectation of life, was clearly a Christian, and merits a resoundingly Christian epitaph. The naming of Barrovadus on the stone points to two,

54 Whithorn: the Latinus stone, CIIC 520 (corrected reading by C.A.R. Radford)

probably three, generations of Christians at Whithorn by *c.*450; and again we are taken back to a community of Christians here around the end of the fourth century.

Some 25 miles (40 km) to the west of Whithorn, in the Rinns, the far south-western peninsula of Galloway, there is a related site. Three more inscribed stones stand now at Kirkmadrine church. A fourth (now lost) is reported to have come from a grave a short way south, at a place called Curgie,[43] and probably all four stones belong originally to a cemetery there. One of the stones is ornamented with an encircled ☧ and an alpha (the part with the omega is broken off), and it commemorates two *sancti et praecipui sacerdotes* 'holy and outstanding bishops' named as Viventius and Mavorius.[44] Another, similar in style, but lacking the A and W, also has two names; one, from which some letters have flaked off, ends in . . .*s* (a short name, like *Iustus*, would fit), the other being *Florentius.*[45] These masculine names, with any patronymics omitted, may well imply as Radford has suggested[46] that these two men, obeying the biblical injunction to call no earthly man their Father, were also priests. The lost, Curgie, stone is said to have borne the name *Ventidius* and the description *diaconus* 'deacon'. The third of the Kirkmadrine stones[47] is, from its lettering, later in the sixth century; it bears an encircled chi-rho, and merely *Initium et Finis*, a verbalisation of the idea expressed by A and W. This stone appears to commemorate an event, or dedication, rather than anyone's grave.

Since it is hardly credible that there could have been *two* bishoprics on adjacent peninsulas, one could hypothesise that Whithorn was one of several Christian sites with cemeteries in the fifth century, and that at a period in the second half of that century the seat was removed, perhaps temporarily, to Kirkmadrine and Curgie. The death of one bishop (*Viventius?*) was perhaps shortly followed by that of a sick or elderly successor (*Mavorius*). Both bishops would be later than Nynia. There is an implication, of course, of an undiscovered Christian site in the Kirkmadrine area.[48]

This, then, is as much as we can infer about the beginning of Christianity in south-west Scotland – among the Novantae of Galloway, who during the fourth century may have learned of Christ and the Gospels from their fellow-Britons of the Carvetii, trading and probably also settling across the placid fishy waters of the Solway and beyond. They were beyond, and outside, the Wall frontier; but what, to such happily insignificant folk, whose major worry would have been Irish bandits, could the wars and rumours of wars across Hadrian's Wall have really meant? They obtained their bishop; in some manner, the episcopate was continued. Nynia's fame, like Patrick's, grew mainly after his death. The ripples of it spread out, notably (after their fifth-century conversions) among the Irish; and despite the handicap of time passing among largely-illiterate communities, something about Nynia was cherished and transmitted, until later generations could embody these traditions in a local, simple, Life – seen in one guise by the *Miracula* poet, in another and much later (English?) version by Ailred. Even some special tale, behind Bede's elusive hints of Pictish conversions, survived; and Alan Anderson, acutely, saw[49] that the English names of the first and third of the Anglian bishops, *Peohthelm* (Pecthelm) and *Peohtwine*, meaning as they do 'Leader of the Picts' and 'Friend of the Picts', may have been adopted by these men on their appointments to the see, with direct reference to this aspect of Nynia's early fame.

But who, and where, were these Picts in the first half of the fifth century? Was Whithorn indeed the sole centre from which their conversion, whatever that implies, was undertaken? To answer this, we must tackle another problem – the course of events in North Britain after the 370s.

The name *Picti* 'the Painted Ones' was applied, probably in the first case by the Roman army, to a group of tribes living north of the Clyde-Forth isthmus. In the tangle of explanations, some straining reason itself, for this label, there is nothing forceful enough to prevent us initially reading it at its face value. We may assume that it gained popularity (after its first recorded instance, a panegyric of AD 297) because these people tattooed both their faces and the visible parts of their bodies, a custom to which there is both early and adequate allusion.[50] The concise view, from field-archaeology and linguistic studies, is that the Picts were an amalgamation: of very early Iron Age incomers concentrated north of the so-called Highland Line, with a large existing native population of Bronze Age or even Neolithic descent. A mixture of this nature is implied by the occurrence, still into historic (post-Roman) centuries, of two languages: one, Celtic Pictish, related to British, perhaps in the degree that broad Scots (English) is related to Standard English, and another whose pitiful remnants indicate that it was of a non-Celtic, and indeed non-Indo-European, type.[51]

John Mann has considered[52] that the peoples named about AD 230 by Cassius Dio – the *Maeatae* (nearer the Wall) and the *Caledonii* to their north – were loosely united as the outcome of continuous Roman pressure into a defensive coalescence of two tribal federations. As late as 367, by which period the Picts are cited, alongside the *Scotti* or Irish raiders, in generic terms for Rome's barbarian enemies, an internal Pictish division into *Dicalydones* and *Verturiones* is still recognisable. Nevertheless, in Mann's words, one could claim that 'the Pictish kingdom was a product of the Roman presence in Britain'.

Throughout the fourth century, the Picts figure as the main enemy beyond the northern frontier. As a *leitmotiv* to Romano–British history, we learn of their conspiratorial arrangements with other barbarians – the *Scotti* and the Saxons. There is some evidence that, though land-based and able to range through Britain north of the Wall, the Picts possessed boats and could attack, in strength, by sea[53] (*cf.* p. 249 above).

The Theodosian reconstitution of the northern frontier took place in 369. The interpretation of subsequent events is uncertain. Dr Miller,[54] in her reading of Claudian's laudatory poem about the consulate (in AD 401) of Stilicho, the Vandal-born general who served Theodosius and Honorius, would reconstruct two slightly later 'Northern Wars'. The first began in 383 with the defection of the usurper Magnus Maximus and his removal of much of the Wall garrisons; the barbarians continually ravaged the area between the two walls. After the news of Magnus Maximus' death (388), the British, who had technically been in a state of revolt, submitted once again to Imperial authority; troops were sent, and by about 390, the Lowlands had been regained. A frontier was now restored further to the north, on the Forth-Clyde (Antonine Wall) line. In 398, the Picts, in concert with *Scotti* and Saxons, attacked once more in force, and regained control of the lands between the Antonine and Hadrianic frontiers. Probably about 400, Hadrian's Wall then became the ultimate *limes*, and so remained while, slowly, it ran down into oblivion.

In theory, then, all that stood between the Picts, and the tracts of land suitable for settlement between the Antonine and Hadrian's Walls in the fifth century, was the fact that these lands were already occupied by at least four named tribal groupings of British – not Pictish – origin, language, and possibly sympathies. In Chapter 10, the various interpretations that can be placed on what Gildas has to say about this region, at this period, were discussed; both in Edward Thompson's, and Dr Mollie Miller's, we find Picts attacking Roman Britons inside Britannia after 400, but Gildas is insufficient as a source if we seek to find what the Picts did when finally expelled from Britannia. We can only presume that the vast majority of them returned to Pictland, as described by Bede for the seventh century; those *septentrionales insulae partes*, northern parts of the island (of Britain), which on the west were bounded by the estuary of the Clyde – a wide arm of the sea, pushing far inland, *qui antiquitus gentem Brettonum a Pictis secernebat* 'which from a very early time divided the British nation from the Picts'.[55]

The chapter of Bede's *Historia* that contains the brief mention of Nynia is essentially about Columba, not Nynia; it describes Columba's coming to Britain, defines the 'northern' and 'southern' Picts as being divided by steep and rugged mountains (the ridge called The Mounth); and provides a further synchronism for Columba in stating that *Bridius filius Meilochon rex potentissimus* 'a most powerful king, Bridei son of Maelchon' had (in Bede's year AD 565) been reigning over the Picts for eight years. Dr Isabel Henderson makes the point that Bede's information about Nynia, in particular the statement that Nynia had *multo ante tempore* 'a long time before' (Columba) preached the Word and brought the Faith to the southern Picts – between the Grampians and the Firth of Forth – need not have come from Whithorn at all. It may well have come from the Picts themselves; directly, or through Bede's friend Trumwine,[56] who in 678 was sent by archbishop Theodore of York as bishop to the kingdom of the Picts 'which at that time was subject to the English'. We know from a later chapter of the *Historia*[57] that Trumwine's seat was not apparently in the conventional land of the southern Picts; it was on the south side of the Firth of Forth at a monastery called *Aebbercurnig*, Abercorn. In 685, the Northumbrian king Ecgfrith led an army into Pictland and was defeated soundly at Nechtansmere; after which the Picts recovered their own lands, which the English had been holding, and many English were either slain, or were taken as slaves, or escaped *de terra Pictorum fuga* 'by flight from Pictish territory'. Trumwine and his companions were among these last.

The implication in Bede's consistent wording, and description of these events, is that at some time after the fourth century land on the *south* side of the Firth of Forth – opposite, and visible from, the north or Fife shore, which was certainly Pictish at an earlier date – was itself part of Pictland. Whether the Northumbrian Angles had, in the generation before the battle of Nechtansmere, managed to seize land on both the north and south sides of the Firth of Forth, or whether, having occupied formerly British coastal lands between North Berwick and approximately Edinburgh, the Angles had pushed westwards (to Stirling, say) and thus taken over a Pictish tract, Bede's statement seems unequivocal. Abercorn was the place chosen for a bishopric for the Picts; Abercorn (about 10 miles or 16 km west of Edinburgh Castle) was in Pictish territory in 685; that territory was in 678 part of a kingdom of the Picts subject to the English; and after 685 the Picts recovered their own lands. Therefore by the seventh century the southern Picts, who may have claimed they had received Christianity from the Briton Nynia *multo ante tempore* (in the fifth century) may have done so in much this area – West Lothian and part of Stirlingshire. They could have occupied this area, some way south of what was traditionally regarded as the true Pictland, in the fifth century, in the aftermath of the 'Northern Wars' or 'Pictish Wars' that modern scholarship would now extract from Claudian's poem on Stilicho's exploits, and Gildas' retrospective northern history. There is nothing objectionable in this suggestion and archaeology offers it minor support. In terms of Christianity, the Pictish claim about Nynia's activities becomes, as we shall see, just believable; whereas Nynia in the role of a fifth-century peripatetic episcopal missionary, preaching on the far shores of the Tay, or even further to the north, is beyond anything that analogy or historical likelihood would allow.[58]

It is unnecessary, and it would be unsuitable, to go into the minutiae of Pictish archaeology, such as it is. Figure 55, however, sets out the known occurrence in southern Scotland between the Walls, and south of the Firth of Forth, of certain items which would be associated with Picts, rather than Britons. Place-names with the prefix *Pit-* (as in Pitcairn, Pitlochry, etc.), otherwise define the ascertainable post-Roman lands of the Picts[59] with such notable concentration as to allow the idea that this is a Pictish-Celtic word (**pett* 'farmstead, land-holding', cognate with Gaulish *petia*, the source of French *pièce* and English 'piece'). The objects called 'Class I stones' are probably approximate parallels to the inscribed memorial stones of the post-Roman British Church, but instead of lettering they bear small groups of symbols, drawn from a pictorial repertoire of disputed origins which is again exclusively associated with the historical Picts.[60] ('Class II' stones employ the same symbols, but with Christian motifs, like the Cross, in addition; are in low relief as well as incised techniques; and must post-date the general, Columban, conversion of the northern Picts in the later sixth century or the earlier seventh.)

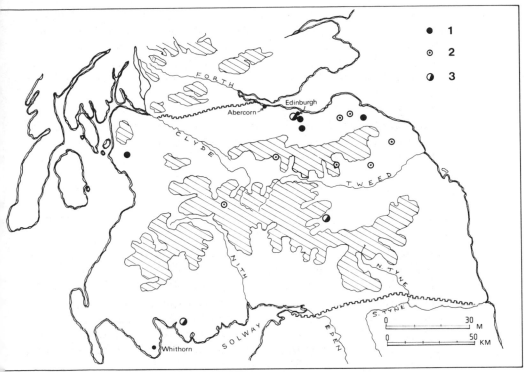

55 Picts and British in sub-Roman southern Scotland, 5th–6th cent.
  1 Place-names in *Pit-* (after Jackson and Nicolaisen) 2 Pictish silver chains (after Stevenson R.B.K. 1955) 3 Class I Pictish symbol stones. Land over 800 ft (250 m) shaded

Even if the Class I stones are not older than the sixth century – and this has been disputed by those who (like the present writer) would see them begin in the fifth – they still ante-date any Northumbrian conquests in the region.

The third group of objects mapped are the so-called 'massive silver chains'; ornamental objects, presumably worn around the neck (by men?), the most likely source being late Roman silver, as in the Traprain Law hoard, and consisting of heavy links fastening with a broad silver ring. They have a limited distribution, and the ascription to the Picts depends partly upon this, mainly upon the fact that two of the terminal rings bear incised Pictish symbols of the same kind as those on the Class I stones. Again they must be of post-Roman date.[61]

The combined distribution is generally north of the Tweed, south of the Firth of Forth, and west of the post-Roman British state of the *combrogi* who lived around the estuary and in the valley of the Clyde – the kingdom of Strathclyde, whose native name has not come down to us.[62] The outliers do not affect this; the Pictish Class I stone in Galloway is, from its context on a rock by a small native fort,[63] patently associated with some far-ranging Pictish raid. What the pattern hints at is an extension of the territories of the southern Picts during the period from, probably, the mid-fifth to early seventh centuries; and presumably this was the *terra* that the Angles captured, made into a short-lived see at Abercorn, and lost again after Nechtansmere. If Nynia preached the Word of God to any Picts, this is the most likely area; though, as we shall see in a later chapter, Picts in the west of this region may not have held to their Christianity over-long. They were Patrick's *Picti apostatae* (p. 342).

Precisely how large or well-defined any settled area of Picts may have been is something that neither or sources nor, still less, so skeletal a map as fig. 55, can tell us. It may have been centred west of Abercorn, the later West Lothian or Linlithgow; Bede tell us[64] that the eastern end of the Antonine Wall was two miles west of Abercorn at a place called *Penneltun* in English, and 'which the Picts call *Peanfahel* – i.e., End of the Wall.[65] Alternatively, by the sixth century Picts may have sparsely occupied higher ground between the headwaters of the Clyde and Tweed, the Lanarkshire Moors; the distribution (not shown) of earth-houses, a kind of subterranean store attached to dwellings of the Roman and later centuries, and common in the Pictish area proper, includes a few examples here as well as south of Edinburgh.[66]

Wherever it was, southern Scotland at this period also has to accommodate the post-Roman British peoples (fig. 56). Strathclyde, which may have had a northern 'frontier' of a minor kind in the Cowal district of southern Argyll, against the *Scotti*, the first Irish settlers,[67] possessed a centre at Dumbarton Rock, the Rock of the Clyde, or as Bede tells us, *Alcluith* in their own language.[68] No particular name is attached to the Galloway coastal plain, unless (as suggested, tentatively, in fig. 49) it formed the westernmost district of Rheged. Where, precisely, the British forerunner of the kingdom or region we know mainly after its late sixth- or seventh-century conquest by the Northumbrians as Bernicia may have been, we cannot be sure. Ptolemy's *Votadini* emerge in the early historic period as another kingdom, *Guotodin*, or *Gododdin* in modern Welsh and customary usage.[69] It is likely that its most prestigious post-Roman centre was *Din Eidyn*, probably the now-obliterated fortified seat atop the Castle Rock at Edinburgh. A much smaller area, *Manau Guotodin*, the Manaw of Gododdin, lay at the north-west end of this kingdom and its centre, as Kenneth Jackson shows, must surely have been a not dissimilar fortified citadel now displaced by Stirling Castle. Finally, there is some reason to suppose that the middle and upper Tweed valley, in the area of Melrose and Peebles, was a distinct district or region; its British name is not apparent, unless indeed this was the original *Bernaccia*, the wider coastal part of which, from the Tweed south, became the Bernicia of the Angles.

Between, roughly, AD 400 and 600, these British kingdoms – and one must suppose any Pictish enclaves – became Christian. The evidence for this assertion was set out in some detail by the present author some time ago[70] and the conclusions alone will suffice here. As well as the Whithorn and Kirkmadrine inscribed stones, there are others – not many, but enough to give an indication – mostly of the sixth century.[71] Of particular interest are two from the Tweed area; one, lost, found centuries ago at Peebles, allegedly with the wording *Locus Sancti Nicolae Episcopi*. The fact that it could be read at all implies Roman capitals or very clear half-uncial, and if the name 'Nicolas' strains credulity, *locus* 'tomb, sacred place' also occurs on a seventh-century stone, possibly commemorating a relic, from Whithorn. More recently, another stone, from Peebles as well, dated to the seventh century, bears (as at Kirkmadrine) the title *sacerdos* and a name *Neitano* that was common to Picts and North British.[72]

It is also just possible to suggest religious centres (fig. 56). The story of Kentigern at Glasgow was encountered in Chapter 9, and if he died in 612 this implies a see in the later sixth century. The medieval Life of Kentigern, by Jocelyn of Furness,[73] contains a passage whose curious features may suggest that it draws on a rather older life, or Glasgow tradition.[74] It purports to describe the establishment (in the fifth century?) of this episcopal church at Glasgow, in a burial-ground *a sancto Niniano quondam consecrato* 'long ago consecrated by St Ninian'. If, as will be argued below, the king Coroticus to whom Patrick addressed a letter – in the writer's view, somewhere around 470 – was the ruler of Strathclyde, Christianity on the Clyde does indeed go back to the later fifth century. We shall also see that Patrick's *Epistola* refers, apparently, to what must have been the neighbouring peoples; they include *Picti apostatae*, once-Christian Picts who had relapsed into paganism (an unforgivable sin), and fig. 55 is at least a hint that some Picts could have bordered Coroticus' kingdom.

Among other candidates for religious centres of the Christian North British might be the Eccles- place-names indicated by Geoffrey Barrow (shown in fig. 49); it may be significant that there are instances near Glasgow, Stirling and Edinburgh. The writer suggested earlier[75] that among the many names of seventh-century Anglian monasteries, mostly known from Bede, a few stand out as *not* possessing Old English names – descriptive, locative, or personal. They include that of *Luel*, the Anglian double-monastery at or close to Carlisle, which seems to be based on the spoken Primitive Welsh form of the Romano–British name *Luguvalium*; and two in southern Scotland. Both of these are British. *Aebbercurnig*, Abercorn, was we know chosen as the seat of Trumwine, when he was sent to an area which the Angles had taken from the Picts to act as bishop for the (Christian) Picti. *Mailros*, Old Melrose, in a bend of the Tweed, a natural site for an enclosure, was by the 640s an Anglian monastery, where St Cuthbert was trained; its position vis-à-vis Peebles and the central Tweed valley is important. Were these already sub-Roman British Christian localities; and is this why, exceptionally, their purely topographical names (the Horned River-confluence: the Bare Promontory) were maintained unchanged?

There is a final piece of archaeological evidence, not fully understood. The coastal tracts on both sides of the Firth of Forth, and further north around the Fife coast and the Tay estuary, have yielded numerous 'longcist cemeteries';[76] rural, often isolated burial-grounds with inhumations, often orientated. One at least, the Catstane cemetery at Kirkliston, near Abercorn and Edinburgh, has a late sixth-century inscribed stone.[77] If any of these are sub-Roman Christian – and this is probable – their extension around the coast of Fife, into southern Pictland proper, may well bear out any Pictish claim retailed through Trumwine or such a figure to Bede that the Picts had received Christian notions before Columba ever visited Inverness.

Earlier in this chapter, it was suggested that the Church in sub-Roman southern Scotland may have been episcopal and diocesan. There is evidence of bishops. In the south-west, we have the Nynia tradition, and the Kirkmadrine *sacerdotes*; from Strathclyde, the late sixth-century Kentigern, who may not even have been the first bishop; and in the Tweed valley, at least the post-600 record of the *sacerdos* Neitano. As in the instance of sub-Roman Britain south of the Wall, a diocese at this time can only have been a fairly loose concept – the notional sphere of influence of a bishop, probably co-terminous with the kingdom or principality (itself not necessarily having strict borders?) at or near whose centre he had his episcopal church or seat.

But, albeit dimly, this is what we may perceive (fig. 56). For Strathclyde, we think of Glasgow. Whithorn may represent a division of Rheged north of the Wall or west of the Nith (with Carlisle standing for the major, southern part?). In the Tweed valley, a tract that may in the fifth century have been within *Bernaccia*, the more likely focus is Peebles (the name derives from Welsh *pebyll* 'tent, pavilion').[78] In the region of Edinburgh, the British *Guotodin* or Gododdin, Abercorn and Ecclesmachan, barely 3 miles apart, lie west of the modern city; and if the district of Manau possessed its bishop, which is less likely, Stirling – with another Eccles – would be indicated.

---

56 Christianity in sub-Roman southern Scotland

1 Significant Christian sites, 5th–7th cent. (see text)   2 Inscribed stones, 5th/6th cent.   3 Inscribed stones, 6th/7th cent.   4 Significant Eccles place-name sites (after Barrow 1973). Names of native states or kingdoms in capitals

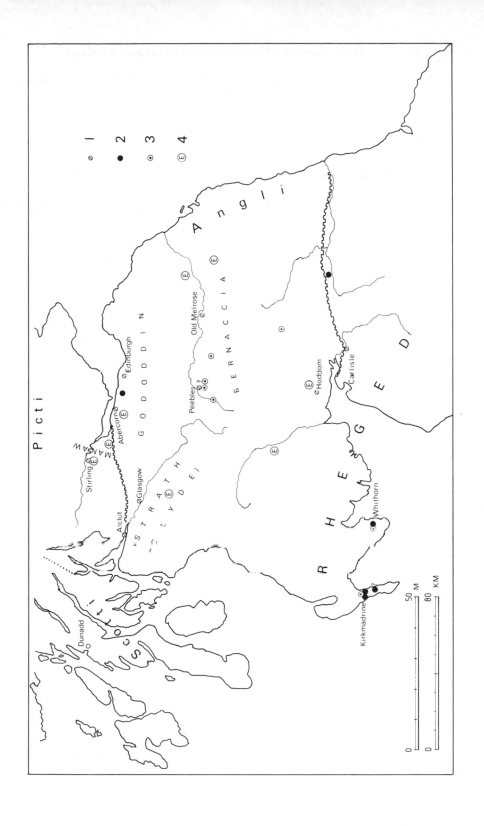

Picti

Scotti

A n g l i

R H E G E D

Dunadd

Stirling ⓔ
ⓔ M A N A W
Alclut
Abercorn ⓔ
Edinburgh
Glasgow

G O D O D D I N

S T R A T H
C L Y D E
ⓔ

Peebles
ⓔ?
ⓔ

B E R N A C C I A
ⓔ
Old Melrose
ⓔ

ⓔ Hodtom
Carlisle

Whithorn

Kirkmadrine
ⓔ?

1 ⊘
2 ●
3 ⊙
4 ⓔ

M
0   50
KM
0   80

How and at what rate Christianity, with its prestigious echoes of *Romanitas* and Latinity, spread – from Whithorn, rather than the western hinterland of the Wall – over much of the Lowlands between *c*.450 and 550, we cannot tell, and we detect the spread itself with difficulty. We need not deny, in their essence, the traditions of Nynia, through whatever channels these came to Bede's notice. Nor need we deny the likelihood that Nynia and his successors influenced Picts, south, west, and even immediately north of the Firth of Forth. But Nynia, if he must be called an apostle at all, could best be represented as the Apostle of the North British.

CHAPTER TWELVE

Britain, Ireland, and Pre-Patrician Christianity

It may be desirable to say a few words in this place on the
uncouth, and seemingly unpronounceable, proper names of
persons and places, which must embarrass every reader of Irish
history who is unskilled in the Celtic languages.
James Henthorn Todd *St Patrick, Apostle of Ireland* (1864)

In all those far-off times when we had no Aer Lingus and British Airways, or their simple predecessors, travel between Britain and Ireland meant sea-crossings; and the early history of that marine travel underlines the importance of all the traditional routes. Most of these in prehistory and protohistory either followed lines of sight, or intelligent deductions (as Shetland from Orkney, or Faroe from Shetland) from the behaviour of cloud-masses. Across the short northern links, from the Antrim coast to the Mull of Kintyre (12 miles or 20km) or from Larne to the Rinns of Galloway (some 25 miles or 40km), one can often see the land opposite. In the last century, Scottish villagers on the west coast of the Rinns peninsula used a steam-packet service, between Portpatrick and Larne, to do their weekly shopping in Co. Antrim. The old traditional crossings, between Holyhead and Dublin Bay, or from Wexford and Rosslare to the Pembrokeshire havens, are now standard commercial routes. Ireland, if far enough from Britain to be a separate country, is nonetheless too close to have experienced a separate history.

In a recent study, Richard Warner suggested that the usual explanation for the occurrence of Roman finds in Ireland – namely, that they indicate a mixture of trade and the loot of *Scotti*, Irish raiders – covers neither the known distributions, nor all the contexts.[1] Such finds, in the early Roman centuries mainly near the north and north-east Irish coasts, can also come from native hill-forts and burials, the latter including the quite remarkable cremation-grave[2] of classic Roman character at Stoneyford, Co. Kilkenny.

Warner contends that we must also consider the possibilities of British refugees from early Roman expansion in Britain; and perhaps native or even non-British auxiliaries from the Roman army, deserting and fleeing to Ireland. (A late Roman refinement might consist of post-360 refugees from areas in North Britain ravaged by barbarians, and we recall Edward

Thompson's hint that not all of the migrating British – from the Mersey? the north Welsh coast? – in the 460s need necessarily have fled to *Gaul*.) Important here, of course, as Warner stresses, is the distinct probability of organised commerce. As early as the late first century AD, Tacitus, describing[3] his father-in-law's projected subjugation of Ireland, remarked that 'its approaches and harbours are known, through commerce and merchants'. In the second century, Ptolemy displayed rather more specific knowledge of the east and south coasts of Ireland than of the, still largely inaccessible, western littoral.[4] He was able to name the greater rivers (*Bououinda* the Boyne; *Birgos* the Barrow) whose estuaries Warner[5] would in the context of potential trade at this period define as 'places where landing is safe, and access to the interior straightforward' (*cf.* fig. 56).

The older catalogue[6] and assessment of Roman material found in Ireland is now superseded by Dr J.D. Bateson's fuller and more critical list;[7] one that offers some attractive grounds for inference. Bateson makes the proviso that, in many cases of individual finds, it is not certain whether the ultimate source lay in Roman Britain or Roman Gaul. Like Warner, Bateson expands the range of explanations. These include: Irishmen who had been raiding Britain, for goods or slaves, or who were returning from mercenary service in the Roman army, or travelling from the (late Roman period) Irish settlements in Britain[8] – or citizens of Roman Britain coming to Ireland as invaders, traders, refugees, adventurers, even as missionaries.

Bateson's map[9] of acceptable finds – it excludes some dubious cases and probably modern losses – shows concentrations in the north-east, opposite the Mull of Kintyre and Galloway; on the coast of Leinster opposite north Wales; and (notably with fourth- and fifth-century objects) over the southern third of Ireland, bringing out Warner's idea of the importance of natural harbours and rivers as waterways.

Some of the northerly finds, including several major hoards that are unquestionably the outcome of raiding or piracy, will be discussed in the next chapter. For the moment, we may look to the eastern and southern coasts. Here, it must now be accepted that fourth-century trade is involved. This brings into sharp focus the recent discoveries at New Grange[10] in the Boyne Valley. Coins and small objects of gold, silver and copper have been recovered in surprising quantities from in and around this mighty prehistoric tomb. Of the 25 coins, 18 are fourth-century (from Maximian to Arcadius and the House of Valentinian or Theodosius (383 × 395)) and they include several gold solidi of great value. It is a very strong inference that their presence at New Grange constitutes votive offerings, which would here be made to *An Daghda Mór* 'the Great Good God', or Jupiter-figure, *optimus maximusque*, of early Irish mythology. R.A.G. Carson thought[11] that the most likely depositors would have been Irishmen. Claire o'Kelly was less confident;[12] and her fellow-excavator of New Grange prefers not to exclude the idea that such particular objects, of such notable value – what Irishmen at this date, in any case, would normally possess near-mint *solidi*? – were deposited publicly and ceremoniously by enterprising *negotiatores* from Roman Britain, in order to secure advantageous positions in a fresh market and to show homage to the indigenous god. We must not press the analogy too hard; but, to many, a parallel case will be that of the Roman coins, mostly gold and silver, found in south India and described by Sir Mortimer Wheeler in a notably brilliant essay.[13]

Others, like Dr Francoise Henry, have suspected[14] that the appearance of certain techniques in fourth-century Irish craftsmanship pointed to 'contacts with the Romans, either those who were in Britain or those on the continent' – and she had in mind contacts closer than might be explained by casual trade. Language may also betray what has been inferred by archaeology and historical likelihood. The matter of ecclesiastical loanwords (from Latin, or even British, into Irish) will be raised again; but this is not all. Professor James Carney, examining[15] some very archaic Irish poems dealing with dynasts from the remote past down to the late fifth century, shows that they contain an early strand of Latin loanwords, none of which is 'of a specifically ecclesiastical character'. These include – the Latin sources in brackets – *arm* (arma), *legión* (legio), *míl*, *cathmílid* (miles), *trebun* (tribunus), *bárc* (barca), *long* (navis longa), *múr* (murus), *ór* (aurum); and, perhaps the most interesting, the use of *Mercúir* (dies Mercurii) and *Saturn* (dies Saturni) for two days of the week (Wednesday, Saturday). As he concludes, these borrowings '. . . show a non-Christian Ireland, having very close contacts with and knowledge of the Roman empire'.

The implication of all these observations is that, whatever causes took Britons to Ireland, or Irishmen to Britain and beyond (and then home again), there were in all probability by the fourth century AD groups of Roman Britons actually living in Ireland; engaged in trade, perhaps managing boats, staffing small mercantile concerns, buying the necessary protection from Irish potentates and priests, and in one degree or another involved in Irish life.

This would not rule out the presence, particularly in the later Roman period and possibly in areas not involved in trade, of large numbers of British (like Patrick and his fellow-sufferers) in the menial capacity of slaves. But enslaved captives cannot offer the sole explanation, even if this happens to be one of the few to which allusion survives from early literature. Nor was the contact unilateral. In the fourth century, perhaps in the later third as well, groups of Irishmen were living in Britain, specifically in such areas as south-west Wales, implanting their own language alongside British and Latin.[16] The sixth-century king Vortipor or Voteporix of Dyfed was a descendant of these immigrants (*cf.* fig. 43); as were, a generation or so earlier, the bilingually-commemorated Christians at Lewannick in east Cornwall (p. 79). Trade presumably flowed in both directions. If the goods offered by Irish traders in British markets were less sophisticated than purely Roman products, we must not suppose that they were any less marketable.

It has long been necessary to posit another link altogether between Ireland and Britain, in the matter of *writing*. The early form of the Irish language, whether as a spoken peasant vernacular or increasingly as an advanced cultural medium, was complex, inflected, and involved distinctive sounds of vowels and consonants that could not have been properly represented (even if the attempt had then been made) by the 24-letter Roman alphabet. The barrier between spoken British and Latin writing was explored in an earlier chapter.

But this does not mean that writing would not have been observed, as a cultural novelty, in fourth-century Ireland. We might think of methods of counting, or of tallies essential for merchants and traders, or that combination of the simple Roman numerals and the Roman cursive script so widely employed by all classes in Roman Britain. Quite apart from the refinement of committing ideas, sentiments and instructions to written form, one can have enumerated lists of trade goods, or creditors and debtors, or the Roman versions of contracts and waybills, where one party might 'sign' or acknowledge with a mark or thumb-print. Was this commercial jotting not seen in fourth-century Ireland – in the hands of Roman traders, or their trained Irish assistants? The finds of Roman material from the early royal centre, the Hill of Tara in Co. Meath (still unpublished) include part of a lead sealing from the kind of box in which waxed tablets of fourth-century accounts – earlier forms of the reconstruction in fig. 2 above – would have been kept.[17] Coins reached Ireland; coins are not just metal discs with portraits – they have writing, to be examined curiously by the illiterate recipient, around their borders. Some of the Roman finds in Ireland, too, are functional. There is a Roman barrel-padlock; a plain bronze ladle from Bohermeen, Co. Meath, and an inscribed fine-stone stamp for use by a herbalist or oculist on his wares from Golden Bridge in Co. Tipperary.

Where both the Irish and the British found common cause in a use for short written passages was in the provision of memorials for the dead – mainly confined to the names of the deceased, with or without his or her parent(s), and very occasionally enriched with epithets. In Atlantic Britain from the fifth century, the use of these has already been examined. But in Ireland, and certain of the regions of Britain settled by Irish in late Roman and sub-Roman times, another script or alphabet was used, one known as *ogom, ogam* or *ogham*. Relatively simple in concept and use, it involved groups of long and short strokes at right-angles to, or diagonally across, a base-line (which could be drawn, or represented by the edge or arris of a stone face); and the letters were arranged in four sets of five letters each. Ogham survived for centuries as an arcane medium of communication.[18] The one fact we can safely deduce from the welter of legend, scholiasts' embroiderings, and cryptic nomenclature of the individual letter-values[19] is that by the period when Christianity and conventional literacy had become fully established, no-one really had any sound notion as to precisely how, or when, this script began.

Ogham deserves a little discussion. Kenneth Jackson has set out his generally-accepted conclusions.[20] It is based on a fourth-century classification of the Roman alphabet, as used by grammarians in the late empire. (The ogham groups are BLFSN; HDTCQ; MGNGZR; and AOUEI — later, five more symbols were added.) Its appearance shows at once that it was adaptable to the easiest modes of incision or carving, on stone, bone or wood; it avoids all the curves and loops inherent in both Roman capitals and the Roman cursive scripts. The inventor(s) may well have been aided by the notions of notches on tallies, or the Roman numeral-groups (like I to IV, or V to VIII) that involve incremental linear strokes. The development must imply a degree of contact in itself between non-literate and literate societies. One might be reminded of a much more recent artificial script of this sort, an affair of ticks, triangles and hooks, used in official Canadian documents to express *Inuit*, the syllabic Eskimo language.

The distribution of ogham-inscribed stones in Ireland, which is mainly southern,[21] and in Britain the notable concentration in south-west and southern Wales,[22] point to the likelihood that the use of ogham, if not the script itself, began in this combined area. Whether it was invented in Ireland by a Roman resident there, or an Irish craftsman working with Roman traders, or in south Wales by an Irish immigrant exposed to Roman schooling, is not really material now. The restrictions imposed by so short an alphabet, and so tersely deployed, do not make it easy to define a starting-date on grounds of linguistics alone; but there seems to be no reason why ogham should not have been current by 400. It could be, and has been, argued[23] that the oldest Irish ogham inscriptions, most of which name the dead in the formula 'Of-A, of the son of B', are not demonstrably Christian, imitate (at some remove) late Roman secular tombstones, and begin in the fourth century rather than the more Christian fifth. The point is not vital; the later ones cannot be other than Christian.

The Roman attitude to Ireland, a barbarian country beyond her *limites*, was not particularly deep or detailed. Early writers knew the Irish mostly as *Scotti*, those Irish who had boats and who used them, alone or in concert with other barbarians, to attack Britannia. But there were many, many more Irish than these – extrapolating crudely from densities of field-monuments, one might guess between a half, and one million in late Roman times, if contemporary Britain held between three and four million people.[24] The vast majority of the Irish never visited Britain in any guise, and probably never thought of it. Traders always prefer to ignore both politics and wars; like those Cornish fishermen who, during the long Napoleonic wars, constantly plied back and forth between Britain and France. If fourth-century *Scotti* were raiding and plundering, north and south of Hadrian's Wall, numerous other Irish were settling – almost certainly as farmers and stockbreeders, as the odd loanword suggests[25] – in other regions of western Britain. There is nothing to preclude us envisaging traders from Roman Britain active around Dublin Bay, and up those rivers navigable from the southern Irish havens and estuaries; traders in constant and profitable contact with Irish producers and British and Gaulish markets.

If a proportion of the late Roman population of Britain was Christian, and if it became increasingly likely that Romano-British Christians were among those taken (as Patrick later was) as slaves to Ireland, it is clearly possible that *some* Christian British were living in fourth-century Ireland. We cannot exclude, either, the chance of Christian communities beyond the official frontier – as at Whithorn – or indeed their augmentation by the occasional native converts. In the generations between about 360 and 430, the Church may, and probably did, gain a real foothold in Ireland.

In the particular year, 431, we see our first sure record of this; though its content tells us that it was the first known external record of Irish *Christianity*, not of the first Christians to live in Ireland. The chronicler and writer Prosper of Aquitaine, able and learned man, friend of St Augustine of Hippo, recorded that Celestine or Caelestinus (Pope 422–32) 'sent Palladius, ordained as their first bishop, to the Irish believers in Christ' *ad Scotos in Christum credentes ordinatus a papa Caelestino Palladius primus episcopus mittitur.* The statement has a slightly wider implication, but for the moment, taking it as it stands, one could make a number of inferences.

It is apparently correct to have assumed that by 431 there were communities, or at least an identifiable community, of Christians in Ireland. They could be called *credentes*, presumably implying baptised and confirmed Christians. They were sufficient in numbers, as was inferred in the instance of Whithorn and Nynia, to warrant a bishop. We do not know whether before 431 they possessed a bishop, any more than we do in the case of Whithorn. It is possible that they, or some authority on their behalf, had requested a bishop and this request attracted Papal interest. The year 431 is significantly close to 429, when Germanus and Lupus visited Britain, to combat Pelagianism (p. 55), an event also recorded by Prosper as having been approved by the same pope *ad actionem Palladii diaconi*; it would be unreasonable not to suppose the same Palladius occurs in both entries. Palladius must have been a person of some significance. We are not in a position to see whether the sending of Palladius to Ireland was an event by-passing, or involving, the Church in fifth-century Britain; but (unlike Nynia) we do not see a *British* bishop being sent to these Christians outside the frontiers of Britannia.

It is Prosper who also provides us with records which fall either side of this, for 431. That concerning Pelagianism in Britain (*cf.* p. 55) and the Germanus visit, for 429, reads (in English), 'Agricola the Pelagian, son of the Pelagian bishop Severianus, corrupted the churches of Britannia by his underhand ways. But at the instance of Palladius the deacon, Pope Celestine sent Germanus, Bishop of Auxerre, to act on his behalf; and having put the heretics to rout he guided the British back to the Catholic faith.' *Catholica fides* is orthodoxy, in opposition to what the *haeretici* held in their own *dogmata*. The second passage, in Prosper's work *Contra Collatorem*, written a year or so (433 × 434) after Celestine had died, expands a comment on the Papal expulsion of certain Pelagians from Italy. It states that, 'Nor, indeed, with any tardier attention' – than Celestine had paid, that is, to driving the Enemies of Grace (p. 56) from Italy – 'did he free Britain from the same plague; for having ordained a bishop for the Irish' (431), 'while he was careful to keep the Roman island Catholic' (429), 'he also made the non-Roman one (*barbaram*) Christian.'

The linking of these events does not necessarily imply that Pelagianism, depicted earlier in this work as a relatively short-lived episode in the fifth-century British Church, had taken root in Ireland to the danger of orthodoxy (though, given the premises made above, Irish Christians would presumably have been aware of the Pelagian Agricola and his followers in (southern) Britain, in the few years preceding 429). Nor does it seem possible safely to infer that Prosper's use of *Christianam* to describe Ireland after Palladius' arrival necessarily means more than just 'Christian', implying by definition what is elsewhere made explicit by *catholicus, catholica fides*. The despatch of Palladius has, perhaps, the appearance of a precaution, or the emphasising of any earlier Papal policies, rather than a particular remedy. It is *Britannias*, the provinces of Britain, and not Ireland – *Hibernia* – that had been affected by the plague of heresy. Palladius, the *primus episcopus*, was surely sent to make the Irish Christians subject to an episcopal diocesan rule; and in his person orthodoxy would most certainly be assured. What none of this can explain for us is why Palladius was the man in question. Why not some lesser, and still orthodox, figure from Britain?

It is not necessary to suppose that Palladius, assuming reasonably that the same man figures in Prosper's entries for 429 and 431, was a Papal deacon, a figure of especial standing in the Papal curia. He is, on any reading of our short but plain sources, much more likely to have been a deacon of the Church at Auxerre; a place where, it appears, events in south-east Britain were followed with concern. Palladius may have been sent (though we can guess this only) from Auxerre to Rome to obtain Papal approval for the sortie; possibly he accompanied Germanus and Lupus to Britain in 429; and was then proposed, from his earlier involvement in the campaign to restore orthodoxy, or for personal qualities, as an appropriate candidate for the Irish see. J.H. Todd, long ago, drew attention[26] to the possibility that other members of a Palladian family were prominent in the fifth-century Gaulish church.

After 431, history is silent about this man. Subsequent tradition – that is, material set down rather later than Patrick's time – showed Palladius as having shortly abandoned Ireland, or having fallen ill and died in Britain or Pictland, or having given up his see by 432, the traditional date of Patrick's arrival in Ireland. This is just a generalised depiction of insignificance and speedy failure, intended to stress, by contrast, Patrick's importance and prolonged success. Hanson has voiced[27] one of the objections to this idea; Prosper's remarks of 433 or 434. It would be curious of Prosper to have said what he did, had the late Pope's emissary in Ireland either died or abandoned his mission in despair. One might conclude that Palladius, whom Prosper may have met or known personally, was then still alive.

There is an early body of Irish belief, which has been given expression in a variety of ways, that there were prominent Christian figures – saints – in a part of Ireland well before Patrick's day, and that they were unconnected with either Patrick or Palladius. These traditions must be seen alongside another, that a people called Corcu Loígde (who by the twelfth century were confined to an area around the river Bandon in Cork – roughly the diocese of Ross) were the first people in Ireland to receive the Faith.[28] At an earlier time, the sixth and possibly fifth centuries, they formed however one of the dominant dynasties in Munster, ruling as far east as Ossory. Patrick's career, as we shall see, was centred on the north and north-east of Ireland; and the essential southern-ness of these non-Patrician traditions, which might be placed with the suspicion that the hinterland of the great southern rivers was a broad focus of commercial contact with late Roman Britain, is interesting. In 1962, Binchy was prepared to hint about 'evidence that considerable areas in the East and South of Ireland had been Christianised by British missionaries before the sending of Palladius (let alone the arrival of Patrick)'.[29]

There is very little factual material about these early, southern, non-Patrician saints. Any surviving Lives are un-historical, bringing them into contact with Patrick and other important people, and providing them with sixth-century obits. We cannot even show that they were historically real, Irish or British, or were regarded as bishops. The saints in question (fig. 57) are: Abbán, of Killaban and Moyarney; Ailbe of Emly; Ciarán of Saighir; Declán of Ardmore; and Ibar, or Iubhar, of Beggery Island in Cork harbour. Kenney, wisely, concluded that 'the only safe general deduction is that before the great development of the Patrick legend there were local legends in various parts of southern Ireland, telling of the Christianising of those districts by saints who knew not Patrick'.[30] Yet we must not dismiss them entirely, if we wish to retain the notion of Romano–British contact; and Binchy also suggested that the first series of Latin loanwords in Irish, borrowed *before* the mission of 431, contained a specifically religious element 'just sufficient to provide a "skeleton service" of Christian terminology'.[31] Examples would include *domnach* 'church', from *dominicum* (*cf.* p. 149 above), *cruimther* 'priest', from the postulated British Latin *premiter*[32] (for *presbyter*), *Cresen* 'Christian', from *Christianus*, etc.; but absent, significantly, is any word of this type or postulated date meaning 'bishop' or representing a similar borrowing of *episcopus*. The Old Irish *epscop* is a borrowing of a later date. 'All this seems to me,' Binchy concluded, 'to suggest that the first stratum of Christian loanwords was already established in the Irish language when the first bishop was sent by Pope Celestine.' Professor Binchy had already made the point about the early (late fourth/early fifth century) horizon of this first stratum of the Latin loanwords in 1958, in reviewing LHEB;[33] and it was accepted, with minor reservations only, by Professor David Greene in 1968.[34] Greene supposed that 'the beginning of the first stratum could hardly be placed later than the middle of the fourth (century)', and that if in truth the religious vocabulary is somewhat skimpy, there are other words which belong here that point rather to trade and material contacts – *clúm* (*pluma* 'feather' (as quill pen?)), *cann* (*panna* 'dish, vessel'), *corcur* (*purpura* 'purple, cloth dyed purple'), *sorn* (*furnus* 'oven: kiln?'), and *siball* (*fibula* 'brooch, safety-pin'). Greene concludes, 'That there was trade between Britain and Ireland during the fourth century seems probable, and that British Christians took advantage of these contacts to spread their faith to Ireland certainly not impossible.'

The area of Palladius' mission was not, as far as we can infer, in the south. Since it must be allowed that its location was known in contemporary Gaul, and presumably in fifth-century Britain, we might search for any region of Ireland where subsequent tradition or legend, however frail, linked Palladius' name with identifiable localities. Where, in Gaul, would be thought an appropriate place for a bishop? In the map of archaeological evidence for Gaulish contacts – and we cannot yet be certain that the imported Class E ware is necessarily as early as 431, though it occurs on what are regarded as fifth-century occupied sites – the area of Dublin Bay can be singled out; Dalkey Island yielded Class E pottery, and since it has also produced[35] fragments of sixth-century wine or oil jars from rather further afield, it may have been some small commercial entrepot. There are odd finds of late Roman material in this coastal belt of Leinster, the east-central province of later Ireland; and three ancient church foundations, later associated in Irish legend with Palladius,[36] lie in this region. There is also a tradition that Palladius landed at the small port of Arklow, on the Wicklow coast.[37] None of this amounts to very much, save cumulatively to remove Palladius and his mission of 431 from the areas, either of the southern non-Patrician saints, or of the slightly later Patrick.

The lingering belief that churchmen from Gaul had brought the Faith to Ireland, and that this event, even if undervalued, was separate from anything in Patrick's life and career, found expression in various ways; not only the Palladian legends, but perhaps an early pride in the link, through Palladius, with Rome. Columbanus, the Irish founder of Luxeuil, Bobbio, and other European monasteries, in a letter written in 613 from Milan to Pope Boniface IV,[38] was at pains to stress this continuous thread of ancient orthodoxy. 'For all we Irish,' he wrote, 'inhabitants of the edge of the world, are disciples of saints Peter and Paul . . . none has been a heretic . . . the Catholic faith (*fides catholica*), *as it was delivered by you first*, who are the successors of the Holy Apostles, is maintained unbroken.'

The final question is: Was Palladius alone in his work? When, considerably after the lifetimes of both Palladius and Patrick, the first Irish annals were compiled, and retrospectively enlarged into supposedly coherent form, entries[39] were constructed for early 'bishops'. In a system that purported to record Patrick's arrival, as a bishop, in 432, and thus confined Palladius to a single year – 431 to 432 – these other persons had to be shown as *in auxilium Patricii* – '(sent) to help Patrick'. From the Annals of Ulster, for example, we have Secundus or Secundinus, arriving in 439 and dying in 447, aged 70; and Auxilius and Iserninus also coming to Ireland in 439, and dying in 459 and 468 respectively. These details are superficially a little suspicious: A, B and C arrive, and then are made to die (in the order of A, B and C) at approximately equally-spaced intervals. This is not quite enough to make us reject all three men as persons; because they are independently associated, in Irish ecclesiastical tradition, with various early churches.[40] Were the sites all in the far west

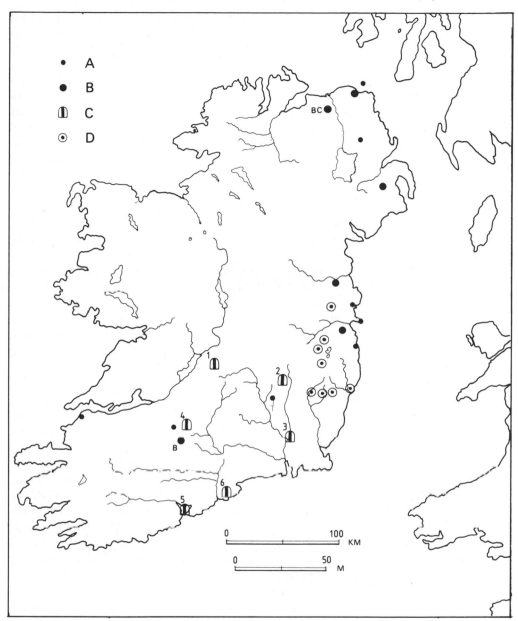

57 Pre-Patrician Christianity in Ireland

A copper and bronze coins and non-precious finds of Roman material (after Bateson)   B Roman gold and silver, 4th–5th cent. (after Bateson)   C Saints of the South. – 1 Ciaran (Saighir)   2 Abban (Killaban)   3 Abban (Moyarney)   4 Ailbe (Emly)   5 Ibar (Beggery Is.)   6 Declan (Ardmore)   D sites of churches traditionally ascribed to Palladius, Auxilius, Iserninus, and Secundinus. Hoards: B (Balline), BC (Ballinrees or 'Coleraine') of Ireland, or the extreme north-west, or remote Co. Kerry, one might think again; but they are not. Their sitings, one (Dunshaughlin) about 20 miles north-west of Dublin, the other four (Killashee, Old Kilcullen, Clonmore and Ahade) between 20 and 40 miles south-south-west from Dublin – all in Leinster – would be more consistent with the notion that these people, if real, were connected with the venture of Palladius, and not Patrick at all. Possibly among them, and among others not named, were priests and deacons accompanying Palladius in 431; we cannot be sure. Of those we know, Secundinus is marginally the least unlikely as Palladius' successor.[41] The weight of current opinion is perhaps in favour of associating Secundinus, Auxilius and Iserninus with Palladius rather than with Patrick.[42] Professor E.G. Bowen suggested[43] that church foundations at St Issells (near Tenby) and Llanhernin in Carmarthen, both in south-west Wales, show early ascriptions to Auxilius and Iserninus respectively. This may well be so; but whether Palladius and his helpers travelled directly by sea from Gaul to Ireland, from Nantes to Arklow or Dublin or any other place, or came partly overland and thus crossed through south-west Wales, it is perhaps a little more likely that such Welsh dedications are some few centuries later in date. They could reflect foundations or additional consecrations, with appropriate relics, by Irish Christians who had moved from, or were still in touch with, the relevant region of Ireland.

What has been discussed is, essentially, an aspect of the early relationship between Ireland and Roman Britain, and also between Ireland and Gaul; a relationship for whose existence, in this Christian detail, there is just enough evidence to permit such a discussion. The evidence, largely archaeological, will continue to increase; and it is probable that it will illuminate a trade, leading to settlements, and the presence of fourth-century Christians in those settlements through which Romano–British interests sought the markets of Ireland. The mission, if we can call it that, of Palladius in 431 offers us a parallel to what was inferred about Nynia; and Palladius, sent with Papal approval as a bishop, beyond the Roman empire, to a Christian community of uncertain size, must be taken to mark the opening of the Christian history of Ireland. If Palladius was, in later centuries, to be eclipsed by the fame, and the accrued legends, of the British bishop Patrick, at least he has not vanished entirely without trace. He, and the other unnamed fourth-century and early fifth-century Christians in Ireland, have merited this separate chapter.

CHAPTER THIRTEEN

St Patrick – His Background and Early Life

O let us never, never doubt
What nobody is sure about.
    Hilaire Belloc, *The Microbe*

The inclusion of two chapters in this book devoted to Patrick, the Apostle of Ireland, would alone be warranted by the facts that Patrick was a Briton and that he lived and worked in the fifth century; but there is also the possibility that, from his career, we can make inferences about the British Church at this period in certain aspects about which little or no other information survives, and this will be explored in Chapter 14.

Few such figures in the Christian history of western Europe have attracted so much posthumous literature, and accrued legend. A complete library of Patriciana would now extend to many hundreds of books – about fifty of which would be worth perusing – and facets of Patrick's life, and mythos, have long been official. The year 1961 was marked as the 1500th anniversary of the saint's death by the Catholic Church and the Irish nation, commemorative postage-stamps and all. Ireland teems with churches, shrines, places of pilgrimage and natural features, the denial of whose direct and authentic connection with the national Apostle would give gratuitous offence. The ecclesiastical primacies of Armagh, both Roman Catholic and Church of Ireland archiepiscopates, have for centuries rested on what are taken to be the undisputed *acta* of Patrick himself, starting about AD 440.

The *historical* Patrick, insofar as we can glimpse him, was a genuine person – considerably more so than 'Arthur', and on a par with more prominent and often better-documented churchmen of that age – and was born within the frontiers of Britannia. His father was called Calpurnius or Calpornius, and was or had been both *diaconus* and *decurio* – a Christian deacon, and the holder of an obligatory civil office. Sources later than his time[1] add, and these points are perfectly credible, that his mother's name was Concessa and that he may have had British names (Magonus, and *Sochet* or Succetus) as well as, or before, his Latin one. Calpurnius owned land, and had servants. Patrick's (paternal?) grandfather, Potitus, had been a priest (*presbyter*), and Patrick himself was successively a deacon and a bishop, and therefore presumably intermediately ordained *presbyter* (though he does not mention this). As a youth not quite sixteen, he was captured presumably by *Scotti*, Irish raiders, and taken to Ireland, *Hiberione*. After six years, he escaped, walked a long distance, joined in a three-day voyage on a boat, and then undertook a further longer trip on foot. Subsequently, he underwent formal training for the canonical orders, became a deacon, and having attained the episcopate he returned to Ireland. It appears that he never left Ireland again, but his work there was not without incident, and he seems to have suffered privations in Ireland, and misrepresentations outside it. He wrote in Latin; he knew his Bible, probably in a mixed form, and a limited range of Christian texts.[2] He would of course have spoken late British, the vernacular of his home region; some Latin; and the vernacular Irish of the fifth century. Throughout his adult life, he was conscious of God's direct and specific guidance, a guidance conveyed to him through dreams and visions, which he describes. He wrote, or dictated to persons whom presumably he had taught to write, his works in Latin. Two of these – the *Epistola*, an 'open letter' to a British king called Coroticus, and a longer work called his *Confessio* – have survived, textually in forms whose general authenticity is beyond question. Like Gildas, Patrick is sparing in the extreme with any references to absolute dates and identifiable place-names. It is clear from the tenor of what does survive that he was a humble, holy and remarkable man. Historically, he is one of the few individual British Christians speaking to us from the fifth century, and in any history of British Christianity the slightest clue or potential inference in what Patrick says is of particular value.

What has just been written constitutes, the lunatic and the extreme sectarian fringes apart, generally accepted common ground. But as soon as one proceeds any further, where inference rather than documentary evidence has to be deployed, controversy begins. This involves Patrick's geographical origins; details of his captivity, escape, and travels (if any) abroad; the sequence of his career; the contexts of his surviving Latin writings; and, above all, his *dates*. So forceful appears to have been, and still to be, the hold that Patrick exercises on historians – notably Irish historians – that the arguments on all such matters have, alas, far too often assumed a distinctly personal flavour. 'Is there a special type of *odium Patricianum* with which even the most genial scholars are likely to be infected?' asked Professor Daniel Binchy.[3] With the marked exception of one great humanist,[4] the answer is plainly, Yes; and the frustration experienced in trying to squeeze yet one more solid fact out of the Patrician corpus has much to do with this. Seen collectively, all these arguments and uncertainties make up what has long been called The Patrician Problem.

Whether or not Patrick was born before, or after, AD 400, all but the most eccentric interpretations of what he says, and of what is otherwise known of the Church, and Ireland, at this period would have Patrick as working and dying within the fifth century. This is the period of Nynia; of Palladius, and of any other non- or pre-Patrician Christian pioneers among the Irish *credentes* (Romano–Britons or Irish); and of Germanus of Auxerre and his two visits to the British churchmen. To a large extent, this must be Patrick's context, too. The present writer, who ventures his own interpretation of the Patrician writings only after much thought and several years of reading and re-reading the relevant material, would wish to explore Patrick in this wider setting; and (as both the late Père Grosjean and Professor James Carney have urged) to look with particular care at what Patrick himself wrote (or did not write) and towards analyses of the structure and content of both *Epistola* and *Confessio*.

The sources for Patrick are varied and have to be clarified at once. The Patrick of current mythology has been put together, partly from a continuous fount of picturesque oral and popular tradition, but mainly from an oblique inheritance from a long series of Lives. The oldest of these, the Life by Muirchú, and the so-called Memoir by Tírechán, were composed – and from a specifically Armagh viewpoint and interest – in the period 661 × 700.[5] Since these were preceded, if at all, in the surviving corpus of Irish hagiography only by the first Life of Brigid of Kildare, by Cogitosus,[6] and thus correspond approximately to the earlier group of pre-Bedan Northumbrian Lives,[7] they are both in themselves important, simply as productions; but both stand some two centuries later than anything Patrick wrote, and that portion of Muirchú's work which alone can safely be approached as a potential historical source is derived from Patrick's *Confessio*. Between Patrick, and these native biographers, may fall certain references to Patrick included or inserted in the various Annals (lost or surviving) that were created and maintained by major monastic Irish churches.[8] Further argument surrounds the question of whether any of such began to be composed and written down as early as the late sixth or early seventh centuries,[9] or not before 'the middle of the eighth century at the earliest';[10] though the balance of reasonable argument would favour what Dr Miller calls 'a Latinate historical horizon', a starting-point for such compositions, between c.550 and 600, more surely c.573 to 600, in the Northern British kingdoms.[11] We cannot, on the strength of Adamnan's Life of Columba alone,[12] deny Irish churchmen at the same period the *ability* to produce written annals; the question is now mainly at what stage it became customary to do so, and c.750 strikes one as unreasonably delayed.

This is important; because the assumption that records of Patrick's death, if not highlights of his life, could have been entered in a computation began as early as *c.*570 – having been gathered from a churchman, who had known some much older churchman who in turn had had some first-hand knowledge of Patrick – forms one quite fair argument for accepting, preferably, the later of the two obits or death-dates for Patrick. But, the later Armagh Lives and potentially-relevant annalistic entries aside, the sole proper source for any fresh enquiry must be Patrick's own writings; and these must be seen as the *Epistola* (*Ep.*) and the *Confessio* (*Conf.*), without certain additional and minor items that have been attributed to him.[13]

Of the two major puzzles in the Patrician problem – his personal geography, and his dates – the former, as slightly the less complicated, can be taken first. Within Ireland itself, all and any traces of his activities are decidedly northern (as opposed to, say, the emphasis in fig. 57). He mentions (*Conf.* 23) a single place-name, *silva Vocluti* 'the wood of Foclut', *quae est prope mare occidentale* 'which is near the western sea'; i.e., is presumably on the north-west or western coast. Debate on the identification has been prolonged[14], but without retracing any of this, it may be stated that a formerly wooded area around Killala in Co. Mayo[15] is the most widely accepted probability. Patrick's connection with Armagh may rest on tradition, but it is tradition of a very early period, and it has no locational rival; and arguments in its favour would include the proximity to *Emain Machae* or Navan Fort, a vast stronghold formerly the seat of the Ulidian kingdom in north-east Ireland.[16] The three traditional resting-places – Saul, Downpatrick and Armagh – are at least in the same part of Ireland. Subsequent, though probably quite early (seventh century?) place-name evidence,[17] would confine Patrick's work mainly to the north-east.

We are told by Patrick (*Conf. 1*) that he was taken captive when he was at his father's *villula*. It is reasonable to suppose that since this was in Roman Britain it lay south of Hadrian's Wall; was nearer to the west, rather than east, coast of Britain; and on the west, approximately opposite that part of Ireland with which Patrick was involved. There is an indication of wealth and substance; his father was a member of the curial class, three generations of his family possessed Latin names, and (*Ep. 10*) *servos et ancillas domus patris mei* 'the male and female servants of my father's house' were captured in the same raid. Whether *villula* is his diminutive for what we would call a 'villa' – a country-house in its farming estate – or, as with the rather earlier case of Tacitus' German chieftain,[18] simply a convenient Latin term for a substantial native farmstead, we cannot tell. The *villula* which Calpornius owned was near (*prope*) a place called *vicus bannavem taburniae*, which has the sad distinction of being the only place-name in Britain that Patrick gives us.

We are therefore, very probably, in the north-west quarter of Britannia, in the late fourth or early fifth century, for reasons stated. This *vicus* – and the word is the commonest term (*cf.* p. 255) for a small settlement or village unimportant enough to lay claim to any better official title or popular description – was somewhere that Calpornius (or Potitus, the grandfather; the sentence is ambiguous) *fuit* 'was, used to be, used to live'. If Patrick's father, the decurion, is implied, there is a further implication that this *villula*, *prope* this *vicus*, was also not unthinkably far from a larger town which would have possessed the civil administrative structure calling for an *ordo*, a 'cantonal council', and the various obligatory grades attendant upon qualifications of wealth and property (*decurio* among them) used to run such a structure and fulfil the offices.

In the north-west, at this period, the only possibility would be Carlisle, *Luguvalium*, which is appropriately near the western coast (and the indicated regions of Ireland) to suggest that Irish slave-raids not unthinkably far inland – in fact, to the paternal *villula* – would accord with what we can infer. A (lost) tombstone from Old Penrith, which is some 13 miles (about 29 km) SSE of Carlisle, confirms the existence of the late Roman *civitas Carvetiorum*, the civitas which can hardly be centred otherwise than at *Luguvalium*.[19] It describes the deceased as *senator* and *qu(a)estorius*, terms which, as R.P. Wright points out, do not for the fourth–fifth centuries exclude civilian interpretations – titles of a member of the curial class, like Calpornius.

The particular reading of the vicus as *bannavem taburniae* is established from a comparison of surviving manuscripts, and the only variant that need be considered – from MS D, the Book of Armagh written shortly after 800 – would be *taberniae*.[20] There is no connection with Latin *taberna* 'inn, tavern'; the better approach is to write the name as /*bannaventaberniae*/ and then to separate the elements. A division into the known forms *banna*, *venta* and *berniae/burniae* at once suggests itself. *Banna* occurs by itself, and in compounds, in Romano–British place-names; *venta*, apparently descriptive, is also found in compound names.

Banna is a British word, and in place-names indicated a notable 'horn', 'spur' or promontory of rock.[21] The Ravenna *Bannovalium* is either Caistor or Horncastle (Lincolnshire), possibly the latter,[22] where the spur is that formed by the junction of two rivers. (In a higher coastal setting, Abercorn, Bede's *Aebbercurnig* (p. 287), also stands on a spur above the juncture or two streams, and employs another British word for 'horn' (**corn-*), adjectivally (**corn-iacos?*)[23] – though W.J. Watson noted that this is the only derivative of **corn-*, as opposed to many from **banna*, **banno*, to have survived in Scotland.) In combination, there *is* a known instance of *Bannaventa*, a small Roman settlement at Whilton Lodge in Northamptonshire mentioned in the Antonine Itinerary; it is suggested[24] that the name was transferred from the neighbouring Iron Age hill-fort (Brough Hill, outside Daventry). This particular place, though of course frequently seized upon as Patrick's father's *vicus*, hardly satisfies any of the requirements discussed above, and cannot seriously be considered.

The element *venta* must describe some variable outward aspect of civilian life common to several Romano–British urban centres; it acts as prefix to the names of three civitas capitals[25] and is the suffix in the *Bannaventa* just cited, and *Glannoventa*, the Roman fort at Ravenglass on the Cumberland coast.[26] What *venta* means is a problem; Kenneth Jackson's earlier discussion[27] rejecting any link with Latin *vendo* 'I sell', late Latin *vendita* 'sale: market?', should now be read with Professors Rivet's and Smith's views. The *word* itself is more likely to be of Celtic, or non-Latin origin; its late Romano–British *meaning*, however, remains obscure and one can only make the informed guess that the semantic area 'meeting-place, local centre, market-place' includes it.

There is, of course, a *Banna* in the north of Britain; it has long been known to have been the name of a fort on Hadrian's Wall, in view of its inclusion in a sequence of place-names inscribed on two metalwork objects, the Rudge Cup[28] and the Amiens Patera.[29] In both, *Banna* comes (reading from west to east) after *Camboglanna (Castlesteads)*. *Banna* was long identified as Bewcastle, 6 miles (9 km) north of the Wall, because *Camboglanna* was identified as the fort at Birdoswald since the *Notitia Dignitatum* garrison attributed to *Camboglanna* was attested at Birdoswald, physically, by inscriptions[30] to the relevant unit.

However, Mark Hassall has now proposed that a gap in the *Notitia* text (damage at the foot of a MS folio) has lost two lines, with the result that *Camboglanna* becomes Castlesteads, and *Banna* is Birdoswald[31] – where a stone inscribed by the *venatores Banniess(es)* 'the Banniensan Hunters' provides some confirmation.[32] We are 15 miles (24 km) only ENE of *Luguvalium*, Carlisle. The *vicus Banna* (*Venta Berniae*) cannot be the fort itself; the name would rather allude to a civilian, dependent settlement, such as that which appears to exist in the area east of the fort.[33] If this is the *vicus Banna*, to which the (distinctive? descriptive local?) term *venta* was added in the late Roman period, one has to explain -*Berniae*.

The element involved has been discussed by Kenneth Jackson;[34] it enters into the names **Bernaccia*, *Bernicia* (*cf*. p. 291), and would be a British stem of the form **berna* meaning, like Old Irish *bern* 'gap, mountain pass'. One can imagine a British Latin **Bernia* serving as a district-name, and thus appearing in the genitive after *vicus Banna Venta*; there are not over-many parallels to this, since the distinctives viewed in, say, *Aquae Sulis* and *Aquae Arnemetiae*, *Venta Belgarum* and *Venta Silurum*,[35] refer to larger towns and are of another order.

However, we do at least know that a more southerly *Bannaventa* existed, on the line of a main road; and, as Jackson has pointed out elsewhere, the persistence of the British, post-Roman name-form *Manau Guotodin* or *Manaw Gododdin* (*cf.* fig. 56) must not lead us to confuse the area so-named with the much larger 'Gododdin'. As he writes,[36] 'Gododdin here is syntactically genitive, and the meaning is literally "Manaw of Gododdin", that is, "Manaw *in* Gododdin"', and the purpose 'of this qualification is to distinguish it from the other Manaw known to the Welsh and Cumbrians in the Dark Ages, namely the Isle of Man'. On a restricted scale, *Banna Venta* (in *Bernia*) would be distinguished from the *Banna Venta* lying on Iter II, VI and VIII. As for the **bern-* itself, the Greenhead pass, between the upper North Tyne at Haltwhistle and the upper gorge of the river Irthing, naturally suggests itself.[37] Calpornius' *villula* was near the *vicus*; a Romano–British estate of Highland Zone character, perhaps on the south side of the Irthing between Birdoswald and Lanercost, would fit this, and is now less inconceivable in view of the discoveries of villas at Old Durham and at Piercebridge.[38] Figure 58 brings all these places together.

Why does this matter? The answer must be that, as we shall see, what Patrick tells us about his later life suggests that he returned to his home district, that this district forms the most probable background for his ecclesiastical training and advancement, and that any inferences we

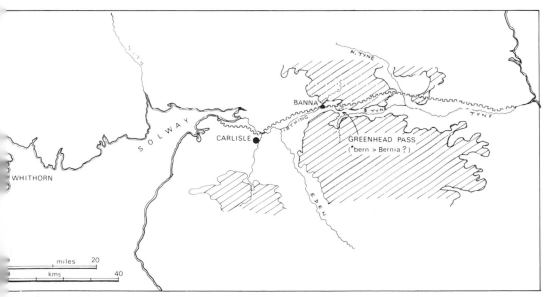

58 Patrick's homeland – Carlisle, the western end of the Wall, Banna (Venta) Berniae and the Greenhead pass (?= **bern*)

choose to make about the Church in Britain at the time of Patrick's episcopate in Ireland acquire point and value only if we can locate them a little more precisely than just within Britannia. There are not enough clues in Patrick's writings to take us further; but the present writer is convinced, now, that the setting of Carlisle for Calpornius and probably Potitus, of around Birdoswald for the *vicus Banna Venta Berniae*, and of this part of north-west Britain for what can be inferred of Patrick's Ireland, entirely outweigh other suggestions (of the Daventry *Bannaventa*, the Severn estuary, Dumbarton, etc.). In time, our next indication is from Muirchú; he adds (but may be only inferring) that *Bannavem Thaburniae* is *chaut procul a mari nostro* 'hardly far from our sea', and glosses it with another place-name that he had been told, given variously as *Ventre*, *Nemthor* (and elsewhere, later, *Nemthur*). Muirchú clearly did not know either the name or location, and it is profitless now to pursue this.[39]

Carlisle may not have been a centre of Christianity before the fourth century but, as has been suggested in earlier chapters, it may have been so early enough to provide a background for the priesthood of Potitus and/or the diaconate of Calpornius, if the civitas centre (rather than the *vicus*) is indicated. Nor given the nature of the lands north of the Wall is it improbable to suppose a force of *Scotti*, landing on the north shore of Solway or in the mouths of the Esk or Eden, crossing the Wall between Carlisle and Birdoswald at some unattended stretch and rounding up captives in the Irthing valley – in expectation of a successful trip back to their boats, and to Ireland.

When we turn to Patrick's dates, we find no real guidance. His reference (*Ep.* 14) to the Franks as being still pagan at the time he wrote – the Franks were converted from 496 onwards – is an unhelpfully late point. The inferred background of a *vicus*, a *villula* with slaves owned by a Christian *decurio* who presumably attended at a nearby still-functioning centre of government, formal education, and an ability to write Latin, is strictly apposite to Patrick only up to the age of 16; but, again, it would be a bold man who claimed that, in north-west Britain, such *romanitas* had necessarily disappeared by 410, or any other certain date.

There are in fact no less than three avenues by which one could explore Patrick's chronology. The first, and least satisfactory, is to use the conflicting evidence of the various Irish annal entries, not one of which (wherever first set down) was committed to writing until considerably after Patrick's time and death. The second, recently favoured by Professor Richard Hanson, is to construct a framework of dates contextually and inferentially; to some extent, but with other results, this was also Bury's method in 1905. The third, attempted below, is to produce a *relative* chronology from the clues contained in Patrick's writings, and then to attach this if possible to some estimated absolute date at one or more points.

For centuries, the traditional view of Patrician chronology rested upon two received dates: one, of 432, for his return to Ireland as a bishop – when almost by definition he would have been at least 30 – and the other, around 492/3, for his death; clearly at an advanced age. The origin of the 432 date has long been seen as connected with modes of constructing annals and chronicles (in the sixth, seventh and later centuries) that used earlier European material to supply the total lack of native records. The Chronicle of Prosper of Aquitaine (Chap. 12), apparently known in Ireland, had clearly stated – and this could not be set aside – that Palladius had been sent, by the Pope himself, as the first bishop to the Irish believers; and in 431. If that year had been pre-empted for Palladius, then 432 was the next best and possible year for Patrick in his champions' eyes, and appropriate later glosses (of Palladius' relative failure, departure, or early death) were added.

The selection of an obit sixty years later is still the main puzzle of the traditional dating; assimilation of the saint's life-span to that of Moses,[40] 120 years, bisected at the age of 60 (in 432), merely elaborates but does not explain the original temporal extension. A complication was the appearance of a *second* obit half-way between these dates, around 461; though as Hanson[41] has hinted, this may mark assimilation to the obit of a much more widely-known fifth-century figure, Leo I, pope 440–61, and the present writer would join others in suspecting that 461 was not originally a Patrician death-date at all.

This 'traditional' chronology was first seriously challenged as late as 1905 by the Roman historian, J.B. Bury. Bury – who accepted the 461 obit – presented a scheme[42] in which the events of Patrick's career, adduced both from Patrick's writings and from those of his later biographers (to some extent, impartially), were accorded absolute dates. These were drawn, by analogy or likelihood, from the history of the later Roman Empire, Bury's own special subject, or less happily from that of early Ireland, as it was then thought to be ascertainable.

On this model, Patrick, born in 389 (not at Daventry, but on the lower Severn) was captured in 405, supposed date of a great raid on Britain by king Niall Nói Giallach, Niall of the Nine Hostages. His escape took place in 411. After the short sea-trip, Patrick's long walk – to be examined below – 'through a deserted countryside' (*per desertum, Conf.* 19) occurred in a part of Gaul laid waste by the Vandals, in 409 × 416. Patrick remained in Gaul; indeed, he travelled in Europe. He was ordained at Auxerre by a person identifiable as bishop Amator, who died in 418. Patrick returned as a bishop to Ireland in 432, as tradition immemorially demanded. He founded the first church at Armagh in 444, and died (aged 72, which is at least more likely than 120) in the traditional year, 461.

Since 1905, as Binchy forcefully reminds us, this scheme, which had behind it all the weight of Bury's authority and the academic recognition of two (432, 461) of the three old, traditional years, became the new orthodoxy; the 'orthodox' as opposed to 'traditional' (432–92) thinking. If most of Bury's synchronisms can now be overturned or picked off, one by one, and his view of the certainty of early Irish dates would be shared by very few people indeed,[43] the Bury model is still held with official blessing by the vast majority of Irishmen and, more effectively, by the Irish ecclesiastical hierarchy.

The complexity of the problem – so far, merely the existence of the pre-Bury and the Bury schemes – was much extended by two separate and later works, T.F. O'Rahilly's *The Two Patricks*[44] and James Carney's *The Problem of Saint Patrick*.[45] Both these distinguished native scholars, for similar reasons, felt that Bury's ideas failed to explain the existence of two, separate, death-dates. Their solutions, in essence reviving a very much older and submerged idea, were not dissimilar; there had to be actually *two* people involved in the Patrick story, and the earlier and older of the two was only much later to be remembered as 'Patrick' or 'Old Patrick' (*senex Patricius*), after his death in 457 or 461 (or thereabouts). The real Patrick – the Briton from *Banna Venta Berniae* who was enslaved, escaped, and came back as a bishop, roughly at the time of 'Old Patrick's' death – himself died later, on 17 March 493, St Patrick's Day. O'Rahilly's choice for the first Patrick was Palladius – the 432 is really the 431 of Palladius' arrival. Carney's was a Gaulish bishop called Secundinus, who first appears only in the early annals, as a companion either of Patrick (proper), or historically more convincingly perhaps of Palladius.

This 'Duo-Patrician' theory, appearing embarrassingly enough in time for 1961, which was celebrated enormously as the Patrician Year, is an attack on the official acceptance of the 461 obit. It offers support for that of 493; and thus, or so common sense would tell us, argument for a Patrician career wholly in the fifth century, involving a return to Ireland totally divorced from the date of 432, and from the largely unconnected (but independently dated) arrival of Palladius.

Much of Carney's book, and of his other varied writing about Patrick,[46] is a great deal more acute and percipient than is always admitted by his critics, some of whom seem to have been put off not by what Carney says, but by the manner of his saying it; and his elevation of the shadowy and indefensible (and unnecessary) Secundinus to the deutero-Patrick rôle in no way detracts from his handling of inferences from Patrick's own writings. This is not the place to elaborate on the nature of the various 457 × 461 entries, which – whether related to Leo I's death or not – contain certain curious features; they will occur again below.

Professor Richard Hanson's view of Patrician chronology[47] is an elegantly-argued balance of probabilities: between a single early Patrick, corresponding to the idea of a person returning to Ireland in 432 and dying in 461, and a single later Patrick, dying in 492. Hanson confines himself initially to a series of arguments and inferences based only on what Patrick himself says or implies and (unlike Bury) does not have recourse to external dated events. The outcome is that the probability of a single early Patrick outweighs any alternative. Hanson's saint would have been born between 388 and 406,[48] would have returned to Ireland as a bishop in 425 × 435 and died about 460[49] – it is emphasised that these are conjectural dates only, but ones reached without any reference to later annals or traditions. The outcome, chronologically, is nonetheless generally that reached by Bury on different grounds.

Objection will be attached, not to the various lines of argument, but to some of the premises on which such lines rest. We are told that Calpornius was both a deacon and a *decurio*; at what period in late Roman Britain is it likely that a member of this curial class could (presumably) take Holy Orders in order to avoid[50] the considerable burden of his obligatory office and yet retain his property (*villula*)? Hanson sees this between Magnus Maximus' unsurpation (388) and the reimposition of Imperial authority (398 × 400? under Stilicho), Patrick being perhaps born in this period. The question of Patrick's knowledge of the Bible text, and which text, in relation to the date at which his ecclesiastical education could have begun, was touched upon earlier; if, as Hanson thinks, this is preferably 420 × 425, when Patrick was aged at least 22, again we place his birth in 388 × 406. Minor points include Hanson's view that Patrick's writings display a sense of the imminence of the end of the world (are eschatological) – this was common in the fifth century, but might suggest that part of the century nearer to 410, the Sack of Rome, an awful event seen as a portent of the Last Days; and Patrick's view of himself as *Romanus*, something having the same chronological implication. There is also the argument that the Coroticus of the *Epistola*, taken (as the present writer would agree) to be a king of Strathclyde and not another person of the same name in Ceredigiaun, west Wales, lived and reigned in a broad bracket of 420 × 470, suggesting any contact with Patrick more probably before, rather than after, 450 × 460. Some stress is laid on Patrick's reference (*Ep.* 14) to Gaulish Christians ransoming captives from the still-pagan Franks with the gold coinage called *solidi*; this possesses little relevance to Patrick's date unless we know at which stage in the past he supposed this to have been common.[51]

One is bound to ask if Hanson's views of the last years of Roman Britain, notably after 400, are necessarily in accord with all the recent evidence on this score. Was the floruit of Coroticus really 420 × 470, or (as others would compute) a shorter and later period? Are we all agreed – and some clearly have not been, or are not[52] – that Patrick's experiences from the ages of 22 to about 35 were exclusively set in Britain? Can we be sure that there were not parts of Britannia where, up to well past 410, persons talked Latin as well as British, thought of themselves as Christian *Romani*, and chose to maintain official titles, only a chance handful of which have survived on inscribed stones[53] or seem to be retrospectively described by Gildas[54]? Did all annals commence to be compiled so late that the obit of 492 – however this arose – was totally invented? Is it not possible, in short, that Hanson's valuable essay provides us not with temporal brackets for Patrick, but merely a number of *termini post quos*: dates after which, and only after which, certain things could have occurred and certain observed conditions could have been fulfilled?

It has long been recognised that within limits a relative chronology can be constructed from the statements in the *Confessio* and *Epistola*. For example, Patrick escaped from Ireland aged (16 plus 6) about 22; he is unlikely to have become a bishop before the age of at least 30 × 35; a statement in the *Epistola* implies it was preceded by a letter send by the hand of a presbyter whom Patrick himself had trained *ex infantia* 'from childhood'. If this means, conservatively, an age of 10, this native priest (aged 30-plus?) had been in Patrick's *familia*, immediate spiritual entourage, in Ireland some twenty years; therefore the *Epistola* postdates by that stretch Patrick's return to Ireland. The *Confessio* very probably, if not certainly, is later than the *Epistola* – that is, was composed when Patrick was older than 50 × 55 – and suggests internally that he was at least seeing himself as an older man. There are other, more subtle, internal dates to be won.

The remainder of this chapter puts forward a historical model: that of the life and career of a single Patrick, a Briton from the area already indicated, who died late in the fifth century – quite possibly in 492, or thereabouts – aged 70 or more.[55] It will require only the assumption that he was born in the fifth century. The sole permissible sources are Patrick's writings; and it will be necessary to look very critically at external events, localities and persons, since the sequence of Patrick's life deduced from what he himself says cannot, if this late dating is claimed, conflict too fiercely with what may be known independently. Certain aspects of his writing – notably their Latinity, possible inferences concerning the contemporary Church in Britain, and the suggestion that other, now-lost writings may be implied by the *Confessio* itself – will be considered in Chapter 14.

Let us assume that a man who died in 490 × 495, at a fair old age, might have been born in the second decade of the century; say in 415, either in the paternal *villula* or possibly in a town house in Carlisle. Demonstrably, Patrick's knowledge of Latin points to[56] formal schooling, of the kind which his family could have afforded; the question of at what date versions of the Vulgate New Testament alongside, or instead of, the Vetus Latina would have been in use is relevant (so Hanson) in that Patrick's pre-captivity schooling would have fallen inside 420 × 430.

It is not material whether 'schooling' means attendance at some *schola grammatici* in Carlisle (a *vicus* would hardly have possessed one), or a tutor at the *villula*. It *is* material that we envisage a period, after 410 rather than within the tumultuous northern-frontier situation in the decade or so preceding that date, and before the mid-fifth century struggles (beginning around 440) inferred by Edward Thompson from Gildas' account (see Chap. 10). The central part of the phase 410 × 440 is one in which, particularly at the western end of the Wall, it may well be that a simulacrum of Roman ways continued. We await further discoveries from Carlisle itself, where the present indications[57] seem to be that town life went on into the fifth century; and in Chapter 11 it was argued that the story of Nynia must be placed in the first half of the fifth century, and that the despatch of a bishop – from Carlisle – to the Whithorn *credentes* should belong to the first quarter. One thinks of a Calpornius born about 390 and a Potitus born about 360, respectively ordained deacon about 420 and priest about 395; in the continuity of Church life postulated throughout this book, the latter event is acceptable and the former, given a period of relative stability in that area, just as probable. How long after 410 we must allow the possibility of an *ordo civitatis Carvetiorum*, and under precisely what modified conditions, functioning in Carlisle, we cannot tell, nor do we know whether *decurio* was merely a jealously-guarded title by 420; but it would be rash to suppose this impossible.

Patrick's capture took place when he was *fere sedecim* 'barely sixteen' (*Conf.* 1) and also involved (*Ep.* 10) the capture of the household servants, and the devastation of his father's *domus*, the *villula*; though other members of his family, not mentioned as involved in this, must have been elsewhere. He was taken *in captivitate* to Ireland, *cum tot milia hominum* 'with so many thousands of people', literally; as Hanson has pointed out, this cannot really mean that this particular raid, or any raid, involved enslavement and trans-shipment to Ireland on this scale, and a better version is 'as so many thousands of (other) people (had been in the past)'. We are therefore, around 430, in a phase of Irish raids, of renewed sporadic attack by *Scotti*, the phase culminating in the major attacks of *c*.440 (p. 249). Since the aims of these incursions, from the third to fifth centuries AD, presumably embraced loot as well as Britons, the fresh examinations of Roman material found in Ireland[58] are timely.

At what periods, argued from archaeology rather than from history, is there evidence for such raiding? Michael Dolley,[59] building on the foundation of Bateson's catalogue, felt obliged to point out that 'there is *prima facie* something unlikely about a Patrician captivity beginning in the early 400s'. (In the orthodox, Bury, scheme, an actual, though un-historical, date of 405 was allotted to Patrick's capture; in Hanson's, much the same date would be implicit.) There are two hoards in Ireland, Balline in Co. Limerick, and Ballinrees (older 'Coleraine') in Co. Londonderry – these are marked as B and BC on the map, fig. 57 – that contain partly-dismembered silver ingots and plate, and must represent the outcome of successful expeditions. The Ballinrees hoard also contains coins, which show that the hoard was deposited in 420×425, and the plate seems to be of North Gaulish or even British origin.[60] Dolley, whose arguments involve history as well as numismatic inferences, suggests that 420×440, rather than 400×420, is the phase when Irish raiding must be envisaged, and by implication supports a captivity of Patrick seen (as here) around 430, against the earlier date of *c*.405. Though Hanson has now countered many of Dolley's points,[61] the date – which is not in dispute, numismatically – and location (fig. 57) of the Ballinrees find show that material of this kind *was* still being taken, and it can hardly be from elsewhere but the north of Britannia, at this late date.

Patrick does not say where, in Ireland, he was in captivity. He was with his master six years (*Conf.* 17), during which we may guess he learnt to speak some Irish. The wording of *Conf.* 23, describing a dream in which Patrick imagined, among other things, that he heard the voices of those (Irish? Irish and fellow-Britons?) who were by the Wood of Foclut which is next to the western sea, ends with these voices exclaiming as one, 'We beg thee, O holy youth, *ut venias et adhuc ambulas inter nos*' – and since this must mean 'to come and walk again amongst us', there is a very strong suggestion that the uniquely-named *silva Vocluti* was within the area of his captivity.

Patrick, son of a landed proprietor, had tended *pecora* (sheep or cattle) in lonely places, and was eventually warned in another dream that the time of his release was nigh and that (*Conf.* 17) 'Behold, your ship is ready'. Upon this, he escaped, and walked to the ship. It was a good 200 *milia* away; the Roman *mille* was shorter than our statute mile, and if one must have distances, this is about 188 miles (300 km). From the region of Killala, Co. Mayo, this suggests the southern coastline, between Bantry and Wexford, rather than the eastern, Leinster coast opposite Britain. We might just allow that Patrick had an idea of distance, derived from the *milia per diem* a man could walk, current in his home-world of Roman roads and the interval-length Roman milestones of the northern frontier.

Here, at some port, Patrick encountered the promised ship. The master and crew were pagans, and he conversed with them (in Irish?); they took him aboard, set sail, and reached land *post triduum* (after a period of three-times-24 hours).

In the factually-bare narrative of Patrick's *Confessio*, this is but one of many fiercely-argued stages. Was this trip to Britain? Against such an idea are many points. Patrick would surely have said so; yet (*Conf.* 23) his eventual return to his native land seems to have taken place rather later (*iterum post paucos annos* 'again, after a few years, (I was in Britain with my kin)'). If what he says, and we have no other guide, suggests the south rather than east coast, this includes the natural harbours where archaeology suggests that trading-ships plied in the fourth and fifth centuries, involving contact with Gaul as much as with Britain (figs. 50, 57). It hardly takes 72 hours to cross the Irish Sea, unless delay follows unusually violent weather, a detail that might have impressed itself upon Patrick's memory but which is nowhere mentioned. The distance in (land) miles from, say, Cork harbour to the nearest landfall in Brittany, *Armorica*, rounding Scilly, is about 270 miles. With only a moderate sea and winds, an average speed of 3–4 miles an hour – reasonable for a small sailing-vessel – would bring a boat to Léon, the north-west peninsula of Brittany, in those 72 hours.[62]

When the boat landed (*Conf.* 19), the captain and crew, with Patrick, left their vessel and travelled on foot; a trading-venture seems the least unlikely explanation. The chronology of this walk is unclear. Patrick's account seems to tell us that it took 28 days in all; that the seamen, if burdened, were not burdened with food but expected to find provisions *en route*; that, against expectation, they found the countryside largely deserted; that they followed a road which at one stage traversed some woodlands (a herd of pigs and some wild honey were discovered); and that this timely encounter with food took place about 16 days after landing, when they were all nearly starving.[63] After this they rested two days, having gorged themselves; for the remaining ten(?) days they appear to have had food in abundance, the means of fire, and fine weather, until they reached *homines* (*Conf.* 22) – human habitations; their goal(?).

The precise details do not matter. Patrick describes this trip as *per desertum* 'through the wilderness', and the implication is of a deserted countryside rather than a spiritual desert. Bury's orthodox model, which placed this escape, sea-trip and walk about 411, saw the *desertum* as part of the devastated Atlantic provinces of Gaul, progressively ravaged by Vandals and other from 407.[64] Precisely what effects this had in the remoter parts – for modern France is a large country – is of course disputable.

The present model has argued, solely on what Patrick tells us, that a landfall in northern Brittany (*cf.* fig. 59, map) is probable. The same model places the walk about 436 × 437, Patrick being now 'barely 16' plus '6 years'. If we are to look for a time when a small band of foot-travellers laden with some kind of merchandise are trudging across Armorica, from Léon to the Loire valley – using, for this trip of about 200 miles (320 km), part of the Roman road-system and crossing the forested spine of the province – we can think of 435–7. At this time the Armoricans, who had previously staged a revolt in 409,[65] were again involved in a widespread movement affecting *Gallia ulterior*, northern Gaul, under the leadership of one Tibatto, their aim being secession from what remained of Roman power in their region.[66] To what extent this may have, temporarily, denuded the province of its inhabitants we cannot say; but Armorica in 436 × 437 is as likely a setting as an unspecified part of Gaul in 411.

Patrick's narrative jumps over entire periods in his life. When, in *Conf.* 23, we read that again after a few years he was *in Brittanniis* with *parentes* who welcomed him *ut filium* – and despite the odd phrasing it is preferable to read this exactly as 'parents' and 'son', with Patrick still only in his twenties – they besought him that after so many tribulations he would not leave them again. Had he therefore been, as one supportable reading of this implies, elsewhere, between his escape and this returning home? Acres of print have been expended on this topic. If one credits, as the present writer does, that the sea-trip was to somewhere other than Britain, clearly there is a chance that the 28-day walk (in Gaul) was followed by a stay, not necessarily longer than *paucos annos*, in Gaul.

Gaul is in fact the only other part of the empire indicated in Patrick's writings (*Galliae*, *Conf.* 43: *Galli*, *Ep.* 14). The embroidery of the late seventh-century writers, and of commentators up to Todd and Bury, extended the Continental visit and travels to Rome, to Lérins, to the Tyrrhenian Sea and of course to Auxerre. One need go no further than to suppose some area in the north-west or north of Gaul, for a year or so, is implicit; and it is precisely such a minimal reading that the percipient

---

59 Patrick's world

ALCLUT

BANNA
CARLISLE

SILVA FOCLUTI
ARMAGH

YORK

HIBERIONE

BRITTANNIAE

185 miles

72 HOURS

GALLIAE

SEINE

28 DAYS

TROYES

LOIRE   TOURS

AUXERRE

NANTES

0   200 M

BORDEAUX

James Kenney favoured.[67] There is however a spectrum of belief or disbelief, ranging from those who regard a stay in Gaul during which Patrick experienced an ecclesiastical (and perhaps, in particular, a *monastic*) training as virtually certain,[68] to others who would see any such visit or stay as no more than possible.[69] Less cogent would be arguments around a further divide, concerning the ecclesiastical and/or monastic training, according to whether Auxerre (Grosjean: John Morris) or Lérins, the island monastery off Cannes (Carney: O'Rahilly), is preferred. These are, largely, arguments from Muirchú and Tírechán, not from Patrick's writings; from external history and not from constructs inferred from what Patrick wrote. The present writer would *infer* a sea-trip to Gaul and a short stay there; it is only speculation to add that a well-born Christian Roman citizen, able to speak some Latin and stranded in Nantes (?) about 436, might look to fellow-Christians there or at Tours or Auxerre (fig. 59). It is still speculative to point out that Auxerre at this time housed Germanus and his circle – already involved in the British Church (429) and probably in Palladius' departure for Ireland (431), and perhaps ready to express an interest in a Christian Briton who had escaped from a still-pagan region of Ireland.

The other, separate, argument for Patrick's stay in Gaul (undated) rests on linguistic inferences – from the nature of his Latin. There is no doubt that Latin was not his first language. At home, this would have been (late) British; in Ireland, perhaps for the larger part of his life, the vernacular Irish of his period. Latin is a language that he would have heard his father speak, heard in Church, heard at school; that he himself must have spoken, and learnt to write. Patrick's two pieces contain two classes of Latin – quotations from versions of the Bible and other Christian literature, and statements or comments which he composed himself. The former class need not have been retained in memory from his pre-captivity schooldays – in *Conf. 1, 9, 10* to some extent Patrick implies this, though it is not entirely clear how we should read his self-deprecations. It may be, as Hanson likes to suppose, that Patrick's Biblical and patristic knowledge was acquired during ecclesiastical training after he was 25 or so; on the present model, after 440 or so.

It is when Patrick writes Latin himself, claiming as he does in later life (*Conf. 9*) that it is *lingua aliena* and that the reader will be only too able to none *qualiter sum ego in sermonibus instructus atque eruditus* 'in what manner I was taught and schooled in such words', that more subtle inferences can be explored. Professor Christine Mohrmann's study of Patrick's Latin[70] has been both quoted and sadly misquoted; since her conclusions make up one of the few really important and independent analyses of the Patrician problem, a précis is required. Some of her points will be recalled in the next chapter. The *Confessio*, a meditative explanation of Patrick's life and endeavours, may (if modelled on anything) be inspired by the Pauline epistles.[71] Patrick was a man *unius libri*, that one *liber* being his Bible. Outside his quotations, direct or slightly paraphrased, his Latin is clumsy and colloquial (and, interestingly, she sees indications – as *Conf.* 9, 18, 32 and 41 – that he was 'thinking aloud' and perhaps dictating unchanged material to an assistant). His own Latin elements are so un-bookish that they must belong to the mainstream of spoken Latin; they derive from personal contact with living, which to Mohrmann means Continental, Latin. She sees pointers to the 'popular Latin', the relatively educated spoken VL, of Gaul, more as it was before rather than after about 450. There are also clear hints, for example his use of the pronoun *ille*, instead of *ipse*, which favour central Gaul and count against any ideas of a stay in southern Gaulish localities like Lérins.

Patrick's uneven bilingualism, indeed trilingualism, is in itself of no little sociolinguistic interest. If we allow, with just about every serious student, that he returned to Ireland aged between 35 and 45 and spent at least thirty more years there, his previous life involved a vernacular sequence of British, then Irish, then British, the two British phases complicated by (spoken and written) Latin; the second and possibly slightly longer period of his life was one of spoken Irish, relieved only by *written* Latin and to a very much lesser extent spoken Latin in whatever form he had earlier acquired this *lingua aliena*. Where, in having to compose (instead of merely Biblically to quote) Latin in old age, did he turn? Mohrmann stresses the total improbability that he could have found, in Ireland, any 'Irish' spoken Christian Latin form. To her, he drew upon a knowledge of colloquial Latin he had earlier acquired; her analysis of what his writings exhibit suggest this was fifth-century Continental VL, probably of central or northern Gaul; and she concluded,[72] 'I cannot explain the structure of Patrick's language if he had no contact with Gaul'.

No serious rebuttal of Christine Mohrmann's forcefully-expressed ideas has yet been made. John Morris tried to suggest[73] that it was really an argument *ex silentio* and that this 'living Latin' could have been British; further, that in fact we possess ample textual evidence of what early fifth-century British Latin was like. This of course depends upon accepting, with Morris, that the Pelagian texts discussed in Chapter 2 are of British authorship, composed in Britain; and few students would be prepared to concede this. Binchy made the legitimate objection[74] that, even if one accepts Mohrmann's main contention, it would nevertheless be hard to accept (with, for instance, Grosjean)[75] that Patrick remained at Auxerre or anywhere else of a corresponding religious and intellectual status in Gaul for a period as long as 418 to 432; Auxerre, to take the commonly-postulated idea, was then the intellectual hub of Gaul and a Latin style acquired at Auxerre over a decade or more would be quite unlike Patrick's own composition. Hanson[76] brought together evidence, supporting in some detail the general conclusions advanced below in Chapter 3, to show that spoken VL persisted even at a most popular and 'vulgar' level in Britain at the very end of the Roman period, and repeated some of Binchy's objections.

But these arguments, in many cases, are applicable only if one supposes that Patrick's sojourn in Gaul (if it happened) was lengthy, beyond the *paucos annos* one would at the most see implied. There must have been a considerable hiatus between the adolescent Patrick who learnt to read and write Latin, knew words like *reguli* (*Conf.* 41) 'chieftains' and the diminutive *villula* doubtless current in fifth-century British VL, and knew how to read some of the New Testament in a provincial North British school approved by his Christian family; and the young man who after six years among the Irish – speaking Irish, thinking and praying (*Conf.* 16) in British – found himself obliged to *converse* in Latin among persons to whom spoken VL was the principal mode of speech. It is of course this *second* Latin phase that Mohrmann seeks to pin down. Was Patrick in the position of some modern English child who, first learning 'Franglais' from a regionally-accented English teacher in the setting of large classes in an English-language school, after some years re-learns colloquial French of his or her own age-group in France at some French college or in a French-speaking family or business? Can we deny, even if it is only a possibility that Patrick spent those *paucos annos* in Gaul, the conclusions reached by Mohrmann?

Hanson has pointed out our difficulty here; we can only discuss our small stock of Patrick's *written* Latin – we have no idea, and his orthography does not tell us, how he pronounced it. We cannot adduce those interesting analogies of the late 1940s and 1950s, when it was possible to detect among English-speaking Germans whether their English had been colloquially acquired from British, or American, forces; or to observe the re-settled Poles in Scotland who spoke, not SE in RP, but English as dialectally spoken north of the Border, like the Italian ex-prisoners in Cornwall who stayed on, and readily acquired even the 'r-coloured vowels' of their hosts.

One must continue, then, to separate Patrick's literary knowledge of Latin – begun before he was 16, resumed ecclesiastically (and, it will be suggested, in northern Britain) after his eventual return – from his knowledge (rusted by long absence from Latinity when it was eventually to be used) of Latin as a means of expression. Whether the latter was due to exposure to fifth-century British VL, if such existed, or its Gaulish equivalent, which did exist, depends upon one's view of what would be spoken in British church circles in the second quarter of the fifth century. But if a two- or three-year sojourn in 'central Gaul', among lively Gaulish

VL unilinguals, is held by one in a position to make such an assertion to underlie Patrick's later composition, it is indeed not impossible to infer from his writings that this sojourn *did* take place. It was suggested earlier, following the single, late, Patrick model, that it fell in the years 436/7 × 440: the *paucos annos* before he returned to the *parentes*. The section of the *Confessio* (23) which introduces his return leads us to the second stage of his life. Chapter 14 will discuss this, in order to see what light is thrown upon fifth-century Britain and Ireland, and the fifth-century Church, by the later life and the writings of this remarkable Christian Briton.

CHAPTER FOURTEEN

St Patrick's Episcopate and the British Church

Given plenty of leisure and a little money, I should try one
day unscrambling the letter of St Patrick known as the Confession and print the resulting text. This would bring out an
important aspect of that famous document . . ..
Paul Grosjean, S. J., Bollandist, (1958)

Patrick's return to his native Britain, an event postulated in the last
chapter to have brought him back from Gaul about AD 440, is only
implicit in his own writings. It is often overlooked that the model of a
totally-collapsed and largely isolated post-410 Britannia ignores a
growing body of evidence to the effect that links by sea, long established
during the Roman centuries, obviously continued in the background.
The incidence of the imported Gaulish pottery groups (fig. 50) apart,
some general route between Ireland and the mouth of the Loire has to be
supposed; it was at Nantes that the Irishman Columbanus, in 610,
awaited passage back to Ireland on the next ship.[1] The shorter Channel
crossings of south-east Britain, quite aside from the likelihood that
London (served by its Thames estuary and waterfront) never lost entirely
its maritime mercantile status, are not only evidenced by St Germanus's
crossings in 429 and 448; the archaeology of Kent alone implies that from
the fourth to seventh centuries such cross-Channel traffic was
commonplace.[2]

The remainder of Patrick's life, from his return to the *parentes* to
whenever, in absolute dates, he died in Ireland, has in the first instance to
be deduced solely from his writings. Students have to assume, as well,
that our texts of the Confession and the Epistle sufficiently represent
what Patrick wrote or dictated, taking into account the history of the
various MSS, none of which is a contemporary copy of either work.[3] The
Confessio is so named by its author, and the title of the shorter piece
derived from its text (an *epistola* to the soldiers of Coroticus). The
convenient arrangement of both into numbered sections or chapters
dates only from the present century.[4]

As Père Grosjean intriguingly hinted, there may have been more than
one version of the *Confessio*, or of much of it; and while it lends itself to
analysis or Grosjean's 'unscrambling', into a series of discrete themes

and topics, these are not wholly coherent nor presented in an expected order. Individual sections which came late in the text hark back to much earlier passages. This degree of overlap appears to result from Patrick's habit of being reminded, in the course of reciting one aspect of his life, of some precept or conclusion he wishes to stress before passing to the next aspect. Here, however, is one such analysis, citing *Confessio* section numbers and arbitrary labels:

1 *My Early Years* – interrupted schooling, capture, gift of Faith
   (1–16, 34, 38–39)
2 *Escape from Ireland* – sea voyage, and walk *per desertum*
   (17–20, 22)
3 *Return to Britain* – deacon, bishop, and back to Ireland
   (23, 28)
4 *Sad Tale of my Youthful Sin and Treacherous Friend*
   (26, 27, 29–30, 32–33)
5 *False Accusations against me, and My Rebuttal*
   (28, 31, 37–38, 43, 44, 46, 48–55, 61)
6 *Details of My Difficult Work in Ireland*
   (21, 35–36, 40–42, 47)
7 *Dreams and Visions, or, God's Special Favour to me Manifested*
   (17, 20–21, 23–25, 29, 45)
8 *Various Conclusions and Affirmations*
   (47, 54, 56–60, 62)

If any reliable translation of the *Confessio* is read in this suggested way, and any similar effort to pick out the main components of the narrative will produce a generally like result, it is clear that some historical truth underlies what Patrick says. It might also be hinted that one section of the *Epistola* (*Ep.* 10), which sits rather oddly between its neighbours, may originally have formed part of the Rebuttal theme (5, above) and could have been displaced early in the textual transmissions.

Certain other conclusions offer themselves. Firstly, there is a strong impression that Mohrmann was right[5] in regarding our text as mainly that of a dictated statement; of an elderly, though in no sense senile, man whose mind was outrunning both his command of compositional Latin and the capacity of his scribe to get down a first version on something akin to the Springmount tablets (p. 84). Secondly, one can receive the *Confessio* in a number of ways. It may be a statement of its author's personal faith; it may, too, as Carney thinks,[6] constitute a solemn affirmation made as part of (or associated with) a Last Will and Testament. But it could also be seen as the partly-repetitive expansion of an earlier document, also written or dictated by Patrick, lost, but to a limited degree reconstitutable.

Thirdly, despite the Gildas-like absence of place- or personal names, clear allusion to dated events, and even much factual content, the work contains a great many clues; some of which, notably during this examination of a historical model of a single late Patrick, may be unexpectedly specific. And lastly, though this would be beyond the scope both of this book and its author's capacity, there is still ample room for comment on the *Confessio*; one has in mind such passages as *Conf.* 35, 42, and 48–53, the relevance of early Irish laws to historical studies, and the tenor of two recent papers by Binchy.[7]

The *Epistola* also lends itself to dissection. Whether or not the *Confessio* had a predecessor, the *Epistola* text makes it clear that as an 'Open Letter' it followed a slightly earlier missive that may have been semi-private. The context is well known, and the work is linked to what must have been a great trauma in Patrick's episcopate. Patrick learns that the *milites*, probably the customary war-band or group of privileged armed followers,[8] of a British king Coroticus had been raiding within the territory of his Christian work. These men plundered and stole, and encountered people who (even if the *milites* could not have known this) had only recently been baptised by Patrick – these baptisms were mentioned in Chapter 8. Some of these native Irish converts and neophytes were slain; others, including women, taken as slaves back to Britain, as Patrick himself had also once been taken to a foreign land by lawless and greedy sea-borne raiders. Worse; they had been sold as slaves to heathens, to apostate Picts and to *Scotti* (the Irish settlers in Britain). Patrick at once sent a party headed by one of his own native clergy, the man he had trained *ex infantia* (p. 318), with a letter to Coroticus explaining to this Roman Christian monarch the circumstances and asking for the safe return of the Irish Christians. This mission was met with jeers; righteously angered, Patrick now publishes his *Epistola* so that all may know what has been done, and in his capacity as the established bishop in Ireland he pronounces what amounts to the excommunication of Coroticus and his guilty followers. Their guilt is that much greater because, like Patrick, they are (nominally) Britons, Roman citizens, and Christians themselves.

The twenty-one sections of the *Epistola* can be indicated:

1	Patrick states who, and what, he is.
2–4	A detailed accusation.
5–7	Excommunication, and a call to all Christians to enforce it.
8–9	Sharp reminders of God's anger at thieves and murderers.
10	(Perhaps an interpolation – see below.)
11–13	Reproach to, and condemnation of, the sinners.
14	Direct address to the sinners.
15	Lament for those enslaved and slain.

16	Rhetorical address to those dragged into slavery.
17–18	Another, to the souls of those who were murdered.
19	On the future fate of the sinners.
20	God, not Patrick, ordains their ineluctable fate.
21	Final pleas, for wide publicity, and for general repentance.

It is into this terse and angry broadside, all of whose components can be related to the burden and purpose, that we have to fit *Ep.* 10. It is not an easy passage to read; but it will take us back to the *Confessio*, to Patrick's career, and to the potential dates one might attach to the events indicated in both works. Translated into modern and slightly colloquial English, *Ep.* 10 would read like this:

> I ask you; did I come to Ireland, except through God? Or did I come because of some prompting of the flesh? Who was it who *made* me come?
>
> I am bound, by the Holy Spirit, not to see anything more of my own kin. I ask you; is it *my* doing that I now extend this holy mercy to those very people who once took me captive, and who made such a havoc of the men and the serving-maids on my father's estate?
>
> What I have been, I have been by right of my birth. I was born the son of a decurion. When I sold off my expectations (and I am neither ashamed, nor sorry, about that) it was entirely for the good of others. And because of all that, here I am now; a slave again myself (but this time in *Christ*!) to that very same foreign race. It is entirely for the sake of the unspeakable glory of that Life Everlasting, which is in Christ Jesu Our Lord.

Now it is difficult to see how this can have any real relevance to the otherwise unbroken flow of the *Epistola's* sequence; or any particular meaning to Coroticus and his followers. Textually, it intrudes, within a passage (*Ep.* 8, 9, 11) devoted to specifically condemning the crimes perpetrated. It also appears to be more in the nature of an answer, and one given in response to certain insinuations that Patrick deeply resents; we shall see what these may have been.

Most Patrician students have noticed that the saint is concerned, among other things, to refute various accusations – these are vague, only because not stated – and that this aspect of the *Confessio* must in some way be concerned with his earlier ecclesiastical career. The present writer inclines to the view that this theme is really the central aspect of the *Confessio* and thus the most important. If so, then the *Confessio* we now have is a version, expanded with the prolixity, righteous indignation, and perhaps the linguistic isolation of Patrick's old age, of an earlier document – earlier, by some little time. No doubt the old man dictated it, and if it was then copied from tablets to papyrus or vellum, this text was not then necessarily revised or changed. If Grosjean's interesting suggestions[9] are followed, it may very well be that different versions of what are taken to represent *Confessio* texts were circulating not long after Patrick's death. (This has nothing to do with later Armagh-based censorships or 'improvements', if these happened.) There is the final version, dictated in old age. The hypothetical earlier document, a copy or draft of which Patrick either kept or memorised, was basically a rebuttal or statement, made in his own defence, ending probably with *Conf.* 54, which is a solemn oath. We must see under what possible circumstances, and when both in his own life and in the fifth century, he would have found it necessary to do this.

When Patrick returned to Britain, we know it was to his home district. He was a few years older than 22; let us suppose, 25. He was now trained for the diaconate, a canonical grade he could be expected to attain at the age of 30 – about AD 445. Presumably he was in the *familia* of the local bishop or other prominent clergy and presumably this took place in somewhere like Carlisle; York would be possible, but York, as far as we can see, was not his home area.

During this period of instruction, in a milieu where late British would be the most likely common speech (though all Patrick's reading and copying would be in Latin), and also before he became a deacon, he confessed to *amicissimus* 'to my dearest friend' – his spiritual instructor, possibly an older priest or even kinsman – a sin committed far back, in Patrick's pre-captivity boyhood. Recent coy hints that this was a sexual peccadillo miss the point; some minor dishonesty was involved, perhaps the childhood theft of church candles. The *confession* of this, by now conscience-inflated, sin – *not* its original commission; this is an important point – fell in Patrick's age of about 25 × 30, on this model about AD 440 × 445, and perhaps near the eve of his becoming a deacon.

Though he does not say so, he presumably went on to become a full presbyter, a priest, at the age of 35 – say in 450. By this time, we can infer with some likelihood that his father Calpurnius, who might have been born about 390, had died. Patrick inherited what he calls *nobilitas mea* (*Ep. 10*). If it is too much to imagine that curial status, even as a vain title, persisted in what was hardly still the *civitas Carvetiorum*, and (if as hardly perceptible) was now presumably part of Rheged, something of value was inherited; the town *mansio* in Luguvalium, the lands of the 430-devastated *villula*. This he sold, for the good of others. The entire context tells us that 'the good of others' was the provision of necessary funds for the Irish episcopate, and at some stage in the decade 450 × 460 Patrick was raised to episcopal rank and designated to this work (*Ep. 1*, *Hiberione constitutum episcopum*).

If one agrees, as our limited clues suggest we should,[10] that Patrick's return as a bishop to a part of Ireland was an action directed and initially governed by the *British* Church, implications arise at once. There is the obvious one, that in some part of Britain, the Church – and this means within an area in a position to hold synods involving bishops and senior clergy – was still functioning in a late Roman style. It has been argued that, perhaps a quarter-century earlier, precisely similar ecclesiastical powers and decisions provided Christians also *extra limites* in Galloway with a British bishop. But, also quarter of a century before, as Europe's major churches would now know, the first bishop *constitutum* for the Irish had been appointed, not from Britain, but by the Pope – Palladius, in 431. Morris considered, in relation to the origin and authority of Patrick's despatch, that 'it was inconceivable that a later bishop should be consecrated [for the Irish] without his [the Pope's] approval; and papal initiative was to be expected'.[11] It may be added that one effect of accepting any such change of authority is to weaken the idea that Palladius's arrival in 431 was followed anywhere nearly as early as 432 by Patrick's despatch.

In this mid-fifth-century phase, centred about 445 × 455, one can detect a number of superficially unrelated, probably relevant, and possibly linked strands. The first is the papacy of Leo I, pope from 440 to 461; as the Annals of Ulster later recorded his accession (under 441), *Leo ordinatus xlii Romanae ecclesiae episcopus*. This forceful and energetic man, a youthful anti-Pelagian,[12] had an effective reign; he sought and accomplished the extension of the Papal power, securing a rescript from Valentinian III recognising his jurisdiction over all the provinces of the Western empire. Since Prosper of Aquitaine, who settled in Rome in 434, later entered Leo's service, it may be guessed that the Papal interest in Britain and Ireland, if any, included knowledge of Palladius' 431 bishopric.

The second event is the *second* visit, to Britain, of Germanus, whose eventful first trip in 429 was discussed in Chapter 2. On this occasion, we learn from Constantius of Lyon,[13] Germanus was accompanied by Severus, 13th bishop of Trier (426–76). Constantius claims that a few promoters of Pelagianism were still active, and implies that a Gaulish synod of bishops urged Germanus to visit Britain and combat this. Germanus did so, is depicted as performing another spectacular public miracle, confuting heresy through public sermons, and arranging to take the now-banished Pelagians back with him to Gaul. Constantius shows us, naturally, a total success; 'even at this time' (i.e., about 480) only orthodox faith is to be seen in Britain.

Constantius did not know the date, and introduces the story with an evasive *Interea* ('Meanwhile'); but, as Plummer noticed,[14] it must have been shortly before Germanus' death at Ravenna (31 July 448) and the circumstances point to a short visit, probably in April and/or May of

448.[15] It may go a little too far to suppose, with Morris,[16] that Germanus secured the deposition (and deportation) of two Pelagian bishops; the most one can suppose is that Constantius believed contra-Pelagianism was involved in this second visit.

The third of the strands to be connected is that, for this period, those who subsequently compiled annals and chronicles in Ireland, or used Irish-based material in similar British endeavours, chose to record a strange variety of entries. Leo's universal prestige will account for any reasonable, later, desire to enter his accession as pope (correctly, 440) and death (correctly, 461). Why, though, did the Annals of Ulster carry, under 441 and after Leo's accession, *et probatus est in fide Catholica Patricius episcopus* 'and Patrick the bishop was *probatus* in the Catholic [i.e., orthodox] Faith'? We might see *AU* (Annals of Ulster) 443, 'Bishop Patrick, ardent in his Faith and Christ's teaching, flourishing in our province', as, like AI (Annals of Innisfallen) 443 *Patricius in Christi doctrina floruit*, mere retrospective, pro-Patrick, pro-Armagh glosses.

The *probatio Patricii*[17] was, to John Morris, a sign that Patrick had successfully appealed to Rome, for confirmation in his office, following circumstances threatening his episcopal position which one might infer from the *Confessio*.[18] Yet all this would place the *Confessio* at or before 440, which on internal evidence alone is simply not possible, even if one accepts 432 as Patrick's return to Ireland; and (so Hanson) *probatio* cannot bear this meaning, whatever the compilers of AU and AI, or their source, supposed the event in question had been.[19] There is no evidence that Patrick appealed, or ever had any intention of appealing, to Rome, or that Leo I ever heard Patrick's name.

We cannot, from lack of materials, infer and we can therefore only speculate that Leo I and his view of the Papacy in the extreme western provinces, Germanus's second visit, the British-originating episcopate in Ireland (filled by Patrick), and lastly Patrick himself, are connected. The annalistic entries suggest, if anything, that very similar speculations were current in Ireland and possibly Britain by the seventh century. In 454, Leo I issued new instructions on the computation of the dates of Easter, a point where mathematical muddles had intruded into doctrinal orthodoxy; and it is evident[20] that these instructions were known in Ireland. The British annalistic compilation, the Annales Cambriae (AC), also contains, under 453 (*recte*, 455), *Pasca commutatur super diem Dominicum cum papa Leone episcopo Romae.* Our speculation could perhaps embrace the idea that not only the 431 mission involving Palladius was known to Leo, possibly before his 440 accession, from Prosper; Rome was aware of later circumstances about this first bishopric, which we do not know ourselves and will never recover. On whatever score a British synod of bishops (and one may infer such) approached the Gaulish church, probably during 447, requesting another visit from no less a person than Germanus, is it possible that Leo – learning in 448 of the outcome, of Britain's secure orthodoxy, and bearing in mind the fate (whatever it was) of Palladius – decided upon another bishopric in another part of Ireland, and also decided that the Church in Britain would be charged with its arrangement? In that period – 448–54, perhaps *in* 454 with the Papal announcement that new Easter tables were in preparation – was such a Papal authorisation transmitted to the surviving metropolitan(s) of Britannia?

This chapter designedly explores the 'late' model of Patrick; and there have been earlier attempts to find, in annalistic records of the period 450 × 460 (or so), any trace of this postulated second British-inspired Irish see and Patrick's arrival. The most curious such trace – curious, because again in an unquantifiable way it seems to be confused with the earlier (and to this writer, secondary) obit of Patrick – is that of a date that wavers between 457 and 461. James Carney has made great play of AC 457 (*recte*, 459?), *Sanctus Patricius ad Dominum migratur.*[21] This is from the *A* text – late tenth or early eleventh century (Harleian MS 3859) of AC; the *B* text reads *Sanctus Patricius obiit*, a straight obituary record, and the *C* text, *Sanctus Patricius in Domino pul(l)ulavit.*

Until a full modern critical edition of AC is available, one can only say, concisely, that what we have may have been finally redacted not later than 956, and that Irish material may in part or whole be derived from a lost Leinster compilation of the seventh century.[22] In the *A* text, *migratur* is an exceptional mode of expressing a death. Between the entries from 444 to 595, deaths otherwise only occur as *quies* (468,521), *pausat* (501,547), *obiit* (570), *dormitatio* (544, 574), and *moritur* (558,580,595). '*Migratur*' is, literally, 'he is removed (from A to B)', though in Classical Latin[23] it can form part of an expression meaning 'he died'. The *C* text *pullulavit* used a verb that can be translated as 'he put forth, came forth, brought forth' – which might have a metaphorical meaning, though hardly 'he died'. One's inclination is to agree, with Carney – and this need not require amending *ad Dominum, in Domino*, to *ad Hiberniam, in Hibernia* – that somewhere behind this may lurk, not a genuine obit at all (easily enough assimilated to that of Leo I, in 461), but some other record centred upon Sanctus Patricius late in 450 × 460.

We left the Saint himself, with the assumption that – in his own part of Britain – he had, after 450, become a priest; was chosen, by a synod of the British Church, to become a new bishop in part of Ireland (where he had been, and where he would know the vernacular); was therefore consecrated as a bishop; and because he knew from his, or general, experience of Irish ways that funds would be needed and perhaps were not easily to hand, he sold what he calls his *nobilitatem* to provide such funds himself. It has also been guessed that it is not in open conflict with the skeletal records of later Annals, nor the general history of the mid-fifth century, to suppose that in initiating this new see the British Church was following a Papal direction, from a Pope who had some interest in Palladius, in British orthodoxy, and indeed in Irish orthodoxy. What do Patrick's writings say, or permit us to infer? Do any such inferences still support the hypothesis that we are, not around 432, but in the late 450s?

Since (p. 329) various themes in the *Confessio* were suggested, and since clearly crucial to any elucidation is that numbered (5), concerning accusations which can only have been that Patrick's mission was misconducted, can we even begin to reconstruct what happened? Let us start with theme (4), that of the Youthful Sin and Treacherous Friend. The sin itself (*Conf.* 27) took place, one day, in the space of an hour, when he was barely 15 – shortly before his capture. He ridded his soul of its burden much later, perhaps when he was nearly 30, to his *amicissimus*. On a still later occasion (*Conf.* 26), one when these accusations about the conduct of his mission were being discussed – as we shall see, a British synod is the only probable context – a factor that swayed feeling against him was the unexpected revelation by the *amicissimus*, by now surely elderly, of what Patrick had confessed. The admitted sin thus bore relevance to some aspect of the accusations, and that aspect was in the area of personal dishonesty (wrongful use of funds, bribery, simony, etc.). Patrick was told about this revelation; it is a strong inference that after the synod British clerics were sent to see him in Ireland. He was deeply shocked and hurt, not least because that confession – the *confession*, not the original commission; as *Conf.* 27 makes clear – took place *annos triginta* 'thirty years' before its public revelation. As on other occasions, the shock resulted in a dream (*Conf.* 29); in this, Patrick, though of course he had not been present at the synod in question, seemed to see *scriptum contra faciem meam sine honore* 'a writing without honour, against my face' – a mental picture of the written accusation being discussed. He was comforted only because in this dream God told him that He had looked with displeasure upon the face of the treacherous friend, *designati nudato nomine* 'of that man, indicated by his revealed name'; Patrick still refrains from identifying his old *amicissimus*.

In *Conf.* 32, Patrick again telescoping time, we revert to the sad affair, in sorrow rather than anger at the incomprehensible behaviour of this friend. Long before the *defensio*, Patrick's phrase for this preliminary airing of the accusations against him, Patrick had had reason to understand this friend in particular would stand up for him. As for the boyhood sin, had this very man not, long ago, pardoned Patrick for it himself when it was confessed? It was this very man, too, who had actually encouraged the hesitant Patrick, uncertain about the whole Irish venture, with such comforting words as *ecce dandus es tu ad gradum episcopatus* 'Look, you really *ought* to be given the rank of a bishop'. And now, what had happened? The *defensio* was not of Patrick's seeking or suggestion; it took place without him, when Patrick was no longer even in Britain. Why – the old Patrick sadly ponders – did his friend, who had once supported him, publicly dishonour him before everyone, good and evil, and in such a very delicate matter; that of Patrick's fitness for, and subsequent conduct of, his episcopate? For *this* was the matter under attack, by *aliquantis senioribus meis* 'some of my old ecclesiastical superiors' (*Conf.* 26), naturally the very people who would constitute a British synod. However, *satis dico* 'enough said' (*Conf.* 33).

What we get here is a reprospective, tangled glimpse of something happening when Patrick was probably aged about 60; that is, something happening about thirty years after Patrick was nearly 30, and on this model, somewhere about 470 × 475. Why did it happen? and can we detect the various, distinct, *scripta*, implied visits, and (most of all) the reasons?

An analogy may clarify this. Imagine that the head and treasurer of some remote overseas Christian mission receives, out of the blue, a long list of accusations about his honesty and conduct of that mission; to which is appended the news that his home-based Committee, having learnt that at the age of 12 he had been once caught shop-lifting, had felt bound to comment on their inclination to think now that such accusations might have substance. Imagine, then, that this unhappy Head of Mission is invited to return at once, and to reply verbally, dealing with matters covering several decades, to these accusations. Imagine, last of all, that these proceedings are tape-recorded; but that because of some muddle, only the *reply* – characterised by alarm, anger, repetition and some irrelevant reminiscences – is recorded. Given a typed transcript of part of that recorded reply, and nothing else whatsoever, how much of the Committee's original and detailed letter setting out the accusations could be reconstructed?

This may well be exactly the dilemma we face; and, to pursue the analogy a stage further, our reconstruction rests, not on this hypothetical one-sided recording transcribed for us, but only from the accused person's rambling memoirs, written a good ten years later.

Nonetheless Patrick does give us – and we can take *Ep.* 10 along with the *Confessio* sections listed as theme no. 5 – a great deal of specific, or easily inferred, information. As a beginning, it is apparent that he always saw himself as quite unworthy, was far from keen to assume the leadership of a new Irish see, and only did so in the end because of God's bidding (*Conf.* 28, 37, 46 *Ep.* 10). In going to Ireland, he took a vow never to return, never to see his British kin again; for God, he would go back into what amounted to a second 'slavery', among strangers, none of whom spoke his own tongue, most of whom were heathen, and some of whom had enslaved him properly when he was a boy.

He made this decision. The mission required funds, probably gold and silver that would in Ireland be more acceptable than money. For not wholly clear reasons (*Conf.* 37) Patrick, even against instructions, refused to accept contributions from fellow-Christians at home, at the risk of hurt feelings. Instead (*Ep.* 10), he raised the funds himself by selling either his inheritance or expectations.

In Ireland, he never took advantage of the Irish – as, given his knowledge of their language and customs, he might well have done – and was always 'faithful to those heathen among whom I live' (*Conf.* 48), avoiding the slightest risk of danger to his converts, or the Church itself and its repute. Patrick would give no handles for criticism by the Irish who had not yet been won for Christ. He had always returned any gifts made to his churches, let alone to himself, even at the risk of offending prominent donors (*Conf.* 49, 50). He challenges *anyone*, any arm-chair critic at home in Britain, to show that he, Patrick, took so much as a brass farthing[24] from a single one of all those Irish he baptised over the years; or, where the price would have been higher – even as much as the cost of a pair of shoes – from any of his converts who wanted to be ordained as clergy.

The irony of such suggestions is that, far from receiving, he had always been obliged to *spend*: on customary gifts to the local rulers; on supporting their sons, whom he was obliged to take around the countryside with him; and on douceurs to the local *brehons*, the custodians of Irish common law and practice (*Conf.* 51–53). There is no need to take just Patrick's word; any of his converts who could understand enough Latin (*Conf.* 55) would bear witness to the truth of all this.

The whole of this rebuttal is partly wound up with an affirmation (*Conf.* 54), drawn from Patrick's favourite Second Epistle of Paul to the Corinthians: *ecce testem Deum invoco in animam meam quia non mentior* 'Lo, I call God as witness, upon my soul, that I do not lie'.

This is not quite all. As to the poverty so consistently mentioned, imposed upon him by his circumstances, and possibly regarded as unfitting to a bishop by other bishops in Britain, he can produce one of his devastatingly simple justifications (*Conf.* 55): *et Christus Dominus pauper fuit pro nobis* 'for Christ the Lord was poor, too, for our sakes'.

Can we not see, even at this remove, the shape of the charges made about the distant Patrick and his work; based on ill-natured rumours and misunderstandings of the special problems of Irish life, but reaching the pitch where they had, at last, to be considered formally by those he calls *seniores* (*Conf.* 26, 37) and again *dominicati rethorici* (*Conf.* 13) – the learned, well-to-do bishops and senior clergy who made up the ruling circle of the Church in mid- or late fifth-century northern and western Britain? Even if, from time to time, chance rumours had reached him in Ireland, we can picture his shock on being presented with a request to answer a string of loose accusations, most of which he would see as fantastic.

Suddenly, after decades among Irish speakers, where the only Latin – and taught, to use familiar modern terminology, through the medium of the Irish language at that – would be a tattered sheaf of Bible parchments, Patrick was faced with a choice. Visitors from Britain, almost certainly fellow-clerics, came to acquaint him with the imminent *defensio*. Would he now return with them to Britain, and answer all these points at a synod? No; he explains (*Conf.* 43) the (to him) overriding reason why he cannot leave Ireland, under any circumstances. God has bidden him to stay, and that is that.

But the very work of God in Ireland, so long guarded in every respect by Patrick, is now externally endangered; some kind of rebuttal must be made. Patrick could hope, in producing one, to pad it out with familiar, and (as he no doubt hoped) appropriate pieces from the Bible; but it would still require a much less easily composed linking text, and here he would have to draw upon a conversational Latin he had almost forgotten. Would it be the half-recalled scraps of spoken British VL of his distant boyhood; or the rather more general vernacular he had once spoken, *paucos annos*, in Gaul thirty or more years beforehand? One can sense, again, the strength of Christine Mohrmann's informed analysis at this point. On top of this dilemma, can we not see a Patrick all too aware of the rusticity of his command of the official language of the Church – *his* Church – and his apprehension that the British *rethorici* would find cause for more sneers at his obvious *rusticitas*?

We face two questions: what did these accusations say? And why, after so long, were they being said at all? The answer to the second question must be: because Patrick had in his *Epistola* chosen to pronounce the excommunication of Coroticus and to make that fact embarrassingly public. This action of his brought matters to a head. Such a statement involves consideration of the absolute date, earlier claimed as around 470 × 475, and we must return to that assertion.

To answer the first question, one can, in all probability, infer the general sense of the *scriptum sine honore*, as containing both general and detailed accusations; and as a lost document of the British Church in the latter part of the fifth century, it possesses some interest. It would have embraced comments along these lines:

General

1 That when, years beforehand, it was agreed that the Church in Britain should establish this new See in Ireland, Patrick arranged to be appointed as its first Bishop for his own purposes, viz. to enrich himself, taking advantage of his local knowledge of the Irish and their language and manners.

2 That Patrick expected to finance the mission in some way not authorised by the Church; because, even though asked, he refused to accept the normal endowments being offered at the time.

Specific

3 That he improperly received valuable gifts (*ornamenta*) from rich Irish converts, notably rich Irish women converts.

4 That he took money from converts when he baptised them.

5 That he took rewards from converted and baptised Irishmen as an inducement subsequently to ordain them.

6 That by all such grossly improper conduct over a number of years he brought our Church into disrepute, and his associates and himself into danger, among hostile and pagan Irish elements.

To all such points, the *Confessio* seems to provide – *seriatim*, and not in any detectable order in the text we have – full and specific answers. The fact that the answers are, apparently, so specific goes far to support the idea that the accusations or charges were much as reconstructed above.

Far the most damaging assertion is that listed as no. 5. This offence, the performance of ordinations for money – understandable in a world where church revenues could be the source of income for clergy alone – is called *simony*, after Simon Magus (*Acts*, viii. 18) who tried to buy the Apostolic power with silver from Peter and John. Its gravity was restated in canon 2 of the Council of Chalcedon in 451,[25] and penalties included forfeiture of the ecclesiastical grade of the person thus selling ordination. If such a charge had seriously been pressed, and proved, Patrick would have been deposed. As he was not, we can be sure that neither this nor any other canonical offence was formally laid against him. Nor can the general accusations, suggested above, have had much force; on the relative dating alone, at any synod of this time there would not have been many still alive concerned with the initial planning and decisions of Patrick's mission.

Our reconstruction, then, might be as follows. Patrick, after many years in Ireland, is visited by British clerics, representing a body (*seniores*) in the British Church whose authority Patrick is still prepared to concede and from whom the authority of his own episcopate originally came, with a letter. The letter, or what these clerics tell Patrick, specifies various accusations. Patrick is invited to return and answer them. He declines; and produces a written Rebuttal, in Latin. This is taken back to Britain – Patrick has kept, or can reproduce, or can recall from memory, the Rebuttal's substance. A later visit of the same kind, perhaps, acquaints him with what happened when this synod met, considered (but apparently eventually dismissed) the accusations – the *scriptum* – and did so despite the friend's betrayal of Patrick's pre-diaconate confession. When, later still, a more aged Patrick dictates his *Confessio*, it contains the distinctive Themes outlined at the start of this chapter, but mixed up with them, and still branded upon his entire consciousness, is the substance of that second lost document, his Rebuttal. The episode of the Rebuttal and the *defensio* in Britain occurred when Patrick was about 60 and this was about 470 × 475.

If Coroticus' raid and its aftermath sparked off these sad happenings, we seek a year – AD X, let us call it – which was slightly *before* any party in the British Church decided it was time to take the rumours about Patrick seriously; and which (because of the cleric trained *ex infantia*) was perhaps twenty years *after* Patrick's return to Ireland. But X + 1, the year of the *defensio*, seems to be thirty years after Patrick's confession of his boyhood sin, implying that his return to Ireland was some ten years after he became a deacon – say, at the age of 40 or so. X is, however, a year in which Coroticus was a British king, was a Christian, possessed a war-band, and was associated with *Scotti* in Britain, and with Picts who had previously been Christian but had now lapsed into paganism, and were apostates (*Ep.* 2). These Picts and *Scotti* were allies of Coroticus and had bought slaves from him.

This suggests that evaluation of Year X in terms of absolute time would be invaluable. The model followed in this chapter places it around AD 470. Is this supportable? The crux is obviously the named Coroticus.

This name was borne by at least two fifth-century British kings: one in west Wales, who gave his name to Cardigan (Ceredigiaun), the other in Strathclyde. In view of all that has been said, of Patrick's geography at home and in Ireland, of the allusions to Picts and *Scotti*, and of the obvious inference that this Coroticus was somewhere that a personal messenger could speedily be sent, the northerner – his realm only 70 miles from the Antrim coast – is surely indicated. In seventh-century Armagh, this was assumed. A chapter-head in the Armagh text of Muirchú's Life[26] is, *de conflictu sancti Patricii adversum Coirtech regem Aloo*. 'Aloo' represents the genitive of *Ail* (*Cluaide*), or *Alclut*, the Strathclyde citadel at Dumbarton Rock.[27]

Any date for this man depends upon estimates, not on factual and individual records. In the past, this Coroticus has been dated – to a floruit of around 450 – by direct reference to the orthodox dating of Patrick.[28]

Independently, there has grown up a little-questioned assumption that Coroticus must be a figure of the early or mid-fifth century; so much so that even Binchy, disposed[29] on balance to favour some 'late' model of Patrick's chronology, felt that on such a basis it would be necessary to exclude the (presumptively earlier) link with the Strathclyde king.

But the combined implication of the most recent studies of these British northern king-lists is clear.[30] The estimates would prefer to see this Coroticus' birth around 440×450, and consequently his floruit – when he did in truth rule, and send his *milites* on raids – more at such a time as 465×475.

There are other reasons why one could prefer a floruit for this person, and an *Epistola*, in the period 465×475, to earlier estimates such as 452.[31] This has nothing to do with the all-too-often sprung trap of dating Patrick by Coroticus, or Coroticus by Patrick. The *Picti apostatae* are accused, by a bishop, of a specific and awful shortcoming; allies of Coroticus, willing to receive Christian slaves from him, they must have been living very close to his kingdom. Yet they, too, had once been Christian.[32] Who were they? These, surely, are among the southern Picts whom, by Bede's time, it was assumed Nynia brought into the fold of Christ – and their proximity to Strathclyde is perhaps indicated in fig. 55. Their settlement in this area is perhaps from the 440s (Chap. 10); their conversion, from the Whithorn direction, is not likely to be before the middle of the century (Chap. 11). An apostasy, awful enough and widespread enough to be common knowledge, sits more comfortably in the 470s than the 450s.

Again, the Scotti who were allies or associates of Coroticus' Britons (*Ep.* 2); were enemies, lived with death, and would willingly buy captive Christians (*Ep.* 12, 14), having no knowledge of God – these, apart from Patrick's use of *Scotti* instead of *Hiberionaci* ('Irishmen') to label them, are the Scotti that the sub-Roman British above all knew and feared. They were the first settlers, in the nascent colonies in Argyll, neighbours of the British in Strathclyde, bordering them in the region now called Cowal[33] (see fig. 55). But, if we are to accept even the provisional chronology of these settlements,[34] then the later within the fifth century we can place them, the better. While Scotti as depicted in Patrick's *Epistola*, neighbours and allies of Coroticus, may be just credible in relatively small, but widely-known, groups by 470, their presence in the earlier period around 450 is perhaps beyond current inferences. Our conclusion, on all these grounds, is that the raid, and the *Epistola*, are indeed around 470.

Why should the publication of Patrick's *Epistola* have led to a climax in some putative, long-drawn history of rumours and accusations about his conduct of Church matters in Ireland? Here one has to guess; but the most tempting guess is that, to the *seniores* of the Church in North

Britain, this detached and difficult bishop had exceeded his authority to a degree that could not be overlooked, and in a manner where there may have been secular as well as ecclesiastical cries to discipline Patrick, and call him to account at last. Coroticus was a Christian, British king – with the *Epistola* we may well be before the time of any Strathclyde bishops at Dumbarton Rock or at Glasgow (a list of whom would later include Kentigern), but his Christianity would be subject to some bishop, and that would not have been Patrick. Patrick had chosen publicly, for whatever reason, to excommunicate the Christian subjects of a Christian king in a diocese other than his own.

In offering a 'late' model of Patrick's life and work, one can do no more than guess at particular dates; it is the general position in time that is being argued. But let us suppose Patrick, consecrated as a bishop, went to Ireland in some such year as 455; that Coroticus sent his *milites* raiding the Antrim coast in 470 (and that Patrick's cleric trained ex *infantia* had been fifteen years with the saint and was now thirty and a deacon, if this is material); that the aftermath of the Epistola – framing of charges, clergy sent to Patrick, Patrick composing his rebuttal, a *defensio* in Britain, and Patrick acquainted of its course and outcome – all fell in, say, AD 471.

Where the British Church is concerned, the implications are that a British synod meeting somewhere in Britain in 447/448 and asking a second time for Germanus' potent help was not the last such synod; not by any means. Something like a synod apparently received, around 600, representations from Augustine. It has been suggested that in the 450s such an ecclesiastical gathering could have been acquainted with the news that Pope Leo intended to change the method of calculating the annual date of Easter – even if, when the cursus of 457 was issued, it appears not to have been adopted or followed in Britain or Ireland, where for two centuries more an increasingly out-dated system was preserved;[35] and that at this time, or near it, the same authorities either decided, or were Papally instructed or permitted, to create a fresh see in Ireland supplementing that created on Papal initiative in 431.

What is now suggested is that, somewhere – and the north of Britain is probably indicated – the Church retained enough of its hierarchy and formal organisation to meet again, perhaps in 471, to consider the irregular excommunication of Coroticus and his followers by Patrick and a series of accusations against Patrick. John Morris, who mostly favoured an early Patrick, was emphatic that on his own view of fifth-century British history it would have been 'next to impossible'[36] for any such meeting to have occurred 'after the disasters of the late 450s'. But if the Church, and Christianity, continued at all in Britain during the later fifth century, and this continuation has been argued at some length, one cannot deny the likelihood of formal conventions. Binchy, in his own examination of the Raid, the *Epistola*, and any aftermath[37] makes the point that in contemporary Canon Law a bishop might be censured or deposed only by the metropolitan of his province, acting in association with the other bishops of that province. If the reconstruction of the most likely accusations aimed at Patrick is a correct reflection of what Patrick says, proof of simony – the sale of ordinations – would be enough to secure deposition; and much of the rest, formal censure.

Since we have no evidence, beyond mere conjecture, that by 400 the senior bishops in each of Britain's *provinciae* were regarded as of metropolitan status, may we suppose that in the fifth century the bishop of any particular centre was generally assumed to head the British Church? It is just conceivable that, still at 471, we might think of York. This was the prime urban centre of the North; if a fifth-century British kingdom, alongside Elmet, preceded (as a purely British *Deira*) the later Deira taken over by the Angles, it forms the most attractive candidate for its centre, with sub-Roman occupation and perhaps a measure of re-fortification in the old fortress north of the river (fig. 29). Might one posit the late fifth-century equivalent of a single 'metropolitan' for the whole *terra* of once-Roman Britain here? There are clues: for example, Eric John's careful analysis of the position of York in English Christianity and the possibility that York's special ecclesiastical status was part of a specific, sub-Roman British tradition taken over by the converted Northumbrians.[38] Did bishops of Deira, ruling first a British and then some uneasily mixed population, claim some such title throughout the fifth century? Here, then, is one place we can begin to imagine a synod in 471; and perhaps one can just go so far as to think of it occurring in that vast *principia* building at York which, as Derek Phillips's excavations have shown, stood, roofed, during the fifth century and for that matter some centuries afterwards.[39]

There are still a few aspects of Patrick, and his life, to be determined. If, with Edward Thompson, we suppose that Patrick like Nynia and Palladius is credible as a bishop, *extra limites*, only on the assumption that he went to minister to existing Christians[40] – with the eventual conversion of the pagan Irish as a joint aim – who were those *credentes*? We could think of the descendants or the successors of fourth-century British traders. In fig. 50, the notable incidence of imported Gaulish pottery, which can symbolise wider imports, in the north-east may partly reflect recent activities in Irish fieldwork, but it is still disproportionate and significant. If Patrick's *tot milia hominum* really meant that, in his youth, British slaves were common in Ireland, Christian Britons (like Patrick) may have been dispersed, but not rare. There is now Thompson's latest suggestion[41] that in the refugee movement from the

Saxons after 446, deduced from what Gildas says, Britons from some north-western port may have fled to Ireland as well as to Gaul. In Gaul, Mansuetus (p. 51) signed as *episcopus Britannorum* in 461, and may have gone with British Christians overseas. Was the known presence of other post-446 British Christian refugees in northern Ireland, opposite those tracts of Britain ravaged by Saxon conflicts, one factor behind a decision to open a new see there? We are talking, presumably, about some such bracket as 446 × 461; and have already postulated Patrick's despatch near the middle of that period. Thompson would go so far as to wonder[42] if Gildas' *transmarina relatio* of DEB 4, the body of tradition preserved overseas about Britain's Roman past, reached Gildas not from Gaul but from Ireland; Gildas, we know, had to draw upon this because there were no literary remains at home – they had either been 'burnt by the enemy, or taken with them some time ago by our fellow-citizens who went into exile'.

Patrick's *Confessio*, a precious and unique piece of fifth-century British Christian Latin, was written or dictated by an old man; it has intimations of mortality and the eventual flowering of his work (*Conf.* 14, 41, 56) and it ends *Et haec est confessio mea antequam moriar*. If, in its course, it recapitulates his rebuttal to those charges, it does so in the course of more general reminiscence and reflection; and if the raid of Coroticus' soldiers, and the British aftermath, be placed in the early 470s, we are reading a document finally committed – as a personal testament; not as an *apologia* – to a publishable form a good few years later. The *Confessio* may have been dictated some time after 480. Between then, and the end of the century, Patrick will have died. If, a century later, the continued use of Latin in Christian circles – now surely reinforced with added contact of many kinds from overseas – for the first time provided a milieu in which the new, partly reforming, monastic establishments were prepared to commence a 'Latinate horizon of historicity' and to enshrine the Christian past in annalistic form, those responsible would have been in contact with men who had spoken to others who knew, and might even have been in the *familia* of, Patrick the Briton. Those annalistic dates, for his death, that cluster around the early 490s may reflect, with some reality, the tradition that he died before the end of the century.[43] Singled out as a possible link is another Briton, Mochta, Mauchte or Maucteus, whose death (Annals of Ulster, 535) is close enough in time to Patrick's. At the end of the next century, Adamnan, composing his life of Columba, still knew enough of this man to describe him as *quidam proselytus brito homo sanctus sancti Patricii episcopi discipulus Maucteus nomine* 'a certain stranger, a Briton and a holy man, disciple of the holy bishop Patrick, M. by name';[44] and to add that a prophecy made by Maucteus had been 'passed down to us from ancient men'. The credible date of

Patrick's death is as likely to have been passed down, too; and the confusions of later reckonings, the Mosaic span of 120 years, the two obits, the two Patricks, stem from that irreconcilable gap between the year after Palladius' coming (which is not a Patrician event) and the time of his death, which is.

Of the aftermath – the elevation of Patrick into the much-travelled wonder-worker of Muirchú and Tírechán, and then the improbable Christian wizard of the later Latin lives – other books can treat, and many have done so. The Patrick of the present book stands for himself, and perforce in a degree for the unsung Palladius and Nynia: a Christian Briton whom the British Church sent, as a bishop, to Irish Christians, who worked there, was wrongly accused, was justified in his own eyes by God, and who died in the 490s, conscious that – whatever he had done or left undone – he had not broken faith, with the Irish, with God, or with himself.

CHAPTER FIFTEEN

'Thoroughly Roman . . . in Origin'

And thorns shall come up in her palaces, nettles and thistles in
the fortresses thereof; and it shall be an habitation of jackals,
a court for ostriches. And the wild beasts of the desert shall
meet with the wolves, and the satyr shall cry to his fellow;
yea, the night-monster shall settle there, and shall find her a
place of rest.
Isaiah, *chap. 34, vv. 13–14*

Where – in Britain's ecclesiastical, rather than political and social,
history – does the real break between Roman times and the early
medieval period fall? The expression 'sub-Roman' has been used many
times in this book. It is an expression that, in its time, has meant many
things to many writers, which may explain its popularity as an historical
label. To *this* writer, it denotes the latter part (after 410, for convenience)
of a whole series of events and practices and attitudes, all of which have
their beginning in the Roman period; and which continue as far as one
see from those beginnings into the fifth century – in certain regions of
Britain, probably into the sixth century. Christianity in southern
Scotland, insofar as its derivation can be made out, sprang from that
early fifth-century see established at Whithorn; and the Whithorn
bishopric, unless some totally eccentric phenomenon is represented,
came out of late Roman Britain. Again, if Palladius himself was from
Gaul, and was sent to Ireland at the behest of the Bishop of Rome,
Palladius came to serve *credentes* whose faith was drawn from Roman
Britain; and Patrick's life, despite its remote and difficult setting, was no
more than a personal extension of the late Roman Christianity of some
such region as the western hinterland of Britannia's northern *limes*.
Within the former Roman civil diocese, of course, the evidence rehearsed
at length in earlier chapters of this work should show why it can now be
contended that the Roman Christianity of Britain was not expunged by
the arrival and assaults of several thousand pagan Germans – any more
than spoken British Latin, or the British people themselves, in their
hundreds of thousands. 'Sub-Roman' in the Christian sense, then, may
well be an apposite phrase after AD 500; until, and unless, any major
change in our ecclesiastical history can be demonstrated.

For the present author, that change – the divide between 'sub-Roman' and what is truly 'post-Roman' in Church matters – is marked by the advent of monasticism. By this is meant the foundation of full monasteries: archaeologically detectable as areas (often enclosed) with one or more churches, the living-quarters and offices of a full-time religious community under an abbot, and eventually a monastic cemetery. Models for such foundations appeared in the fourth century around the eastern and southern shores of the Mediterranean; by the end of that century, Gaul began to show its own isolated attempts to reproduce what was known to be occurring in the Wadi Natrun, the Thebaid, Palestine and Syria. On present evidence monasticism reached Britain not before the latter part of the fifth century – first, probably, in south-west Britain and south Wales, and then during the early sixth century, Ireland.

The horizon we can use to separate sub-Roman and post-Roman Insular Christianity then opens about 475. The particular fashion spread through time, as well as in space. It was in 563 that Columba founded Iona, among the Scotti of Argyll; it was not until the 630s that monasteries, essentially of this Atlantic-Irish type, appeared in Northumbria, starting with Lindisfarne. This is the real division, in terms of our Church history, and the division spans at least a century. In labelling the title of this book 'to AD 500', the author had it in mind to suggest, rather than (as the French so usefully say) *préciser*, a point at which the present narrative can be assumed to close. The later history and archaeology of Insular Christianity must be reserved for another, and differently-constructed, study.[1]

This choice, of the advent of monasticism, is not just one of convenience. Its appearance, perhaps at such south-western coastal sites as Tintagel[2] (Pl. 8) where a starting-date of about 475 is derived from diagnostic sherds of imported pottery, is not isolated; it forms part of a New Wave of innovations. Such things, which involve renewed literacy, and art, and reflections of the Mediterranean development of the martyrial cult of relics, are in Britain and Ireland manifested to us as small finds, or artistic motifs, or through field-archaeology. Behind them all lies the importation of new *ideas* – and ideas hailing not so much from Atlantic Gaul and Iberia as from North Africa and the Levant. Once more, we infer that small trading-boats were the means of transmission. It is a moot point whether the trade (in material of Mediterranean provenance) provided handy transport for Insular pilgrims who returned home with these seminal ideas, and helped to put them into practice; or whether trade followed new demands, created by such pilgrims back from the Holy Places and Desert Fathers.[3]

The distributional pattern of material finds that results, and its delineation can be counted among the minor triumphs of (British and Irish) protohistoric research over the last few decades, speaks for itself (fig. 60). It differs so radically from underlying patterns of the maps earlier used to illustrate Roman Christianity that we sense at once it must belong, not to a final chapter, but to the next volume in the story. The imported Mediterranean wares Classes A and B – fine red dishes and bowls of late Roman colour-coated type, and jars for wine and oil[4] – the use on inscribed stones of words such as *nomen, nomina*, and *memoria* (favoured in North Africa)[5] and, in the first Christian ogham-inscribed stones of south-west Ireland the primitive Irish equivalent of *nomen*, *ainm(anm)*,[6] with indications of simple external memoriae and 'slab shrines' in Christian cemeteries also of south-west Ireland[7] – all these, with the emphasis on a sea-borne introduction looking south beyond Gaul, can be used to make up such a map.

These remarks may not suffice to wither that hardy perennial, the notion than monasticism came to Britain in late Roman times. The agents proposed range from Victricius of Rouen (p. 51) onwards. There are these strange ideas that Nynia did, in person, visit Martin of Tours before the latter's death in 397, returned to Whithorn, and promptly founded a physical imitation of Martin's pioneer monastery. It has been claimed that minute scrutiny of Patrick's wording reveals that he himself was proto-monastic and diffused monastic ideas among his Irish converts; even that Gildas was a monk and wrote with a basic monastic tinge. None of this will stand critical scrutiny, still less gain any support from prolonged archaeological investigation.

Martin of Tours was in his monastic ideals, as in other ways, a lone figure; the unique power of this extraordinary Pannonian man of God still reaches us, penetrating the jejune biography of Sulpicius Severus with his Dialogues and Letters[8] and the inflated mythology retailed by Gregory and others. The bonfires lit by Martin were of those crowds of souls of *urban* Gallo-Romans, who maintained *romanitas* and then Roman Christianity in the cities, among a still pagan rural Gaul. Not even Martin would have succeeded on this scale in fifth-century Britain. As for the claims about British monasticism, the sheer improbability that Nynia had any personal connection with Martin was raised in Chapter 11. The inscribed stones apart, one cannot find anything now visible of pre-Anglian Whithorn. As Christine Mohrmann pointed out,[9] 'There are no traces in Patrick's Latin of the special terminology of monasticism', and nothing supporting any traditions of contact with early fifth-century monasticism in Gaul. Gildas, who in all likelihood was not a monk but a regular priest,[10] describes a British Church (from 530-odd back to the mid-fifth century) where, as W.H. Davies showed,[11] 'the monastic element seems small' even at the time of composition, when monasteries had been founded for a generation.

Progressively from Chapter 10 – and implicitly, here and there, in the

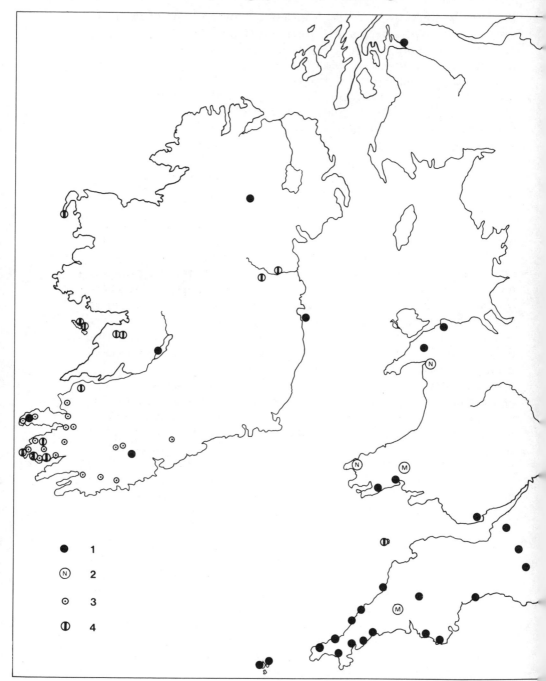

1

N 2

3

4

conclusions of earlier chapters – the assertion of this book has been one of continuity, from Roman to sub-Roman times. If Continuity (of the British Romans, their life and languages, and of Britannia) is the horse that draws this vehicle into the fifth century, the Church is the rider. One cannot see any other, *single*, facet of fourth-century Britain likely to have preserved Latin, and literacy, and the sense of community with an empire beyond Britain. The theme propounded is not however that British Christianity survived and continued in precisely the manner in which it lasted, unbroken or modified, in parts of Gaul or Spain. Patently this was never the case. It is that some measure of survival, of continuity, dimly glimpsed because of defective sources, is an explanation for what we encounter in the sixth and seventh centuries; and an explanation preferable to another in which Christianity of Roman Britain was extinguished (in 410? 425? 441?), and subsequently, undemonstrably, re-introduced.

To state this is to countermand those numerous statements of recent years which, in contrasting the political fate of Roman Britain with that of other provinces in the west, would have us see the Church dying along with the old order.[12] No-one could suppose that the fifth-century British circumstances were like those in Gaul. The radical distinction must be our virtual collapse of urban life. One can argue that London and Canterbury almost certainly, and a few other places (York? Gloucester? Carlisle?) quite possibly, have never been entirely deserted since their Roman origins; but even these will have participated in the national run-down of the Roman towns and cities, whose later phase is obliquely pictured by Gildas. There will have been many people in fifth-century Britain who, reading the words of the prophet Isaiah used to introduce this chapter – they are part of his terrible curse on the land of Edom – took their force with particular and localised poignancy. That odd group of 'Rat's Castle' place-names, for deserted habitations of old, may well go right back to such times, since they occur in the British languages as well as in English.[13]

But sub-Roman Britain, like Roman Britain, was as to nineteen-twentieths (or more) of its composition a rural, agrarian society. A Church which, at the end of the fourth century, might have provided means of worship at Icklingham, or surviving villa estates, or northern vici, or at whatever sub-Roman settlements the Eccles-names imply,

---

60 Start of post-Roman Insular, monastic Christianity – Mediterreanean imports and ideas from the later 5th cent.

1 Classes A and B Mediterranean pottery   2 Inscribed stones, *nomen or memoria*   3 Ogham-inscribed stones with *anm*   4 Small memoriae, cellae and slab-shrines, of ultimate Mediterranean inspiration

could have stabilised itself here and there in the setting of rural life, outside the cities and major towns. For it is in this sphere of *rural* settlement that so much interest, and research effort, has now been attracted. There is increased attention paid to tenure; the dividing-up of land in the first place, the relative permanence of those units through time, and the suggestions that estates passed from Roman Britain, to sub-Roman British and then to English landlords, in largely unaltered form – and, ecclesiastically, implying that sooner or later one of our many parish churches known to stand on Roman foundations will be shown to *be* sub-Roman in origin.

The earlier maps (figs. 47, 49) show, and show significantly, the areas in which percipient students might choose to concentrate any such enquiries; and these are indeed those areas in which continuity becomes apparent. In the north of Britain, there is the Greater Yorkshire, if one can call it that, with its Deira and Elmet;[14] over the Pennines to the west, Cumbria, with its British language until Norman times.[15] In Wales, by far the most fascinating region is the southern coastal plain, where a high degree of sub-Roman life seems to have followed the fourth century[16] and where it would be rash and hasty to deny a succession from Roman Christianity, through a fifth-century episcopal church, to monasticism.[17] In the south-west of Britain, where Rome's hand lay light and where, as a corollary, it is not easy to see the Church established before sub-Roman times, a British kingdom of sub-Roman origins lasted until Alfred's day, and a British language until the Hanoverian kings. Perhaps of the greatest fascination are those challenges posed by potential continuity in such areas as the later Dorset and Somerset, and Cotswold[18] – and ultimately, though only for the hardiest and best-equipped of explorers, Wheeler's sub-Roman triangle of 1935, and Kent itself.

What, then, has this book tried to show? Firstly, that there *is* a Christianity of late Roman Britain, substantial enough to warrant a description through four hundred pages; and that despite peculiarities of detail which one might ascribe to some innate tendency to accept, modify and express new ideas in a specifically British idiom, this Christianity must be set within the wider picture of the late Roman empire in the West. Secondly, that the evidence for survival – in the face of early English settlements – of the Church, and of much of Late Roman Britain with its Latinity and its romanised population, is now rather stronger than any evidence that the Romano–British church died out completely during the fifth century. Thirdly, though this is only a technical comment, that advances in our knowledge will now be won in the field, probably at an increasing rate; from archaeological discoveries, from further field-work and probably too from fresh interpretations of material we already have.

In the first chapter, limited allusion was made to the *message* of Christianity as it might have appeared to the less privileged classes of fourth-century Britain. Are we in any better position – looking backwards from the year 500, over the complex scene that has been reconstructed – to expand this theme? What *was* the rôle of the Church, in the changing social conditions of Britain during the two centuries before Gildas wrote? We could, for instance, as William Frend has recently done,[19] contrast the Church in post–370 Gaul when Martin of Tours raised Christianity from 'a largely urban and aristocratic' movement to the status of a popular, militantly anti-pagan one, incidentally laying the foundations of an eventual parochial system, with the apparent absence of any such wave in Britain. Or, with Frend again, we could point to the evidence for the late fourth-century revival of paganism, and Britain's supposed reception (though this was denied in Chap. 2) of Pelagianism, features not encountered in contemporary Gaul. Frend rightly asks, 'How was it that the *ecclesia Britannorum* failed to provide foundations for the *ecclesia Anglicana* even in Kent?' To this legitimate question there may be several answers: a language barrier, the depth of mutual antagonism between British and English, the non-coincidence of individual Christian sites, and the reason given by Bede (below). But would it be wholly true to state that Christianity failed to emerge as the predominant religion in Britain in the first half of the fifth century – insofar as there *was* any 'predominant religion' at that time? And Frend concedes[20] that 'a complete blank' in continuity is not conceivable today; that, gradually, features linking Romano-British and Anglo-Saxon Christianity (as, for instance, at St Albans) are beginning to emerge.

We possess so little direct information that we must be wary of exceeding proper inference. What Patrick's writings may tell us about the fifth-century Church in North Britain is something won only with difficulty (Chap. 14) and then only inferentially at best. What Gildas really tells us is open, and will long remain open, to much questioning. One might, rashly perhaps, sum it up in saying that Gildas looks back with imperfect historical knowledge over a gradual amalgam of the Christian hierarchy and the more powerful elements in our sub-Roman society, one that (to him) had been to the detriment of Christianity rather than to the enrichment of social conduct. Yet on another level there are clues. If, as the native kingdoms slowly replaced the *respublicae civitatum Britanniae*, rare individuals emerge named as Venedotians or Elmetiacans, no longer Brigantians or Dumnonians, then at the lower stage of the rural settlement the membership of a church – an *ecclesia* or an *eglēs* – may have fed that need not only for overt participation in a community larger than the common agricultural bond, but also of some kinship with the dissolving past – seen, nostalgically, as so often in

Gildas' words, as an age of relative stability and lawfulness. Some measure of popular support for the Church there must have been. We have absolutely no information as to how late fourth- or fifth-century British bishops were elected – it would go far beyond our evidence to adduce contemporary Gaulish practice here[21] – but, as we have seen, we may suppose that the British episcopate and with it some form of the territorial diocesan system continued. This would have required general Christian approval as much as aristocratic patronage; and even in the coastal parts of Wales we cannot confirm the rise of powerful monastic houses – aspects of a system which, in some degree, eclipsed the older diocesan one – before the end of the fifth century.

But how did individual British Christians see themselves? What did Patrick – our earliest source here – mean (*Ep.* 2) by the term *civis*? Richard Hanson argued that Patrick meant (or, one might cautiously say, 'still' meant) any civilised adherent of a complex of the Christian Church and the Roman empire.[22] 'All Christians automatically entered Romania.' And it may well be that, scantily, this view was particularly welcomed within the British Church; where one facet, at least, of Christian membership after 400 could have been identification with the distant Imperial centres that had nurtured and recognised such a Faith, provided its language, its texts and symbolism, housed its patristic giants, and constructed within Britannia the framework that, imperfectly, such adherents strove to preserve. In the occasional glimpses of synodal dealings between Britain and Gaul after 400 there is no sign of particular British humility; rather, perhaps, help and advice between equals. A solitary early fifth-century text of indisputably British origin – and we cannot as yet give this label to any of the supposedly British Pelagian tracts – might reveal more of British sentiments than any quantity of guesswork.

Lastly, we just begin to perceive the quantitative nature of the growth of Christianity in Roman Britain and afterwards. If future research allows us to expand, refine and systematise such maps as figs. 15 and 49 above, future students will hardly be content with such phrases as 'a minority religion', unqualified either by date-brackets or any more detailed estimate. Yet one senses that this entire book has necessarily been discussing a minority religion; and that not much before 500, and then only in certain regions implicit in the map, fig. 49, were Christians of all sorts more numerous within a given principality or native state than the practitioners of any one other, distinct, form of religion.

It has already been explained why the end of the fifth century, a date chosen to stand for the initial establishment in Ireland and western Britain of full monasticism, closes this part of the Christian history of Britain and Ireland. But it is only permissible to end here because of the progress of research in the last fifty years on all the Insular monastic phenomena and the rich associated archaeology and art.[23] In 1912 Hugh Williams ended his study with the notion of 'Two Churches' – this was in 600, not 500, with a British church of Roman origin in the north and west, and the new Roman church of Augustine in the south-east. These had in common the Faith, and Latin; but their members had differing backgrounds, mutually incomprehensible languages, and on the British side the inheritance of all the memories of the previous two hundred years. That British irreconcilability to all the descendants of the Saxons who had broken faith, ruined so much of Britannia, and seized so much of Britain's lands, was still too strong to allow a common Christian doctrine to bridge the gap. In Gildas' day, the distinction had been absolute; the Saxons were by definition pagans. In Bede's, British and English Christian kingdoms existed in the same small island, as did the gap between them. If we were not specifically told this by Bede, in whose gentle soul the enormity of British Christianity's failure to hold out the light of the Gospels to the incoming English rankled until the very end, we could have guessed as much from a string of clues, that enigmatic first meeting at Augustine's Oak among them. It is a bizarre reflection on the course of Insular history that Hugh Williams' 'two churches' were in the seventh century first brought together to any extent by the *Irish* – Christian descendants of those pagan Scotti who had settled in the lands of the Picts and the North Britons. But, behind this, from the late fourth to the early seventh century, the old indigenously developed Christianity of Britain was no more than submerged; not extinguished. In 1953, many people regarded Jocelyn Toynbee as over-bold when she stated that 'the so-called Celtic Church, surviving continuously in the north and west, was thoroughly Roman in creed and origin; Roman, too, initially, in its organization and practice'.[24] Today, three decades later, this is no more than the conclusion to which the balance of probabilities leads us.

Bibliography

Abbreviations of titles of journals follow the system used by the Council for British Archaeology (in *British Archaeological Abstracts*, etc.). In citing items from series, BAR = British Archaeological Reports (Oxford), CBA = Council for British Archaeology (London), and RR = Research Reports – of the body indicated.

Adams, G.B. 1970 'Language and Man in Ireland,' *Ulster Folklife 15/16*, 140–71

Addyman, P.V. & Morris, R., eds. 1976 *The Archaeological Study of Churches*, CBA RR *13*

Addyman, P.V. 1977 'York and Canterbury as Ecclesiastical Centres', in: Barley, M.W., ed. (1977), 499–509

Alcock, L.A. 1967 'Roman Britons and Pagan Saxons: An Archaeological Appraisal', *Welsh Hist Rev 3*, 229–49

Alcock, L.A. 1971 *Arthur's Britain. History and Archaeology* AD *367–634* (London)

Alcock, L.A. 1976 (Note on) 'Dumbarton Rock', *Medieval Archaeol 20*, 176

Anderson, A.O. 1948 'Ninian and the Southern Picts', *Scot Hist Rev 27*, 25–47

Anderson, A.O. & M.O. 1961 *Adomnan's Life of Columba* (London & Edinburgh)

Anthony, I.E., ed. 1968 'Excavations in Verulam Hills Field, St Albans, 1963–4', *Hertfordshire Archaeol 1*, 9–50

Atkinson, D. 1951 'The Origin and Date of the *Sator* Word-Square', *J Eccles Hist 2*, 1–9

Atkinson, D. 1957 'The Cirencester Word-Square', *Trans Bristol Gloucestershire Archaeol Soc 76*, 21–31

Bannerman, J.W. 1968a 'The Dál Riata and Northern Ireland in the sixth and seventh centuries', in: Carney, J. & Greene, D., eds., *Celtic Studies: Essays in memory of Angus Matheson* (London), 1–11

Bannerman, J.W. 1968b 'Notes on the Scottish Entries in the early Irish Annals', *Scot Gaelic Stud 11.2*, 149–70

Bannerman, J.W. 1974 *Studies in the History of Dalriada* (Edinburgh & London)

Barker, P.W. 1975 'Excavations on the site of the Baths Basilica at Wroxeter 1966–1974: An Interim Report', *Britannia 6*, 106–17

Barker, P.W. 1979 'The latest occupation of the site of the Baths Basilica at Wroxeter', in: Casey, P.J., ed. (1979), 175–81

Barley, M.W., ed. 1977 *European Towns – Their Archaeology and Early History* (London & New York)

Barley, M.W. & Hanson, R.P.C., eds. 1968 *Christianity in Britain 300–700* (Leicester)

Barrow, G.W.S. 1973 *The Kingdom of the Scots – Government, Church and Society from the eleventh to the fourteenth century* (London)

Bateson, J.D. 1973 'Roman Material from Ireland: a reconsideration', *Proc Roy Ir Acad C 73*, 21–97

Bateson, J.D. 1976 'Further Finds of Roman Material from Ireland', *Proc Roy Ir Acad C 76*, 171–80

Baynes, N.H. 1929 *Constantine the Great and the Christian Church* (London)

Beckerlegge, J.J. 1953 'Ancient Memorial Inscription on a Stone at Hayle', *Old Cornwall 5.4*, 173–8

Beckwith, J. 1963 *Coptic Sculpture, 300–1300* (London)

Behrens, G. 1950 *Das Frühchristliche und Merowingische Mainz* (= R-G.Z.M. *Kulturgeschichtliche Wegweiser 20*) (Mainz)

Bettenson, H. 1943 *Documents of the Christian Church* (Oxford)

Biddle, M. 1976 'The Archaeology of the Church – a widening horizon', in: Addyman, P.V. & Morris, R., eds. (1976), 65–71

Biddle, M. 1979 *St Albans Abbey. Chapter House Excavations 1978* (Fraternity of the Friends of Saint Albans Abbey, Occas. Paper. 1)

Biddle, M. & Kjolbye-Biddle, B. 1980 'The Medieval Chapter House of St Albans Abbey, and its Excavations in 1978', *Expedition, 22.2* (Philadelphia), 17–32

Biddle, M., Hudson, D., & Heighway, C. 1973 *The Future of London's Past* (= *Rescue* Publication 4) (Worcester)

Bidwell, P.T. 1979 *Exeter Archaeological Reports 1 – the Legionary Bath-house and Basilica and Forum at Exeter* (Exeter)

Bieler, L. 1942 *Codices Patriciani Latini: a descriptive catalogue of Latin manuscripts relating to St Patrick* (Dublin)

Bieler, L. 1943 'The problem of Silua Focluti', *Irish Hist Stud 3*, 351–64

Bieler, L. 1947 'Der Bibeltext des heiligen Patrick', *Biblica 28*, 31–58, 239–63

Bieler, L. 1949a *The Life and Legend of St Patrick* (Dublin)

Bieler, L. 1949b 'Sidelights on the chronology of St Patrick', *Irish Hist Stud 6*, 247–61

Bieler, L. 1950 'Studies on the Text of Muirchú – I. The Text of Manuscript Novara 77', *Proc Roy Ir Acad C 52*, 179–220

Bieler, L. 1952 *Libri Epistolarum Sancti Patricii Episcopi*, 2 vols. (Dublin)

Bieler, L. 1953 *The Works of St Patrick* (= Ancient Christian Writers, vol. 17) (Westminster, Md., & London)

Bieler, L. 1954 'St Patrick a Native of Anglesey?' *Éigse, 7*, 129–31

Bieler, L. 1959 'Studies on the Text of Muirchú – II. The Vienna Fragments and the Tradition of Muirchú's Text', *Proc Roy Ir Acad C 59*, 181–95

Bieler, L. 1962 'A Linguist's View of St Patrick', *Éigse, 10*, 149–54

Bieler, L. 1963a *The Irish Penitentials* (= Scriptores Latini Hiberniae vol. V) (Dublin)

Bieler, L. 1963b *Ireland – Harbinger of the Middle Ages* (London)

Bieler, L. 1964a 'Christianity in Ireland during the Fifth and Sixth Centuries: a study and evaluation of sources', *Ir Eccles Rec 102*, 162–7

Bieler, L. 1964b 'Patrician Studies in the *Irish Ecclesiastical Record*', *Ir Eccles Rec 102*, 359–66

Bieler, L. 1967a *St Patrick and the Coming of Christianity* (History of Irish Catholicism, fasc.I.i) (Dublin)

Bieler, L. 1967b 'Interpretationes Patricianae', *Ir Eccles Rec 107*, 1–13

Bieler L. 1968a 'St Patrick and the British Church', in: Barley, M.W. & Hanson, R.P.C., eds. (1968), 75–86

Bieler, L. 1968b 'The Christianization of the Insular Celts', *Celtica*, 8, 112–25

Bieler, L. 1979 *The Patrician Texts in the Book of Armagh* (= Scriptores Latini Hiberniae, vol. X) (Dublin)

Binchy, D.A. 1958 (Review of: LHEB = Jackson 1953), *Celtica*, 6 288–92

Binchy, D.A. 1962 'Patrick and His Biographers, ancient and modern', *Studia Hibernica 2*, 7–123

Binchy, D.A. 1966 'The date of the so-called *Hymn of Patrick*', *Ériu 20*, 234–8

Binchy, D.A. 1975–76 'Irish History and Irish Law', *Studia Hibernica 15*, 7–36, and 16, 7–45

Birley, A. 1977 *Life in Roman Britain*, 5th impr. (London)

Birley, E. 1961a *Roman Britain and the Roman Army* (Kendal)

Birley, E. 1961b 'A Christian monogram from Brough-under-Stainmore', *Trans Cumberland Westmorland Antiq Archaeol Soc n.s. 61*, 298–9

Blair, P.H. 1954 'The Bernicians and their Northern Frontier', in: Chadwick, N.K., ed. (1954), 137–72

Böhner, K. 1958 *Die Fränkischen Altertümer des Trierer Landes*, 2 vols. (Berlin)

Bonner, G., ed. 1976 *Famulus Christi; essays in commemoration of the Thirteenth Centenary of the Birth of the Venerable Bede* (London)

Bonnet, C. 1974 'Genève, capitale burgonde', *Archeologia 66*, 12–17

Boon, G.C. 1957 *Roman Silchester. The Archaeology of a Romano–British Town* (London)

Boon, G.C. 1960 'A temple of Mithras at Caernarvon-*Segontium*', *Archaeol Cambrensis 109*, 136–72

Boon, G.C. 1962 'A Christian monogram at Caerwent', *Bull Board Celtic Stud 19*, 338–44

Boon, G.C. 1974 *Silchester, The Roman Town of Calleva* (Newton Abbot)

Boon, G.C. 1976 'The shrine of the head, Caerwent', in: Boon, G.C. & Lewis, J.M., eds., *Welsh Antiquity: Essays . . . presented to H.N. Savory* (Cardiff), 163–75

Boppert, W. 1971 *Die frühchristlichen inschriften des Mittelrheingebietes* (Mainz)

Bowen, E.G. 1969 *Saints, Settlements and Seaways in the Celtic Lands* (Cardiff)

Bowman, A.K. 1974 'Roman Military Records from Vindolanda', *Britannia 5*, 360–73

Brailsford, J.W. 1951 *Guide to the Antiquities of Roman Britain* (British Museum, London)

Branigan, K. 1967 'Romano–British Rural Settlement in the Western Chilterns', *Archaeol J 124* 129–59

Branigan, K. 1971 *Latimer – Belgic, Roman, Dark Age and Early Modern Farm* (Chess Valley Archaeol & Hist Soc)

Branigan, K. 1977 *Gatcombe Roman Village* (BAR 44, Oxford)

Breeze, D.J. & Dobson, B. 1976 *Hadrian's Wall* (London)

Bromwich, R. 1954 'The Character of the Early Welsh Tradition', in: Chadwick, N.K., ed., (1954), 83–136

Bromwich, R. 1976 'Concepts of Arthur', *Studia Celtica* 9/10, 163–81

Brooks, N.P. 1977 'The Ecclesiastical Topography of Early Medieval Canterbury', in: Barley, M.W., ed. (1977), 487–96

Brown, P.D.C. 1971 'The Church at Richborough', *Britannia* 2, 225–31

Brown, P.R.L. 1967 *Augustine of Hippo – a biography* (London)

Brown, P.R.L. 1977 *Relics and Social Status in the Age of Gregory of Tours* (Stenton Lecture 1976) (Reading, 1977)

Bruce-Mitford, R.L.S., ed. 1956 *Recent Archaeological Excavations in Britain* (London)

Bultmann, R. 1956 *Primitive Christianity in its Contemporary Setting* (London)

Burrow, I.C.G. 1974 'Tintagel – Some Problems', *Scot Archaeol Forum* 5 (Edinburgh), 99–103

Bury, J.B. 1905 *The Life of St Patrick and His Place in History* (London)

Butler, R.M., ed. 1971 *Soldier and Civilian in Roman Yorkshire* (Leicester)

Cameron, K. 1968 'Eccles in English Place-Names', in: Barley, M.W. & Hanson, R.P.C., eds. (1968), 87–92

Cameron, K., ed. 1975 *Place-Name Evidence for the Anglo-Saxon Invasion and Scandinavian Settlements* (English Place-Name Soc.)

Cameron, K. 1980 'The Meaning and significance of Old English *walh* in English place-names', *J Engl Place-Name Soc* 12, (1979–80), 1–53

Campbell, J. 1975 (Review of Morris, *The Age of Arthur*) *Studia Hibernica* 15, 177–85

Campbell, J. 1979 'Bede's Words for Places', in: Sawyer, P.H., ed., *Names, Words and Graves: Early Medieval Settlement* (Leeds), 34–55

Carney, J. 1955 *Studies in Irish Literature and History* (Dublin)

Carney, J. 1959 'Comments on the Present State of the Patrician Problem', *Ir Eccles Rec* 92, 1–28

Carney, J. 1961 *The Problem of St Patrick* (Dublin)

Carney, J. 1971 'Three Old Irish Accentual Poems', *Ériu* 22, 23–80

Carney, J. 1975 'The Invention of the Ogom cipher', *Ériu* 26, 53–65

Carpenter, H.J. 1943 'Creeds and Baptismal Rites in the first four centuries', *J Theol Stud* 44, 1–11

Carson, R.A.G. 1976 'The Water Newton hoard of gold solidi', *The British Museum Yearbook, 1: The Classical Tradition*, 219–20

Carson, R.A.G. & O'Kelly, C. 1977 'A Catalogue of the Roman Coins from Newgrange, Co. Meath', *Proc Roy Ir Acad C* 77, 35–55

Casey, P.J., ed. 1979 *The End of Roman Britain* (BAR 71, Oxford)

Chadwick, N.K., ed. 1954a *Studies in Early British History* (Cambridge)

Chadwick, N.K. 1954b 'Intellectual Contacts between Britain and Gaul in the Fifth Century', in: Chadwick 1954a, 189–253

Chadwick, N.K. 1954c 'A Note on Faustus & Riocatus' in: Chadwick 1954a, 254–63

Chadwick, N.K. 1955 *Poetry and Letters in Early Christian Gaul* (Cambridge)

Chadwick, N.K., ed. 1958a *Studies in the Early British Church* (Cambridge)

Chadwick, N.K. 1958b 'The Name *Pict*', *Scot Gaelic Stud* 8, 146–76

Chadwick, N.K. 1966 *The Druids* (Cardiff)

Chadwick, N.K. 1969 *Early Brittany* (Cardiff)

Chadwick, O. 1954a 'The Evidence of Dedications in the Early History of the Welsh Church', in: Chadwick N.K. 1954a, 83–136

Chadwick, O. 1954b 'Gildas and the Monastic Order', *J Theol Stud n.s. 5*, 78–80

Chandler, J.H. 1976 *Christianity in Roman Britain: A Bibliography, 1960–1975* (College of Librarianship, Wales, Aberystwyth)

Chandler, J.H. 1978 'The nature of Christianity in Roman Britain' (lecture, Dorchester, December 1978)

Charlesworth, D.H. 1961 'Roman jewellery found in Northumberland and Durham', *Archaeol Aeliana, 4 ser, 39*, 1–36

Charlesworth, D.H. 1978 'Roman Carlisle', *Archaeol J 135*, 115–37

CIIC = see Macalister, R.A.S.

Clarke, G., ed. 1979 *Pre-Roman and Roman Winchester, Part II, The Roman Cemetery at Lankhills* (= Winchester Studies 3) (Oxford)

Clarke, L.C.G. 1931 'Roman Pewter Bowl from the Isle of Ely', *Proc Cambridge Antiq Soc 31*, 66–72

Clarke, R.R. 1960 *East Anglia* (London)

Collingwood, R.G. & Myres, J.N.L. 1937 *Roman Britain and the English Settlements*, 2nd edn. (Oxford)

Collingwood, R.G. & Richmond, I.A. 1969 *The Archaeology of Roman Britain* (London)

Colyer, C. & Gilmour, B. 1978 'St Paul-in-the-Bail, Lincoln', *Curr Archaeol 6.4* (= 63), 102–5

Colyer, C. & Jones, M.J. 1979 'Excavations at Lincoln, 2nd Interim Report: Excavations in the Lower Town 1972–78', *Antiq J 59*, 50–91

Coquet, (Dom) J. 1978 *L'Interêt des Fouilles de Ligugé*, edn. revue & augmentée (Ligugé, Vienne)

Cowen, J.D. 1936 'An Inscribed Openwork Gold Ring from Corstopitum', *Archaeol Aeliana, 4 ser, 13*, 310–9

Cowen, J.D. 1948 'The Corbridge Gold Ring: a Footnote', *Archaeol Aeliana, 4 ser, 26*, 139–42

Cross, F.L. & Livingstone, E.A. 1977 *The Oxford Dictionary of the Christian Church*, 2nd edn., corrected repr. (Oxford)

Crowe, C.J. 1979 *Monastic and early church settlement in north-west England from the Dee Valley to the Solway: a survey of selected sites* (MA thesis, Faculty of Arts, University of Manchester)

Crummy, P.J. 1973 (Note on Colchester excavations) *Medieval Archaeol 17*, 140

Crummy, P.J. 1974 *Colchester: Recent Excavation and Research* (Colchester)

Cumont, F. 1922 *After Life in Roman Paganism* (Yale)

Cunliffe, B.W., ed. 1968 *Fifth Report on the Excavations of the Roman Fort at Richborough, Kent* (Society of Antiquaries, RR 23) (London)

Curle, A.O. 1923 *The Treasure of Traprain.* (Glasgow)

Curwen, E.C. 1943 'Roman Lead cistern from Pulborough, Sussex', *Antiq J 23*, 155–7

Dalton, O.M. 1911 *Byzantine Art and Archaeology* (Oxford)

Dalton, O.M. 1921 *A Guide to the Early Christian and Byzantine Antiquities*, 2nd edn. (Brit Mus, London)

Dalton, O.M. 1922 'Roman Spoons from Dorchester', *Antiq J* 2, 89–92

Dalton, O.M. 1927 *The History of the Franks by Gregory of Tours*, 2 vols. (Oxford)

Daniels, C.M. 1967 *Mithras and his Temples on the Wall*, 2nd edn. (Newcastle upon Tyne)

Davies, J.G. 1952 *The Origin and Development of Early Christian Church Architecture* (London)

Davies, J.G. 1962 *The Architectural Setting of Baptism* (London)

Davies, Wendy 1978 *An Early Welsh Microcosm – Studies in the Llandaff Charters* (Roy Hist Soc, London)

Davies, Wendy 1979 'Roman settlements and post-Roman estates in south-east Wales', in: Casey P.J., ed. (1979), 153–73

Davies, W.H. 1968 'The Church in Wales', in: Barley M.W. & Hanson R.P.C., eds. (1968), 131–50

Day, M. 1979 (Note on sub-Roman Canterbury) *Rescue News 19*, 4

De Beer, (Sir) G. 1958 'The Inhabitants of Switzerland', *J Roy Soc Arts*, 106, 408–24

De Palol, P. 1967 *Arqueología Cristiana de la España Romana* (=España Cristiana, I) (Madrid & Valladolid)

De Plinval, G. 1943 *Pélage, ses écrits, sa vie et sa réforme* (Lausanne)

De Rossi, J., ed. 1857–61 *Inscriptiones Christianae Urbis Romae septimo saeculo antiquiores*, 2 vols. (Rome)

De Ste Croix, G.E.M. 1963 'Why were the Early Christians Persecuted?' *Past & Present 26*, 6–38

Dickinson, T. 1979 'On the Origin and Chronology of the Early Anglo-Saxon Disc Brooch', in: Hawkes, Brown & Campbell, eds. (1979), 39–80

Dieulafoy, M. 1914 'Basilique constantinienne de Lugdunum Convenarum', *Comptes-rendues de l'Academie des Inscriptions & Belles-Lettres 14* (Paris), 59–90

Doble, G.H. 1943 *St Dubricius* (= Welsh Saints no. 2), (Guildford & Esher)

Dolley, R.H.M. 1976 'Roman Coins from Ireland and the Date of St Patrick', *Proc Roy Ir Acad C 76*, 181–90

Doppelfeld, O. 1950 'Zur Vorgeschichte der Georgskirche in Köln', in: Zimmerman, W., ed., *Die Kunstdenkmäler des Rheinlands*, 2 (Essen), 90–104

Dumville, D.N. 1973 'Biblical Apocryphra and the Early Irish: a preliminary investigation', *Proc Roy Ir Acad C 73*, 299–338

Dumville, D.N. 1977 'Sub-Roman Britain – History and Legend', *History 62* (= no. 205), 173–92

Duine, F. 1914 *Questions d'Hagiographie et Vie de S.Samson* (Paris)

Dunnett, B.R.K. 1971 'Excavations in Colchester 1964–68', *Trans Essex Archaeol Soc, ser 3*, 3, 1–130

Dyggve, E. 1951 *History of Salonitan Christianity* (=Instituttet for Sammenlignende Kulturforskning, ser. A XXI) (Oslo)

Eagles, B.N. 1979 *The Anglo-Saxon Settlement of Humberside* (BAR 68, Oxford)

Elkington, D.H. 1976 'The Mendip Lead Industry', in: Branigan, K. & Fowler,

P.J., eds., *The Roman West Country* (Newton Abbot), 183–97

Ellison, A. 1978 *Excavations at West Hill, Uley, 1977. The Romano–British Temple; Interim Report* (= CRAAGS Occ. Paper 3) (Bristol)

Engleheart, G.H. 1898 'On some buildings of the Romano–British period discovered at Clanville, near Andover', *Archaeologia 56*, 1–20

Engleheart, G.H. 1924 'On some Roman buildings and other antiquities in a district of North-West Hants', *Proc Hampshire Fld Club Archaeol Soc*, 9, 214–15

Evison, V.I. 1979 *Wheel-Thrown Pottery in Anglo-Saxon Graves* (Roy Archaeol Inst, London)

Farrar, R.A.H. 1957 (Note on the Frampton 'villa'), *Proc Dorset Natur Hist Archaeol Soc 78*, 81–3

Faull, M.L. 1974 'Roman and Anglian Settlement Patterns in Yorkshire', *Northern History 9*, 1–25

Faull, M.L. 1975 'The Semantic Development of Old English *Wealh*', *Leeds Studies in English 8*, 20–44

Faull, M.L. 1976 'The Location and Relationship of the Sancton Anglo-Saxon Cemeteries', *Antiq J 56*, 227–33

Faull, M.L. 1977 'British Survival in Anglo-Saxon Northumbria', in Laing, L.R., ed, *Studies in Celtic Survival* (BAR 37, Oxford), 1–56

Fawtier, R. 1912 *La Vie de Saint Sampson* (Paris)

Ferguson, E. 1979 'Inscriptions and the Origin of Infant Baptism', *J Theol Stud n.s. 30*, 37–46

Finberg, H.P.R. 1964 *Lucerna – Studies on some Problems in the Early History of England* (London)

Finberg, H.P.R. 1972 (ed.) *The Agrarian History of England and Wales, I.2 –* AD 43–1042 (Cambridge)

Finney, P.C. 1978 'Gnosticism and the Origins of Early Christian Art', *Atti del IX Congreso Internazionale di Archaeologia Cristiana 1975* (Rome), 391–405

Fisher, J.D.C. 1965 *Christian Initiation: Baptism in the Medieval West* (London)

Fletcher, (Sir) E. & Meates, G.W. 1969 'The Ruined Church of Stone-by-Faversham', *Antiq J 49*, 273–294

Fletcher, Lord (Eric), & Meates, G.W. 1977 'The Ruined Church of Stone-by-Faversham – Second Report', *Antiq J 57*, 67–72

Fletcher, W.G.D. 1904 'A Fourth Century Christian Letter from (?) Uriconium', *Trans Shropshire Archaeol Soc, 3 ser 5 (= 28)*, i–ii

Fontaine, J. 1973 *L'Art Préroman Hispanique I* (= Nuit de Temps 38), (La Pierre-Qui-Vire, Yonne)

Forbes, A.P. 1874 *Lives of S. Ninian and S. Kentigern* (= Historians of Scotland vol. V) (Edinburgh)

Fox, (Lady) A. 1952 *Roman Exeter. Excavations in the War-Damaged Areas 1945–1947* (Manchester)

Frend, W.H.C. 1952 *The Donatist Church* (Oxford)

Frend, W.H.C. 1955 'Religion in Roman Britain in the Fourth Century', *J Brit Archaeol Ass, 3 ser 18*, 1–18

Frend, W.H.C. 1959 'The Failure of the Persecutions in the Roman Empire', *Past & Present 16*, 10–30

Frend, W.H.C. 1965a *Martyrdom and Persecution in the Early Church* (Oxford)

Frend, W.H.C. 1965b *The Early Church* (London)

Frend, W.H.C. 1968 'The Christianization of Roman Britain', in: Barley M.W. & Hanson R.P.C., eds. (1968), 37–50

Frend, W.H.C. 1979 'Ecclesia Britannica: Prelude or Dead End?' *J Eccles Hist* 30, 129–44

Frere, S.S. 1966 'The end of towns in Roman Britain', in: Wacher, J.S. ed. (1966), 87–100

Frere, S.S. 1972 *Verulamium Excavations I* (= Society of Antiquaries, RR 28) (London)

Frere, S.S. 1975 'The Silchester Church: The Excavation by Sir Ian Richmond in 1961', *Archaeologia 105*, 277–302

Frere, S.S. 1978 *Britannia. A History of Roman Britain*, rev. edn. (London)

Fulford, M. 1979 'Pottery production and trade at the end of Roman Britain: the case against continuity', in: Casey, P.J., ed. (1979), 120–32

Gelling, M. 1978 *Signposts to the Past – Place-Names and the History of England* (London)

Gillam, J.P. & MacIvor, I. 1954 'The Temple of Mithras at Rudchester', *Archaeol Aeliana, 4 ser 32*, 176–219

Gilmour, B. 1979 'The Anglo-Saxon church at St Paul-in-the-Bail, Lincoln', *Medieval Archaeol 23*, 214–18

Goddard, E.H. 1922 'Roman Lamp with cross emblem, Tidworth', *Wiltshire Archaeol Natur Hist Mag 41*, 424

Goodburn, R. 1972 *The Roman Villa, Chedworth* (Nat Trust, London)

Goodburn, R. & Bartholomew, P. eds. 1976 *Aspects of the Notitia Dignitatum* (BAR Supp 15, Oxford)

Goodchild, R. 1953 'The Curse and the Ring', *Antiquity 27*, 100–02

Goodenough, Erwin 1953–1958 *Jewish Symbols in the Graeco–Roman World* (8 vols: Bollingen Foundation, N.Y.)

Gose, E. 1958 *Katalog der Frühchristlichen Inschriften in Trier* (= Rhein. Landesmus. Trier, Trierer Grabungen u.Forschungen, III) (Berlin)

Gould, J. 1973 'Letocetum, Christianity, and Lichfield', *Trans S Staffordshire Archaeol Hist Soc 14*, 30–1

Grabar, A. 1946 *Martyrium* (2 vols., 1943–46) (Paris)

Grabar, A. 1967 *The Beginnings of Christian Art 200–395* (= Engl transl of 1966 French orig) (London)

Green, C.S.J. 1977 'The significance of plaster burials for the recognition of Christian cemeteries', in: Reece, R., ed. (1977), 46–53

Green, C.S.J. 1979 *Poundbury – A Summary of Recent Excavations at Poundbury, Dorchester* (Dorchester)

Green, M.J. 1976 *The Religions of Civilian Roman Britain* (BAR 24, Oxford)

Green, M.J. 1977 'Theomorphism, and the role of divine animals in Romano–British cult art', in: Munby J. & Henig M. eds. (1977), 297–326

Greene, D. 1968 'Some Linguistic Evidence relating to the British Church', in: Barley M.W. & Hanson R.P.C., eds. (1968), 75–86

Greene, K. 1974 'A Christian Monogram from Richborough, Kent', *Britannia 5*, 393–5

Grimes, W.F. 1956 'Excavations in the City of London', in: Bruce-Mitford, R.L.S., ed. (1956), 111–44

Grimes, W.F. 1968 *The Excavation of Roman and Medieval London* (London)

Grosjean, P. 1957 'Notes d'hagiographie celtique', *Analecta Bollandiana 75*, 158–226

Grosjean, P. 1958a 'Les Pictes Apostates dans l'Épitre de S. Patrice', *Analecta Bollandiana 76*, 354–78

Grosjean, P. 1958b 'The Confession of St Patrick', in: Ryan, J., ed. (1958), 81–94

Grover, J.W. 1867 'Pre-Augustine Christianity in Britain, as indicated by the discovery of Christian symbols', *J Brit Archaeol Ass, 1 ser 23*, 221–33

Guy, C. 1977 'The Lead Tank from Ashton', *Durobrivae 5*, 10–11

Haarhoff, T.J. 1958 *Schools of Gaul* (Witwatersrand Univ., Johannesburg)

Haddan, A.W., & Stubbs, W. 1871 *Councils and Ecclesiastical Documents relating to Great Britain and Ireland*, (3 vols., 1859–1871) (Oxford)

Hamp, E.P. 1975 'Social Gradience in British Spoken Latin', *Britannia 6*, 150–62

Hanson, R.P.C. 1968 *Saint Patrick – His Origins and Career* (Oxford)

Hanson, R.P.C. 1970 'The Church in Fifth-Century Gaul: Evidence from Sidonius Apollinaris', *J Eccles Hist 21*, 1–10

Hanson, R.P.C. 1977 'The D-Text of Patrick's *Confessio*: Original or Reduction?', *Proc Roy Ir Acad C 77*, 251–6

Hanson, R.P.C. 1978 'The Date of St Patrick', *Bull John Rylands Lib Univ Manchester 6*, 60–77

Harbison, P. 1970 'How Old is Gallarus Oratory?' *Medieval Archaeol 14*, 34–59

Harden, D.B. 1960 'The Wint Hill Hunting Bowl and Related Glasses', *J Glass Stud 2*, 45–82

Hassall, M.W.C. 1976 'Britain in the *Notitia*', in; Goodburn R. & Bartholomew P. eds. (1976), 103–18

Haverfield, F. 1914 'Roman Silver in Northumberland', *J Roman Stud 4*, 1–12

Hawkes, C.F.C. 1947 'Roman Ancaster, Horncastle and Caistor', *Archaeol J 103*, 17–25

Hawkes, S.C. 1961 'Soldiers and Settlers in Britain, Fourth to Fifth Century', *Medieval Archaeol 5*, 1–70

Hawkes, S.C. 1973 'A Late Roman Buckle from Tripontium', *Trans Birmingham Warwickshire Archaeol Soc 85*, 146–59

Hawkes, S.C. 1976 'A Late-Roman Nail-Cleaner with Peacock', *Durobrivae 4*, 17–18

Hawkes, S.C. 1979 'Eastry in Anglo-Saxon Kent: Its Importance, and a Newly-Found Grave', in: Hawkes, S.C., Brown, D. & Campbell, J., eds. (1979), 81–113

Hawkes, S.C., Brown D, & Campbell J. eds., 1979 *Anglo-Saxon Studies in Archaeology and History I* (BAR 72, Oxford)

Hayes, J.W. 1972 *Late Roman Pottery* (London)

Heighway, C.M., Garrod, A.P. & Vince, A.G. 1979 'Excavations at 1 Westgate Street, Gloucester, 1975', *Medieval Archaeol 23*, 159–213

Henderson, I. 1967 *The Picts* (London)

Henig, M. 1974 *A corpus of Roman engraved gemstones from British sites* (BAR 8, Oxford)

Henry, F. 1956 'Irish Enamels of the Dark Ages and the cloisonné techniques', in: Harden, D.B., ed., *Dark-Age Britain* (London), 71–88

Heurgon, J. 1951 'The Amiens Patera', *J Roman Stud 41*, 22–30

Hewitt, A.T.M. 1971 *Roman Villa, West Park, Rockbourne...Report* (Fordingbridge, Hants)

Higham, N.J. 1978 'Continuity Studies in the First Millenium AD in North Cumbria', *Northern History 14*, 1–18

Higham, N.J. 1979 'Continuity in North-West England in the First Millenium A.D.', in: Higham, N.J., ed., *The Changing Past* (Dept Extra-Mur Stud Univ Manchester), 43–52

Hill, D.H. 1977 'Continuity from Roman to Medieval: Britain', in: Barley, M.W., ed. (1977), 293–302

Hillgarth, J. 1962 'Visigothic Spain and Early Christian Ireland', *Proc Roy Ir Acad C 62*, 167–94

Hind, J.F.G. 1980 '*Elmet* and *Deira* – Forest Names in Yorkshire?' *Bull Board Celtic Stud 28*, 541–52

Hoare, F.R. 1954 *The Western Fathers* (London)

Hogan, E. 1910 *Onomasticon Goidelicum* (Dublin & London)

Hogg, A.H.A. 1964 'The Survival of Romano–British Place-Names in Southern Britain', *Antiquity 38*, 296–9

Hogg, A.H.A. 1965 'Rheged and Brigantia', *Antiquity 39*, 53–5

Hogg, A.H.A. 1974 'The Llantwit Major Roman Villa: A Reconsideration of the Evidence', *Britannia 5*, 225–50

Hood, A.B.E. 1978 *St Patrick. His Writings and Muirchu's Life* (= Arthurian Period Sources 9) (London & Chichester)

Hope-Taylor, B. 1979 *Yeavering. An Anglo-British Centre of Early Northumbria* (London)

Howorth, H.H. 1913 *St Augustine of Canterbury* (London)

Hubert, J., Porcher, J., & Volbach, W.F. 1969 *Europe in the Dark Ages* (= Engl transl of 1967 French orig) (London)

Hughes, K. 1972 *Early Christian Ireland: Introduction to the Sources* (London)

Huskinson, J. 1974 'Some pagan mythological figures and their significance in early Christian art', *Papers Brit School Rome 42*, 68–97

Jackson, K.H. 1948 'On some Romano–British place-names', *J Roman Stud 38*, 54–8

Jackson, K.H. 1953 *Language and History in Early Britain* (= LHEB) (Edinburgh)

Jackson, K.H. 1954 'The British Language during the Period of the English Settlements', in: Chadwick, N.K., ed. (1954a), 61–82

Jackson, K.H. 1955a 'The Britons in Southern Scotland', *Antiquity 29*, 77–88

Jackson, K.H. 1955b 'The Pictish Language', in: Wainwright, F.T., ed. (1955), 129–60

Jackson, K.H. 1958a 'The Sources for the Life of St Kentigern', in: Chadwick, N.K., ed. (1958a), chap. vi

Jackson, K.H. 1958b 'The Site of Mount Badon', *J Celtic Stud 2*, 152–5

Jackson, K.H. 1963 'Angles and Britons in Northumbria and Cumbria', in: Lewis, H. ed., *Angles and Britons* (Cardiff, 1963), 60–84

Jackson, K.H. 1969 *The Gododdin: The Oldest Scottish Poem* (Edinburgh)

Jackson, K.H. 1970 'Romano–British Names in the Antonine Itinerary', *Britannia* 1, 68–82

Jackson, K.H. 1973 'The British languages and their evolution', in: Daiches, D. & Thorlby, A., eds., *Literature and Western Civilisation: II, the Medieval World* (London, 1973), 113–26

Jalland, T.G. 1941 *The Life and Times of St Leo the Great* (London)

Jarrett, M.G. 1956 (Note on stone from Maryport) *J Roman Stud* 46, 148

Jarrett, M.G. & Dobson, B., eds. 1965 *Britain and Rome: Essays Presented to Eric Birley on his Sixtieth Birthday* (Kendal)

Jedin, H., Latourette, K.S. & Martin, J. 1970 *Atlas zur Kirchengeschichte – Die Christlichen Kirchen in Geschichte und Gegenwart* (Freiburg)

Jenkins, F. 1965 'St Martin's Church at Canterbury; a survey of the earliest structural features', *Medieval Archaeol* 9, 11–15

Jenkins, F. 1976 'Preliminary Report on the Excavations at the Church of St Pancras at Canterbury', *Canterbury Archaeology 1975–76*, 4–5

Jensen, G.F. 1977 'Place-Names and Settlement History: a Review with a select bibliography of works mostly published since 1960', *Northern History 13*, 1–26

Jessup, R.F. 1959 'Barrows and Walled Cemeteries in Roman Britain', *J Brit Archaeol Ass, 3 ser 22*, 1–32

John, E. 1970 'The Social and Political Problems of the Early English Church', in: Thirsk, J., ed., *Land, Church & People – Essays Presented to Prof. H.P.R. Finberg (= Agr Hist Rev, 18 suppl)*, 39–63

Johns, C. & Carson, R.A.G. 1975 'The Waternewton Hoard', *Durobrivae 3*, 10–12

Johnson, S. 1980 *Late Roman Britain* (London)

Johnston, D.E. 1977 'The Central Southern Group of Romano–British Mosaics', in: Munby, J. & Henig, M., eds. (1977), 195–215

Johnstone, P.K. 1962 'A Consular Chronology of Dark Age Britain', *Antiquity* 36, 102–09

Jones, A.H.M. 1959 'Were Ancient Heresies National or Social Movements in Disguise?', *J Theol Stud n.s. 10*, 280–98

Jones, A.H.M. 1963 'The Social Background to the Struggle Between Paganism and Christianity' in: Momigliano, A, ed. (1963), 17–37

Jones, A.H.M. 1964 *The Later Roman Empire 284–602*, 3 vols. (Oxford)

Jones, A.H.M. 1968 'The Western Church in the Fifth and Sixth Centuries', in: Barley, M.W. & Hanson, R.P.C., eds. (1968), 9–18

Jones, G.R.J. 1975 'Early Territorial Organisation in Elmet and Gwynedd', *Northern History 10*, 3–27

Jones, G.R.J. 1976 'Historical Geography and Our Landed Heritage', *Univ Leeds Review 19*, 53–78

Jones, M.E. 1979 'Climate, nutrition and disease; an hypothesis of Romano–British population', in: Casey, P.J., ed. (1979), 231–51

Kelleher, J.V. 1962 'Early Irish History and Pseudo-History', *Studia Hibernica* 3, 113–27

Kenney, J.F. 1929 *The Sources for the Early History of Ireland: I, Ecclesiastical* (New York)

Kent, J.P.C. & Painter, K.S. 1977 *Wealth of the Roman World – Gold and Silver* AD *300–700* (British Museum, London)

Kerlouégan, F. 1968 'Le Latin du *De Excidio Britanniae* de Gildas', in: Barley, M.W. & Hanson, R.P.C., eds. (1968), 151–76

Khatchatrian, A. 1962 *Les baptistères paléochrétiens; plans, notices et bibliographie* (Paris)

Kirby, D.P. 1962 'Strathclyde and Cumbria: a survey of historical development to 1092', *Trans Cumberland Westmorland Antiq Archaeol Soc, n.s. 62, 77–*

Kirby, D.P. 1966 'Bede's Native Sources for the *Historia Ecclesiastica*' *Bull John Rylands Lib Univ Manchester 48,* 341–71

Kirby, D.P. 1973 'Bede and the Pictish Church', *Innes Review 24,* 6–25

Kirby, D.P. 1976a 'British Dynastic History in the Pre-Viking Period', *Bull Board Celtic Stud 27,* 81–113

Kirby, D.P. 1976b '…per universas Pictorum provincias', in: Bonner, G., ed. (1976), 286–313

Krämer, K. 1974 *Die Frühchristlichen Grabinschriften Triers* (= Trierer Grabungen u. Forschungen, 7) (Mainz)

Krämer, W. 1958 *Neue Ausgrabungen in Deutschland* (Berlin)

Krautheimer, R. 1965 *Early Christian and Byzantine Architecture* (Pelican History of Art)

Krautheimer, R. 1979 *Rome: Profile of a City* (Princeton)

Laing, L.R. 1969 'Dark Age timber halls in Britain – some problems', *Trans Dumfriesshire Galloway Natur Hist Antiq Soc 46,* 110–127

Laistner, M.L.W. 1935 'The Library of the Venerable Bede', in: Thompson, A.H., ed. *Bede. His Life, Times and Writing* (Oxford, 1935), 237–66

Last, H. 1952 'The Rotas-Sator Square; present position and future prospects', *J Theol Stud n.s. 3,* 92–97

Leach, P. 1975 *Interim Report, Ilchester 1975* (CRAAGS, Bristol)

Leask, H.G. 1955–60 *Irish Churches and Monastic Buildings,* 3 vols. (Dundalk)

Lehner, H. 1978 'Die Ausgrabungen in der Kirche Biel-Mett (BE)', *Archäologie der Schweiz 1,* 149–54

Levison, W. 1941 'St Alban and St Albans', *Antiquity 15,* 337–59

Lewis, M.J.T. 1966 *Temples in Roman Britain* (Cambridge)

Liebeschuetz, W. 1963 'Did the Pelagian Movement have Social Aims?', *Historia 12,* 227–41

Liebeschuetz, W. 1967 'Pelagian evidence in the Last Period of Roman Britain', *Latomus 26,* 436–47

Lindsay, J. 1948 *Song of a Falling World: Culture during the Break-up of the Roman Empire (*A.D. *350–600)* (London)

Lindsay, J. 1958 *Arthur and His Times* (London)

Liversidge, J. 1959 'A New Hoard of Romano–British Pewter from Icklingham', *Proc Cambridge Antiq Soc 52,* 6–10

Liversidge, J. 1977 'Recent Developments in Romano–British Wall Painting', in: Munby J. & Henig M., eds. (1977), 75–104

Lucas, A.T. 1967 'The Plundering and Burning of Churches in Ireland, 7th to 16th century', in: Rynne, E., ed. *North Munster Studies* (Limerick, 1967), 172–229

Mâle, E. 1950 *La Fin du Paganisme en Gaule, et les plus anciennes basiliques chrétiennes* (Paris)

Mann, J.C. 1961 'The administration of Roman Britain', *Antiquity, 35*, 316–20

Mann, J.C. 1971 'Spoken Latin in Britain as evidenced in the Inscriptions', *Britannia 2*, 218–224

Mann, J.C. 1974 'The Northern Frontier after A.D. 369', *Glasgow Archaeol J 3*, 34–42

Mann, J.C. 1976 'What was the Notitia Dignitatum for?' in: Goodburn R. & Bartholomew P., eds. (1976), 1–9

Mann, J.C. & Jarrett, M.G. 1967 'The Division of Britain', *J Roman Stud 57*, 61–4

Markus, R.A. 1974 *Christianity in the Roman World* (London)

Maxwell, G.S. 1976 'Casus Belli: Native Pressures and Roman Policy', *Scot Archaeol Forum 7* (Edinburgh), 31–50

Meates, G.W. 1955 *Lullingstone Roman Villa* (London)

Meates, G.W. 1956 'The Lullingstone Roman Villa', in: Bruce-Mitford, R.L.S., ed. (1956), 87–110

Meates, G.W. 1979 *The Roman Villa at Lullingstone, Kent. Vol. I: The Site* (Kent Archaeol Soc)

Merrifield, R. 1977 'Art and Religion in Roman London: an inquest on the sculptures of Londinium', in: Munby, J. & Henig, M., eds. (1977), 375–406

Miller, M. 1975a 'Historicity and the Pedigrees of the Northcountrymen', *Bull Board Celt Stud 26*, 255–80

Miller, M. 1975b 'Relative and Absolute Publication Dates of Gildas's *De Excidio* in Medieval Scholarship', *Bull Board Celtic Stud 26*, 169–74

Miller, M. 1975c 'Stilicho's Pictish War', *Britannia 6*, 141–50

Miller, M. 1975d 'Bede's Use of Gildas', *Engl Hist Rev 90*, 241–61

Miller, M. 1976 'Date-Guessing and Pedigrees', *Studia Celtica 10/11*, 96–109

Miller, M. 1977 'Starting to Write History: Gildas, Bede and Nennius', *Welsh Hist Rev 8*, 456–65

Miller, M. 1978a 'Date-Guessing and Dyfed', *Studia Celtica 12/13*, 33–61

Miller, M. 1978b 'The Foundation-Legend of Gwynedd in the Latin Texts', *Bull Board Celtic Stud 27*, 515–32

Miller, M. 1978c 'The last British entry in the *Gallic Chronicles*', *Britannia 9*, 315–18

Moeller, W.O. 1973 *The Mithraic Origins of the Rotas/Sator Word-Square* (Leiden)

Mohrmann, C. 1961 *The Latin of St Patrick* (Dublin)

Momigliano, A., ed. 1963 *The Conflict between Paganism and Christianity in the Fourth Century* (Oxford)

Morgan, (Rev.) D. 1969 *St Bride's Church, Fleet Street, in the City of London* (St Bride's Restoration Fund)

Morris, J.R. 1965a 'Pelagian Literature', *J Theol Stud n.s. 16*, 26–60

Morris, J.R. 1965b 'Dark Age Dates', in: Jarrett, M.G. & Dobson B., eds. (1965), 145–85

Morris, J.R. 1966 'The Dates of the Celtic Saints', *J Theol Stud n.s. 17*, 342–91

Morris, J.R. 1968a 'The date of St Alban', *Hertfordshire Archaeol I*, 1–8

Morris, J.R. 1968b 'The Literary Evidence', in: Barley, M.W. & Hanson, R.P.C., eds. (1968), 55–74

Morris, J.R. 1973 *The Age of Arthur: A History of the British Isles from 350 to 650* (London)

Munby, J. & Henig, M., eds. 1977 *Roman Life and Art in Britain*, 2 vols. (BAR 41, Oxford)

Murray, M. 1977 'Art and the Early Church', *J. Theol Stud n.s.* 27, 303–45

Myres, J.N.L. 1960 'Pelagius and the End of Roman Rule in Britain', *J Roman Stud 50*, 21–36

McCarthy, M. 1979 'Carlisle', *Curr Archaeol 6.9(= 68)*, 268–72

MacDonald, J.L. 1977 'Pagan religions and burial practices in Roman Britain', in: Reece, R., ed. (1977), 35–38

Mackreth, D.F. 1979 'Durobrivae', *Durobrivae 7*, 19–21

McNamara, M. 1973 'Psalter Text and Psalter Study in the Early Irish Church (AD 600–1200)', *Proc Roy Ir Acad C 73*, 201–98

MacNeill, E. 1923 'Silua Focluti', *Proc Roy Ir Acad C 36*, 249–55

MacNeill, E. (ed. Ryan, J.) 1964 *Saint Patrick* (Dublin)

MacQueen, J. 1961 *St Nynia – a study of literary and linguistic evidence* (Edinburgh)

MacQueen, J. 1962 'History and Miracle Stories in the Biography of Nynia', *Innes Review 13*, 115–29

MacQueen, W. 1960 'Miracula Nynie Episcopi', *Trans Dumfriesshire Galloway Natur Hist Antiq Soc 38*, 21–57

McRoberts, D. 1965 'The ecclesiastical significance of the St Ninian's Isle Treasure', in: Small, A., ed., *The Fourth Viking Congress* (Aberdeen 1965), 224–46

McRoberts, D. 1973 'The Death of St Kentigern of Glasgow', *Innes Review 24*, 43–50

Nash-Williams, V.E. 1930 'Further Excavations at Caerwent, Monmouthshire, 1923–5', *Archaeol Cambrensis 80*, 229–88

Nash-Williams, V.E. 1950 *The Early Christian Monuments of Wales* (= ECMW) (Cardiff)

Nash-Williams, V.E. 1953 'Excavations at Caerwent and Caerleon', *Bull Board Celtic Stud 15*, 165

Noll, R. 1954 *Frühes Christentum in Oesterreich* (Vienna)

Norman, A.F. 1971 'Religion in Roman York', in: Butler, R.M., ed. (1971), 143–51

O'Kelly, M.J. 1958 'Church Island near Valencia, Co. Kerry', *Proc Roy Ir Acad C 59*, 57–136

O'Kelly, M.J. 1975 *Archaeological Survey and Excavation of St Vogue's Church, etc., Carnsore, Co. Wexford* (Electricity Supply Bd, Dublin)

O'Rahilly, C. 1924 *Ireland and Wales: Their Historical and Literary Relations* (London)

O'Rahilly, T.F. 1942 *The Two Patricks. A Lecture on the History of Christianity in Fifth-Century Ireland* (Dublin)

O'Rahilly, T.F. 1946 *Early Irish History and Mythology* (Dublin)

Ó Ríordáin, S.P. 1947 'Roman Material in Ireland', *Proc Roy Ir Acad C 51*, 35–82

O'Sullivan, D.M. 1980 *A Reassessment of the Early Christian Archaeology of Cumbria* (MPhil thesis, Dept of Archaeol, University of Durham)

O'Sullivan, T.D. 1978 *The De Excidio of Gildas – its authenticity and date* (Columbia Studies in the Classical Tradition, vii) (Brill, Leiden)

Oulton, J.E.L. 1940 *The Credal Statements of St Patrick* (Dublin)

Padel, O.J. 1978 'Cornish names of Parish Churches', *Cornish Studies* 4/5 15–27

Painter, K.S. 1964 'Excavation of the Roman Villa at Hinton St Mary, 1964', *Proc Dorset Natur Hist Archaeol Soc 86*, 150–4

Painter, K.S. 1965a 'Excavation of the Roman Villa at Hinton St Mary, Dorset, 1965', *Proc Dorset Natur Hist Archaeol Soc 87*, 102–03

Painter, K.S. 1965b 'A Roman silver treasure from Canterbury', *J Brit Archaeol Ass, 3 ser 28*, 1–15

Painter, K.S. 1968 'The Roman site at Hinton St Mary, Dorset' *Brit Mus Q 32*, 15–31

Painter, K.S. 1969 'The Lullingstone Wall-Plaster: An Aspect of Christianity in Roman Britain' *Brit Mus Q 33*, 131–50

Painter, K.S. 1971a 'Villa and Christianity in Roman Britain', *Brit Mus Q 35*, 157–75

Painter, K.S. 1971b 'A Roman silver spoon from Biddulph, Staffordshire' *Antiq J 51*, 323–4

Painter, K.S. 1973 'The Mildenhall Treasure: a Reconsideration' *Brit Mus Q 37*, 154–80

Painter, K.S. 1975a 'A Roman Christian silver treasure from Biddulph, Staffordshire', *Antiq J 55*, 62–9

Painter, K.S. 1975b 'A Fourth-Century Christian Silver Treasure found at Water Newton, England, in 1975' *Rivista di Archeologia Cristiana 3–4*, 333–45

Painter, K.S. 1976a 'The Design of the Roman Mosaic at Hinton St Mary', *Antiq J 56*, 49–54

Painter, K.S. 1976b 'The Waternewton Silver Treasure', *Durobrivae 4*, 7–9

Painter, K.S. 1977a *The Mildenhall Treasure: Roman Silver from East Anglia* (Brit Mus, London)

Painter, K.S. 1977b *The Water Newton Early Christian Silver* (Brit Mus, London)

Palmer, L.R. 1961 *The Latin Language*, 3rd corr. impr. (London)

Patten, T. 1974 'The Roman cemetery on London Road, Carlisle', *Trans Cumberland Westmorland Antiq Archaeol Soc n.s. 74*, 8–13

Pearce, S.M. 1978 *The Kingdom of Dumnonia – Studies in History and Tradition in South Western Britain AD 350–1150* (Padstow)

Peeters, C.J.A.C. 1969 *De liturgische dispositie van het Vroegchristelijk Kerkgebouw* (Assen)

Perrat, C. 1962 'Listes épiscopales et premiers édifices chrétiens de Lyon', in: *Hommage à Albert Grenier (Coll. Latomus)* (Bruxelles, 1962), 1213–71

Phillips, D. 1975 'Excavations at York Minster, 1967–73', *Friends of York Minster 46 Ann Rep 1975*, 19–27

Piggott, S. 1968 *The Druids* (London)

Plummer, C. 1896 *Venerabilis Baedae Opera Historica*, 2 vols. (Oxford)

Powell, D. 1972 'St Patrick's Confession and the Book of Armagh' *Analecta Bollandiana* 90, 371–85

Price, J. 1978 'Trade in Glass', in: Du Plat Taylor, J. & Cleere, H., eds, *Roman Shipping and Trade: Britain and the Rhine Provinces* (CBA RR 24, London), 70–8

Prinz, O. 1960 *Itinerarium Egeriae – Peregrinatio Aetheriae*, 5th edn. (Heidelberg)

Radford, C.A.R. 1935 'Tintagel; the Castle and Celtic Monastery, Interim Report', *Antiq J* 15, 401–19

Radford, C.A.R. 1950 'Excavations at Whithorn, 1949', *Trans Dumfriesshire Galloway Natur Hist Antiq Soc* 27, 85–126

Radford, C.A.R. 1951 'St Ninian's Cave', *Trans Dumfriesshire Galloway Natur Hist Antiq Soc* 28, 96–8

Radford, C.A.R. 1957 'Excavations at Whithorn (Final Report)', *Trans Dumfriesshire Galloway Natur Hist Antiq Soc* 34, 131–94

Radford, C.A.R. 1967 'The Early Church in Strathclyde and Galloway', *Medieval Archaeol* 11, 105–26

Radford, C.A.R. 1968 'The Archaeological Background on the Continent', in: Barley, M.W. & Hanson, R.P.C., eds. (1968), 19–36

Radford, C.A.R. 1971 'Christian Origins in Britain', *Medieval Archaeol* 15, 1–12

Radford, C.A.R. 1975 *The Early Christian Inscriptions of Dumnonia* (Cornwall Archaeol Soc, 1975)

Radford, C.A.R. 1977 'The earliest Irish Churches', *Ulster J Archaeol* 40, 1–11

Raftery, B. 1969 'A late Ogham inscriptions from Co. Tipperary', *J Roy Soc Antiq Ireland* 99, 161–4

Rahtz, P.A. 1968 'Sub-Roman Cemeteries in Somerset', in: Barley M.W. & Hanson, R.P.C., eds. (1968), 193–6

Rahtz, P.A. 1971 'Castle Dore – a re-appraisal of the post-Roman structures', *Cornish Archaeol* 10, 49–54

Rahtz, P.A. 1977 'Late Roman cemeteries and beyond', in: Reece, R., ed: (1977), 53–64

Rahtz, P.A. 1978 'Grave orientation', *Archaeol J* 135, 1–14

Rahtz, P.A. & Watts, L. 1979 'The end of Roman temples in the west of Britain', in: Casey, P.J. ed. (1979), 183–201

Ramm, H.G. 1971 'The end of Roman York', in: Butler, R.M., ed. (1971), 179–200

Reece, R., ed. 1977 *Burial in the Roman World* (CBA RR 22, London)

Reynaud, J-F. & Vicherd, G. 1976 'Fouilles récentes de l'ancienne Eglise Saint-Laurent de Choulans, a Lyon', *Comptes Rendus de l'Académie des Inscriptions & Belles-Lettres* (Paris 1976) 460–91

Richards, M. 1960 'The Irish settlement in south-west Wales – a topographical approach', *J Roy Soc Antiq Ireland* 90, 133–52

Richards, M. 1962 'Welsh *Meid(i)r*, *Moydir*, Irish *Bóthar*, "Lane, Road"' *Lochlann* 2, 129–34

Richmond, I.A. 1935 'The Rudge Cup: II, The Inscription', *Archaeol Aeliana*, 4 ser 12, 334–42

Richmond, I.A. 1956 'The Cult of Mithras and its temple at Carrawburgh on

Hadrian's Wall', in: R.L.S. Bruce-Mitford, ed. (1956), 65–86

Richmond, I.A., ed. 1958 *Roman and Native in North Britain* (Edinburgh & London)

Richmond, I.A. 1959 'The Roman Villa at Chedworth, 1959–59', *Trans Bristol Gloucestershire Archaeol Soc 78*, 5–31

Richmond, I.A. & Gillam, J. 1951 'The Temple of Mithras at Carrawburgh', *Archaeol Aeliana, 4 ser 29*, 6–92

Rivet, A.L.F., ed. 1969 *The Roman Villa in Britain* (London)

Rivet, A.L.F. & Smith, C.C. 1979 *The Place-Names of Roman Britain* (London)

Robertson, A.S. 1970 'Roman Finds from Non-Roman Sites in Scotland', *Britannia 1*, 198–226

Rodwell, W.J. 1977 'Churches in a Historic Town' (= Colchester), in: Rodwell, W.J. & K., eds. *Historic Churches – A Wasting Asset* (CBA RR 19, London), 24–41

Rodwell, W.J. & Rowley T., eds. 1975 *Small Towns of Roman Britain* (BAR 15, Oxford)

Rodwell, W.J. & Wright, R.P. 1972 'A Roman-Christian Monogram from Wickford, Essex', *Antiq J 52*, 338–40

Rogers, C.F. 1903 'Baptism and Christian Archaeology', *Studia Biblica et Patristica 5* (Oxford), 239–362

Ross, Anne 1967 *Pagan Celtic Britain* (London)

Runcie, (Bp) R., ed. 1977 *Cathedral and City – St Albans ancient and modern* (St Albans)

Rutherford, A. & Ritchie, J.N.G. 1975 'The Catstane', *Proc Soc Antiq Scotland 105*, 183–8

Ryan, J., ed. 1958 *Saint Patrick* (= *Thomas Davis Lectures*) (Dublin)

Salway, P. 1965 *The Frontier People of Roman Britain* (Cambridge)

Schauman, B. 1979 'Early Irish Manuscripts' *Expedition, 21.3* (Philadelphia), 33–47

Sedgley, J.P. 1975 *The Roman Milestones of Britain* (BAR 18, Oxford)

Sennhauser, H.R. 1974 'L'Eglise primitive en Suisse et le Haut Moyen Age', *Archaeologia 66* (Dijon), 18–33

Sherlock, D. 1976 'The Roman Christian Silver Treasure from Biddulph', *Antiq J 56*, 235–7

Sherwin-White, A.N. 1952 'The Early Persecutions and Roman Law Again', *J Theol Stud n.s. 3*, 199–213

Sherwin-White, A.N. 1963 *Roman Society and Roman Law in the New Testament* (Oxford)

Sjoestedt, M-L. 1949 *Gods and Heroes of the Celts* (trans. M. Dillon, 1940 French orig) (London)

Smith, A. 1978 'St Augustine of Canterbury in History and Tradition' *Folklore 89*, 23–38

Smith, A. 1979 'Lucius of Britain: Alleged King and Church Founder' *Folklore 90*, 29–36

Smith, C.C. 1979 'Romano–British Place-Names in Bede', in: Hawkes, S.C., Brown, D. and Campbell, J., eds. (1979), 1–19

Smith, D.J. 1969 'The Mosaic Pavements' in: Rivet, A.L.F., ed. (1969), 71–126

Smith, D.J. 1977 'Mythological Figures and Scenes in Romano–British

Mosaics', in: Munby, J. & Henig, M. eds. (1977), 105–94

Smith, D.J. 1978 'Regional aspects of the winged corridor villa in Britain', in: Todd, M., ed. (1978), 117–48

Smyth, A.P. 1972 'The Earliest Irish Annals', *Proc Roy Ir Acad C* 72, 1–48

Stead, I.M. 1971 'Beadlam Roman Villa: an interim report', *Yorks Archaeol J* 43, 178–86

Steer, K.A. 1972 'Two Unrecorded Early Christian Stones', *Proc Soc Antiq Scotland 101*, 127–9

Stevens, C.E. 1937 'Gildas and the Civitates of Britain', *Engl Hist Rev 52*, 194–203

Stevens, C.E. 1941 'Gildas Sapiens', *Engl Hist Rev 56*, 353–73

Stevens, C.E. 1976 'The Notitia Dignitatum in England', in: Goodburn, R., & Bartholomew, P. eds. (1976), 211–24

Stevenson, J. 1965 *A New Eusebius – Documents Illustrative of the history of the Church to* AD *337* (London)

Stevenson, J. 1966 *Creeds, Councils and Controversies – Documents illustrative of the history of the Church* AD *337–461* (London)

Stevenson, R.B.K. 1955 'Pictish Art', in: Wainwright, F.T., ed (1955), 97–128

Stevenson, R.B.K. 1966 'Metalwork and some other objects in Scotland and their cultural affinities', in: Rivet, A.L.F., ed., *The Iron Age in Northern Britain* (Edinburgh, 1966), 17–44

Swinson, A. 1971 *The Quest for Alban* (Fraternity of the Friends of St Albans Abbey)

Taylor, H.M. & Taylor, J. 1965 *Anglo-Saxon Architecture*, vols I, II (Cambridge)

Taylor, H.M. 1978 *Anglo-Saxon Architecture*, vol. III (Cambridge)

Taylor, T. 1925 *The Life of St Samson of Dol* (London)

Thomas, C. 1959 'Imported Pottery in Dark-Age Western Britain', *Medieval Archaeol 3*, 89–111

Thomas, C. 1961 'Excavations at Trusty's Hill, Anworth, Kirkcudbs., in 1960', *Trans Dumfriesshire Galloway Natur Hist Antiq Soc 38*, 58–70

Thomas, C. 1964 'The Interpretation of the Pictish Symbols', *Archaeol J 120*, 31–97

Thomas, C. 1966 'Ardwall Isle; the excavation of an Early Christian site of Irish type', *Trans Dumfriesshire Galloway Natur Hist Antiq Soc*, 43, 84–116

Thomas, C. 1968 'The Evidence from North Britain', in: Barley M.W. & Hanson, R.P.C., eds. (1968), 93–122

Thomas, C. 1969a 'Lundy, 1969', *Curr Archaeol 2.5 (= 16)*, 138–42

Thomas, C. 1969b 'Are These the Walls of Camelot?' *Antiquity 43*, 27–30

Thomas, C. 1971a *The Early Christian Archaeology of North Britain* (Oxford)

Thomas, C. 1971b 'Rosnat, Rostat and the Early Irish Church', *Eriu 22*, 100–06

Thomas, C. 1972 'Irish Colonies in post-Roman Western Britain: a survey of the evidence', *J Roy Inst Cornwall n.s.* 6, 251–74

Thomas, C. 1973 *Bede, Archaeology and the Cult of Relics* (Jarrow)

Thomas, C. 1976 'Imported Late-Roman Mediterranean pottery in Ireland and western Britain; chronologies and implications', *Proc Roy Ir Acad C 76*, 245–56

Thomas C. 1979a 'Saint Patrick and fifth-century Britain; an historical model explored', in: Casey, P.J., ed. (1979), 81–101

Thomas, C. 1979b 'Hermits on Islands or Priests in a Landscape', *Cornish Stud* 6, 28–44

Thomas, C. 1980 'Churches in Late Roman Britain', in: Rodwell, W.J., ed. (1980), *Roman Temples and Religion in Lowland Britain* (BAR, Oxford)

Thompson, E.A. 1956 'Zosimus on the End of Roman Britain', *Antiquity 30*, 163–7

Thompson, E.A. 1958 'The Origins of Christianity in Scotland', *Scot Hist Rev* 37, 17–22

Thompson, E.A. 1977 'Britain AD 406–410', *Britannia 8*, 303–18

Thompson, E.A. 1979 'Gildas and the History of Britain', *Britannia 10*, 203–26

Thomson, R.L. 1964 'Celtic Place-Names in Yorkshire,' *Trans Yorks Dialect Soc 11*, 41–55

Todd, J.H. 1864 *St Patrick, Apostle of Ireland* (Dublin)

Todd, M. 1975 'Margidunum and Ancaster', in: Rodwell, W.J. & Rowley, T., eds. (1975), 211–23

Todd, M. 1977 '*Famosa Pestis* and fifth-century Britain', *Britannia 8*, 319–26

Todd, M., ed. 1978 *Studies in the Romano–British Villa* (Leicester)

Toller, H. 1977 *Roman Lead Coffins and Ossuaria in Britain* (BAR 38, Oxford)

Tolstoy, N. 1962 'Who was Coroticus?' *Ir Eccles Rec 97*, 137–47

Tomlin, R.S.O. 1974 'The Date of the Barbarian Conspiracy', *Britannia 5*, 303–10

Tonnochy, A.B. & Hawkes, C.F.C. 'The Sacred Tree Motive on a Roman Bronze from Essex', *Antiq J. 11*, 123–6

Toynbee, J.C.M. 1953 'Christianity in Roman Britain' *J Brit Archaeol Ass, 3 ser* 16, 1–124

Toynbee, J.C.M. 1962 *Art in Roman Britain* (London)

Toynbee, J.C.M. 1964a *Art in Britain under the Romans* (Oxford)

Toynbee, J.C.M. 1964b 'The Christian Roman Mosaic, Hinton St Mary, Dorset', *Proc Dorset Natur Hist Antiq Soc 85*, 116–21

Toynbee, J.C.M. 1964c 'A New Roman Pavement found in Dorset', *J Roman Stud 54*, 1–14

Toynbee, J.C.M. 1968 'Pagan Motifs and Practices in Christian Art and Ritual in Roman Britain' in: Barley, M.W. & Hanson, R.P.C., eds. (1968), 177–92

Toynbee, J.C.M. 1971 *Death and Burial in the Roman World* (London)

Traube, L. 1907 *Nomina Sacra* (Munich)

Turner, B.R.G. 1979 'Roman Christians at Witham', *Rescue News 18*, 2

Van der Meer, F. & Mohrmann, C. 1958 *Atlas of the Early Christian World* (London)

Vendryes, J. 1956 'Sur un emploi du mot AINM 'nom' en Irlandais', *Études Celtiques 7*, 139–46

Victory, S. 1977 *The Celtic Church in Wales* (London)

Vieillard-Troiekouroff, M. 1976 *Les monuments de la Gaule d'après les oeuvres de Grégoire de Tours* (Paris)

Wacher, J.S., ed. 1966 *The Civitas Capitals of Roman Britain* (Leicester)

Wacher, J.S. 1974 *The Towns of Roman Britain* (London)

Wacher, J.S. 1978 *Roman Britain* (London)

Wagner, H. 1971 'The Archaic *Dind Rig* Poem and Related Problems', *Ériu 28*, 1–16

Wainwright, F.T., ed. 1955 *The Problems of the Picts* (Edinburgh & London)

Walker, G.S.M. 1957 *Sancti Columbani Opera* (= *Scriptores Latini Hiberniae* 2) (Dublin)

Wall, J. 1965 & 1966 'Christian Evidences in the Roman Period: The Northern Counties, Parts I and II', *Archaeol Aeliana, 4 ser 43*, 201–25: *4 ser 44*, 147–64

Wall, J. 1968 'Christian Evidences in Roman South-West Britain', *Trans Devonshire Assoc 100*, 161–78

Walters, B. & Phillips, B. 1979 *Archaeological Excavations in Littlecote Park, Wiltshire, 1978: First Interim Report* (Littlecote Park)

Ward Perkins, J.B. 1966 'Memoria, Martyr's Tomb and Martyr's Church', *J Theol Stud n.s. 17*, 20–37

Ward Perkins, J.B. & Goodchild, R.G. 'The Christian Antiquities of Tripolitania,' *Archaeologia 95*, 1–84

Warner, R.B. 1976 'Some Observations on the Context and Importation of exotic material in Ireland, from the 1st cent. BC to the 2nd cent. AD', *Proc Roy Ir Acad C 76*, 267–92

Waterman, D.M. 1967 'The Early Christian Churches and Cemetery at Derry, Co. Down', *Ulster J Archaeol 30*, 53–75

Watson, W.J. 1926 *The History of the Celtic Place-Names of Scotland* (Edinburgh and London)

Weidemann, K. 1968 'Die Topographie von Mainz in der Römerzeit und dem Frühen Mittelalter', *Jahrbuch Röm.-German. Zentralsmuseum Mainz 15*, 146–9

Weidemann, K. 1970 'Zur Topographie von Metz in der Römerzeit und im frühen Mittelalter', *Jahrbuch Röm.-German. Zentralsmuseum Mainz, 17*, 147–71

Wells, C. 1960 'A study of cremation', *Antiquity 34*, 29–37

Wenham, L.P. 1968 *The Romano–British Cemetery at Trentholme Drive, York* (London)

West, S.C. 1976 'The Roman Site at Icklingham', *East Anglian Archaeol 3*, 63–126

Wheeler, R.E.M. 1935 *London and the Saxons* (London)

Wheeler, R.E.M. 1946 *London in Roman Times* (London)

Wheeler, R.E.M. & Wheeler, T.V. 1932 *Report on the Excavations of the Prehistoric, Roman, and Post-Roman Site in Lydney Park, Gloucs.*, (Soc of Antiq RR 9, London)

Wheeler, R.E.M. & Wheeler, T.V. 1936 *Verulamium. A Belgic and Two Roman Cities* (Soc of Antiq RR 11, London)

Whitaker, E.C. 1960 *Documents of the Baptismal Litany* (London)

White, N.J.D. 1905 'Libri Sancti Patricii: the Latin writings of St Patrick', *Proc Roy Ir Acad C 25*

White, N.J.D. 1918a *Libri Sancti Patricii. The Latin Writings of St Patrick* (= Texts for Students 4) (London)

White, N.J.D. 1918b *A Translation of the Latin Writings of St Patrick* (Texts for Students 5) (London)

Whitelock, D. 1976 'Bede and His Teachers and His Friends', in: Bonner, G., ed. (1976), 19–39

Whitwell, J.B. 1970 *Roman Lincolnshire* (= History of Lincolnshire II) (Lincoln)

Wightman, E.M. 1970 *Roman Trier and the Treveri* (London)

Wild, J.P. 1972 *The Romans in the Nene Valley* (Peterborough)

Wild, J.P. 1976 'Loanwords and Roman expansion in north-west Europe', *World Archaeol 8.1*, 57–64

Wilkinson, J. 1971 *Egeria's Travels, newly translated, etc.* (London)

Williams, H. 1901 *Gildas: The Ruin of Britain, etc.* (London)

Williams, H. 1903 'Heinrich Zimmer on the History of the Celtic Church', *Zeitschrift für Celtische Philologie 4*, 527–74

Williams, H. 1912 *Christianity in Early British* (Oxford)

Wilson, D.R. 1968 'An Early Christian Cemetery at Ancaster', in: Barley, M.W. & Hanson, R.P.C., eds. (1968), 197–200

Wilson, D.R. 1975 'Romano–Celtic Temple Architecture', *J Brit Archaeol Ass, 3 ser 38*, 3–27

Wilson, P.A. 1964 'St Ninian and Candida Casa: Literary Evidence from Ireland', *Trans Dumfries Galloway Nat Hist Antiq Soc 41*, 156–85

Wilson, P.A. 1966a 'Romano–British and Welsh Christianity: Continuity or Discontinuity?' *Welsh Hist Rev 3*, 5–21, 103–20

Wilson, P.A. 1966b 'On the use of the terms Strathclyde and Cumbria', *Trans Cumberland Westmorland Antiq Archaeol Soc n.s. 66*, 57–92

Wilson, P.A. 1968 'Eaglesfield; the place, the name, the burials', *Trans Cumberland Westmorland Antiq Archaeol Soc. n.s. 78*, 47–54

Winterbottom, M. 1979 (ed. transl.) *Gildas: The Ruin of Britain and other works* (= Arthurian Sources 7) (London & Chichester)

Wright, R.P. 1975 'A Roman–Christian Monogram from York Minster', *Antiq J 55*, 129–30

Zimmerman, W. 1958 'Ecclesia lignea und ligneis tabulis fabricata', *Bonner Jahrbuch 158*, 441–47

References

1 **The Approach and the Religious Background**
(*pages 17–34*)
1 Toynbee 1953; Frend 1955
2 R.G. Collingwood, *The Idea of History* (Oxford 1946)
3 E.H. Carr, *What Is History?* (1962), 24
4 Collingwood (1946), 252ff.
5 Thomas 1973
6 Collingwood (1946), pt. v (*passim*)
7 Sedgley 1975
8 M.L. Ryder, 'The History of Sheep Breeds in Britain', *Agric. Hist. Review*, 12 (1964), 1–12, 65–82; 'Parchment: its History, Manufacture and Composition', *Journ. Soc. Archivists*, 2 (1964), 391–9
9 Green M. 1976
10 Lewis 1966
11 Ross 1967
12 Sjoestedt 1949
13 Chadwick N.K. 1966; Piggott 1968
14 Mann, pers. comm., 1968
15 Tacitus, *Germania*, 43
16 Chandler 1978
17 Illus. Green 1976, pl. XI b, c
18 Mann, *op. cit.* n. 14
19 De Ste. Croix 1963, 11
20 Mann, in *JRS* 69 (1979), 176
21 Lewis 1966; Wilson D.R. 1975
22 Ross 1967; Green M. 1977
23 As at Caerwent – Boon 1976
24 Jessup 1959
25 Toynbee 1971, chap. iv
26 Jones A.H.M. 1964, 895
27 De Ste. Croix 1963, 17
28 Lewis 1966; Meates 1979
29 Bultmann 1956, 175–9
30 Smith D.J. 1977
31 Chandler 1978
32 Toynbee 1968
33 Green M. 1976, chap. 4
34 Bultmann 1956, 156–71
35 Jones A.H.M. 1964

2 **The Historical Evidence**
(*pages 35–60*)
1 Collingwood 1946, 49ff.
2 The bibliography of Gibbon and his critics is most complex; best accessible account is still the *Encyclopaedia Britannica* article s.n. 'Gibbon, Edward', signed 'J.B.B.' (= J.B. Bury)
3 Longmans, London, 1844; 2nd edn., 1846
4 Macmillan, London, 4 vols., 1892
5 Carr 1962, 145
6 Thompson 1979, 208
7 Haddan & Stubbs 1869–71 (3 vols.)
8 Plummer 1896
9 Williams 1903
10 Kenney 1929, 77
11 Williams 1912, 441
12 Stevens 1937; Stevens 1941
13 Morris 1973; Miller 1975b, 1975d; Dumville 1977; Winterbottom 1978; O'Sullivan 1978; Thompson 1979
14 Wheeler & Wheeler 1932
15 Wheeler & Wheeler 1936
16 Wheeler 1935
17 *Cf.* Isabel Henderson, *A list of the published writings of Hector Munro Chadwick and of Nora Kershaw Chadwick* (Cambridge 1971)
18 Toynbee 1962; Toynbee 1964
19 Barley & Hanson 1968
20 Mostly listed in Binchy 1962
21 E.g., Radford 1971; Painter 1972
22 Kent & Painter 1977
23 E.g., Grabar 1946; Grabar 1967
24 Khatchatrian 1962
25 Krautheimer 1965
26 Davies J.G. 1952; Davies J.G. 1962

27 Ward Perkins & Goodchild 1953; Ward Perkins 1966
28 Williams 1912, chap. ii
29 HE i. 4; Plummer 1896, ii. 14
30 Williams 1912, 60–6; *cf.* also Smith A. 1979
31 Haddan & Stubbs 1879–81, i. 3–13
32 Rivet & Smith 1979, 49–102
33 Williams 1912, 96–100
34 Frend 1955; Frend 1968
35 Frend 1965b, ch. xiii; documents, Stevenson 1966, index s.n. 'Arius'
36 Rivet & Smith 1979, 49–50
37 Frend 1959; Frend 1965a
38 De Ste. Croix 1963
39 *Ibid.*, 24
40 Sherwin-White 1952; Sherwin-White 1963
41 De Ste. Croix 1963, 17
42 Frend 1959, 15–16
45 E.g., Carthage – Stevenson 1965, 250
44 Bettenson 1943, 19; Stevenson 1965, 267
45 Bettenson 1943, 20–1
46 Jones A.H.M. 1963
47 Frend 1959, 18–19 & refs
48 Bettenson 1943, 21–2; Stevenson 1965, 296
49 Bettenson 1943, 22–3; Stevenson 1965, 300–02
50 Stevenson 1965, 302–04
51 Frend 1952; Frend 1965, 139ff. (origins)
52 DEB 10
53 DEB 12
54 HE i. 7
55 Smith C. 1979, 6–8
56 Williams 1912, 103
57 Williams 1901
58 Williams 1912, chap. vi
59 *Carmina* viii. 3
60 *Cf.* Morris 1973, 88–92; and see chap. 14 below
61 Levison 1941; *cf.* also Swinson 1971 and Runcie 1977
62 Morris 1968a
63 Morris 1973, 336
64 Hanson 1968, 143–5 & refs; Morris 1973, 335–8
65 So Hanson 1968, 144
66 Bieler 1952, ii. 149
67 Williams 1912, 282; Hanson 1968, 21–65; Morris 1973, 88–93, map 4, 557
68 LHEB chap. 1, esp. 13
69 *Epistolae* IX. ix, sect. 6
70 Generally treated in Williams 1912, chap. xv: Chadwick N.K. 1954b: Chadwick N.K. 1955, index s.nn.: Hanson 1968, chap. 2
71 Thompson 1968, and refs
72 Thomas 1971a, 108, fig. 50
73 Chadwick N.K. 1954c
74 Prinz 1960: Wilkinson 1971
75 Haddan & Stubbs 1879–81, i. 14
76 *Peregrinatio Egeriae* iii. 7
77 Useful bibliogr., Morris 1965; Cross & Livingstone 1977, 1059; *cf.* Stevenson 1966, 217–19 (Pelagius' doctrines)
78 Myres 1960, 21
79 Morris 1965
80 Brown P.R.L. 1967; Stevenson 1966, 222 (Augustine on Grace)
81 *Vita Germani* cap. xii
82 Myres 1960
83 Cross & Livingstone 1977, 586
84 Myres 1960, 26
85 Morris 1965, 55–6
86 Ibidem
87 Morris 1966: Morris 1973, index s.n. 'Pelagius'
88 Morris 1965, 34–6
89 Hanson 1968, 41ff.
90 Thompson 1956
91 Williams 1912, 230ff.; Chadwick N.K. 1958, 110–20
92 Myres 1960, 34; Hanson 1968, 49–51
93 Jones A.H.M. 1959, 295
94 Morris 1973
95 Liebeschuetz 1963
96 Liebeschuetz 1967
97 Thompson 1977; Thompson 1979
98 Williams 1912, 210; Haddan & Stubbs 1879–81, i. 15; Hanson 1968, 47
99 Thompson 1979, 211

3 **Languages, Literature and Art** *(pages 61–95)*

1 LHEB 5ff.; Jackson 1954
2 Jones M. 1979
3 Adams 1970 (only full-ranging discussion of this point)

4 Collingwood & Richmond 1969, 206
5 Jones A.H.M. 1964, ii. 986ff.
6 LHEB 99–100
7 Rivet & Smith 1979, 14–18
8 Greene D. 1968, 86
9 De Beer 1958 (historical origins of Swiss multilingualism)
10 LHEB 97–106; Jackson 1973
11 Cf. Birley A. 1977, 114ff.; Wacher 1978, 84, 191
12 Hanson 1968, 158–70; Frere 1978, 350–2; Rivet & Smith 1979, introduction
13 LHEB 101–05
14 Thomas 1972; LHEB *passim*
15 LHEB 105
16 Recently, Tomlin 1974
17 H. Pilch, *Studia Celtica* 6 (1971), 138ff.
18 Useful and inexpensive introductory works: Peter Trudgill, *Sociolinguistics – An Introduction* (Penguin 1974); J.B. Pride & Janet Holmes, edd., *Sociolinguistics – selected readings* (Penguin Education, 1972); David Crystal, *Linguistics* (Penguin 1971)
19 Mann 1971
20 E.g., Shiel 1975
21 Hamp 1975
22 Bloomfield 1935, 52
23 Hamp, *BBCS* 24 (1972), 481–2
24 LHEB 76–82
25 Bloomfield, 1935, chap. 26
26 Alcock 1971, 49
27 LHEB chap. 3
28 LHEB 87
29 LHEB 109: Jackson 1973, 117
30 LHEB 119
31 Faull 1978; Cameron 1980
32 Gelling 1978, chap. 3
33 Jackson 1973
34 Jones A.H.M. 1959, 287
35 Thompson 1979
36 Faull 1974; Jones G.R.J. 1975
37 LHEB 79
38 Greene D. 1968, 77
39 Green D., *op. cit.*
40 LHEB 304
41 LHEB 395
42 Mann 1971
43 Hamp 1975
44 Hamp 1975, 157
45 Hamp 1975, 159
46 LHEB 175
47 Williams 1912, 316ff.; Morris 1973, 357
48 Cross & Livingstone 1977, 169 (BIBLE, English versions)
49 Williams 1912, chaps. iv, xxiv
50 Williams 1912, 421; LHEB 269. Old Cornish *oferiat* 'priest', Welsh *offeiriad*, are particular derivatives
51 Hillgarth 1962: Dumville 1973
52 Hillgarth 1962; Thomas 1976
53 Bieler 1947; Mohrmann 1961, iii: Hanson 1968
54 Oulton 1940; Bieler 1952
55 Dumville 1973; for Jerome on the Vulgate, see Stevenson 1966, 167–8
56 Cross & Livingstone 1977, 1451
57 Bowman 1974, esp. fig. 1
58 Hanson 1968, ch. vi
59 Davies W.H. 1968, 140, n. 103
60 Bieler 1947
61 Williams 1912, chap. iv
62 McRoberts 1973
63 Armstrong & Macalister 1920; Hillgarth 1962, 183–4; McNamara 1973 – text, pp. 213–14, appendix by Maurice Sheehy; Schauman 1979
64 McNamara 1973, 214
65 Schauman 1979, 37
66 Toynbee 1968
67 Stevenson 1965; cf. however the view in Murray 1977, 306
68 De Rossi 1861
69 Branigan 1977, 109, fig. 23 (no. 369)
70 Cf. Warner, *Cornish Archaeology*, 6 (1971), 29–31, and refs
71 CIIC ii, nos. 912–15; for the Nomina Sacra, Traube 1907
72 Thomas 1971, chap. 4
73 Thomas, *op. cit.*, fig. 49: Boppert 1971 (corpus)
74 Goodenough 1953–58
75 Grabar 1967
76 Dalton 1911
77 Toynbee 1962, 64
78 Cross & Livingstone 1977, 514
79 Hewitt 1971, pl. vi (A), p. 11 – note that the 'altar' is a chip-carved table; *Britannia*, 10 (1979), 169ff.

80 Hawkes S.C. 1973
81 Toynbee 1968, 181
82 Liversidge 1977, 99, fig. 5.9
83 De Palol 1967, lam. lxxxviii; Fontaine 1973, 7
84 RCAMS (Selkirk), frontis. and p. 69
85 Toynbee 1968, 178–80

4 The Material Evidence – First Part

(pages 96–122)

1 *The Reader's Digest Complete Atlas of the British Isles* (1965), 121
2 Barley 1977; Weidemann 1968; Weidemann 1970
3 By Harlan Beach & Charles Fahs, Bartholomew (London), 1925
4 Jedin Latourette & Martin 1970
5 Van der Meer & Mohrmann 1958
6 Ross 1967
7 Lewis 1966, fig. 130
8 Green M. 1976
9 *Ibid.* 75–81
10 *Ibid.* chap. 3
11 *Ibid.* map 16; *cf.* Ross 1967, index, *s.vv.* 'Horned Deities'
12 Green M. 1976, 156–261, indexed
13 Thomas 1968 (maps): Thomas 1971a, 10–14, map fig. 1
14 E.g., Johnson S. 1980, fig. 122
15 Toynbee 1953
16 Atkinson 1951; Atkinson 1957; Toynbee 1953, 2–3, fig. 1; Moeller 1973. See also Stevenson 1965, 7–8; Last 1952
17 *Sunday Times*, 9 July 1978: *Britannia*, X (1979), 353, pl. XXb
18 *Op. cit*, 1979, n. 70
19 Brailsford 1951, 46, fig. 21: Toynbee 1953, 19, n. 6
20 Biddle Hudson & Heighway 1973, 18
21 Curle 1923
22 *Cf.* Wall 1966, 147–50
23 Bateson 1973, 63–73
24 Most fully now, Painter 1977a
25 Toynbee 1953
26 Toynbee 1962; Toynbee 1964
27 Smith D.J. 1969, fig. 3.30, 119 (refs)
28 *Ibid.*, Johnston 1977
29 Smith D.J. 1977
30 Finney 1978 (with full bibliography)
31 Listed – Smith D.J. 1969, 84(d)
32 Smith D.J. 1969, pl. 3:27
33 Detailed description, Smith D.J. 1977; Toynbee 1964, 250–2
34 Toynbee 1964b: Toynbee 1964c: Painter 1964: Painter 1965a (site re-examined): Painter 1968 (aperçu of site and pavement): Painter 1976 (new hypothesis about design)
35 Toynbee 1964b
36 Brandenburg, cited Painter 1969, n. 17; Huskinson 1974
37 Chandler 1978
38 Wacher's plan – Butler 1971, 169 fig. 24
39 Wall 1965, 214
40 Goodburn 1972, pl. 11
41 Wall 1965, 213–14
42 Rodwell & Wright 1972
43 Wright 1975
44 *Britannia* 7 (1976), 387
45 *Antiq. J.*, 7 (1927), 321–2 illus.
46 Fox 1952, 92, pl. IXA
47 Brannigan 1977; the sherd, fig. 23
48 Frend 1968, 41, 48 n. 53
49 I am grateful to Miss Catherine Johns for confirming this
50 *JRS* 50 (1960), 239
51 Kent & Painter 1977, 57 & refs
52 Painter 1971b
53 Painter 1977a, 30–1
54 Helen Waugh, *Antiq. J.*, 46 (1966), 60–71 (spoon: pl. xvii. b)
55 Engleheart 1898
56 Finberg 1972, 23
57 Brailsford 1951, 42 illus.
58 Liversidge 1959
59 Illus. also Toynbee 1962, pl. 136
60 *Cf.* Kent & Painter 1977, 42 (illus.); and Traprain, Curle 1923
61 Painter 1971b: Painter 1975a; Sherlock 1976: *Britannia*, 3 (1972) 61: *Britannia*, 7 (1976), 392
62 Charles J. Jackson, *Illustrated History of English Plate, etc.* 2 vols., London (1911): ii. 479, figs. 566–7.
63 Painter 1975a, pl. xvi: Sherlock 1976, fig. I.1
64 Painter 1965b, 11
65 Kent & Painter 1977, 42 (no. 83)
66 McRoberts 1965
67 Rivet & Smith 1979, 513

68 Dalton 1922: RCHM *Dorset* II.3 (1970), 536, 562–3 illus.
69 Kent & Painter 1977, 57
70 Haverfield 1914
71 *Ibid.*, frontisp.; *cf.* Wall 1965, 216 (refs)
72 *Observer* 15 June 1975, *Times* 11 Sept 1975, *Sunday Times* 14 Sept 1975, *Church Times* 19 Sept 1975
73 *Durobrivae* 3 (1975), 30
74 Painter 1975b
75 Painter 1976b
76 Painter 1977b
77 Johns 1977
78 See Painter 1977b, 25ff.
79 Catalogue: Kent & Painter 1977
80 *Britannia*, 7 (1976), 385–6; *Britannia*, 8 (1977), 448
81 *Cf.* Mackreth 1979 – plan
82 Johns and Carson 1975: Painter 1977b (summary): Carson 1976
83 Painter 1977b (nos. 1 to 28)
84 Best illus., Kent & Painter 1977, 31 (no. 35)
85 So Painter 1977b
86 Kent & Painter 1977, 30
87 *Britannia*, 8 (1977), 448–9, n. 147
88 Wheeler & Wheeler 1932, 101, pl. xxxiv; RIB 307
89 Kent & Painter 1977, 30
90 H. Barker *et al.* in Painter 1977b, 25–6
91 *Ibid.*
92 Wild 1972
93 Mackreth 1979
94 'probably . . . looted from a shrine somewhere on the line of Ermine Street' (RIB)
95 Toynbee 1964, 328–30, pl. lxxvi
96 Green, *Britannia*, 44 (1973), 325; in Rodwell & Rowley 1975, 201, 207–09
97 Chandler 1978
98 Curwen 1943
99 Christopher Guy, *Britannia* (forthcoming)
100 Curwen, *op. cit.*, pl. xxviiii
101 Toller 1977
102 *Ibid.*, 46–47 ('section 3')
103 West 1976
104 Guy 1977; *Britannia*, 8 (1977), 443–4
105 Toynbee 1964, 353–5

5 **The Material Evidence – Second Part**
(pages 123–142)

1 *Trans. Birmingham & Warwicks. Arch. Soc., 50* (1927), 50, pl. xiii (original note): Gould 1973
2 Boon 1962
3 *Proc. Cambs. A.S., 41* (1948), 79, pls. 26–7
4 Wheeler 1946, 25, fig. 2.i, 119
5 *Cf.* Liversidge 1959, 7
6 Clarke L.G.C. 1931: Toynbee 1962, pls. 137–8
7 Clarke, *op. cit.*, 72–3
8 Greene K. 1974
9 Hawkes 1946, 23 fig. 4; Whitwell 1970, 72; Toynbee 1964, 355
10 *JRS* 45 (1955), 147: Toynbee 1964, 355, pl. lxxxi(a)
11 *JRS* 37 (1947) 180–181
12 Toynbee 1964, 355
13 Toynbee 1953, 19, pl. V.2
14 Goddard 1922
15 Toynbee 1953, 21, fig. 7
16 Toynbee 1953, 17, with refs
17 Boon 1974, 163, fig. 24.7
18 RCHM *Eboracum*, 73, pl. 65 no. 150; Toynbee 1968, 191
19 Toynbee 1953, 17
20 Fletcher 1904; for Arius, Cross & Livingstone 1977, 87
21 *Cf.* Wall 1966, 153–6
22 Toynbee 1953, 14
23 Patten 1974; Charlesworth 1978, 124
24 *Cf.* Salway 1965, 216
25 Birley 1961a, 176
26 Green C. 1977
27 Ramm 1971
28 Green C. 1979
29 Wall 1966, 151, fig. 1
30 Toynbee 1953, 17
31 Now illus. by Henig; Munby & Henig 1977, pl. 15.iii
32 Tonnochy & Hawkes 1931
33 Hawkes S.C. 1973
34 Stead 1971
35 Hawkes S.C. 1976
36 Hawkes S.C. 1973, refs
37 Harden 1960
38 Toynbee 1962, 185–6, fig. 161
39 Price 1978; distributions generously up-dated (*in litt.*) by Jennifer Price

and Dorothy Charlesworth
40 Wall 1965, 216–25
41 Cowen 1936: Cowen 1948;
Charlesworth 1961
42 *Op. cit.*, 1965
43 Charlesworth 1979, 131 no. 20;
Henig 1974, no. 772
44 Toynbee 1953, 19; best illus., Clarke
R.R. 1960, pl. 39
45 Toynbee 1953, pl. IV.5 (shows both
ring and impression)
46 Palmer 1961, chap. vii – a crucial
discussion of the whole topic
47 Goodchild 1953; Boon 1957, 130–1
48 Wheeler & Wheeler 1932, 100, fig.
28.6
49 Dalton 1921, 58, figs. 33–4; RCHM
Dorset III.2 (1970), 94 illus.
50 Boon 1957, 131
51 Engleheart 1924, 214
52 Painter 1965b, 2 (no. 15)
53 Cunliffe 1968, 98–9; drawing, pl. xlii,
160
54 Henig; in Munby & Henig 1977, 352
55 Birley 1961b; Wall 1965, 223
56 Wall, *op. cit.*, 223 and fig. 7
57 Bede, HE i.30
58 Ellison 1978 (and later interim notes)
59 Boon 1960
60 Grimes 1956: Grimes 1968
61 Toynbee 1964, 315
62 Grimes 1968
63 Merrifield 1977; *contra*, Grimes 1956,
141
64 Richmond & Gillam 1951:
Richmond 1956: Wall 1966: Lewis
1966, 99ff.; Daniels 1967
65 In Richmond 1956, 65–9
66 Gillam & MacIvor 1954
67 Lewis 1966, 143–5
68 Cunliffe 1969, 4
69 Frend 1968, 47

6 **Churches in Late Roman
Britain – the Background**
(*pages 143–154*)
1 This, with Chap. 7, is partly
foreshadowed by Thomas 1980
2 Miller 1975b
3 DEB 3
4 DEB 12
5 DEB 24

6 Miller 1975d
7 Thompson 1979
8 DEB 26
9 DEB 66
10 Miller 1975d: *cf.* Smith C. 1979,
Campbell 1979. For the library at
Jarrow, Laistner 1935; Kirby 1966;
Whitelock 1976
11 HE, Preface
12 HE i.7
13 HE i.26
14 HE i.33
15 HE ii.14: Phillips 1975, 24
16 HE ii.16
17 Colyer & Gilmour 1978; Gilmour
1979
18 HE i.20
19 HE ii.14
20 HE ii.14
21 HE iii.17
22 Hope-Taylor 1979
23 HE iii.25
24 HE iii.4
25 Zimmerman 1958
26 Plummer 1896, I.Lxxiii, n.l
27 Eddius Stephanus, *Vita Wilfridi* cap.
17
28 *Cf.* Morris 1968: Thomas 1971a,
chap. 7
29 Wild 1976, with further refs.
30 *Cf.* Palmer 1961, esp. 183–7
31 DEB, Preface, 4, 28
32 DEB, Preface, 12, 26, 34
33 HE i.20
34 Hogan 1910, 349–54
35 Bowen 1969, 126–7, fig. 30
36 Cross & Livingstone 1977, 1392–3
37 *Confessio* 49
38 DEB 27, 28
39 Jackson 1969, 117, 130
40 On the Risley Park lanx (Catherine
Johns, forthcoming), *eclesia* may
form part of a non-British
inscription.
41 Leask 1955–60, I
42 E.g., Thomas 1971a, chap. 3
43 Harbison 1970
44 O'Kelly 1958
45 O'Kelly 1975 (the date is HAR-1380)
46 Thomas 1967
47 Thomas 1971a, chap. 4
48 Radford 1977
49 Thomas 1979b, esp. fig. 4

50 Harbison 1970, map
51 Thomas 1976, figs. 1 and 2
52 Thomas 1971a, 151
53 E.g., the 'Derry Churches', Co. Down – Waterman 1967
54 Lucas 1967; *cf.* also Murray 1979
55 Smyth 1972
56 Leask 1955–60, I.6–7
57 *Cf.* Thomas 1971a, chap. 7
58 Stokes 1887
59 Anderson & Anderson 1961
60 Radford 1977
61 Bieler 1963b, 28
62 Thomas 1971a, 145ff., fig. 65, 207ff.
63 Laing 1969
64 Morris P. 1979 (*cf.* figs. 35–41)
65 Barker 1979 (plan now in Johnson S. 1980, 165, fig. 18)
66 Rahtz 1971
67 Alcock 1971, 225–227
68 Barker 1975; Barker 1979

7 **Churches in Late Roman Britain – Analogies, Examples and Conclusions**
(*pages 155–201*)

1 Krautheimer 1965; Ward Perkins 1966
2 *Historia Francorum* (ed. O.M. Dalton 1927); *Monumenta Germaniae Historica, Scriptores Rerum Merovingicarum* series, I, *Libri historiarum* (ed. Krusch & Levison, 1937–1951), II, *Miracula et opera minora* (ed. Krusch, 1885). A good modern aperçu is 'The work of Gregory of Tours in the light of modern research', J.M. Wallace-Hadrill, *The Long-Haired Kings* (1962), chap. 3; for individual sites see Vieillard-Troiekouroff 1976
3 *HF* x.31
4 *HF* i.31
5 Wightman 1971, 229ff.
6 *Cf.* J.J. Wilkes, *Dalmatia* (1969), esp. 427ff., and fig. 16; Jedin Latourette & Martin 1970, map 17.
7 Grabar 1946; Dyggve 1951; Davies J.G. 1952; Krautheimer 1965; Peeters 1969
8 Excellent and broad demonstration – Barley 1977
9 On the legal position of all such *collegia*, *cf.* P.W. Duff, *Personality in Roman Private Law* (Cambridge 1938), ch. v
10 Van der Meer & Mohrmann 1958, map 27: Jedin Latourette & Martin 1970, map 16; Krautheimer 1979
11 Jones A.H.M. 1964, 900ff.
12 Mâle 1950
13 Tomlin 1974 discusses Jovinus's part in the affairs of 367
14 Wightman 1971, 110ff., plan fig. 8
15 Dieulafoy 1914: Mâle 1951, 129: Hubert Porcher & Volbach 1969, plan, 299
16 Hubert Porcher & Volbach 1969, plan, 294; Bonnet 1974, 12–17
17 Böhner 1958 (vol. ii, map 3)
18 Wightman 1971, 228ff.
19 Bonnet 1974, plan, 16
20 Weidemann 1968: Weidemann 1970
21 Krämer 1958: Radford 1968, plan, 34; see also Biddle, in Runcie 1977
22 Radford 1968, 32, illus.; Böhner, in Barley 1977, 198ff.
23 Weidemann 1970
24 *Epistolae*, II.x
25 Reynaud & Vicherd 1976: plan in Hubert Porcher & Volbach 1969, 307. There has been much work at Lyon; *cf.* Reynaud's papers in *Archeologia* 48 (1972), 47–50, and *CRAI* (1973), 346ff. on St Just, also Audin & Perrat in *Bull. Mon.* (1959), 109–18
26 H. von Petrikovitz (unpubl.)
27 Behrens 1950; Böhner 1958; Boppert 1971; Krämer K. 1974
28 Ausonius, II (= *Ephemeris*), ii
29 *Epistolae*, xxii
30 Chadwick N.K. 1955, esp. chaps. iii, iv: Hanson 1970
31 Eygun 1967; Coquet 1978
32 Nash-Williams 1930; Nash-Williams 1953; *cf.* Radford 1971
33 Alcock 1963, 63 n.
34 Boon 1976, 175 n. 28
35 Boon, *op. cit.*
36 HE i. 33
37 Taylor & Taylor 1965, 148: Brooks 1977
38 Rodwell 1977, 30
39 Bidwell 1979, 110ff.; *cf. Britannia*,

10 (1979), 324, fig. 15

40 HAR-1614, HAR-1613, respectively

41 Lincs. Archaeol. Trust, *4th Ann. Rep.* (Lincoln, 1976), 16: now Colyer & Jones 1979, 52–4, fig. 2 (plan)

42 Brown P.D.C. 1971

43 Frere 1975

44 Boon 1974, chap. 5

45 Radford 1971, 1

46 Wheeler & Wheeler 1936

47 Frere 1972

48 Wheeler & Wheeler, *op. cit.*, 122–3, pl. xxxv

49 HE i.26

50 Taylor & Taylor 1965, 143–5

51 E.g., Howorth 1913

52 *Cf.* Plummer 1896, ii. 42

53 Jenkins 1965

54 These figures are taken from the admirable *Topographical Maps of Canterbury* folder (Cant. Archaeol. Trust, 1980)

55 Brooks 1977, 49

56 So, as a compromise, Howorth (1913, 47)

57 Chadwick O. 1954a

58 *Cf.* Taylor & Taylor 1965, 134ff. and refs

59 HE, Preface

60 Taylor & Taylor 1965, 146–8

61 Howorth 1913, 70ff.

62 Jenkins 1976

63 Plummer 1896, ii. 58–9; Howorth 1913, 71

64 Howorth 1913, 72

65 Rodwell 1977, 25ff.

66 Rodwell, *op. cit.*, 39

67 Crummy 1973: Crummy 1974; Rodwell 1977, 38

68 Green C. 1977; Green C. 1979

69 *Cf.* Sennhauser 1974

70 Biddle Hudson & Heighway 1973, 18ff.

71 *Cf.* also Biddle 1976, 65–7; Morgan 1969 (for St Bride's)

72 Anthony 1968

73 Meates 1955; Painter 1969: Meates 1979

74 Meates 1979, period plan – 138

75 This chronology now follows Meates (1979, 24)

76 Smith D.J. 1978, 128ff.

77 Smith, *op. cit.*, fig. 39

78 Farrar 1957

79 Smith 1969, pl. 3. 16

80 Walters & Phillips 1979

81 Smith 1978, 135

82 Walter & Phillips 1979, fig. 5

83 Painter 1976a

84 Painter, *op. cit.*

85 Brannigan (variously); Painter 1968, 26

86 Fletcher & Meates 1969; Fletcher & Meates 1977

87 Jenkins 1965, 12

88 Crummy 1973, 140, fig. 55

89 Lehner 1978

90 Peeters 1969, 389 (translated)

91 *Guardian*, 19 June 1967: *Yorks. Arch. Journ.*, 42 (1967–70), 117

92 Bradwell on Sea: Canterbury, Sts Peter and Paul, St Mary, St Pancras phase II; Reculver: Rochester (Taylor & Taylor 1965) – St Paul-in-the-Bail, Lincoln (Gilmour 1979)

93 Krämer 1958

94 Frere 1975, 292ff.

95 Brown P.D.C. 1971 (with plans)

96 Doppelfeld 1950

97 Well summarised by Mâle, 1950, 110ff.

98 *Cf.* Lewis 1966, esp. 185, 193; and refs. in chap. 5 above, under 'negative evidence.'

99 Respectively, from Frere 1978, fig. 13; chap. 10 below; and Campbell J. 1979

100 RCHM *Eburacum*, 51b (no. 18)

101 See n. 91 above: and *cf.* Norman 1971

102 *Cf.* Colyer & Jones 1979, fig. 2

103 Based on maps in Van der Meer & Mohrmann 1958

104 Jones, M. 1979

105 Jones, *op. cit.*, 244

106 C. Green (in Frend 1979, 134 n. 29) estimates the fourth-century Christian community in Dorchester at 5–10 per cent, or between 200 and 400 people

107 Mann 1961: Rivet & Smith 1979, 49–50

108 Mann, *op. cit.*; Hassall M. 1976, 109ff. (Johnson S., 1980, 5–6, curiously reverses the positions of

these in a somewhat over-specific map); *cf.* also Mann & Jarrett 1967

109 Hassall, *op. cit.*

110 For details of these entries *cf.* Frend 1955: Frend 1979: Hanson (below): Haddan & Stubbs 1869–71, i. 7–10

111 Hanson 1968, 32–34

112 *De Laude Sanctorum*, i – Jack Lindsay's translation (Lindsay 1958, 96)

8 Baptism and Baptisteries
(pages 202–227)

1 Fisher 1965

2 Davies, J.G. 1962

3 Davies, *op. cit.*, 23ff.

4 Van der Meer & Mohrmann 1958, fig. 397

5 Davies 1962, 26

6 *Cf.* Grose 1958, nos. 102, 103 & 174

7 Davies 1962, 23–6; Khatchatrian 1962

8 Mâle 1950, chap. vii; Hubert Porcher & Volbach 1969, 294–307

9 Rogers 1903

10 *Cf.* now Whitaker 1960, *passim*; earlier, Carpenter 1943

11 Davies 1962, 18–22

12 Mainly in Khatchatrian 1962

13 Bieler 1952, 195

14 *Cf.* I Timothy, iii. 6

15 Bieler 1953; *contra*, Hughes 1966, 44–9, arguing for the later 6th century

16 Bieler 1963; Hughes 1972, 88 (2nd or 3rd quarter, sixth cent.)

17 Ferguson 1979

18 Bieler 1963

19 Bieler, *op. cit.*, 10; Kenney 1929, 245

20 HE ii. 2

21 Smith A. 1978, 25–6

22 Plummer 1896, ii. 75; Williams 1912, 87ff., 473

23 Whitaker 1960, 218

24 McRoberts 1973; for the Life, see Forbes 1874

25 *Cf.* Jackson 1958a

26 Jackson, *op. cit.*, 342

27 MacQueen J. 1956

28 Thomas 1971a, 216–19

29 Fawtier 1912; Duine 1914, 38–9; Taylor 1925; Morris 1973, esp. 357ff.

30 MacQueen W. 1960; MacQueen J. 1962; Thomas 1966

31 *Vit. Germani*, caps. 17, 18; HE i. 20

32 HE ii. 14

33 Dalton 1927, esp. ii. 555

34 HF ii. 20

35 Canon 20 – see Whitaker 1960, 213

36 Frere 1976, pls. lix, lxi.b

37 Cited by Frere, *op. cit.*, 279

38 Radford 1971, 3

39 Boon 1974, 181ff.

40 Frere 1976, 295 n. 2

41 Boon, *op. cit.*

42 Boon, *op. cit.*, 182

43 Brown P.D.C. 1971, 225 n.

44 It was popularly published almost at once, by Miss Jessie Mothersole (*The Saxon Shore*, Bodley Head, London, 1924; fig. 13): *cf.* Brown, *op. cit.*, pl. xxx,a & b

45 West 1976

46 West, *op. cit.*, 71, fig. 35

47 West, *op. cit.*, 74–6

48 Turner 1979 (preliminary note): stone relief, *Britannia, I* (1970), 267

49 Lewis 1966, fig. 112

50 Lewis 1966, fig. 8

51 Goodburn 1972, 34, pl. 10. 2

52 Grover 1867, pl. 10, i, ii: Goodburn 1972, pl. 11

53 Wall 1966, 154–155

54 Toller 1977, 3, map 1

55 Elkington 1976

56 Toynbee 1962, 179

57 *Cf.* Toller 1977, 19ff.

58 C. Guy, *Britannia*, forthcoming

59 Toynbee 1962, pl. 143: Painter 1971a, pls. lxvi.b, lxvii

60 Toynbee 1964, 354

61 Van der Meer & Mohrmann 1958, fig. 467

62 Toynbee 1962, 164, pl. 95: *cf.* Lewis 1966, 116

63 Van der Meer & Mohrmann 1958, fig. 551

64 Ward Perkins & Goodchild 1953, 58, fig. 28

65 Plans in Khatchatrian 1962

66 In *The Sign of Four*

67 Noll 1954, 110ff., pl. 26: Khatchatrian 1962, 92, fig. 323b

68 West 1976, 67, 74

69 *Cf.* Thomas 1971a, 190–8

9 Burials and Cemeteries
(pages 228–239)

1 Chadwick N.K. 1966, index s.v. "Immortality": Piggott 1968, 120–122
2 Cumont 1922
3 Toynbee 1971
4 Wenham 1968
5 Clarke G. 1979
6 Green C. 1977: Green C. 1979, and report in preparation
7 *Cf.* Biddle's uncompromising remarks, Biddle Hudson & Heighway 1973
8 Jones M. 1979
9 E.g., Radford 1967; Radford 1968; Radford 1971
10 Toynbee 1971
11 In Collingwood & Richmond 1969, chap. ix
12 Reece 1977
13 Wacher 1974
14 Rodwell & Rowley 1975
15 Toller 1977
16 Toynbee 1962; Toynbee 1964
17 Wells 1960
18 Rahtz 1979, 12–13
19 Clarke G. 1979, 424ff.
20 *Ibid.*, 371–2
21 *Ibid.*, 425–6; *cf.* Jones A.H.M. 1964, 80ff; Stevenson 1965, 297–8
22 Clarke G. 1979, 427
23 *Cf.* Rahtz 1968; Rahtz 1977
24 Rahtz 1977, 55
25 Rahtz 1968, Rahtz & Watts 1979
26 Wilson P.A. 1978; Crowe 1979; O'Sullivan 1980
27 Especially Faull 1976; Faull 1977
28 Thomas 1968
29 Hope-Taylor 1979, chap. 6, esp. 251–5
30 Rahtz 1977, 53
31 Hogg 1974
32 Thomas 1971a, chap. 3 (fuller definitions)
33 Wilson D.R. 1968; Todd 1975; the place is not the RB *Causennae*, so Rivet & Smith 1979, 164
34 Wilson D.R. 1968, 198
35 Rahtz 1977, 54
36 Clarke G. 1979. 97ff., with plan
37 *Ibid.*, 429ff.
38 *Ibid.*, 430
39 Frend 1979, 133
40 Wenham 1968, 45
41 *Cf.*, for the moment, Green C. 1979
42 Illus., Munby & Henig 1977, i. 99

10 Fifth-Century Britain and the British Church
(pages 240–274)

1 Thompson 1979, 208; Gildas was probably a priest, not (as sometimes claimed) a monk – Chadwick O., 1954b. O'Sullivan 1978, an important summary, was unfortunately not accessible to the author until after this book was written.
2 DEB 3
3 Morris 1965a: Morris 1973; Dumville 1977; Thompson 1977; Frere 1978
4 Stevens 1937; Stevens 1941; Stevens 1976
5 Hawkes S.C. 1961; Hawkes S.C. 1973
6 Miller 1975d
7 Cited ASC, by page (see Abbreviations: Whitelock, Douglas & Tucker 1961)
8 Thompson 1956; Morris 1973; Dumville 1977; Miller 1978d
9 Fulford 1979
10 Miller 1975a; Kirby 1976a
11 Morris 1973, maps 3, 6, 18
12 LHEB 220–222
13 DEB 19–25
14 Wacher 1974, 411–22; *contra*, Todd 1977
15 LHEB chap. 1
16 Morris 1973; Thompson 1979
17 DEB 25
18 DEB 25
19 Dumville 1977, 183–186
20 DEB 20; for the site itself, *cf.* Jackson 1958b
21 Morris 1973, 95ff., map 5 (*Ambros* place-names)
22 ASC 10
23 Dumville 1977, 188
24 Thomas 1969b
25 DEB 31
26 Miller 1978a: *cf.* Morris 1973,

index, s.n.

27 Morris 1965b; Morris 1966; Morris 1968b

28 Best (short) obituary, *Times*, 10 June 1977 (of *Age of Arthur* – 'bold, fascinating and underrated book'): *cf.* Campbell 1975

29 Morris 1968b

30 Miller 1978c

31 Miller 1975b

32 Miller 1975c; Thompson 1956; Thompson 1977

33 Miller 1977a

34 Miller 1975c

35 DEB 25

36 Thompson 1979

37 *Ibid.*, 225

38 Bromwich 1976, with refs

39 Jones G. 1975; Miller 1978b

40 Barker 1979; Barker's plan, Johnson S. 1980, 165, fig. 18

41 *Cf.* LHEB 701–705

42 S. Johnson (1980, 66) claims that *venedotis cive* is now 'established' (*fide* a Mr White) to be a ninth-century addition for propagandist purposes; but Johnson's own reading of *venedotis* as 'of the Votadini' (!) hardly inspires confidence

43 Alcock 1967, 239

44 Gelling 1978, chap. 3

45 Gelling, *op. cit.*, 85, fig. 2

46 Campbell J. 1979

47 Faull 1975

48 Cameron 1980

49 Gelling 1978, 95–6

50 M. Todd, appendix to Cameron 1980

51 Biddle Hudson & Heighway 1973

52 Frere 1966; Brooks 1977; Day 1979

53 Boon 1974

54 Frere 1966 (with refs.)

55 Heighway Garrod & Vince 1979

56 Barker 1975: Barker 1979

57 McCarthy 1979

58 Pers. comm., Prof. G.D.B. Jones

59 Frere 1966; *cf.* Alcock 1967

60 Rivet & Smith 1979, 346–8

61 HE ii. 3; for *Hrofi-*, see LHEB 267

62 Jones G.R.J. 1975; *cf.* Jones G.R.J. 1976 (instances); and see now Hind 1980, for 'Elmet' and 'Deira' as

originally British forest-names

63 Branigan 1967; *cf.* remarks in Branigan 1971, chaps. v & vi This is the *desertae Ciltine* ('Chiltern deserts') of Eddius' *Life of Wilfrid*, cap. 42 – *cf.* Plummer 1896, ii. 228 (HE iv. 15); *Cf.* also Collingwood & Myres 1937, chap. xxii

64 Wheeler 1935, 50ff., fig. 2

65 In Biddle Hudson & Heighway 1973

66 *Cf.* Hawkes S.C. 1979

67 Evison 1979

68 Dickinson 1979

69 Cameron 1968

70 Cameron 1975

71 Jensen 1977

72 LHEB 227, 412

73 LHEB 227

74 Cited in Cameron 1968, 87

75 Gelling 1978, 72ff.

76 HF i. 33

77 Thomson 1964

78 Wilson P.A. 1978

79 Pers. comm.

80 Barrow 1973, chap. 1

81 W.F.H. Nicolaisen, *Scottish Studies*, 13.1 (1969), 47–58

82 Thomas 1971a, chap. 3, esp. 85ff.; *cf.* now Padel 1978

83 Painter 1971a, 157–8 (for additions, see caption)

84 *Cf.* Rahtz & Watts 1979

85 E.g., Margaret Murray, *The Witch-Cult in Western Europe* (Oxford, 1921); *The God of the Witches* (Faber, London, 1931)

86 *Cf.* Davies, W.H., 1968

87 Thomas 1968, 102–05: add now the (late 7th?) *Neitano sacerdos* stone, Peebles (Steer 1972, illus.)

88 Doble 1943: *cf.* Morris 1973, index, s.n.

89 Davies W. 1979

90 HE i. 27, sect. vii

91 HE ii. 2

92 HE ii. 4

93 Morris 1973, index, s.n.

94 *Cf.* Rahtz 1971 (site, post-Roman halls)

95 Williams 1912; Wilson P.A. 1966a; Davies W.H. 1968; Victory 1977

96 Pearce 1978, chaps. 3 & 4

97 RCHM *Dorset II.2 (South-East)* (1970), 303–07; *cf.* Radford 1975
98 Thomas 1976 (with maps and refs.)
99 CIIC i. 479 (corrected reading, upper lines)
100 RIB 2233 (dated 306–07)
101 RIB 2254; the back, CIIC i. 407 = ECMW no. 258
102 ECMW no. 104 (Penmachno), and no. 33 (Llantrisant, Anglesey): *cf.* also Johnstone 1962
103 Thomas 1976, 254 (appendix)
104 *Cf.* Kenney 1929, 142–3

11 St Ninian, and Christianity in Southern Scotland
(*pages 275–294*)

1 Anderson & Anderson 1961
2 Samples – 'St Columba, the apostle of the Scots in Alba, but not of the country now called Scotland' (1927); *cf.* 'St Ninian, Apostle to the Picts of Scotland' (1951), etc.
3 Richmond 1958, chap. vi; Rivet & Smith 1979
4 Maxwell 1976
5 Watson 1926, chaps. i & ii
6 Maxwell, *op. cit.*, 47
7 Robertson 1970
8 Mann 1974, esp. 35
9 Breeze & Dobson 1976, 231ff.
10 Richmond 1958a, 124–5
11 Frere 1978, 392; *cf.* his fig. 13, 398
12 Bromwich 1954; Jackson 1963a; Miller 1975a
13 Since, e.g., Chadwick H.M. 1949, 142
14 Jackson 1955a, 80; *pes*, from Latin *pexa tunica*, 'woollen cloak'
15 Jackson 1955a; Miller 1975a; Kirby 1976
16 Mann 1974
17 Jackson 1955a, 80
18 Hassall 1976
19 Curle 1923; Wall 1966, 147–50
20 HE iii. 4
21 MacQueen J. 1961, 23ff.
22 Thomas 1966
23 Thomas 1973
24 Wilson P.A. 1964; Thomas 1971b
25 Wilson P.A., *op. cit.*
26 HE iii. 4; the date may be 563,

Anderson & Anderson 1961, 66–67
27 MacQueen J. 1961, 8
28 MacQueen W. 1960 (text & transl.); MacQueen J. 1962, Thomas 1966, 111–12 (commentaries)
29 *Vita Martini*, cap. x; *cf.* Hoare 1954, 24
30 Radford 1951 (last excavation); Thomas 1967, 158–9 (date of incised crosses)
31 Chadwick O. 1954, esp. 177–81
32 Numerous writers; *cf.* Morris 1973, 337
33 Radford 1967, 110
34 MacQueen J. 1961, 8–12, with refs.
35 So Radford 1950, 91–2
36 Henderson 1967, 210
37 Radford 1950, 119: Radford 1957, 181; Radford 1967, 110
38 Chadwick N.K. 1963a, 165 n. 13
39 Thompson 1958
40 Ministry of Public Building & Works, Scotland (as it then was), and Mr. P.R. Ritchie: *The Scotsman (Week-end Magazine)*, 4 May 1963 p. 1, art. by Stewart Cruden; *cf.* Thomas 1966, 105–06. Best plan of site; Radford 1957
41 Anderson 1948, 45–6: Wilson P.A. 1977
42 CIIC i. 520: better (standard) reading, Radford 1957, 170ff., & fig. 9
43 CIIC i. 516–518: for Curgie, see Thomas 1968, 103, nn. 40–2
44 CIIC i. 516 – *cf.* above, fig. 21, 4
45 CIIC i. 517 – fig. 21, 2
46 Radford 1975
47 CICC i. 518 – fig. 21, 3
48 But, from intensive field-work, not apparently at or around Kirkmadrine church itself
49 Anderson 1948, 43
50 Thomas 1964, 88–93; *cf.* now Rivet and Smith 1979, 438–40
51 Jackson 1955b; *cf.* Adams 1970
52 Mann 1974
53 Chadwick N.K. 1958b
54 Miller 1975c
55 HE i. 1
56 HE iv. 12; *cf.* also Kirby 1973, esp. 22ff; Kirby 1976b
57 HE iv. 26; but *cf.* here Blair 1954

58 *Cf.* Thomas 1968, esp. 94–6 and refs.
59 Jackson 1955b, map 6; Henderson 1967, 29–30
60 Stevenson 1955; Thomas 1964; Henderson 1967
61 Stevenson 1955
62 *Cf.* Wilson P.A. 1966b; Kirby 1962
63 Thomas 1961 (suggesting a late sixth-early seventh century raid)
64 HE i. 12
65 *Cf.* Watson 1926, 346–7
66 Stevenson R.B.K. 1966, 33, fig. 6
67 Miller 1975d, 243 n. 1, proposes such a frontier
68 HE i. 12: recent excavations, Alcock 1976
69 Jackson 1969 (for this and all other tribal and territorial names mentioned)
70 Thomas 1968
71 CIIC. i, 498, 510, 511, 514, 515
72 Steer 1972
73 Forbes 1874
74 *Cf.* Thomas 1971a, 218–19
75 Thomas 1968, 114–16
76 Thomas 1968, 107–08 (with map)
77 Recent re-excavation, Rutherford & Ritchie 1975
78 Watson 1926, 383

12 Britain, Ireland and Pre-Patrician Christianity

(pages 295–306)

1 Warner 1976
2 Bateson 1973, 72 (a fresh study, by Richard Haworth, is promised)
3 *Agricola*, 24 – *per commercia et negotiatores*
4 O'Rahilly 1946, 1–42: Tierney 1976; Rivet & Smith 1979, chap. 3
5 Warner 1976, 284
6 Ó Ríordáin 1947
7 Bateson 1973; supplement, Bateson 1976
8 Summarised, Thomas 1972, with refs.
9 Bateson 1973, 33
10 Carson & O'Kelly 1977
11 *Ibid.*, 42
12 *Ibid.*, 49; and pers. comm., Professor M.J. O'Kelly
13 R.E.M. Wheeler, 'Roman Contact with India, Pakistan and Afghanistan', in: Grimes, W.F., ed., *Aspects of Archaeology in Britain and Beyond* (London, 1951), 345–81
14 Henry 1956, esp. 76
15 Carney 1971 (*cf.* also Wagner 1977)
16 Summaries – O'Rahilly C. 1924; Thomas 1972. Wales in more detail - Richards 1960; Richards 1962
17 Bateson 1973, 69; pers. comm. also from Professor C.F.C. Hawkes, who first identified and catalogued this material
18 An extraordinary late instance – Raftery B. 1969
19 Carney 1975
20 LHEB 151ff.
21 CIIC i. 502 (map – requires updating)
22 Richards 1960, 140 (map)
23 Thomas 1971a, 96–7
24 *Cf.* Jones M.E. 1979
25 Discussed in Thomas 1972
26 Todd 1864, 278ff.
27 Hanson 1968, 52–4
28 MacNeill 1919, 162; Kenney 1929, 323; O'Rahilly 1946, 3, 48–9
29 Binchy 1962, 165
30 Kenney 1929, 309ff.; Bieler 1964a; Bieler 1968b
31 Binchy 1962, 166
32 Greene 1968, 80
33 Binchy 1958
34 Greene 1968, 80–1
35 Thomas 1976, 250, fig. 3
36 Ryan 1958, 80; Bowen 1969, 121–4
37 Todd 1864, 286–7: Bury 1905, 300
38 Walker 1957, 38–9
39 Conveniently, in Hanson 1968, appendix I
40 Kenney 1929, 169–70
41 Binchy 1962, 164–6
42 Binchy, *loc. cit*; Kenney 1929, 260; Hanson 1968, 195–6
43 Bowen 1969, 124

13 St Patrick – his Background and Early Life

(pages 307 – 327)

1 Muirchú: see Hood 1978; Bieler 1979
2 Oulton 1940; Bieler 1947; Morhmann 1961
3 Binchy 1962, 15

4 Ludwig Bieler (not one of whose extensive Patrician writings display this)

5 Kenney 1929, 329–34: Bieler 1979, 1–2, 42

6 Kenney 1929, 359–60

7 Listed, Thomas 1971a, 213–14, 225–6

8 Conveniently in Hanson 1968, app. 1

9 So Hughes 1972, chap. 4; Smyth 1972 – e.g. Iona after 563?; cf. Bannerman 1968b

10 *Contra*, Hanson 1978, 74

11 Miller 1975a

12 Anderson & Anderson 1961, cf. 90, 109–10

13 Bieler 1953, 48–54

14 MacNeill 1923; Bieler 1943, 351 n. 4 (list of places suggested)

15 Irish Nat Grid, G 2030

16 Binchy 1962

17 Bowen 1969, 126

18 Tacitus, *Annales* iv. 73 (I owe this to Prof. Malcolm Todd)

19 RIB 933, and comment, pp. 310–11; Jones, G.D.B., *The Carvetii* (forthcoming)

20 Bieler 1952, 56

21 Rivet & Smith 1979, 262

22 Rivet & Smith 1979, 265–6

23 Watson 1926, 461

24 Rivet & Smith 1979, 262–5

25 *Venta Belgarum, Venta Icenorum, Venta Silurum*

26 Rivet & Smith 1979, 367

27 Jackson 1970, 80

28 Richmond 1935: Breeze & Dobson 1976, pl. 9

29 Heurgon 1951

30 E.g., RIB 1898, 1904, 1909

31 Hassall 1976, 113–14: Breeze & Dobson 1976, 273ff.; Rivet & Smith 1979, 262 ('not only acceptable, but . . . obvious')

32 RIB 1905

33 Salway 1965, 96

34 LHEB 704–05

35 Bath and Buxton: Winchester and Caerwent – two spas and two civitas capitals

36 Jackson 1969, 71

37 I am grateful to Prof. G.D.B. Jones for pointing this out

38 *Cf.* Clack, P.A.G. & Gosling, P.F., *Archaeology in the North* (Northern Archaeol. Survey, Durham, 1976), 32–6

39 Bieler 1979, 66–67: Bury 1905, 322–5 (note that Bury saw *berniae* as the name of 'a district (or perhaps river) added to distinguish B. from other places of the same name' (*ibid.*, 323))

40 Deuteronomy, xxxiv. 7

41 Hanson 1968

42 Bury 1905

43 So Kelleher 1962

44 O'Rahilly 1942

45 Carney 1961

46 E.g., Carney 1955, chap. ix: Carney 1959

47 Hanson 1968: Hanson 1978 (a further article is adumbrated – pers. comm., April 1980)

48 Hanson 1968, 178–84

49 Hanson 1968, 188

50 Stevenson 1965, 304–05, 334

51 Hanson 1978, 68–9

52 Bury 1905: MacNeill (ed. Ryan) 1964; Bieler 1949; O'Rahilly 1957; Mohrmann 1961; Morris 1966, 366–7

53 Inscribed stones – ECMW no. 103 (*magistratus*); CIIC 476 (*tribunus*)

54 Davies W.H. 1968, 140

55 Foreshadowed to some extent in Thomas 1979a

56 Mohrmann 1961

57 Charlesworth 1978; McCarthy 1979

58 Bateson 1973; Bateson 1976 (replacing Ó Ríordáin 1947)

59 Dolley 1976

60 Bateson 1973, 63–4, with refs.

61 Hanson 1978, 73–4

62 Nautical friends in south-west Britain who have done such trips readily confirm this estimate

63 Following Carney 1961, 62ff.

64 Bury 1905, 338–42

65 Thompson 1977, 310

66 Thompson 1956; Chadwick N.K. 1969, 150–7; Thompson 1977, 311

67 Kenney 1929, 168

68 Bury 1905; Bieler 1959, 65, 74; Bieler 1968, 123; O'Rahilly 1957 (referring to his 'second' Patrick): Grosjean

1957 174–5; Carney 1961
69 Chadwick N.K. 1954b, 214–15
   (hinting that *Spain* is as likely!);
   Mohrmann 1961; Binchy 1962, 90;
   Morris 1966, 366–7: Hanson 1968,
   129–30
70 Mohrmann 1961
71 *Ibid.*, 6 (specifically, 2 Corinthians?)
72 *Ibid.*, 54
73 Morris 1966, 366 n. 2
74 Binchy 1962, 88–90
75 Grosjean 1975, 175
76 Hanson 1968, 160–70

14 St Patrick's Episcopate and the British Church
(pages 328–346)

1 Columbanus, *Ep.* iv – Walker 1957,
   xxvii, 35
2 Evison 1979, chap. 4
3 Bieler 1942; Bieler 1952
4 White 1905; White 1918a; White
   1918b
5 Mohrmann 1961, 12–15; *cf.* also
   Grosjean 1958b
6 Carney 1962, 153
7 Binchy 1975: Binchy 1976
8 Miller 1975a
9 In Grosjean 1958b
10 With Morris 1966, 361–3; Hanson
   1968, 133–4; Bieler (1948: 1968, 127)
   hovers between Britain and Gaul
   here
11 Morris 1966, 361
12 Jalland 1941 full discussion of
   Leo's policies and attitudes
13 Constantius, *Vita Germani* 25–27;
   Bede, HE i. 21, used the later Life of
   Lupus of Troyes
14 Plummer 1896, ii. 34
15 So now Thompson 1977, 311 n. 35
16 Morris 1973, 346–7
17 Kenney 1929, 168
18 Morris 1966, 364–5; Morris 1973,
   349
19 Bieler 1968, 28; Hanson 1968, 100–03
20 Williams 1912, 468; Hanson 1968,
   68ff; the tables or *Cursus Paschalis*,
   prepared by Victorius of Aquitaine,
   came into general use (though not
   apparently adopted in Britain or

Ireland) in 457.
21 Carney 1955, 342ff., esp. 371
22 Chadwick, N.K. 1958, 46ff.
23 Cicero, *ex vita migrare* 'to die';
   morte migratur 'he dies'
24 *dimidio scriptulae, Conf.* 50: 'half a
   scruple', a minute coin of the
   smallest weight, *scripulum*, Irish
   screpall
25 Stevenson 1966, 324ff.
26 Bieler 1969, 66, 251
26 Bieler 1969, 66, 251; since this book
   was completed, E.A. Thompson ('St
   Patrick and Coroticus', *J Theol Stud
   n.s. 31* (April 1980), 12–27) has
   propounded with ingenuity and force
   a fresh possibility – that Coroticus
   (a *third* C., neither of Strathclyde
   nor Cardigan) and his *milites* were
   British outlaws living in N. Ireland
27 Post-Roman occupation, Alcock 1976
28 E.g., Tolstoy 1962
29 Binchy 1962, 167
30 Miller 1975a esp. 278 n.i. (using,
   and defending use of , 27-year
   generations); Kirby 1976, 100 ('this
   seems to carry C. inescapably into
   the 2nd half of the 5th cent.');
   implicitly, Dumville 1977, 179, 191
31 As Hanson 1968, 101–02
32 Patrick's *apostatae* cannot be mere
   abuse; Grosjean 1958a: Bieler 1953,
   91 n. 4
33 So Miller 1975d, 243 n.i, indicating
   possible frontier
34 Bannerman 1968a: Bannerman 1974
35 Hence one theme of the Synod of
   Whitby – Bede, HE iii. 25
36 Morris 1966, 363
37 Binchy 1962, 90–5
38 John 1970
39 Phillips 1975
40 Thompson 1958
41 Thompson 1979, 222
42 *Ibid.*, 223
43 A.P. Smyth (1972, 44) goes further
   still; the 492/3 obit is in a
   'continuous and reasonably reliable
   sequence of events' (as finally
   entered in AU)
44 *Vit. Columbae*, second preface:
   Anderson & Anderson 1961 discuss
   him (index, s.n. 'Maucte').

15 'Thoroughly Roman . . . in Origin'
(pages 347–355)

1 Thomas 1971a (written in 1969) now requires considerable revision
2 Radford 1935; but not discounting Burrow 1974
3 The start – Haddan & Stubbs 1869–71, i. 14
4 Thomas 1959: Thomas 1976 (both with refs.)
5 ECMW, introduction, notes these
6 Vendryes 1956
7 Thomas 1971a, chaps. 4 & 5: Thomas 1973
8 Hoare 1954, conveniently, with good intro.; (p. 5) 'Sulpicius did not 'create' Martin, though he certainly exploited him'
9 Mohrmann 1961, 47ff.
10 Chadwick O. 1954b
11 Davies W.H. 1968, 142
12 *Cf.* such comments in Frend 1955; Frend 1968; (even) Frend 1979; Painter 1971a, 166; Radford 1967: Radford 1971
13 Crawford, and Gover (*Antiquity* 2 (1928), 327)
14 Eagles 1979; Faull 1974; Faull 1977; Hope-Taylor 1979; Jones G.R.J. 1975; Jones G.R.J. 1976
15 Barrow 1973; Higham 1978; Higham 1979; Jackson 1963
16 Davies W. 1979
17 Davies W.H. 1968: Williams 1912 (throughout): Wilson P.A. 1966a
18 E.g., Finberg 1974 (and other essays); Pearce 1978
19 Frend 1979
20 *Ibid.*, 143
21 Brown, P.R.L. 1977
22 Hanson 1968, 114
23 Summarised in Thomas 1971a
24 Toynbee 1953, 24

INDEXES

I

Places, and Persons (Classical, Medieval and Modern) Named
or Cited (ancient writers and Romano-British place-names
italicised)

Abb., abbot: bp, bishop: dcn, deacon: k., king:
q., queen: St, saint

II

Words and Phrases other than in English

GREEK

chrismon 86
Christos 87, 92
ekklēsia 147
Iesous 90, 92
*ichthū*s 92

marturos 45
philtron 130
sōter 92
zēseias 130

LATIN

Classical, Christian and Medieval including Greek loanwords

altare 77, 81, 116, 121, 149
ancilla 116, 207, 311
angelus 131
anima 128
antistes 41
apostatus 290–1, 342
ara 31, 81

baptizo, -atus 77, 131, 207
basilica 48, 148
benedictio 77
bracchium 72
bucca 72

candidus, -a 282
candidatus 208
cantharus 93
caritas 77
castellum 241
catechesis 203
catechumen, -on 203–5
catholicus, -a 301, 304, 334
caudex 82, 84
cella 171, 185
civis 246, 252, 354
civitas 98, 133, 193, 255, 259, 267
c(h)risma, -re 208, 211
chrismarium 205
Christianus 263, 301

Christus 87
clerus 77, 125, 131
clocca 77
codex 82
coepiscopus 268
collegium 30, 157
c. illicitum 31
colonia 63, 250
columba 92
combustio 152
competens 203
confessio 345
corona 87
credentes 300
curialis, -es 75, 242

defensio 336–7
defixio 131
desertae 387
diabolus 77
diaconus 77, 131, 197, 267, 284, 301, 307
diocesis, -es 158
dogma(ta) 301
dominicus, -a, -um 148-9, 153, 264, 303
dominicatus 267, 339
Dominus (noster) 77, 90–1, 108, 127, 148
durante vita 132

VULGAR LATIN

IRISH (all stages)

BRITISH

PICTISH

WELSH (all stages)

CORNISH (Old and Middle)

BRETON

OLD ENGLISH

III

General
RB, Roman Britain: PR(B), Post-Roman (Britain):   SR(B), Sub-Roman (Britain)